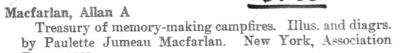

TREASURY OF MEMORY-MAKING CAMPFIRES

ALLAN A. MACFARLAN

TREASURY OF

ASSOCIATION PRESS • NEW YORK

MEMORY-MAKING CAMPFIRES

ILLUSTRATIONS AND DIAGRAMS
BY PAULETTE JUMEAU MACFARLAN

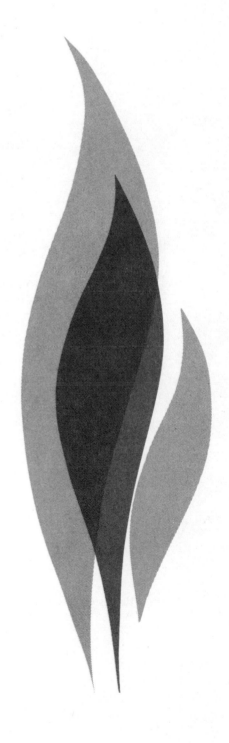

A TREASURY OF MEMORY-MAKING CAMPFIRES

Other books by
ALLAN A. MACFARLAN

CAMPFIRE AND COUNCIL RING PROGRAMS

CAMPFIRE ADVENTURE STORIES

INDIAN ADVENTURE TRAILS

LIVING LIKE INDIANS

BOOK OF AMERICAN INDIAN GAMES

NEW GAMES FOR 'TWEEN-AGERS

MORE NEW GAMES FOR 'TWEEN-AGERS

FUN WITH BRAND-NEW GAMES

FUN IN THE SUN BOOK OF CAMPING, CRUISING,
AND ADVENTURING

16263

Association Press, 291 Broadway, New York 7, N. Y.

Publisher's title stock number: 1520   Library of Congress catalog card number: 63-10380

Printed in the United States of America

Dedicated to

MY WIFE

Campwise and trailwise comrade on land and water trails, and
illustrator of this book.

CONTENTS

Handicap Twirl, Ball Duel, Possum Race, Two-Rope Trick Pull, Row Ball, Back-to-Back Balloon Race, Informer!, Anchored Hoop Pass

Crab Run, Hobbled!, Tumbleweed, Tumbleweed Drive, Puff Ball Kick, Triple Ball Drive, Dance Bell Ambush, Fire Tender

III. CONJURING THE STORY SPELL

IV. WHEN THE SPIRIT SOARS

Contents

V. OUR INDIAN HERITAGE

INTRODUCTION

SEATED around a glowing campfire, one feels at peace with the world. Sparks drift starward, and the mysterious night sounds in the dark forest arouse thoughts of other memory-making campfires which forge links between the near present and the distant past. The deep woods; the fragrant, spiralling smoke of a wildwood fire; the fun of cookouts, games, songs; and the *camaraderie* of fire-friendships—such experiences live long in our memories.

Despite the generous helping hand of nature, and her incomparable background for the fire, much of its success depends upon good planning and upon the program and gaiety inspired by campfire leaders. This involves carrying out camping and activity ideas which are original, workable, and pretested for popularity among campers. To assist leaders in carrying out their task with confidence, TREASURY OF MEMORY-MAKING CAMPFIRES introduces brand-new, fully detailed and illustrated program activities for both campfire and council fire.

Written for the novice as well as for the experienced camp director, this TREASURY OF MEMORY-MAKING CAMPFIRES gives careful attention to such basic matters as choosing campfire and council ring sites, laying and lighting fires—from the simplest to the most impressive novelty fires—and effectively opening, conducting, and closing campfire and council fire programs. Some of the thrilling, authentic activities derived from the little-known Northwest Coast Indians will blaze a new trail into modern camping circles, to the delight of modern "braves" of all ages.

Frequently, the forest setting may not be available to youth leaders—when there's "rain on the roof," or when programs are scheduled in the playground or auditorium. Most of the special activities in TREASURY OF MEMORY-MAKING CAMPFIRES are adaptable to whatever environment is at hand. City recreation directors as well as "chiefs in the forest" can stage exciting, colorful events by making use of the games, drama, storytelling, pageantry, and dance program suggestions detailed in these chapters. Camping and firecraft, campfire fun-fare, magic council fires, canoe ceremonies, and similar activities are, of course, for outdoor campers.

Nearly all activities seem to be enhanced by the magic of the out-of-doors. When the crimson flame of the fire fades into a warm glow toward the end of a campfire, a spirit of fellowship prevails. Campers are inspired by the surrounding forest, the serene stars, and the glorious sunset just past. It is small wonder that the tired, busy adult joins hands with the child in the eternal search for that primeval peace which radiates from the heart of a campfire.

PART 1

FIRE MAGIC
AND MYSTERY

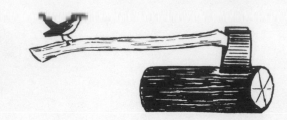

campfire call

There are magic nights when the ember campfire-pictures will glow brighter, will appear clearer, more thrilling, and meaningful—a time when fire-friendship means more. On such nights the mysterious, compelling Call of the Campfire is more insistent. No longer can one resist its imperative, ever louder whisper—

> *Come!*
> > *Come!*
> > > *COME!*

It is with such nights in heart and mind that this book has been written.

chapter 1

creative campfires

GETTING AWAY FROM IT ALL" becomes more and more difficult as time goes on. The shadows of cities and towns seem to encircle us—until they are swallowed by the shadows formed by the flickering flames of the campfire. A fire brings out something of the primordial in man, releases some intangible quality in his nature that reverts to his fur-clad forbears. When one is seated in the charmed circle of the campfire, civilization with its restless crowds and its worries is left far behind.

Seers have predicted that evolution will eventually bring man back from overheated apartments in over-crowded cities, to the tranquility of the campfire once more. Even though the campfire site and surroundings may not be ideal in some cases, nevertheless when all is blanketed by night, the campfire glow dominates the scene. The campfire circle, big or small, whether shared by two or twenty, is a realm apart, where fire-friendships are formed in nature's temple, lit by the golden glow of the fire and made fragrant by the incense of woodsmoke.

CHOOSING THE CAMPFIRE SITE

The responsibility for establishing an ideal site should not rest entirely on the shoulders of the camp director and his assistant, though naturally they will have their say before it is finally selected. The hike and nature leaders should be called into conference when a new site has to be located or a change in site contemplated. The suggestions of a good caretaker, who should know the entire layout of the camp property better than most people, may prove helpful in actually pinpointing the sort of site desired.

There are many things to be considered carefully before the site is decided upon. One of the most important things is the selection of a suitable campfire site which is within a few hundred yards of the main camp buildings. A site in as close proximity to the camp buildings as possible is desirable, chiefly on account of sudden rain storms and having a short distance to travel in the dark when the campfire ends. Another reason for having a campfire circle reasonably close to the camp buildings is that when a play involving dressing up and change of costumes is being staged and props—or benches for adult spectators —have to be transported from the main buildings, the short distance between the main camp and campfire will prove convenient. When special lighting is required or a sound recorder has to be used, the proximity of the electric connections is important. These "blessings of civilization" features do not mean that the campfire site should be placed so that it is dominated by the main camp buildings. An ideal campfire area is one situated on rather high ground in a wooded or lightly wooded spot with a natural woodsy background which makes the campfire twice as enticing as when it is set up in an open field, for instance.

Great care has to be exercised in order that the approach to the campfire circle is not swampy or too wet after a heavy rain prior to campfire night. Equal care must be taken that an apparently fine, dry site is not chosen and worked on in rainless weather only to find that the spot is damp in showery weather and practically under water in wet weather. The author has seen such abandoned sites often enough to feel that he should sound the warning here.

The mistaken idea sometimes exists that the further a campfire circle is away from the main camp buildings the better and more romantic it becomes. Regarded from the "distance lends enchantment" theory the idea seems sound, but it is not always so. Not infrequently one sees fine close-to-camp-center campfire sites neglected for less suitable ones selected further afield. It is a fact that much of the glamour of a campfire is lost when it burns in a circle within plain view of camp buildings—though this may be offset by planting a screen of fair-sized, fast-growing evergreen trees to surround the campfire circle. The search should be for a suitable and convenient spot on the camp property as far out of earshot and eyeshot from civilization as conditions permit. Many such sites exist, though they may often be overlooked until someone skilled in campcraft points them out. On some camp properties, lovely sites for the campfire are available on gently sloping hillsides, on hilltops, on the shores of lakes, on the bank of a river, or on a peninsula.

Be wary about campfire circles dug out of level ground or in hillsides. The anticipated convenience of tiers of natural "benches" formed in excavating the circle can be too easily offset by a heavy rain, even when some sort of drainage has been installed.

In some camps, the site of the campfire is decided by the age of the campers who will sing around it. This is not an unwise plan provided it is not influenced by the very youngest campers. Quite often a convenient spot can be chosen especially for the freshman campfire. These little folk should be introduced to campfires even at their early stage of camp life, but it is better not to allow them to participate in the real campfires until they have a few seasons of camping to their credit. This gives them something to look forward to and keeps them camp-conscious.

CAMPFIRE CIRCLE BACKGROUNDS

When the best campfire site available has been found—let us assume that it is one on fairly high, level ground, surrounded by at least a few trees not more than 40 or 50 feet distant from the actual *fire site*—half of the mission is accomplished. The surrounding trees will allow the suspension of the wires described in Chapter 4 for the lighting of "magic" fires and the performance of various stunts for which the wires are basic props. When few trees surround the campfire site, some camps plant additional fast-growing young trees in the area, at least 15 feet outside of the outer edge of the campfire circle, in order to assure the intimacy and promote the natural background so helpful in creating the ideal campfire circle. Natural-wood, closely strung picket-fence-type backdrops at least 6 feet high can be erected at the parts of the circle which are most bare of vegetation, in order to add to the decor. These types of screens are not nearly so necessary for campfire circles as they are for council fire areas, and many camps get along very well by simply using special large and suitably painted backdrops for the various campfire nights planned. Some ideas for these are given in Chapter 15.

LAYING OUT THE CAMPFIRE CIRCLE

Once the actual spot has been decided on, it is not difficult to lay out and level off the actual inner circle surrounding the fire. The diameter of this circle should never be less than 30 feet, and some camps use circles of 40 to 50 feet in diameter successfully. The larger circle offers additional advantage for games and staging the more grandiose events, such as pageants, that are not infrequently part of the campfire activities. With the author's system of staging simultaneously as many similar events as possible on all four sides of the fire, the campfire circle becomes a four-ring circus with every seat, comparatively speaking, a ringside one. Suggestions for this will be found in "Quadrupling Campfire Fun," in Chapter 6.

An easy way to lay out the actual circle is first of all to drive a stout stake into the exact center of the desired circle, put a small loop on one end of a wire or strong cord over it, and fasten the other end of the 15- or 20-foot length of the cord or wire to the blunt end of a pointed stake or metal rod. Be certain that the distance between the center stake and outer edge of the inner circle is the one desired, and then mark out the campfire circle by tracing the circumference on the ground with the point of the marking stake or metal rod. A weed-killing flame-thrower may be used to burn along the mark left by the point of the stake, and it works well when the site is weed or grass covered. Should there be no easy way of burning the circle outline clearly, it may be marked with a liquid lime solution. This marking plainly indicates the inner circle, from which all stones and projecting roots have to be removed as the ground is carefully leveled and beaten down until it is perfectly smooth and flat. Of course, when the campfire circle makers find a suitable piece of level ground covered with grass, there is no need for the work just mentioned. True, the grass will have disappeared after a few campfires, but the ground will still be smooth, solid, and even. If this inner circle is surrounded by the first row of benches or logs or similar seating arrangement at a distance of about 3 feet from its edge, there is no need for further marking. If there is no such seating arrangement, a lime solution may be used to outline the edge. This is a far safer method than marking the inner circle with logs, rounded stones, or any other markings over which campers may trip and be injured. Even a low rail type of fence around the inner campfire circle can be hazardous while games are being played, and for that reason it is not recommended.

pity to use such civilized seating methods unless there is absolutely no suitable wildwood material available.

CAMPFIRE CIRCLE ILLUMINATION

Of course, a bright, flaming fire is the traditional and ideal way to illuminate a campfire circle, but at times some additional lighting is required in order that all campers may see some special features or pageants more clearly than by campfire light alone. Effective camp-made

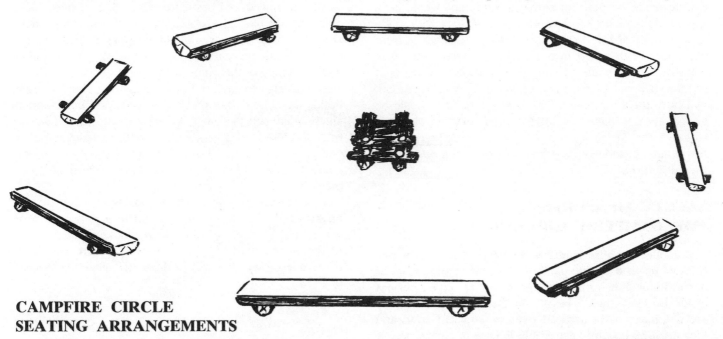

CAMPFIRE CIRCLE SEATING ARRANGEMENTS

Quite a number of good camps which have fine campfire circles are informal about seating arrangements, and the campers simply bring ground sheets on which they sit in rows around the circle. Other camps may have enough benches taken from the recreation hall to form two or three rows of seats around the circle, with another row of smaller campers seated on blankets in front of the first row of benches. Some of the camps with the simplest campfire seating arrangements have rows of built-in wooden or log benches installed in the council fire circle. Seats made from up-ended logs or large posts are rather uncomfortable and difficult to place firmly in position at times. Natural or squared-off logs of varying thickness in 10- to 20-foot lengths, securely pegged to the ground, make good seating when such logs are available. It is bad conservation to cut down live trees, even when timber is plentiful, to provide such seating; but in some states, unfortunately, a great number of formerly fine trees are dead or dying, and they serve the purpose of log seats very well. Seating may also be built in the form of bleachers or by using stringers with built-on seats, but it is a

torches or lanterns, rather than "store bought" lamps, will do a satisfactory job. Most torches made by using cloth soaked in kerosene prove smoky and smelly. Melted paraffin wax gives a better and cleaner light. A good way to use the melted paraffin wax is to dip into it strips of gauze bandages from 1 to 3 inches wide and then wrap these strips around the top of the stick or pole which is being used as the handle for the torch. The strip should not cover more than the top 3 or 4 inches of the handle. All sticks and poles used for handles should be green whenever possible and should range from 1 to 1½ inches in diameter. The lengths of these torch sticks or poles vary from 3 feet, when they are being carried, to 8-foot poles, when one end is driven into the ground. The fact that these paraffin wax torches are dripless is another point in their favor.

Good torches can be made from cattails, which are found on marshy ground and around some lakes and ponds. The "tails" are big enough for use from the end of July onward and are simply prepared, as they do not need to be dried, by just soaking the fuzzy end in melted paraffin or kerosene. Of course, they will only burn for a comparatively short time without the reed burning through, so they should only be carried in their natural state during brief ceremonies. When they are required for a longer period, the top part of the cattail can be wired onto green sticks so that the torches will burn much longer.

Older campers should be given the responsibility of torch-bearing, and instructed in advance to hold their torches out to the side when the campers are walking in line, so that the torch will burn neither the torch-bearers nor other campers.

Much longer-burning torches, which are not carried, can be made by pouring kerosene into cans which have short, bottlelike necks. A short length of thick wick made from lengths of soft, heavy cord braided together or from absorbent cloth rolled into a wick, is inserted into each can. The wick should fit snugly, and about ¾-inch of it should stick out of the neck of the can. A half-pint can will burn for a long time. Torches of this kind should be almost entirely buried in little mounds of clay, earth, or stones before being lighted. *Of course, absolutely no attempt must be made to add kerosene to such torches while they are burning!*

SAFETY MEASURES
FOR CAMPFIRE CIRCLES

An alert campfire leader will always have one or two buckets of sand or fine earth and a pail or two of water in the immediate vicinity of the campfire circle, but not inside it. They should be set on the ground where they are not likely to be tripped over or knocked over, and they must be instantly accessible in case of emergency. A couple of old folded blankets should also be placed beside the fire-fighting buckets. The chances may be slim that these fire precautions will be needed in the course of a season, but if they are not on hand when required, the result could be disastrous. Suppose a flammable costume of paper or cloth worn by an entertainer suddenly caught fire—and such things always happen suddenly and when completely unexpected! Having a blanket handy to smother the fire could save a life. Naturally, the first precaution should be for the campfire director to endeavor to prevent performers from wearing inflammable costumes or accessories, but it is difficult at times to be quite certain that all such things are not flammable, especially the improvised addition which a performer may don or snatch up at the last minute.

SAFETY MEASURES
FOR COUNCIL FIRE AREAS

Around the council fire there is even greater need for preparedness to fight fire than at the average campfire,

because of the nature of the activities which take place in the council circle. Some modern would-be Indians use flaming hoops and torches in their dances. Such dances are not covered in the chapter on dances because of a certain risk they entail not only to the performers but also to the spectators when the dances are not carried out with the utmost precaution by seasoned dancers who have developed hoop and torch control; even then accidents can happen.

The author has seen a flaming hoop slip from a dancer's hand and encircle a brave-in-council when there was no old blanket ready for such an emergency and, on that hot night, no blanketed braves in council. At another council fire, a fringed and bustled dancer fell into the middle of a brightly blazing fire. He had of course intended to clear the blaze in a triumphant leap as a finale to his dance; but his moccasins slipped as he started his jump, and he landed on his chest in the heart of the fire. There were buckets of water and old fire-fighting blankets right beside the chief's chair on this occasion and quick-witted chiefs in council that night, so what might have ended in tragedy closed on a less serious note, despite a rather badly burned brave, who left the acrid smell of burning goose feathers behind as he was taken off to the hospital.

In a council ring there should always be one or two buckets full of sand or fine dry earth, a pail or two of water, and a couple of old folded blankets placed close to the chief's chair at a point where they are not likely to be overturned and will be instantly available in case of need.

BASIC FIRES

The log cabin fire, as illustrated in the drawing, is perhaps the best type for both campfire circle and council ring. The heavy logs with which it is built form a firebox into which much smaller "logs," sawn from branches in correct lengths, may be carefully dropped as the fire needs refueling. These days more than ever the necessity to use only dead trees, or trees which have been blown down, for firewood should be strictly observed. Dead trees will burn more easily and brightly than fresh-cut green timber, and the use of dead trees is good conservation practice.

The fireplace, which should be about 4 feet square, is set directly in the center of the campfire circle. The actual fire bed should be dug down to mineral soil to prevent roots of trees or bushes from carrying the fire underground. The earth or clay, free from roots, is stamped down into the hole, and sufficient earth or clay can be added on top of it to raise the 4-foot square about 6 inches above the completely level ground surrounding it. This fireplace can be edged with a frame of hardwood logs, using two 4-foot logs about 8 inches in diameter with two shorter logs, say 2 feet 8 inches long and 8 inches in diameter, fitted between them, one at each end. These shorter logs are fitted flush with the ends of the two longer logs, and metal strips may be nailed to these four logs where they join, to hold them firmly together. The fire is built inside this frame, but the fire may also be built without a frame.

The base logs of the fire should be 3 feet long and from 8 to 10 inches in diameter. Oak, maple, poplar, and elm are among the woods which burn well. The two base logs should be placed on the ground about 2 feet 6 inches apart and the next two logs laid crosswise on top of them, about one foot from the ends, in log cabin style. Other hardwood logs from 4 to 6 inches in diameter are laid crisscross on top of them, as shown in the drawing. The logs should be a little shorter with each tier. When the first three tiers have been placed in position, it is time to build a very flammable heart in the fire.

Although the author believes that only wildwood material should be used for kindling in all campfire and council fires, he has been forced to alter his opinion at times. For instance, when there is nobody really skilled in fire-building and the rain has fallen during the day, but despite this the fire must blossom into immediate flame when lighted, the fire may require artificial encouragement. Dry newspapers rolled into little balls about 2 inches in diameter may be concealed in the heart of the fire, to which is added wildwood material, such as strips of birch bark from a dead paper birch, very dry grass, small dry branches of fir, spruce, or pine. Dry fir, pine, and spruce cones, especially when impregnated with kerosene or dipped in melted paraffin wax to meet the situation described above, make fine additional kindling; small, dry poplar or basswood twigs also burn well as fire-starters.

it burns a little longer before fresh fuel has to be added. Thick sticks of dry maple, beech, white hickory, or ash should be built, when available, into the fire, finding support on the main crosslogs. A few small "logs" about 3 or 4 inches in diameter and just long enough to overlap the top row of logs should be laid a few inches apart on the very top of the fire. A fire a little over 3 feet tall is high enough for most camp and council fire use, but an extra tier of logs can always be added when desired. As the heart of the fire burns down, miniature logs should be dropped gently, never thrown, in through the top of the fire by a firekeeper. This should be done in a way that does not interfere with any activity going on in the circle.

CAMPFIRE FIRE TENDERS

Though one may think of firekeepers or fire tenders chiefly in connection with Indian council fires, it is a good idea to have an efficient one to take care of the campfire too. He or she will assure a brightly burning fire during the program, and there will be no haphazard feeding of the fire, usually at the wrong moments, to mar campfire fun.

A campfire should almost never be built in bonfire proportions, except perhaps for one special celebration during the camping season; the fire's burning brilliance is far more important than its size.

MAKING SHORT LOGS LOOK LONGER

Frequently, the author has to build log cabin fires for park camp groups, where logs are provided by the park

BASE LOGS

ANGLE LOGS

The heart of a fire built as described may save the awful fiasco of a camp or council fire which will not flame instantly when a light is applied to it. When a well-filled box fire of this sort is lighted above the second log level

authorities. Such logs are often only 2 feet long instead of 3 feet. When the logs are arranged as shown in the drawing, they will form a sturdy fire frame of standard size. The four base logs are arranged on the ground so that there is a space of about 6 inches between them at each corner. Four more of these 2-foot logs are laid, one at each corner, at an angle across the base logs, as illustrated. This arrangement adds length and width to the fire when the next tier is laid. The angle logs do not detract from the log cabin shape of the fire, since the next tier of the framework, four more short logs, fits easily and correctly into the log cabin pattern, as do the remaining tiers of logs. This fire-building pointer is equally useful for council fire chiefs.

FIRE-BUILDING VARIATIONS

There are a number of suitable ways of building fires for both campfire and council ring use, in addition to the log cabin fire described above.

TRIANGLE FIRE. This little-known fire can be used for campfires, YMCA fires, and Y-Indian Guide fires. It can either be built in the shape of an actual triangle, as illustrated, or can be slightly squared off at the pointed

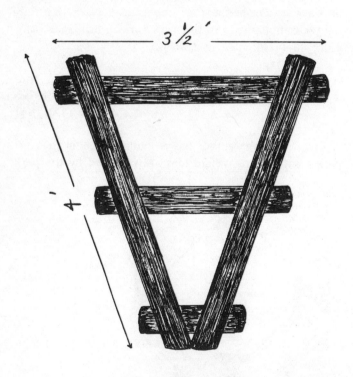

end by opening the two logs at that end 12 to 18 inches and placing a short log under them. The framework log base should be made with logs at least 8 inches in diameter, and the two top logs can be nailed or attached by metal strips to the three underneath logs. This arrangement allows for a circulation of air beneath the fire. The

rest of the fire framework is built up in the triangle shape and in the manner of the log cabin fire already described. This type of fire serves for symbolic fires and is useful when the area in which a campfire has to be built is more or less oblong in shape.

TEPEE FIRE

THE TEPEE FIRE. Although used by some campfire and council fire groups, the tepee fire is not recommended here, for two good reasons. It does not steadily illuminate the council fire area as well as the log cabin fire, and even when well built it has a tendency to shed logs or collapse while being fed fresh fuel. For this fire, about a dozen logs around 3 feet 6 inches long and from 4 to 7 inches in diameter at the butt end, or somewhat thicker if the logs are split in two before building the fire, are needed for the outer framework. The split logs burn better and faster than the unsplit ones, but whichever kind are used they should be placed on the ground in tepee formation, as shown in the drawing, and held in place about three-quarters of the way up by a strand of strong, hard wire wound several times around all of the logs to hold them in place. Of course, this is done after the kindling, smaller sticks, and miniature logs have been carefully built into the heart of the fire. What has been said about building the interior of the log cabin fire applies here also.

Another way to build the framework of this tepee fire is to build the outer logs onto one or two stout greenwood crotches which are driven firmly into the ground in the center of the fireplace before starting to build the fire. One suitable stick with a double fork, not always easily found, is better than two separate ones. A durable metal support rod with one or two crotches at the top is a still better way of setting up the tepee fire. The recommendation is that this fire be used only when necessary for some symbolic reason, as it is not so well adapted for campfire and council fire use as the other types mentioned.

THE OBLONG FIRE. Illustrated here is an excellent fire when it has to be built in a campfire or council fire area which is oblong rather than circular in shape. What

OBLONG FIRE

this fire lacks in width it more than makes up for in length. It is built in the same way as the standard log cabin fire, and with similar logs, but it can range from 4 to 6 feet in length even when it cannot be built more than 2 feet in width. The fire box is as strong as that of the square log cabin fire. This oblong fire can be fed with longer logs than the square type fire, but short logs will make just as good, and a somewhat brighter-burning, fire. The heart of this fire is built in exactly the same way as that described for the log cabin fire.

STAR FIRE. The pioneers used this handy fire, as did outdoorsmen on cold nights. It is mentioned here because it makes a good story fire for small groups of older campers who enjoy an hour or two of storytelling by soft firelight.

The quickest way to get this type of fire going is to light a small, hot fire in what will be the center of the star fire and, when the small fire has burned brightly for ten minutes or so, gently push in the thinner ends of five or six dry hardwood or softwood logs from 6 to 10 feet long and from 6 to 10 inches in diameter at the thick ends. These logs should be arranged in star formation, as shown in the drawing, and when the ends in the fire burn through, the rest of the logs are gradually fed into the fire in the center by pushing on the unburnt ends. It is well to have a few replacement logs of the right size handy.

Here is a good way to make a star fire when a corn or potato roast winds up the storytelling. A round hole about 18 inches in diameter, sloping slightly from the outside edge to a depth of about 6 or 8 inches in the center, is dug. A brisk fire is lit in the hole, and short lengths of stout, dry sticks are laid across it when it is well alight. These sticks should just rest on the ground at the edge of the hole. When the flames rise above ground level, the star fire logs are placed in position, with the ends of the logs almost touching over the center of the fire hole. Soon the ends of these logs will flame and burn, adding their hot ashes and live coals to those already in the fire hole. By the time the logs have been pushed toward the fire until about half of their lengths have been burned away, a hot, glowing bed of embers will be ready in the fire hole to receive the storytellers' potatoes, which may be baked in a large can sunk in the embers when the campers wish to add the grand hotel touch. A further stride in that direction is to thoroughly grease the potatoes before putting them into the can. The potatoes will not taste better to real outdoors people, but they will require less watching. On such a fire, corn may also be cooked in the embers or arranged upright in a can.

COLOR AND "MAGIC" FIRES

Color fires are beautiful for occasional use, and they are easily made. There are a number of chemical powders and cubes on the market which produce multicolored fires when placed on the main logs of the fire or dropped into it when it is burning. Although a few of the chemicals are rather expensive, when bought in half-pound or pound quantities they will last for an entire camp season or longer, depending on how they are used. Colors are produced as follows:

red	strontium chloride
orange	calcium chloride
yellowish	sodium chloride (salt)
blue	copper oxide
green	copper, boron, borax, boric acid or barium chloride

blue-green to purple	copper sulphate or copper chloride
mauve to violet	potassium chloride
crimson to purple	lithium chloride

These chemicals can be readied for use by mixing one pound of the chemical with one gallon of water. Pine cones and lengths of dry, porous sticks are steeped in the solutions, overnight or for longer periods, and when dried are ready for use.

Already prepared color-fire chemicals can be recommended, as they save considerable experimentation and work. These color-fire agents come in various powders, grains, cones, and sticks, with complete directions for use on the packages. All of these chemicals produce a variety of excellent color effects and may be bought in small or larger quantities at reasonable prices.

Camps situated near to the sea will find that logs washed into shore, when dried in the sun, will brighten a campfire with rainbow hues when used as fuel.

FIRE LIGHTING BY BOW DRILL AND BY FLINT AND STEEL

There is no reason why either of the following fire-lighting methods should not be used for lighting both campfires and council fires. Both savor of the outdoors and are arts which are fast becoming lost to many lovers of the open places. Both fires should be lit by a camp director or counselor who has acquired skill in firecraft. The bow drill fire is a friction type which can be lit speedily with some practice—and the correct equipment. The speed with which this fire can be lit, from the time the drill touches the fireboard until the spark ignites the tinder, has been reduced from thirty seconds to a matter of a few seconds, chiefly by the use of almost explosive sorts of tinder. Fortunately, the lighter of the campfire need not try for a record, and the majority of campers will be intrigued to see the tinder blaze after one minute or more of effort on the part of the fire-lighter.

The wildwood instruments used for lighting this fire have been so frequently described that they are not detailed here, nor is this particular method of fire lighting. The necessary bow, thong, drill, socket, fireboard, and tinder may be bought in a number of outdoor supply stores. As a rule such outfits do the job, but often one can find much better natural tinder than that supplied with the outfit.

Flint and steel is another good primitive method of lighting a campfire. Here again, good tinder is of prime importance. The nest of a field mouse, thoroughly dry, or dried fluffs such as dandelion down, or milkweed silk, or charred linen rags, make excellent fire-starters. Thoroughly dry grass mixed with finely shredded cedar or birch bark also makes a fine natural tinder. When the sparks fall on any of these tinders, they should be blown into flame with gentle breath, and the well-prepared campfire ignited. Flint and steel kits can be bought; but improvised sets, kept in a little fire-bag, can be made from a piece of broken file, a similar piece of steel, or the back of a knife blade. As a substitute for flint, a suitable piece of quartz, agate, or jasper can be used, among other stones or minerals.

TRICK FIRE LIGHTING

Though some camps are inclined to reserve trick fire-lighting methods for council fire use, there is no good reason why some of these spectacular fire-lighting ways should not be used when lighting campfires on gala occasions. This is especially true when a camp has no Indian council fire area and all of the fire activities are centered around the campfire. Stress need not be put on the Indian angle of the opening feature in such cases, but it may be highlighted by having one or more "Indians," or a medicine man in full regalia, conduct a brief opening of the campfire ceremony.

FIRE BY FIREBALL

This striking way of lighting a campfire or council fire proves very popular when staged effectively. A fine wire is strung tightly from a branch of a leafy tree to a stake driven into the center of the fire, after an ordinary spool or photographic film spool has been threaded onto the wire. The spool is wrapped around with cotton wool or gauze bandage which has been thoroughly soaked in melted paraffin wax or kerosene. The height of the branch of the tree to which one end of the wire is attached depends on the distance the spool has to travel before reaching the fire. Sometimes the entire effect of the Fireball is spoiled by being released from a branch so high that it reaches the fire almost before the onlookers have time to follow its descent. The only way to assure a certain but reasonably slow descent of the spool into the fire is to try its traject from various heights from a suitable tree or pole in advance of the campfire or council fire. A fairly long run is, of course, far more spectacular than a short one. An older camper or camp leader, well concealed in the tree, lights the spool on a prearranged word or signal from someone in charge of the fire-lighting ceremony. Immediately prior to lighting the spool the camper releases it from a wire guard, made from a loop of wire, which holds it in place. Someone who can be really trusted should do the lighting, as occasionally the spool comes down without being lighted, and sometimes the spool lighter "comes down" without lighting the spool.

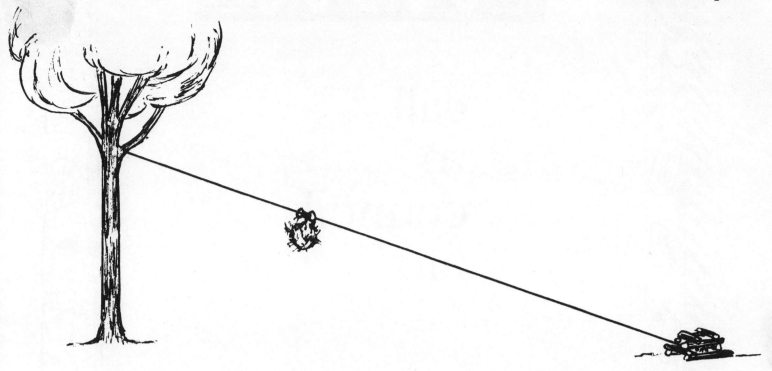

LIGHTING DELAYED-ACTION FIRES

This method of lighting mystifying fires is equally good for lighting either campfire or council fire on special occasions, and the astonishment of the campers as the fire apparently lights all by itself is worth the comparatively small amount of effort taken to prepare the surprise. Once a campfire leader in charge of fire lighting has figured out exactly how long it takes for these saltpeter impregnated fuses to burn, he can "light" a fire by simply placing his fingers for a few moments on the red head of a camper, or in other amusing ways.

This way of ignition is carried out by using a simple delayed-action fuse made from soft white string which has been thoroughly soaked for several hours in a soupy solution of saltpeter and water and then allowed to dry thoroughly in the sun. Two teaspoonfuls of powdered saltpeter dissolved in about one tablespoonful of very hot water, mixed together in a glass lid, will impregnate

at least 10 feet of string, enough for many delayed-action fuse types of fires. A 9-inch length of soft white string ⅛ inch in diameter burns for *approximately* five or six minutes, when burning upward. Ordinary soft white string about 1/16 inch thick will burn for *approximately* the same time, but there is more chance that a thin fuse of this sort may go out at some part of its burning length unless it has been very well and evently impregnated with the saltpeter solution.

The fuses will burn a little faster or a little slower, according to how well they have been impregnated by the saltpeter and the strength of the mixture. The author usually rubs the tiny saltpeter crystals from the string, when it is the ⅛-inch thick absorbent white string fuse, in order to slow down the burning time and make the slight glow on the string practically invisible. The flakey crystals should be left on the cotton tinder-strips, used as the tinder which starts off the fire by igniting the regular tinder used for fire lighting, as these crystals doubly assure their inflammability.

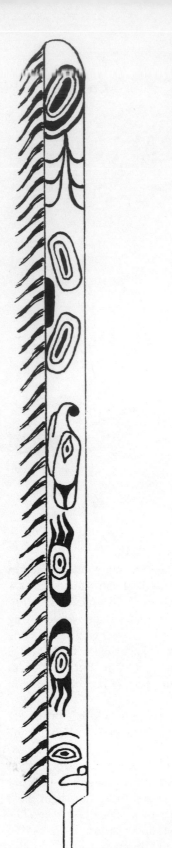

call to council fire

Night magic is in the air! It hovers above the unlit council fire waiting for the iridescent tongues of flame to tell of other strong magic— the magic of the age-old Brotherhood of the Fire. Soon braves file silently through the trees to the council ring. The call of an owl, wrapped in his soft blanket of darkness, merges with the insistent Call of the Forest, which echos the Call to Council. Shadows silently steal from the scarlet and gold of the leaping flames, and the warriors-in-council sense spirit-magic and the many mysterious things unknown to those who have never experienced the wonder of a council fire. Multicolored sparks float skyward like bright-jeweled prayers to the Great Spirit who gave his children life—and the Fellowship of Fire.

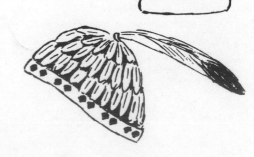

chapter 2

woodsmoke from indian fires

As The First American Indians sat around their council fires, the mystery and peace of the fire inspired wonder which later crystallized into thought. Then they sought the reason why grass was green and the ghost flower white, and why regal white wolves trailed along with the buffalo herds. Thought developed into belief, and in the glow and warmth of fire-friendship the Indians acquired a very precious thing—the secret of mental serenity within, despite physical insecurity without. Campers of today, too, far from the noise and distraction of cities, can develop some part of that priceless trait—by campfire light.

Before the smoke spirals and the sparks soar skyward, one must locate a council fire site to perpetuate the spirit of those of bygone days.

IDEAL COUNCIL FIRE SITES

Advice regarding the choice of best sites for campfire circles has been detailed in Chapter 1, and much of it is also applicable to sites for council fires.

A council fire site can often be further away from the main camp buildings than a campfire circle, because it is more frequently used by older campers. Many camps do not let campers under twelve years of age participate in council fires, and in a number of camps council fire activities are carried out by considerably older camper groups. Being able to select a council fire area further afield offers more scope than when one is faced with the necessity of finding a site considerably closer to the camp center. This is fortunate, as a council fire site in a wooded area, or at least in a secluded one, adds greatly to the romance of the council fire.

A council ring surrounded by trees at a convenient distance, say forty or fifty feet away from the actual *fire site,* is ideal not only for the woodsy effect so helpful in creating the right atmosphere but also because the trees,

even when sparse, offer the means of suspending the overhead wires necessary for lighting the "magic" fires described in Chapter 4, and for staging various magic effects in some of the Indian story plays given in Chapter 18. In the absence of trees, big rocks or a cliff background setting is effective as a natural council ring surrounding.

LAYING OUT THE INNER CIRCLE OF THE COUNCIL RING

A council fire circle 40 feet in diameter is the ideal dimension for the inner circle, with the warriors-in-council seated in rows beginning about 2 or 3 feet away from the outer edge of the inner circle. Many council rings have been constructed with an inner circle diameter of only 30 feet. While this is intimate, it is frequently inadequate, and it will be found that the larger circle offers welcome additional space for staging pageants and ceremonies and for carrying out many of the clan challenges which the smaller ring does not permit. The smaller, 30-foot circle will be found quite adequate for smaller Indian bands. The theory that a larger ring loses in intimacy is easily discounted by staging two less active clan challenges in the bigger circle at the same time or having four man-to-man challenges in action at the same time. With these contests going on, on all four sides of the fire at once, it not only creates an over-all picture of activity but allows considerably more contestants to take part in the various activities and gives each warrior-in-council a ringside seat.

The best council ring is perhaps one with only one entrance. The entrance can be of any reasonable width, and an additional means of entering and leaving the circle can be provided through a doorway or other opening in a large backdrop, such as the entrance of a tepee, longhouse, or Northwest Coast house, described and il-

lustrated in the following pages. For those Indian groups which feel the necessity of an additional entry and exit other than those just mentioned, a narrow passage just back of the chief's chair can be kept clear for emergencies and messengers.

Laying out the circular council ring can be done in exactly the same way as that described for campfire circles in Chapter 1. Council rings do not always need to be, and sometimes cannot be, built in the circular form. Fine council fire areas are frequently built on rather narrow peninsulas and in other sites where the area must be oblong rather than round. The Northwest Coast Indian council fire areas, laid out in the oblong or near-square shape of their huge houses, may give some council fire chiefs an idea for something new in council fire areas. Throughout the winter months, the Indians of the Northwest Coast held their council fires, magnificent ceremonies, and dances indoors. Drawings and diagrams of these areas and how they may be decorated with appropriate backdrops, screens, and totem poles are given in detail in this chapter. It is interesting to note that some of the Northwest Coast tribes used circular outdoor dance rings when the weather permitted.

COUNCIL FIRE SEATING ARRANGEMENTS

A number of seating arrangements are described in the campfire section of this book, but it should be said here that the use of logs of various diameters as seats or, better still, stout, natural, hardwood planks from 8 to 14 feet long, about 10 inches wide, and at least 2 inches thick, adequately supported on sawed-off logs, are probably the best form of seating for council fire onlookers. These plank benches should be graded in height to assure a clear view of the council fire area. Despite elaborate seating in some council rings, many happy warriors in others are simply seated on ground sheets when the group is small and there are only two or three rows of braves in council.

DECORATIVE SHIELDS FOR COUNCIL FIRE AREAS

Shields are useful for several purposes: decorative, dance, and pageant. When used as decorations, they may be hung on trees or poles surrounding the council ring or placed on tripods, such as the one shown in the illustration, on the outside edge of the council fire area. Each council fire tribe can adopt a suitable totem and paint it on their shield. Quite often the designs painted on Indian shields were protective medicine symbols, so that their owners would be less likely to be wounded in battle when carrying them. There were also commemorative shield designs, representing their owners' battles and escapes.

All that is required to make picturesque shields is canvas or other strong, tight-woven cloth, preferably white or buff in color. This cloth is cut in circles about 12 inches more in diameter than the size of the framework of the shield, to allow a 6-inch overlap all around. The Indian shields varied in size from about 14 inches to 30 inches. A good size for council fire use is 18 to 20 inches in diameter.

A suitable framework for shields can be made from strong, narrow hoops or wider, wooden hoops sawed in two all around, or from pliable tree branches bent into a circle with the two overlapping ends tied securely together with strong twine. The unfavorable thing about this type of frame is that it is likely to warp, even when carefully made and dried before use, spoiling the symmetry of the shield. The author has found that the best way to mount the canvas on the shield is to use either a circle of thin plywood or, when the shield is not exposed to rain, a circle of *heavy* cardboard. When heavy cardboard is not available, gluing two circles of lightweight cardboard together will serve the purpose. Holes are pierced with a big sharp nail or icepick about 1 inch from the edge of and all around the cloth, about 4 inches apart. The canvas cover is then laced in the back with a heavy cord, so that the cloth is stretched smoothly over the front of the shield. The Indians painted the design on both the shield and the cover, which was removed just before battle, but the shields for modern council fire decoration need only be painted on the canvas cover. Some Plains shields are shown in this chapter. Strips of colored cloth, colored feathers, and tufts of colored hair may be attached to the shield for further decoration.

BACKDROPS
FOR COUNCIL FIRE AREAS

The drawings of the various dwellings of the Indians of the United States and Canada which appear in this book will, when painted on large sheets of canvas in correct or reduced scale, serve as as effective backdrops to place behind the chief's chair or at one end of the council fire area on a night when a council fire is being held in honor of the Indians whose dwelling serves as a background. These backdrops can have real doorways cut in them, so that they can be used as means of entry and exit when necessary during the program. They also make a good screen behind which warriors can prepare to make their entry into the council ring.

Council fire chiefs may find it a good idea to stage different Indian nights in the council ring. By this means the participating warriors will learn much of the way of life of different tribes about which they may know little. All the braves or a group of "visiting" braves may become Woodland, Northwest Coast, or Southwest Indians, instead of belonging to Plains tribes.

LONGHOUSE BACKDROP. At one council fire, braves can belong to the proud Nation of the Iroquois. The backdrop will remind them that the all-powerful League of the Five Nations ruled the land for two hundred years. The Confederacy was respected by the other nations and tribes of the United States and Canada during that time. The League was invincible in war, when war was necessary, but they were good friends and neighbors to other tribes throughout the many years when the smoke of the peace pipes rose skyward.

PUEBLO BACKDROP. To be People of the Pueblo for a night will be an interesting and probably new experience for many of the warriors gathered around the council fire. Costumes are easily made, and it should be remembered that many tribes throughout the width and breadth of the United States wore breechclouts for convenience's sake on hot nights—except on ceremonial occasions, and all Pueblo nights need not be too formal. There is a wealth of Pueblo material, games, dances, and other activities to assure an interesting, pleasurable night. Younger warriors seeking information for background purposes for a Pueblo night will be surprised to discover how brave and artistic these Indians of the Southwest were. They too had their great chiefs and indomitable warriors, magnificent ceremonial occasions, and artisans who were famed for their weaving, pottery, and silversmith work.

A sandpainting makes a colorful and artistic fireplace decoration for a Southwest Indian night. An illustration of a simple sandpainting design will be found in Chapter 20, along with details on how sandpainting can be adapted to suit council fire areas without being obliterated during activities or taking up too much room. When a Southwest Indian night opens, a Navaho sandpainter artist can kneel before the completed sandpainting on canvas and let the last remaining grains of sand trickle through his fingers to complete the painting, apparently, as the flame-fingers spiral skyward.

CHICKEE BACKDROP. With a backdrop of a Chickee, the typical dwelling of the Indian settlers of Florida, the Everglades, brave Seminole warriors and their redoubtable Chief Osceola come to mind. Thrilling stories of their prolonged battles for freedom from white man's rule, and their adventures with alligators and bears in their Swampland fastness which they knew so well, can make up part of the program. As a finale, the warriors-in-council will be interested to know that the Seminole are the only Indians in America who did not sign a peace treaty with the government.

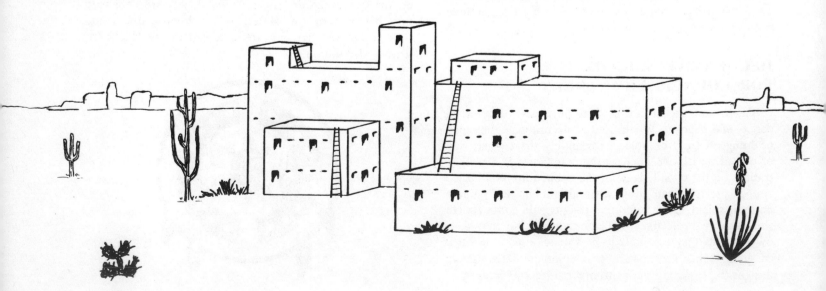

TEPEE BACKDROP. Tepee backgrounds, especially ones with a close-knit, stockaded fence on each side as shown in the illustration, make effective, space-saving backdrops in addition to providing a sort of auxiliary dressing room. A real tepee, when one is available, can take the place of the backdrop replica, but the mock-up saves space and time. The Plains tepees were very similar in appearance. They were made from buffalo skins as a rule, until the white man destroyed the vast buffalo herds. Usually these dwellings were set up on thirteen poles, each pole representing one of the moons in the Indian year. The chief point requiring care when the tepee backdrop is used is that the correct designs for the various tribes be painted on the tepee. Seasoned council fire Indians would be much surprised to see tepees decorated with Blackfoot designs in a Sioux encampment, or Kiowa-Apache decoration on tepees in a Crow camp.

NORTHWEST COAST HOUSE BACKDROP. On another night to be remembered, the warriors can meet before a magnificent Northwest Coast House backdrop, attired as Haida, Nootka, Tsimshian, or Coast Salish warriors; or the main group of Plains or other tribes can entertain a visiting clan from one of these tribes. Costuming is easy, and there is a wealth of material for programs to be found in these pages about these splendid tribes. A switch to the Northwest Coast or woodland areas will give many modern council fire chiefs and braves a chance to lay aside war bonnets weighed down with unearned coup feathers and meet their peers on even ground as they engage in new tribal and man-to-man challenges with their new-found brothers. Totem poles make a striking decor for such nights.

The oblong fire described in Chapter 1 is a fine fire for a Northwest Coast type of council fire area or for use when a council fire area has been rigged up to look like the inside of a great Northwest Coast house. The "inside" illusion is easily created by the setting up of a backdrop or backdrops and one or two inside house screens and posts, and the arrangement of the chief's chair and seating of the warriors-in-council. Such backdrops and screens are described and pictured in the following pages.

NORTHWEST COAST COUNCIL FIRE AREAS

Council Fire chiefs who have carried out their American Plains or Woodland council fire activities in a circular council fire area will wonder how they can best carry out a Northwest Coast Indian council fire in such an area. Some of the circular areas have fixed seats or benches set into the ground for the warriors-in-council, built in a circle surrounding the council fire, apparently making the transformation even more difficult. The answers—for there are several of them—as to how the Northwest Coast setup can be fitted in are simple. The easiest way of all is to change very little of the original layout. In spring, summer, and fall, some of the Northwest Coast tribes carried out dances and ceremonies in a circular council fire area. It was the bitter winds of winter that drove the Indians indoors, so that the winter ceremonies had to be carried out in rectangular spaces inside the huge houses rather than in the open. The illusion of making a circular council fire area appear oblong is not hard to achieve. It can be done by adding one or two additional rows of benches at the sides and ends of the circular area. This is easy when a camp uses movable benches. Another way to obtain the oblong effect, without the use of benches, is to have the first two rows of the warriors-in-council sit on the ground in oblong formation.

CHIEF'S CHAIR BACK

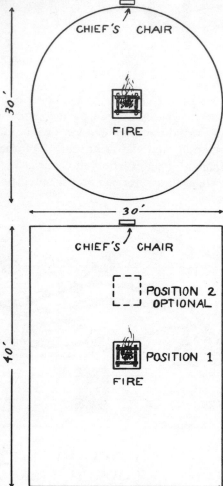

any one of which can be hung up, or set up, behind the tribal chief's chair. The question as to whether the backdrop is merely made of canvas painted and hung on a framework of strong poles, which can be hung up on the night of the council fire, or a mock-up built from light plywood or other wood, which can be stowed away easily at the end of the camp season, is something for the council fire chief to decide.

When the backdrop of an interior is used it must be imagined that the council fire is burning inside the tribal chief's great house and that the warriors-in-council are sitting inside it. A chief's chair with a colorful back is set beside the fire, as illustrated in the drawing. The back can be made from plywood, or even strong cardboard when there is already a wooden back on the chair or short bench used by the chief. Drawings illustrate suitable chair backs, which should be colored chiefly in red, black, and yellow, though other colors may also be used.

A small oval hole about 30 inches high and 18 inches wide cut directly in the center of the backdrop about 8 inches above the ground will prove very useful as a doorway. It can be used by chiefs, shamans, and others who wish to gain direct access to the council fire area, or to leave it after having entered by the usual entrance. A housefront pole, when one is available, can be set up directly at one side of the oval doorway.

A Northwest Coast backdrop of a housefront, with a suitable crest and other paintings on it, can be set up directly behind the tribal chief's chair. This arrangement will give the impression that the council is being held in the open in front of the chief's house. If the original Plains Indian council fire circle possessed totem poles, which is unlikely if authenticity was sought in building the Plains Indian setup, one pole may be dug in immediately in front of the center of the housefront. Other poles could be placed on either side of the housefront, or at the entry to the council fire area. If the camp has no totem poles, they can wait for a while. The drawings show suggestions for housefronts and an interior screen,

HOUSE SCREEN

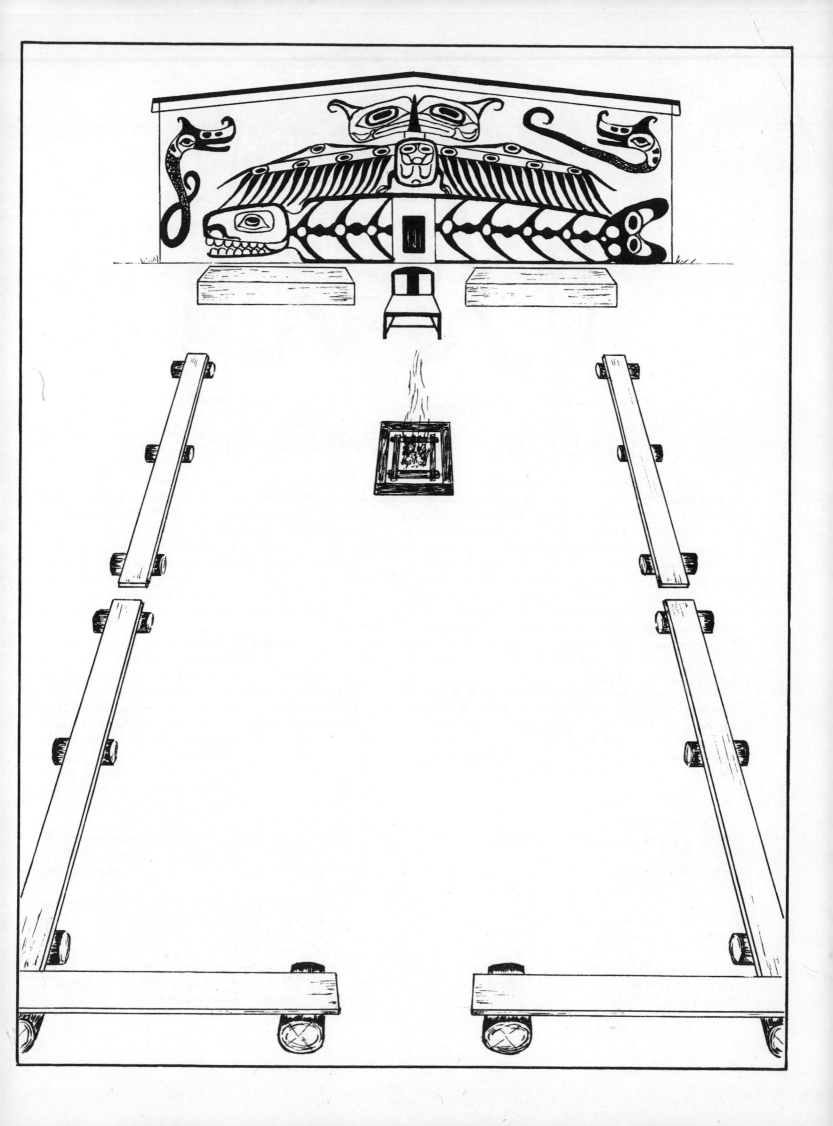

CHIEF'S CHAIR BACK

Council Fire chiefs who wish to build a regular Northwest Coast council fire area should figure on one about 40 feet long and 30 feet wide, inside measurements. As a good circular council fire area is about 30 feet in diameter, inside measurements, there is little difference in the space required to build a rectangular one. The width required for the rows of seats for the warriors-in-council will be decided by the number of warriors who generally attend the council fires. How small these council fire area dimensions seem when compared with the huge Northwest Coast houses, some of which were 500 feet long and 70 feet wide! This left a lot of room for both pageantry and people.

The fire in a council fire area measuring 40 feet by 30 feet may be placed in either of the positions shown in the drawing. If the central position is chosen, there will be a good-sized space of 15 feet on each side of the fire and 20 feet of space at each end. The chief should place the fire where it best meets his needs.

THE ART OF
THE COUNCIL FIRE TENDER

Some Indian tribes of the Northwest Coast completely disregarded cost and ladled eulachon oil, which had a high trading value, onto the council or ceremonial fires when brilliance was most required. At less important moments they dropped oil-soaked torches into the fire. This was done by the fire tenders at just the right moments, not only to illuminate but to heighten the dramatic effects of the ceremonies and other major activities in progress.

Modern council fire chiefs can learn a worthwhile lesson from these tribes, even if they don't have candle-fish oil handy. Too many of the best effects during ceremonial council fires are lost through lack of sufficient illumination. Some council fires have only a few extra sticks of wood lying beside them to last throughout an hour or more of activities. When more wood is needed, often urgently, it has to be sought with a flashlight in the surrounding woods. This is poor council fire management.

Every council fire should have one or two keepers of the fire—fire tenders—who are responsible for the fire. They should be cued as to when the fire should be brightest and when it should be allowed to dim a little. The fire tenders should never be conspicuous. They should sit on the outside edge of the area and try to feed the fire, when necessary, between the events as much as possible. A soft, flickering fire is fine for storytelling, when the stories are not being acted out. When they are, it is a waste of talent and material to have the actions in the council fire area only half seen by the warriors-in-council because of insufficient light. Perhaps the council fire chief can see what is taking place quite well, because he is close to the action, but what of the fourth row of warriors-in-council? For them the most thrilling parts of the action may be lost.

Such conditions need not exist. Pine cones soaked in liquid paraffin or kerosene may be dropped into the fire when brightness is required at a moment's notice. Miniature torches made from dry, softwood sticks such as pine—from 8 to 10 inches long, ½ to 1½ inches in diameter, with from 4 to 6 inches of one end wrapped in paraffin-wax-soaked gauze bandage—will also assure instant-bright illumination. These little torches should be lit at the fire and dropped inside it at the right moment. Rather loosely rolled paper balls which have been saturated in liquid paraffin wax or dipped in kerosene and then allowed to drain, are other means of making the invisible visible. Of course, an overzealous keeper of the fire has to be warned against producing a "bright as a sunlit day" effect at wrong moments. Such unexpected brightness may not be appreciated by a shaman who is working big medicine which shows up better by not being showed up; but even medicine-man magic usually benefits rather than suffers from adequate light.

Colored fire effects are cleverly used at Northwest Coast council fires. The Indians cleverly produced color-fire effects by dropping minerals and specially treated natural woods, which gave off colored flames, into the fire. Some of the most splendid Northwest Coast Indian council fires which the author has attended were made even more effective because logs which had been soaked by ocean water, then sun-dried on the beach, were burned throughout the council fire ceremonies. The wonderful, ever changing colors would be hard to duplicate by artificial or chemical substitutes.

COUNCIL FIRE AREA ILLUMINATION BY TORCHES

Torches make an excellent auxiliary method of adding light to the area on special ceremonial occasions, or at any time when additional light is desirable. Various sorts of torches are described in detail in Chapter 1.

INVITATION STICKS

These sticks were sent out by many tribes as invitations to a ceremonial council fire or other important Indian activity. The workmanship on some of the more elaborate invitation sticks was artistic and beautiful, like most of the Indian craftsmanship.

Invitation sticks are easily made and are a picturesque way of inviting guests to a council fire. The sticks varied in length, size, and design and can be made from straight, smooth sticks.

The Dakota and some other Plains tribes used sticks about 3 feet long with feather and horsehair tuft decorations. These sticks can be painted and further embellished with Plains designs or burnt stripes around them.

The invitation sticks of the Ojibway were short, not more than a foot in length, and were not decorated.

Some medicine societies used short sticks, ranging from 6 to 10 inches in length. They were thin and bore no decoration of any kind. The invitation sticks given out by council fire groups can be collected when presented by the guests on arrival, or the guests may be allowed to keep the sticks as souvenirs of the event to which they have been invited.

COUNCIL FIRE ETIQUETTE

This feature of the council fire program is very important though not at all complicated, except perhaps on special ceremonial occasions in which all warriors-in-council participate. The chief requirements of council fire etiquette are courtesy, good sportsmanship, and common sense. The essentials can be taught to the braves before the first council fire of the season, or learned through a talk by the council fire chief just outside the council ring immediately before the first fire flames. They must learn that no brave may cross the council fire area without first asking for and receiving permission from the council fire chief to do so. No brave may interrupt the council fire ceremonial programs by audible talk or whispering. There will be plenty of opportunity for showing approval in Indian fashion following dances and songs and during challenges. When a brave wishes to speak or take part in a challenge or other activity, when volunteers have been asked for, he stands, raises his right arm above his head, palm of hand pointing outward, and waits until he is noted by the chief and called upon to speak. A real brave does not question decisions made by the chief regarding challenges and other contests. Should the brave be right and the chief wrong at times, the brave who accepts the decision without protest counts grand coup within himself, and he will earn many more silent coups of approval from his brothers-in-council who realize what has happened. A brave shows approval and applauds by saying "How! How!" or "Ho! Ho!" and disapproval and dissent by exclaiming "Wah! Wah!" Braves will soon act with dignity and decorum, as did the Red Men in council under the spell of the council fire.

Young children and pets should never be present at a council fire, and even a well-behaved dog belonging to a chief may bring more trouble than atmosphere to a council fire. They should be left to guard the lodge.

When subchiefs or one or more warriors are chosen to participate in some way in the proceedings at the council fire, they should be briefed in advance so that they know exactly what to do in an Indian manner and just when to do it. Different council fire groups have

INVITATION   STICKS

different rules and rituals, and these should be introduced and learned before the first council fire to assure the smooth flow of council fire proceedings.

NORTHWEST COAST COUNCIL FIRE ETIQUETTE

Council fire etiquette was as strict as potlatch etiquette on the Northwest Coast. The rules followed at these ceremonies are not difficult for the modern warrior to learn, however, since they were based on common sense, good manners, respect for chiefs, shamans, and other leaders, and good sportsmanship during clan challenges and coup-counting events. The warriors were quiet and alert in council. They remained in their places after the entry into the council fire area and did not leave or cross it at any time during the ceremony without permission. A warrior raised a hand when he wished to speak or take part in a challenge. He waited until he was noticed by the tribal or a clan chief and given permission to carry out his wish. The ruling of a chief regarding the winners of challenges was never questioned by the warriors in council. The decisions were accepted without protest, even when it appeared that the chief was mistaken. An alert chief will generally find this out for himself and correct the wrong that he has unintentionally done by a faulty decision. Warriors should not clap their hands, stamp their feet, or whistle during a council fire. They may show approval and encourage their clan warriors to greater efforts in the coups and challenges by shouting "Hai! Hai!" or "Ho! Ho!" or "Klosh!" which in the Chinook Jargon means "Well done!"

COUNTING COUP

Because the term "counting coup" will be mentioned frequently, it may be well to tell how it originated and give a typical example of how the Plains tribes counted coup. Coup derives its meaning from the French word "coup" (pronounced *coo*), which means an effective stroke, or achievement. The word is used daily in the French newspapers—*coup de grâce, coup d'état,* or *coup de soleil.* The French explorers saw some tribes, the Dakota and others, count coup by striking a pole with a tomahawk or war club. Such a ceremony is described later, in Chapter 20.

The word coup was adopted by a number of tribes of American Indians to describe their achievements and exploits in war. Some tribes merely had a candidate for coup honors stand up in council and recite the exploit or exploits accomplished by him for which he considered himself worthy to count coup. Other tribes, including those of the Blackfoot Nation, cast sticks when counting coup. The following is an account of how two young

Blackfoot boys "threw the sticks" to proclaim coup.* It gives a good idea of how two young, modest warriors-to-be proclaimed their very real achievements. Many older braves were far more loquacious and far more boastful in seeking recognition for far lesser feats of valor. The two young braves in the story had captured, from an eagle trap and with their bare hands, two full-grown golden eagles which they wished to train and keep as pets.

"This young warrior-to-be would count coup, Sun Arrow," Yellow Horse told the medicine man.

Without speaking, the medicine man took two short sticks, which were used in coup-counting ceremonies, from a beautifuly beaded medicine bag which he wore. He handed them to Little Wolf.

This maker of magic even knows the number of coups I would count, thought the boy as he nervously took the sticks. He saw his father glance proudly at him, and his hands steadied.

"Chiefs, medicine man, warriors of the Blackfoot Nation," began the boy, "my words are but little, hidden behind the big deeds which your coup feathers proclaim. While the sun traveled the width of a lodge pole, I was able to catch an eagle. It is now on my horse. For this I count coup." As Little Wolf spoke, he threw one of the sticks which Sun Arrow had given him on the ground. "When I was chased by the band of Chief Yellow Horse, I was afraid and saw only dark clouds. When my pony could no longer carry me away from those who pursued, I thought the son of a chief should not turn his back on the enemy. It is a good day to go fighting to The Sand Hills. Then I turned to fight. I was not alone, for Young Hawk pointed his arrow with mine. Because I turned, I count coup."

As Little Wolf threw his second stick to the ground a great shout of "Hau, hau" came from chiefs and warriors alike. Now that his ordeal was over, the boy's knees felt suddenly weak. He would have left the circle, but Yellow Horse motioned him to remain, then signed to Young Hawk to stand in the center of the ring where his companion had counted coup a moment before.

Young Hawk walked forward with a far-distant look in his eyes. He stopped mechanically in front of Sun Arrow. The medicine man handed him two coup sticks. He dropped them on the ground, then nervously picked them up, clutching them even more firmly than he had held the legs of his eagle. He spoke: "Chiefs, medicine man, Blackfoot braves. I feel as a prairie mouse must feel when it meets a buffalo. I am not the son of a chief. I can but speak as a boy who is frightened by things too big for him. I count coup for an eagle which I caught."

As Young Hawk made the statement he threw the stick from him with such force that it sailed high over

* From *Indian Adventure Trails,* by Allan A. Macfarlan (New York: Dodd, Mead & Co., 1953).

the heads of the chiefs in the inner circle. "I can but count a small coup for this second stick," he continued. "Had not Little Wolf turned to fight, I would not have done so. Should I count coup for such a thing?" His voice quavered as he asked the question. The loud shouts of approval from the chiefs and warriors within earshot caused him to throw the second stick from him as forcibly as he had thrown the first. He would have run from the circle, but Yellow Horse stopped him. The boy moved over to Little Wolf and they stood close together. Short Bull, Yellow Horse, and the medicine man spoke quietly together.

PLANNING AND DIRECTING COUNCIL FIRE ACTIVITIES

When it comes to working out a striking council fire program from scratch, one can resort to Albert Einstein's statement that "Imagination is more important than knowledge." Usually there is a fair kernel of actual knowledge in the circle of council fire chiefs who arrange for and direct a council fire. At times the combined knowledge may border on virtuosity, but even that may not help matters so much as might be anticipated unless the knowledge is skillfully used. It requires much imagination, forethought, and planning before a really fine tentative council fire program is even born. After that comes the actual work of screening the available talent, material, and suggestions which have been advanced in the first creative huddle of the planners. Some chiefs believe that a simple, stereotyped council fire opening ceremony, a rather vague talk about Indians in general, a dance or two, a song or two, and a hackeneyed closing ceremony comprise a good enough council fire program. It may be an adequate one, but it certainly is not a good one.

A few council fire chiefs, who stage such programs, have not learned to "give like a chief!" as our American Indian brothers say. These chiefs have found an easy way out, but what of the braves-in-council who take pains to dress, paint in Indian fashion, and *anticipate?* Surely these young warriors deserve something more inspiring, more thrilling, more authentic, more Indian-like? And does not our tremendous unpaid debt to the American Indians somewhat obligate us to give our modern council fire braves a truer, better picture of these splendid peoples?

In the Western Hemisphere, only Canada can look the Indian in the eye with a reasonably clear conscience. With the courageous help of a handful of the Northwest Mounted Police—since known as the Royal Canadian Mounted Police—instead of an army, Canada policed, sheltered, and fed the broken remnants of the once proud tribes which were hunted to its very border by the American Army, and welcomed all Indians in distress with no mental reservations because of color or creed. The sun must have shone strong in the heart of the Great Spirit at this humane treatment of his broken people, who no longer had room to spread their blankets in a land which was rightfully theirs.

Today, in the United States, the young descendents of these tribes have not the chance to study the former splendid handicrafts of their people, because they have practically no worthwhile specimens to place in their own little museums. The reason for the scarcity is easily explained. Throughout America today, many white men's museums, despite their comprehensive exhibits, have huge, hidden surplus stocks of such material comprising literally thousands of genuine American Indian costumes, headdresses, moccasins, and other artifacts stored away, for reasons unfathomable to common sense. Were it not for this unfair "dog in the manger" attitude, American Indian children would have the opportunity to see, marvel at, and feel proud of these objects of infinite art which are but an infinitesimal part of their rightful heritage.

In the face of these truths, it would seem a duty on the part of those who endeavor to teach youth the ways of the American Indians to make a sincere effort to recapture some of their ways of life, their past glory, their outstanding qualities, such as truth, high courage, *camaraderie,* loyalty, and their many arts of pageantry, painting, song, dance, and handicrafts.

The suggestion, born of obligation, that council fires be memorable and the outcome of much thought, preparation, and planning is neither practical nor helpful without some concrete, tested material to draw on. This is given in detail in other chapters, so that very considerable choice is offered for selection by all council fire groups. The suggested programs of ceremonies and activities in Chapter 20 are frameworks on which many worthwhile programs can be built.

chapter 3

CAMPFIRE SMOKE FLOATS lazily skyward like an amethyst veil. Light and shadow play and dance, weaving mysterious patterns in the charmed circle of the campfire. Fire friendships are made wherever the campfire burns, whether on hilltop, by a lakeshore, or in a valley. The everyday world soon fades into unreality by campfire light, troubles take wing, and the fun, story, games, and songs of the campfire circle become happy reality.

PLANNING AND DIRECTING CAMPFIRE PROGRAMS

This job requires more thought, planning, skill, and tact than may be imagined by those who like to think that an impromptu campfire program can always be put across with a bang. Occasionally such programs are successful, even memorable, but this is the exception rather than the rule. Too much talent among the campers makes program planning almost as difficult as when there is a lack of talent. In either case, considerable forethought and planning are advisable in order to turn out a really worthwhile program, pleasing to the large majority of the spectators. There should be something for the mind, eye, ear, and body, in order to round out a fine program.

Whenever possible, programs should be carefully worked out well in advance, and care should be taken to fit them to the age groups participating. Despite this suggestion for advance preparation, a program need not always be hard and fast, as leeway should be allowed to take care of worthwhile turns which may crop up at the last moment; and some allowance should be made for anticipated events which fail to materialize for one reason or another at the last minute. Programs may be filled with variety or specialistic affairs to meet the needs of the particular campfire audience for which the program is staged. A program made up largely of singing will prove poor entertainment for a circle of campers who care little for singing, and this applies to almost any specialty program. Variety and a change in pace from time to time are aids to fine programs. A good master of ceremonies is another must for a really good campfire program. Showmanship, sense of humor, ability at repartee, and tact are important parts of successful campfire leadership technique.

The actual program should scarcely ever be longer than one hour and a half, and a shorter period is best for younger groups. The program can be composed of selected group and solo singing, games, short stories, amusing or very interesting quizzes, a short play or skit, and some brief pageantry if easy to arrange and stage. It is surprising how many of these entertaining features can be included in a well-planned, fast-moving program. A real "singing camp" will have a good time with a program consisting largely of musical festival numbers; while a more athletically inclined camp will find top pleasure in a games tournament program where all of the campers at the fire have an opportunity to play and compete in some of the active, competitive, and amusing games which make up the program.

Modern campers are far less likely to be content with the old material which has served nobly, and too well, though it may have pleased their fathers, and perhaps grandfathers, for many decades. Brand-new, worthwhile material is what is required today. A campers' council and senior campers should be given a share in the planning of campfire programs, because if they do not know just what the campers like best at campfires they will soon find out. A top-flight leader, while avoiding needless censorship, will do well to acquaint himself with just what sort of "special" act or songs some senior campers wish to introduce, as a surprise, for the next campfire. They should be reasoned out of staging numbers which are too off-beat, offensive to good taste, likely to cause embarrassment, or too trite to be worthwhile. Some immature counselors are also prone to such numbers.

campfire fun-fare

There are an infinite number of sorts of campfire programs, but practically all of them can be classed under two general headings, formal and informal. Usually the first is a mass, camp-wide affair in which ceremony and camp tradition play a major part, but for either event there should be something inspirational, nostalgic, legendary, dream-inspiring, and thrill-provoking which will not only add to the splendor of the program but will also contribute to the *esprit de camp*.

Multileadership is usually required when a number of completely different types of campfires are planned for a camp season. A leader who can run a formal campfire splendidly may be at a disadvantage when a Carnival Night campfire, a Games Tournament campfire, or a Storybook Campfire night is under way. It is then that the camp director or usual campfire director has the task of choosing the right leader for the campfire night planned.

Underlying the glamour of campfire programs there should be an unobtrusive core of really worthwhile things. Friendship, good fellowship, loyalty, good sportsmanship, conservation, and other sterling qualities can be promoted at campfires which will bear fruit years after the last sparks from the fires which inspired them have risen skyward like pinpoints of luminous brilliance into the sable darkness of night.

Stories and singing around the campfire are as much in the activity class as games and stunts. Some camps try to get along with only singing and stories as entertainment in their programs of campfire activities. Other camps, with wider vision, have a program of much greater scope and find place for games, plays, stunts, entertaining talks on nature, astronomy, woodcraft, and similar interesting and educational features, in addition to regular storytelling and singing. There is little doubt as to which is the more satisfactory program, especially when taking into consideration the fact that the average camp holds seven or eight campfires each season. The varied programs mentioned can be spread out over that period.

OPENING THE CAMPFIRE

Many camps in daylight saving time zones turn the clocks back to Eastern Standard time when camp opens, to assure at least semidarkness for the opening of campfires, council fires, and other evening activities. This also makes it easier to send the younger campers to bed at an hour that eliminates the stigma of having to go to bed by daylight.

The campfire may be opened in a number of ways, and although each opening should be given considerable thought and showmanship, this is especially true of the first campfire at the beginning of each camp season.

Something really special is demanded for such occasions. A few suggestions follow.

From 30 to 50 feet behind the campfire circle, a big fire-sign such as the one shown in the illustration is set up just before campfire time. The letters are made from thin, dry slats of soft wood, covered with strips of cloth which have been well soaked in liquid paraffin wax. The letters can range in size from 2 feet to 4 feet. The letters are strung onto heavy wires running along the top and bottom of them, each letter being fastened on at the right distance from the next one, and the whole sign fastened by the ends of the heavy wires onto two tall posts with pointed ends, ready to be driven into the ground. This sign is not too noticeable when the campers take their places around the first campfire of the season. If it is still too light because of the early hour of the start of the event, the sign can be camouflaged. There are various ways of doing this, a simple one being to drape a piece of cloth over the letters until it is time for the sign to be lit; the cloth used to cover the letters can be of the camp colors. This makes the campers realize that they are welcome at all hours, and few will suspect that the letters will become letters of fire when darkness falls. The sign is touched off in several places by two counselors with wax tapers, or long matches, when the light-up time comes. As the sign flares up into a flame of welcome, it tells the campers in no uncertain way that they are "Welcome to Camp _____."

Another striking way to open the first campfire, when the position of the campfire circle permits, is to have four or more automobiles placed in a circle around the campfire circle, about sixty feet distant from the campers. When the campers are seated and their attention is directed toward the unlit campfire, a flashlight or whistle signals each driver, who has been crouching on the driver's seat, to switch on his full-power headlights at the same instant. The bright glare surprises the campers and dazzles their eyes; and when all headlights are suddenly switched off at the same instant, after about twenty seconds, the campers dimly see that the campfire has been taken over by five or six Indians, robots, pirates, or spacemen in white. These mysterious figures, who have crept into the campfire circle just as soon as the lights were switched off, proceed with the fire lighting and dance and caper while it is being lit, chanting in strange voices, "Welcome to _____." They then file out silently and disappear into the darkness.

Another spectacular campfire opening is assured with the Bell Tower Fire, described in the following section.

BELL TOWER FIRE

The drawing shows a simple form of tower, which is used to fit completely over a standard log cabin type of fire. Those in charge of campfire arrangements can easily build this tower with a few narrow planks for the framework and the slats from two or three orange crates or old boxes for the four sides. The top of the tower should rise about 2 feet above the concealed log cabin fire. The roof should be made of fairly thick wood at least ½ inch thick. It should jut out 4 inches on all sides of the top of the tower. The completed tower can be painted black outside for added effect. The space between the inside walls of the tower and the actual fire should be filled with pieces of lightly crumpled newspaper and dry tinder sticks reaching not more than three quarters of the way up the tower. This fire, when lit through the lower slit or from directly under the foot of the wall of the tower, will of course ignite the inner log cabin fire, which will add to the effect. The dim light of campfire time will hide all defects in the framework of the tower.

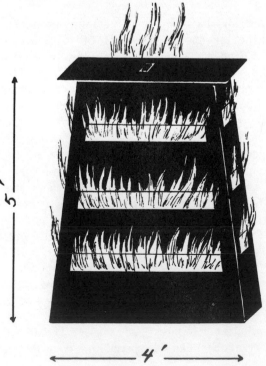

The Bell Tower Fire presents a striking spectacle as it burns, with tongues of flame licking through the slits, but this is not the only impressive feature. The campfire director or storyteller tells a short but dramatic and well-timed story, starting just as the fire is lit, about a *Spirit of Happiness* which has become a prisoner in the Bell Tower. This spirit, it is told, used to give off colored flame before it became a prisoner, but since its captivity the colored flame has died. Only freedom, the legend tells, will renew the spirit's flame and happiness. By burning the prison tower, it is hoped to release the spirit, which cannot be harmed by the flames. Whether it can be freed or not, nobody knows, but because the spirit sometimes tinkled like a bell when it was free, campers with good ears may, if they listen closely, hear the tinkle of the spirit if it is freed by the flames.

At this point or shortly before—if the story has moved at the right pace, the tower has been built well, and the fire co-operates—colored flame will be seen coming from the roof of the Bell Tower, since a flat package containing colored flame powder or cubes wrapped in flammable black paper has been placed on the center of the roof of the tower, outside, just before campfire time.

As the colored flames rise and the tower goes completely up in flames, invisible bells suddenly tinkle joyously high in the air, and the campers know that the *Spirit of Happiness* is free again.

The tinkling bell effects are best obtained by suspending one or more small bells on a short length of fishline from a high branch on a tree just outside the campfire circle. A long, strong black thread leads from the fishline to a point where a leader is concealed from the campers, perhaps behind a bush or tree, ready to jingle the bells at the crucial moment. The leader's cue to act as bell ringer, if he cannot watch the progress of the fire from his hiding place, can be given by the storyteller exclaiming, "Look! the colored flames! the *Spirit of Happiness* is free again!" A few moments later, to maintain suspense, the bells tinkle clearly.

For variation, several bells can be hung high up in trees at various distances from the campfire circle. Two or three bell ringers operate the bells, the bell closest to the campfire ringing first and the others pealing in order of distance away from the fire. The effect, as the campers hear the bell notes die in the distance, is striking; and the final tinkle of bells, repeated from the cluster *closest* to the fire, often brings a cheer from the younger campers, who are glad that the *Spirit of Happiness* has returned to their campfire circle.

THE RAFT FIRE

A forest fire is a terrifying and destructive monster. To avoid any possibility of one during an unusually dry summer in Maine, the author built and operated a successful Island, or Raft Fire. On a windless night, a large buoyant raft about 8 feet square was built. It was covered with earth, and a regular log cabin type fire was built on its center. The raft was anchored offshore, about 50 feet from the edge of the lake, at a point where the shore rose several feet above lake level. The campers, seated in rows in a semicircle, enjoyed an unusual campfire which they had found picturesque. The fire was lit by a leader from a canoe, but it could have been set alight by the Fireball method of campfire lighting—by having a spool wrapped in a strip of cloth soaked in paraffin wax slide down a wire from the bank, at a spot free from trees or vegetation, onto the fire. This method is quite spectacular, with the lake as a background, especially when the fireball is released from a height which does not make its descent into the fire too rapid. A well-built and stoked log cabin type fire should burn brightly for about forty-five minutes without its being refueled. It can then be fed very small chunks of dry wood by a fire tender in a boat or canoe.

"MAGIC" EFFECTS FOR CAMPFIRES

Some of the "magic" stunts described in Chapter 4 can be adapted and used to advantage as a spectacular part of campfire programs. The ideas which follow are a few of the many which can be successfully used to add sparkle to campfire entertainment.

BELL EFFECTS. Bells of various kinds and of varied chimes, hung high and low in trees at varying distances from the campfire circle—as described in the Bell Tower Fire—can be made to chime or tinkle effectively at the right moments in a story, stunt, or play in which bells play a part. A strong black thread, attached to the black thread or fishline from which the bell or peal of bells is suspended from the branch of a tree, can be operated by a counselor from some point which the campers cannot see. The bells are miniature bells, from ½ inch to 2 or 3 inches in diameter, and even the smaller bells chime out quite clearly in the still night air.

Various larger bells, suspended out of sight high in the trees, can be used to good effect when telling the old Chinese folk tale of Ko-Ai, also known as Kong Gay, the little Chinese girl who gave her life to make a bell tone sweet in order to save her father, the Maker of Bells, from execution by order of the Emperor. Three bells are important to the story. The first of the three final bells peals discordantly and angers the Emperor; the second bell has a different sound but still peals with an unmusical tone; the third, final and fatal, bell chimes with sweet and silvery tone, after Ko-Ai's supreme sacrifice, as it echoes her call for her little silken slipper. To narrate this story to the best advantage, the storyteller may appear to be quite oblivious to the bell chimes introduced into the tale to make it more vibrant and graphic. The real artistry, when the peals are ignored, lies in the pauses and timing, which must be carried out in close co-operation with the unseen bell ringer.

PHONOGRAPH AND TAPE RECORDINGS. A spring-action phonograph hidden under some natural prop on the ground or securely fastened up in a tree just outside the campfire circle, with a suitable record or tape ready to be played, can be triggered into playing at the right moment by an off-stage pull on a strong black thread or black nylon fishline. Tape recorders can also be used to produce striking effects when there is an electrical outlet not too far distant.

LUMINOUS PAINT. Luminous paint is suitable for painting moths, fireflies, butterflies, or birds made from lightweight paper, tissue paper, or light cardboard, to be used in campfire stunts when the campfire is allowed to burn low for a little while. The birds and insects can be suspended from an overhead line such as the one described in Chapter 4, if convenient branches do not hang over the campfire circle at some points, and triggered to swing above the campfire circle when required. The effect is colorful and surprising, especially when a light breeze is blowing to heighten the effect of gliding flight. The thin black threads by which the insects are suspended

are quite invisible to the campers seated within the campfire circle. Some luminous paints carry instructions that the objects painted should be exposed for ten minutes or so to strong electric light prior to use, and usually they remain luminous for quite a while after such treatment. Only experimentation a night or two in advance of the fire will determine such technicalities. Other luminous paints do not require exposure to light before use, and they too will remain brightly luminous for a considerable length of time despite exposure to the air. The various colors produced by the different paints and the most effective ways of using them are stated on the containers. These paints are quite reasonably priced.

OUT-OF-CAMP CAMPFIRES

Campfires which will be long remembered can be held out of camp, when the actual camp property is limited and the off-camp conditions are favorable. Campfires within camp bounds but away from the usual campfire circle can be made interesting when the camp property is large enough to include areas which are unknown to the average camper in that particular camp.

Such campfires need not even be held after dark in order to make them interesting and outstanding. One can be held on a hilltop to watch the sunrise, and breakfast can be cooked out of doors after the sun has risen, or the fire can be held just before sunset, from some vantage point, and supper made and served after the sun has gone down.

SUNDOWNER CAMPFIRE

For this campfire, older campers from "down under" waltz their "tucker bags" to the top of a hill, cliff, or other elevation with a view, just before sundown. They build a fire on the hilltop, prepare a hot supper there, and later on eat sandwiches, toast marshmallows, and enjoy hot cocoa made in a big billy by one of the counselors. To keep this event in character, stories of the Australian bush can be told; Australian songs such as the stirring "Waltzing Matilda" can be sung, and all of the hilltop Sundowners can join in the "Kookaburra" round.

Returning to camp in the dark from the out-back is a part of the outing which will appeal to the campers' spirit of adventure. Additional thrills can be added when the bush-wise leader in charge of the expedition apparently encounters difficulty in knowing which trail leads safely to camp. His "If worst comes to the worst, Diggers, we can always sleep here in the bush and find our way back to camp in the morning," adds the excitement and zest which turn a prosaic hike into an adventure. (Note: The Sundowners always do get back to camp safely in time for Taps.)

LANTERN-LIGHT CAMPFIRE HIKE

Before the return hike to camp from this cook-out campfire supper, each camper is given a small Japanese or Chinese lantern, fitted with a short length of stubby candle. The campers follow their leader back to camp in a picturesque Indian-file procession, their path lighted by the soft glow of multicolored lanterns. A leader can take the campers who are not assigned to this particular hike to a point of vantage on the camp property in order to watch the colorful line wind its way back to camp.

LAKESHORE OR BEACH CAMPFIRES

Wonderful times can be had on an ocean beach by arriving at a suitable site in the afternoon, having a swim

and beach games, followed by a campfire cook-out supper. With older campers, a real campfire can be lit as darkness falls, and the campers can enjoy songs and stories while watching the iridescent blaze caused by salt-water-impregnated logs which have been washed up on the beach.

A somewhat similar program can be carried out on the beach of a suitable lake, minus the multicolored flames unless a leader has brought along some powder or crystal "color fire" to be put on the campfire logs.

Swimming should be carried out only before dusk and under constant alert and careful adult supervision.

RIVER, STREAM, AND WATERFALL CAMPFIRES

Campfires can be a delight when staged on the bank of a river or stream, and sometimes a site can be selected at the foot of or overlooking a waterfall or cascade, which adds additional pleasure to the outing. If the site permits, there can be swimming before the cook-out supper. Later in the evening, a song and story campfire can be held as close to the water as caution and safety permit.

Naturally, some of the attractive outings suggested can only be carried out when the camp is situated close enough to one of the spots mentioned to permit a rather easy hike to and from the site selected. The convenience of the spot will decide the age groups of campers who can participate. The younger campers who cannot go will be better camp prospects for the following season after they hear of the fun that the older campers had.

COURTESY AND CARE WILL ASSURE PERMISSION AND FUN. No experienced camp owner or camp director ever tries to arrange for any sort of outing or campfire outside of camp limits without first of all asking for and receiving permission from the owner of the property on which he wishes the event to be held. The same golden rule holds good for a camp outing in state forests or similar property. No counselor should be permitted to lead any of the outings mentioned above to a spot where it is assumed that "nobody will mind." Too frequently it transpires that the "nobody" does mind—a lot! A camp can lose a very precious thing, the good will of its surrounding neighbors, by ignoring this courtesy, and one careless group which litters a site, fails to extinguish the campfire completely, and ignores proper care of a site can cause owners to refuse further permission not only to that camp but to more worthy groups as well.

CLOSING THE CAMPFIRE

Unlike the exciting opening of a campfire, the closing should be as peaceful as a soft breeze sighing through pine branches or the ripple of wavelets on the edge of the lakeshore. Such a ceremony can be as effective as the brilliant opening and have a lasting effect on the campers, in addition to preparing them for quick and untroubled sleep.

Before the campers sing "Taps," some campfire directors like to round off the more exciting campfire with a short, interesting, and suitable story, certainly not one of ghosts or Indian attack. In some camps a counselor or senior camper recites a few verses of an appropriate outdoor poem, such as the following entitled "Thanks."

Having one or more singers sing a verse or two from a suitable song or hymn, such as Brahms' "Cradle Song" or "Now the Day is Over," from a distance so that the words reach the campers clearly yet softly, is another good way to close a campfire. A well-played cornet solo, a restful one played from a distant point, is another effective way of saying good night.

For those who like to close their campfire activities with a simple benediction, an outdoor-mood blessing on the campers may be patterned after the following:

May the Peace of the Forest, the Song of the Birds, the Inspiration of the Hills, the Warmth of the Sun, the Strength of the Trees, the Fragrance of the Flowers, the Joy of the Wind, the Calm of the Lake, in all of which is the Creator of all good things, be in your hearts tonight and always.

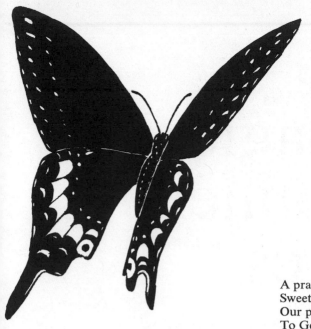

THANKS

An Outdoor Prayer

A prayer of thanks for bird-song clear,
Sweet choirs that chorus, "Dawn is here!"
Our prayer flies up on woodland wings
To God, who gives us all good things.

For furred and feathered forest folk,
For fragrant spruce and sweet woodsmoke;
For cloud-kissed peaks, majestic, free,
Our grateful hearts give thanks to thee.

A prayer of thanks for sun and shade,
For towering cliffs and fern-filled glade;
Wood-winds that play on muted strings:
We thank thee, Lord, for all these things.

For butterflies and wildflowers bright,
Rivers and brooks for our delight;
For lakes and valleys, hills and sea;
For all these good things, thanks to thee.

A prayer of thanks for woods and streams,
Forest and fields where sunlight gleams;
For placid pools, the starry sky
And shimmering sea's soft lullaby.

For brotherhood 'round campfire bright,
For woodland voices, soft moonlight;
For cool and calm at eventide,
Our thanks rise up to thee, our Guide.

A prayer of thanks for flickering fire,
Bright flames, to picture heart's desire;
Tall trees that breathe night's whispered sigh,
Soft breezes murmuring, "God is nigh."

For shelter, food, a fire, a friend,
A welcome earned at journey's end;
God of outdoors, earth, sky, and sea,
Please hear this humble prayer to thee.

A. A. M.

41

chapter 4

magic council fires

WIND-STIRRED BRANCHES brush the stars in the serene sky. Soon the flame-flowers of magic fires will bloom in the darkness. The Thunderbird will swoop down, silent as a moon shadow, and nest in the flaming fire. Past fires, flickering faint as a misty memory, will burn for a heartbeat in the minds of the braves-in-council, then fade and soar skyward, silent as smoke, as magic fires which the warriors have never seen before glow and grow in the enchanted circle of the council ring.

MAGIC FIRES

Three of the spectacular fires which follow have not before appeared in print. All four fires are equally suitable for either a Northwest Coast or a Plains Indian council fire.

Before going into the subject of the so-called magic fire, or any other fire or fire effects used in either campfire or council fire activities, a word of caution makes a good introduction. *"Playing with fire" is always beset with some danger,* whether the element of risk is occasioned by Indian warriors juggling with blazing hoops or torches in the council fire area, a Fireball fire-lighting method which backfires, or a brave stumbling and dropping a lighted torch on the dry forest floor as he speeds from the West toward the council fire with the torch to be used in the Fire-from-the-Sun fire-lighting ceremony. Careful supervision on the part of mature chiefs responsible for council fire operations and the choice of alert, older warriors to carry out the various fire-lighting methods should completely eliminate all risk from such activities.

OVERHEAD LINES
FOR MAGIC FIRE-LIGHTING FEATS

The overhead line required in operating the Thunderbird, Flying Torch, Flaming Feather—and some of the illusions described in Chapter 21, such as the *Dance of The Lightning Snake, The Coming of the Ducks,* the *Magic Feather Dance,* and others—is fully described at this point to avoid further detailed reference elsewhere. These overhead suspension lines are basic and very helpful in staging many magic fires and feats. The lines are invisible at twilight and almost invisible even in daylight, in addition to being entirely out of the way of all other events staged in the council fire area. A few trees at least 30 feet high just outside and around the council fire area are necessary in setting up the overhead line conveniently, though tall poles can be used, or even nearby buildings, when there are no trees available. At times it is necessary to use trees quite a long distance apart, but this difficulty may be overcome by using a considerably longer and stronger length of wire or fishline. The chief necessity for the tensile strength of the stronger line in such instances is so that it will not snap under the strain of the additional pull required to prevent the line from sagging in the middle when it has to be stretched for 70 feet or more.

The overhead line shown in the drawing illustrates how a number of the magic fires are carried out at a council fire. The best overhead line is made of thin but strong black or dark rustproof annealed wire. Number 22 gauge, which is about 1/32 of an inch thick, or even No. 24, about 1/50 of an inch thick, should prove serviceable and last through the entire camping season. These gauges of wire come in various lengths, including handy spools of about 150 feet to a spool. Absolutely no kinks or knots should be allowed to form in the wire while stringing it in position. The second best choice, and a very good one, for an overhead line is 20- to 30-pound-test black nylon fishing line. The line should be a new one, and it should be tested for defects before it is strung in place.

The overhead line is stretched high up across the council fire area, as close to the center as possible, and attached to two trees as nearly opposite each other as possible, the trees being on different sides of the council fire. The line can be tied to a suitable branch or fastened

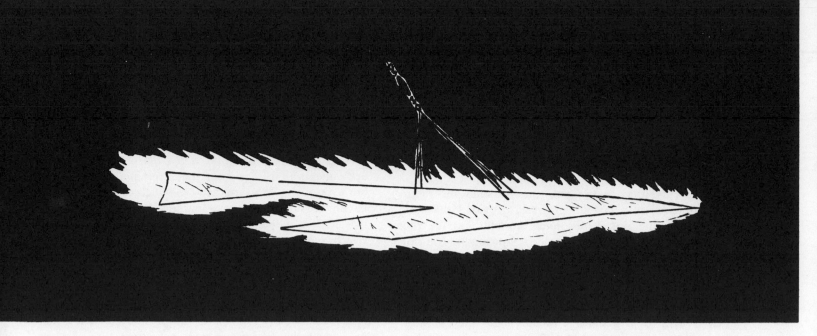

to a dark screw eye screwed into the tree trunk or into a branch which is conveniently situated. The height of the line may have to be decided by the length of the longest safe stepladder in camp. A good height is at least 30 feet, higher if possible. The stepladder will prove useful not only for the initial erection of the line but whenever the line is used later on. Sufficient slack should be left at one end of the line so that it may be lowered close to the ground when the operator's line, the purpose of which is described later, has to be threaded through a ring on the overhead wire. The surplus line is wrapped around the tree trunk or a convenient branch. With a suitable stepladder, operator's lines may be threaded without lowering the overhead line.

When an overhead line is used *only* for staging the Magic Feather Dance, a very thin nylon line or even strong black thread may be suspended above the council fire area above the place where the dance is to be performed. The feather itself may be manipulated by a length of thin, strong black nylon thread.

OVERHEAD LINE RINGS. The rings attached to the overhead line are used to assure easy manipulation of the operator's line, which is threaded through the ring. The rings should be of black metal or black enameled metal which will remain rust-free. These rings should be about ¼ or ½ inch in diameter, inside measurement.

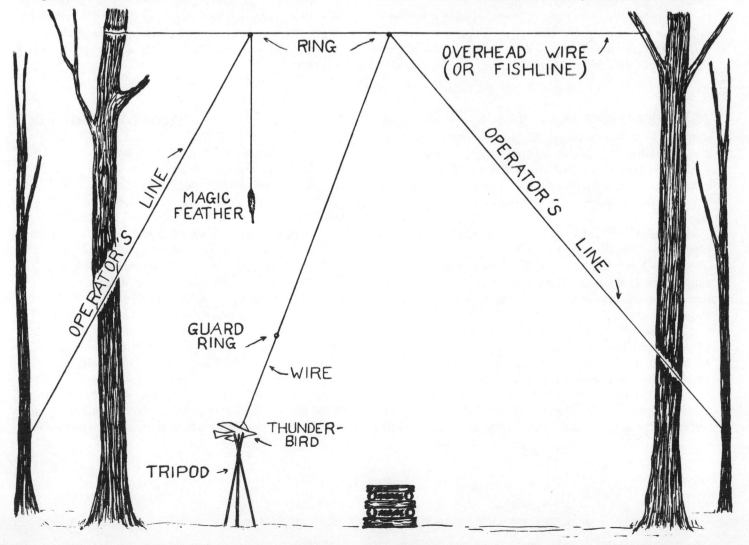

Two or more rings may be fastened onto the overhead line, one *directly* above the council fire for magic fire lighting, and the other ring about 6 feet away from and opposite the chief's chair, to be used for other magic feats.

These rings may be tied onto the overhead line before it is stretched into position for use, provided the chief who strings the line is absolutely certain that the ring or rings hang directly over the desired positions. If a ring is fastened to the overhead wire in a wrong position, it is necessary to remove it and refasten it onto the exact place required in order to assure the perfect working of the feat to be carried out at the council fire.

It is best to tie the rings directly onto the overhead line, using a stepladder to reach the line, *after* the line has been correctly strung in place. The ring should be tied on with a short length of thin nylon fishline so that it hangs down directly under the overhead line. When the ring is whipped in that position, by wrapping a short length of line only around the line which holds the ring to the main overhead line, it will assure its remaining in the exact place desired.

In the performance of some of the medicine-man-magic feats the ring is fastened to the overhead line above the spot where the illusion is to be performed, *but* in the staging of the Thunderbird, Flying Torch, and Flaming Feather fires the ring *must* be suspended *directly above the council fire*. The position of the ring can easily be checked by passing a length of fishline through it, then fastening a weight to one end of the line to act as a plumb line. Should the ring not be *exactly* in place above the center of the council fire, it can easily be moved into the right position from the top of a high safe stepladder.

THE OPERATOR'S LINE. This line is used in conjunction with the overhead line for performing feats of magic and lighting the magic fires. It is best made from 10- to 15-pound-test black nylon fishline. When the line is new and of good quality, the 10-pound line is strong enough to operate all types of magic fires and feats successfully.

When using the overhead line and operator's line for all fire lighting, the chief or his assistant simply pulls in the operator's line after the length of wire with its guard ring, which is mentioned later, has been burnt from the fire end of the operator's line. Nothing then remains to show how the fire was lit.

Last but not least, it is most important that the chief who manipulates the operator's line keep the two parts of the line from twisting around each other. The line from which the Thunderbird, Torch, or Flaming Feather is suspended *must not* be allowed to twist, even once, around the part of the line which extends from the operator to the overhead line ring. A glance at the accompanying diagram shows the correct positions of the line. One can visualize what would happen if the Thunderbird or any other fire-lighting apparatus became twisted around the part of the line which the chief uses to operate them. It will be seen that even if the line is not burnt through by the contact—in which case there would be no possibility of the apparatus lighting the fire—a twisted line makes it impossible to operate any device which requires the operator's line to provide motion. Great care has to be taken especially when the operator sets up his line, perhaps in semidarkness, in preparation for the performance at the council fire. If the two parts of the line are left twisted at that time, nothing can be done, without revealing how the illusion is carried out, to correct the situation when it is time to make the Thunderbird or similar device perform at the required moment when the warriors are in council.

THE GUARD RING. This small black metal ring is fastened to the top end of the length of wire fastened to the Thunderbird, Torch, or Feather. The operator's line is made fast to this ring, which prevents the length of wire from pulling through the ring on the overhead line, thus preventing an overhead line made of nylon fishline from being burnt through by contact with the flaming device. The *outside* measurement of this guard ring can be ½ inch in diameter or any other suitable size, as long as it cannot be pulled through the ring on the overhead line. This guard ring is fastened to the upper end of the length of wire attached to any fire-lighting device. It is to this guard ring that the end of the operator's line is also tied.

THUNDERBIRD FIRE

The Indians seated in the dark council fire area know that the Thunderbird is winging its way toward them. Has not the tribal chief just told them that it will light the council fire if the Spirit Eagle looks on them with favor? They shiver, half in fear, half in expectation. A shaman chants in a low solemn voice, and a drum sounds a slow rhythm somewhere outside the council fire area.

Suddenly there is a bright flash from somewhere close to and behind the tribal chief's chair. Then a cry of wonder bursts from the warriors-in-council when they see that a flaming Thunderbird is circling the council fire area. It flies above and apparently close to the heads of the seated Indians. They shrink from the circling Thunderbird in fear and wonder. Not only does it fly around the council fire but it flies higher, then lower, as it wings its fiery way. After circling the fire several times, flying closer and closer to it as it circles, the Thunderbird hovers over the fire, rising and falling as though trying to decide whether to use the dark framework as a nest or fly away and seek one elsewhere.

The shaman cries in a loud voice, "Give us fire, O Sky Chief! It is our prayer!" As though it has heard these words, the flaming bird, which has been rising ever higher above the fire, hovers for a moment directly above the unlit fire, then swiftly drops onto it and remains nested. Brightly colored flames shoot high from the fire, into which the flaming Thunderbird slowly disappears.

HOW TO OPERATE THE THUNDERBIRD

The operation of this spectacular method of fire lighting is quite simple, once the overhead line is in position. A length of about 100 feet of 10- to 15-pound-test black nylon fishline is passed through the ring on the overhead line which hangs *directly* above the council fire. This line is called the operator's line, and its length will vary according to the size of the council fire area and the point of concealment from which the line is operated. The line can be used many times throughout the season for this and similarly operated "magic" fires. Once one end of the operator's line is brought down through the ring, it is securely attached to the top end of the double swivel on the end of the short length of wire fastened to the top side of the Thunderbird. The bird is now placed on its tripod perch with its tail on one of the three legs and part of a wing balanced on the top of each of the other two legs. The other end of the operator's line is taken to the side of the council fire area directly opposite the fire if possible. The side which offers the best concealment for the chief who operates the line is the one to choose. A tree trunk, a big log, or a small clump of bushes provides ample cover for an operator wearing dark clothing. Great care must be taken not to let the operator's line cross at any point of its entire length.

When the operational point has been selected, about 15 feet of the fishline which has been brought to that spot is securely tied to, and then wound around, a short smooth stick or an empty thread spool. The stick or spool should be hung from a nail with a large head driven into the tree trunk about 4 feet above the ground. Of course, the stick or spool is hung elsewhere if a tree has not been chosen as the place from where the operator will work. A small disc of white paper or cardboard should be fastened a little to one side of the nail to make it easy for the operator to locate the position of the spool of line in the dim light at council fire time.

The Thunderbird is now ready to take wing, and the chief who is responsible for its flight should get in some practice as soon as possible, when there are no onlookers in the vicinity to see how the "magic" works. The unlit bird will perform just as well in daylight as it will when making its flaming flight to light the council fire.

The flash of fire seen just outside the council fire area before the Thunderbird's appearance was one of the methods used by the shaman to distract the attention of the onlookers at the very moment that the Thunderbird was being lit behind a screen and launched into the council fire area from the opposite direction from that in which the flash was seen. Sometimes a loud, unearthly shaman cry given by a shaman hidden behind the spectators, or the loud alarm call of an animal or bird, drew the attention of those present at the council fire away from the area from which the Thunderbird flew in. Although the skillful Indian operators launched the Thunderbird from well outside the council fire area and made it fly in a wide circle around the entire council fire area, this method of operation is too difficult to carry out safely and successfully to be recommended for modern council fire use. A much easier, entirely safe and sure method of launching the Thunderbird, is the tripod-perch described a little further on.

Once the Thunderbird has been lit by either the torch or delayed-action-fuse method, all that the chief who operates the bird has to do is to give a sharp, long pull on the fishline when the Thunderbird is well alight, and it should flame in a flash. The sharp pull on the line immediately causes the bird to rise upward from its tripod perch and fly toward the fire. By a series of pulls, jerks on the line, and releases of a few feet of line from time to time, the bird can be kept swinging and circling around the fire, rising as close to the overhead line as the guard ring will permit and dropping to within 6 feet of the ground—but never closer, for fear of a possible collision with the log cabin fire which will be the Thunderbird's nest. The spectacular finale comes when the operator is ready to make the bird set the fire alight. As the Thunderbird hovers over the council fire, it may be raised rapidly as though flying upward from the fire, lowered slowly, then raised again, keeping the warriors-in-council in suspense. At last, by raising the bird high and keeping a taut operating line, the operator may drop the bird from high above the council fire, directly onto it. This nesting part of the ceremony can be highlighted by a medicine man, with arms extended toward the sky, offering a prayer that the Thunderbird honor the tribe by nesting on its fire.

Care must be taken by the operator that the bird does drop *directly* onto the fire, and a little practice will assure this taking place. Should the bird miss the fire when dropped, because of faulty operation during a quick drop in the final fire-lighting stage, speedy action must be taken so that the operating line does not get burnt through while the bird is momentarily on the ground. This can usually be avoided by pulling the bird up so quickly after it misses the nest that it swings up over the unlit fire and is dropped onto it before the operating line burns through. It is wise to play safe and operate the Thunderbird so that it does not actually touch the ground or collide with the fire at any time. A rather slow, majestic, certain drop onto the fire is far better than a fast uncertain drop which may cause the bird to miss its mark. Fast drops onto the fire nest can be done with fair certainty, but it requires some practice and assurance on the part of the operator to guarantee a perfect performance. Each operator must work out his own technique, and a glance at the drawings descriptive of how this fire is lit and the simple gear required will prove helpful.

Once the fire is lit, the chief who controls the operating line should wind it in when he feels certain that the fishline above the short length of wire is burned through by the fire which the bird has started. A slight tug or two on the line will tell at once whether the line is free from the bird or not. If the guard ring on the line has been burned off, the operator will be able to pull the line through the ring on the overhead wire and wind all of it in. If by chance—and it is most unlikely—the guard ring still remains on the operator's line, then all that he needs to do is gently pull in the line until the ring on the operator's line is held by the ring on the overhead line, and then wind the end of the line which he holds around the the nail in the tree, or anything else handy. This assures that the line will be high above the council fire area and out of sight, so that it will not interfere with other activities around the council fire. The medicine man or chief in charge of lighting the Thunderbird Fire should wait for a minute or two after the fire blazes up before calling chiefs and warriors into the area. This gives the operator time to dispose of his line, so that nobody around the council fire will become entangled by it.

That the Thunderbird Fire can be carried out with spectacular results and neither technical difficulty nor risk of any sort has frequently been proved. All that is required to assure the success of the novice who lights this fire for the first time is some practice in making the Thunderbird, setting up the simple apparatus, and launching the unlit Thunderbird in a series of trial flights prior to the big event. The operator will be well repaid by a flawless performance which will astonish and delight the warriors-in-council when the time comes.

HOW TO MAKE THE THUNDERBIRD

The Thunderbird can be cut from a piece of thin, rigid plywood or any lightweight wood from ⅛ to ¼ inch thick, or from a piece of thick, strong cardboard. If necessary, the Thunderbird may be made in two or three pieces, using one piece of wood for the body and another piece or two for the wings. However, if this second-choice construction method is used, the various parts must be strongly fastened together with thin wire nails, since most glues will not withstand the heat when the bird is in flames.

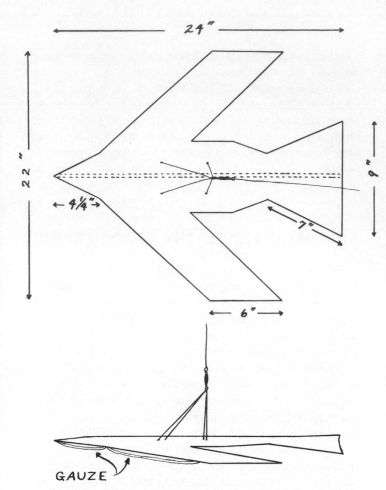

GAUZE

The drawing shows a bird 24 inches long. A Thunderbird of this size produces a striking effect and covers the top of a standard log cabin type of council fire as it nests on it. Slightly smaller birds will light the fire too, but they are not so spectacular. On special occasions the author has built and lit council fires with Thunderbirds 4 feet in length. The rib under the body of the bird, shown by the dotted lines in the sketch, is important if the bird is made from light wood or cardboard, because it keeps the bird rigid. The rib can be made from a piece of light wood about ½ inch wide and ¼ inch thick, and it should be long enough to reach from near the bird's beak to the end of its tail. This rib is nailed securely to the underside of the Thunderbird, in the exact center.

Four screw eyes are fastened into the top of the bird at the points shown in the drawing. They should have shanks from ¼ to ½ inch long so that they hold securely in the bird. When the bird is of cardboard, it is best to have the shanks go entirely through it, so that a piece of thin, flexible wire may be wound around the point of each shank to make certain that it will not pull out of the bird when it is liberally sprinkled with kerosene and in flight. A 7-inch length of strong, thin wire is firmly fastened to each of the two screw eyes nearer to the beak of the bird, and a 5-inch length of wire is fastened to each of the rear screw eyes. The length of these wires is important, since it is the two shorter, rear wires which provide the tilted-forward, sweeping motion and balance which affect the flight of the bird. All four ends of these wires are now fastened firmly to the lower ring on a large metal, barrel-type swivel about 1½ to 2 inches in overall length. This swivel is the sort used by fishermen, but any similar double-ring swivel will do.

A 4-foot length of strong, flexible black wire is now securely attached to the top ring on the swivel. The other end of this wire is securely fastened to a small black guard ring the same size as the ring on the overhead line, directly above the council fire. The free end of the operator's line is passed down through the center ring, directly above the council fire, and is also attached securely to the guard ring.

The guard ring should be considered a *must* for all magic fire lighting which requires the use of the overhead line. When the overhead line is made of nylon fishline, the guard ring prevents a too energetic operator from pulling the flaming Thunderbird too close to the line, burning it through so the bird falls to the ground without lighting the fire, and rendering the overhead line useless for the entire council fire.

The only thing which now remains to be done is to make the Thunderbird thoroughly flammable, so that it will blaze instantly when lit. All parts of the bird should be wrapped with strips of gauze bandage 2 or 3 inches wide, cheesecloth, or strips of any lightweight porous cloth held in position with short lengths of thin wire, or stapled. The cloth is soaked in kerosene and squeezed lightly to remove surplus fluid, shortly before council fire time. To make the bird burn with a colored flame, sprinkle some powder or tuck small cubes of colored-flame-producing chemicals between the two or three layers of wrapping, so that the colored flames burn through the flaming wrappings as the bird circles the fire. Such chemicals are mentioned in Chapter 1.

When the Thunderbird is swiftly lit by a torch, two kerosene-impregnated gauze bandage streamers should be loosely fastened under the body and wings of the bird so they hang down about 1 inch. The purpose of these streamers is to make the bird flare instantly as the flame runs along them. How to light the Thunderbird "magically" by concealed, delayed-action fuse is told a little further on. If the delayed-action fuse should go out in spite of precautions, the swift touch of a small torch or taper will do the trick.

It should be noted that in all fire-lighting methods requiring the use of kerosene or similar flammable fluids, the objects used to ignite the fires must be impregnated with these fluids a short time before using them as fire lighters. If this is not done, these flame-producing liquids are so highly volatile that as the liquid evaporates, its flame-producing quality becomes less and less effective. When the impregnated materials become dry, they are almost entirely ineffective.

HOW TO MAKE THE THUNDERBIRD PERCH

The perch for the Thunderbird is made from 3 straight poles each 6 feet 6 inches long and 1 inch thick. They are lashed together 12 inches from the top, and the legs spread out slightly when the perch is stood upright on the ground to form a tripod. The ends of the legs can be sharpened a little and pushed down into the ground, but this is not necessary with a well-built tripod.

The perch is placed from 8 to 12 feet away from the council fire, and the Thunderbird is balanced securely on top of the tripod with its tail resting on one upright and a wing resting on each of the other two. The wire which runs upward from the ring on the double swivel above the bird must not be allowed to twine around any part of the bird, because the Thunderbird must rise directly upward on the first pull on the operator's line.

The tripod should be removed after the fire has been lit by the Thunderbird.

HOW TO MAKE THE THUNDERBIRD FIRE-NEST

The fire on which the Thunderbird is made to alight is the usual log cabin type of fire. The only difference is that special tinder sticks or dry shavings, which have been dipped in kerosene shortly before council fire time, should be laid conspicuously on top of the fire, so that they will ignite instantly just as soon as the Thunderbird alights on them. Twisted newspaper tapers or short lengths of rope, impregnated with kerosene, should lead from the tinder on top of the fire down into its heart, to assure the actual fire lighting. The purist who is loath to use a little kerosene on a council fire even on special occasions may end up with the Thunderbird alighting on the nest without starting the fire.

HOW TO LIGHT THE THUNDERBIRD BY TORCH

The easiest, and yet effective, way for the medicine man or chief to light the Thunderbird is by the use of a small, brightly burning torch. The slightest touch of a finger of flame, after a number of close passes, will cause the Thunderbird to flare up instantly, especially if it passes just under the bird. Frequently the mistake is made of trying to light flammable things from on top instead of from underneath. When the bird blazes, the medicine man jumps back with a surprised shout, as the bird rises swiftly into the air. The Thunderbird may also be lit with a match, in an inconspicuous way, while the attention of the warriors-in-council is directed elsewhere

by a loud shaman shout from another part of the council fire area. Their eyes will then turn to the Thunderbird only when it bursts into flame and takes flight.

LIGHTING THE THUNDERBIRD BY DELAYED-ACTION FUSE

This is a surprise "magic" method of igniting the Thunderbird which requires a little preparation. It is well worth the slight effort needed, since it takes the warriors-in-council by surprise and makes them think of medicine-man magic, as the bird suddenly bursts into flame and flies upward without anyone in the council fire area standing near to or approaching it. How to make the fuse is described under "Delayed-Action Fires" in Chapter 1.

It may be well to state here that if a saltpeter fuse comes in contact with kerosene or any liquid flammable fluid, the spark traveling along the fuse will instantly go out without igniting the kerosene. So thoroughly, if inexplicably, is the work of extinction done that even a well-made, heavy fuse impregnated just a little with a flammable fluid will not burn again even when dried. It is most important to remember this when attaching the delayed-action fuse to the Thunderbird, Flying Torch, or Flaming Feather. It is for this reason that explicit details explaining the precaution necessary when attaching one end of a delayed-action fuse to the Thunderbird, Flying Torch, or Flaming Feather are given in the section on the "Delayed-Action Fuse Cylinder." The instructions there also tell how to combine the fuse and cylinder so that truly mystifying and spectacular fire lighting is the result.

DOUBLE FUSES. There is the inevitable worry as to whether a fuse will burn throughout its entire length and ignite the fire or object to which it is attached. By using a double fuse, actually two fuses of the same length, a two-to-one chance of success is assured. This applies to all four "magic" fires described. The simple saltpeter delayed-action fuse has proved the most practical for council fire use, despite the need of precaution to prevent its becoming damp and consequently ineffective when used in conjunction with kerosene and similar flammable fluids. The use of several large match heads, as described in the following section, as the terminal target of such fuses makes them sure-fire.

HOW TO MAKE THE DELAYED-ACTION FUSE SPARK-CONCEALING CYLINDER. An ordinary cardboard tube, such as is used for mailing calendars or magazines, can be used to completely conceal the fuse as the spark moves slowly up the fuse on its way to light the Thunderbird or Flying Torch. The creeping spark is absolutely invisible as it climbs upward inside the cylinder. The prepared fuse is hung down through the cylinder with just enough of its end showing at the foot of the tube to be easy to light. The length of the fuse is decided by the time element, how long it will take the warriors to file into their places at the council fire. The length of the easily made cylinder can be decided by the same factor.

Generally speaking, the cylinder should be from 1 to 2 inches in diameter, 10 inches long, and painted black on the outside. It is lashed onto one of the legs of the tripod so that the top of the cylinder is in line with the top of a tripod leg. It almost touches the tail or wing of the Thunderbird, to which one end of the fuse has been fastened. The cylinder is shown lashed to the tripod leg in the drawing. A piece of cotton cloth about 6 inches square, which has been well soaked in a thick, soupy solution of saltpeter and water and then allowed to dry thoroughly, is folded into a loose wad about 1½ inches in diameter and attached to the part of the Thunderbird which is touched by the end of the fuse fastened to the bird. Another excellent way of making a sure connection between fuse and wad is to fold the end of the fuse inside the wad and then attach the wad to the Thunderbird. This assures that the pad will be set alight when the fuse burns up to the wad through the cylinder. To make doubly sure, the heads of five or six unlit big wooden matches, with enough stick left on each to tie them together by, are fastened with very thin wire to the wad. This is the best and surest way to assure a flame which will set fire to the Thunderbird.

As has been pointed out, if the delayed-action fuse, or

even the wad, becomes moist from kerosene, the spark on the fuse will immediately go out just as soon as it reaches the moist spot. The spark will also fail to operate, even when the moist section of the fuse has become thoroughly dry. For this reason, it is best to have a half-sheet of really dry, crumpled newspaper fastened to the underside of the Thunderbird in a place which has not been impregnated with kerosene, so that the fuse is sure to continue burning so that it sets the match heads and wad alight. From there on, the kerosene-soaked streamers described in the directions on how to make the Thunderbird will take over, and the bird will be ablaze in a flash.

FLYING TORCH FIRE

"Tonight," says the tribal chief to the warriors sitting silently around the unlit council fire, "our medicine man will ask the Great Chief to use his power of fire to make our fire flame." He beckons to the medicine man, dressed in full regalia, who advances to the fire.

The medicine man stretches his arms upward and prays, "O Sahalee Tyee, Great Chief above, let it be that our fire may be lit, as are our hearts, by thy above Power. As the fire flames, we will know that no spirits of evil nor enemies lurking in the dark forest can harm us in soul or body. Hear our humble prayer and give us, we pray thee, fire."

Just as the medicine man ends his prayer, a flash of flame springs up for a moment on the edge of the forest, just outside the council fire area, opposite the entrance. The warriors' heads all turn toward the flash. Then their eyes turn swiftly toward the council fire as they hear a loud, shrill cry from the shaman. They see that he lies flat on his face on the ground, while high above him a blazing torch flies backward and forward, from the direction of the entrance to the council area to where the flash came from a moment before. The flaming torch not only flies but flies at various heights. The length of flight gradually shortens, until the torch swings like a pendulum above the fire. Slower and slower it swings, until it remains motionless directly above the unlit fire. Then slowly, very slowly, it begins to rise above the fire as though about to fly up into the black sky of night and leave the fire unlit.

The shaman springs to his feet, lifts his arms toward the rising torch, and cries; "FIRE, give us fire! We asked the Sky Chief to send fire!" As he says these words, the blazing brand stops its upward movement, moves slowly downward toward the fire, then swift as a loon dives it drops into the heart of the fire, which bursts into brightly colored flames as the flaming torch reaches its heart.

HOW TO MAKE AND HARNESS THE FLYING TORCH

The preparation for and the operation of this spectacular fire-lighting method is almost exactly the same as that employed in the Thunderbird Fire. The torch is suspended from the overhead line and launched from the tripod, with the few modifications mentioned in the following paragraphs. A few trial performances by the operator in daylight and at dusk are all that is required to assure a spectacular lighting of the council fire by the Flying Torch method. Though the Indians made the torch fly in from outside the council fire area, this is not recommended for modern council fires; a safer and simpler way of carrying out the feat is given.

A suitable torch can easily be whittled from a pine or spruce branch or any other soft, dry wood. It should be 18 inches long and tapered from 2 inches at one end to about ¾ inch at the other end. A short time before lighting the council fire, a 4-foot-long strip of 1-inch-wide gauze bandage is soaked in kerosene, squeezed out lightly, and wound securely around the thicker end of the torch for a height of about 12 inches. To assure its staying in place, the strip should be tacked lightly or wired to the torch. The torch itself may be dipped in melted paraffin wax before the strip is put on, so the entire torch will burn brightly.

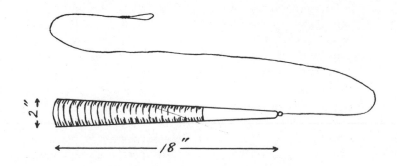

A strong screw eye, with a screw about ¾ inches long, is screwed into the exact center of the thin end of the torch. A 4-foot length of thin, black, flexible, strong wire is securely fastened at one end to the screw eye. A barrel-shaped type of swivel with a ring at each end and about 1½ inch in over-all length is firmly fastened onto the free end of the wire. The free end of the operator's line is passed down through the ring in the overhead line *directly* above the council fire. Then the guard ring, recommended for all fires of this type, should be tied about 1 inch from the free end of the operator's line, and the end is then fastened to the top ring on the double swivel. The purpose of the guard ring, as has been pointed out, is to prevent the flaming torch from being pulled so high up in the course of manipulation that it will burn through the overhead line, if it is made from nylon or other fishline, and not only make the torch fall to the ground without lighting the fire but also put the overhead line out of business.

The best way to keep the torch in flight and finally light the council fire by it is to follow the instructions given under "How to Operate the Thunderbird."

There are various ways of igniting the torch. It may be left suspended about 6 feet above the council fire, by the concealed operator giving his end of the line a couple of hitches around the nail in the tree or bush from which he will manipulate the torch. A more spectacular way is to set up the torch on the tripod used as the perch for the Thunderbird in the Thunderbird fire. A necessary precaution when using the perch as the torch rest is to *wire* the three legs of the tripod together, as the string binding suggested for the Thunderbird perch can be burned through by the blaze of the torch immediately when it is lit. The second thing to be done—and this is another *must*—is to stretch a short length of thin wire between the tops of any two poles of the tripod. This wire should be tied about 2 inches from the top of each of the two poles. Its purpose is to support the torch in an upright position when its butt is placed on the point of the tripod where the three poles are wired together. The torch is *not* fastened in any way to this support wire; it merely leans against it. It is easiest to light the Flying Torch, in either the suspended position or as it rests on the tripod, by attaching a short streamer of gauze bandages 2 or 3 inches long to the thick end of the torch. The streamer hangs down, so that when the end is lit it will flame upward and set fire to the flammable wrapping on the torch. These lightings should be carried out in one swift movement by a chief or medicine man who uses a small torch to ignite the streamer.

In the use of the "magic" of a delayed-action fuse, the torch may be lit either in the suspended position above the council fire or as it rests on the tripod. In the latter method, the spark-concealing cylinder may be used to completely screen the spark as it travels up the fuse.

When the fuse is lit, as it should be, some minutes before the warriors take their places around the council fire, the moving spark is so small that it is almost invisible and should escape the notice of even the most eagle-eyed warriors-in-council. When the spark-concealing cylinder is used for the Flying Torch fire, the cylinder must be lashed to one of the tripod legs, with the top of the cylinder just level with the butt of the torch. After the fuse has been fastened to the end of the torch, it is carefully dropped down inside the cylinder, being lit either before or after it is lowered into place.

The usual problem of how to keep the delayed-action fuse free from kerosene or any other flammable fluid dampness crops up again in this method of lighting the torch. One method of assuring the ignition of the Flying Torch by the delayed-action fuse is to make certain that no kerosene-impregnated strip touches the extreme end of the torch—and of course when the fuse is used, no streamer is attached to the torch end. One end of the fuse is wrapped into a wad of porous cloth which has been well soaked in a soupy solution of water-dissolved saltpeter and then thoroughly dried. The cloth should be folded into a loose wad about 1¼ inch square, with four or five big match heads folded into it. This makes a certain fire-trigger, since the match heads will burst into flame even if the treated wad only smoulders instead of breaking into flame, as it usually does. The wad, with the fuse hanging down from it, is fastened to the butt of the torch by tacks or thin wire nails. The length of the fuse, which should be made from heavy, soft white string thoroughly treated with the saltpeter solution and thoroughly dried, is decided by the length of time which it is required to burn.

As a sure-fire precaution, a *double* fuse, each one of the same length, may be used here, as in *all* cases where a delayed-action fuse is used. If one fuse inexplicably stops burning, the other traveling spark will continue to target, assuring a two-to-one chance of success.

FIRE BY FIRE SNAKE

A very natural-looking snake lies coiled on three round 18-inch-long logs, each about 4 inches in diameter, placed at the edge of the council ring a few feet from the chief's chair. The medicine man stands just behind it, lit torch in hand. He sets the snake aflame, from underneath its belly, and implores it to bring good weather and good hunting by lighting the council fire. After some eloquent persuasion, the snake stirs, slowly uncoils, glides from the logs, and starts in a leisurely manner toward the fire. It stops once or twice on the way and the braves-in-council utter exclamations of disappointment. Then once again it slithers toward the fire, stops just before reaching it—and quickly glides into it. The fire bursts into flame, and the medicine man voices his thanks.

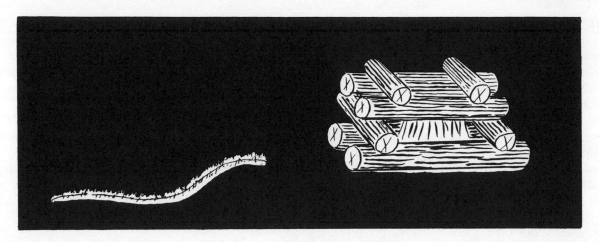

HOW TO MAKE AND OPERATE THE FIRE SNAKE

The snake is made from a 3- or 4-foot length of rope a little over 1 inch in diameter. Whether it is made to look very much like a real snake or not depends on the illumination, by torch or other means, of the council fire ring. The effect of the illusion is heightened when the rope is covered with colored cloth to represent a black snake or a rattlesnake. It is important that a loop of strong, thin wire be securely attached to the snake's mouth, as it is to this loop, a very small one, that the length of strong, flexible black wire is attached by which the snake is pulled into the fire. The rope and snake-covering cloth are impregnated with melted paraffin wax, kerosene, or some other safe flammable substance prior to the fire lighting. As paraffin wax will not burst into flame immediately when the torch is applied to the snake's belly—*not back*—it is best to leave a short loose end of wax-impregnated cloth hanging from under the snake. This very short strip will flame immediately and carry the fire up to the snake.

To mobilize the Fire Snake, a strong screw eye is securely fastened into the second base log of the fire, on the inside and on the opposite side from which the snake approaches the fire. Naturally, the fire should not be stoked tightly at the point between this screw eye and the lower log on the direct opposite side of the fire, because a length of strong black fishline passes through this section of the fire, in order to be threaded through the screw eye. There must be enough of the fishline to reach twice from the fire to a point outside the council ring from which the concealed operator pulls on one end of the line in order to manipulate the snake from the edge of the council ring into the fire. When both ends of the line are brought back to the edge of the council ring, one end is tightly fastened to a 3-foot length of

supple black wire, the other end of which is securely fastened to the loop on the end of the snake's nose. When the operator pulls on the free end of the fishline, once the snake is ablaze, from his point of concealment behind a bush or tree, the snake approaches the fire. By an advance tryout one must make very certain that the burning snake cannot ignite the pulling cord as it goes toward the fire. A dry run or two will indicate the point where the two lines come closest together. Should the operator have, for some good reason, to lie concealed at a point outside the council ring where there is danger of the blazing snake setting fire to the pulling line because they come too closely together, a length of strong thin, rather supple black wire can be used instead of the fishing line. As it is considerably easier to manipulate the fishing line so that the snake moves in a lifelike manner, it is always better to work out the concealed position of the chief so that fishing line can be used instead of wire.

A more elaborate fire lighting of this sort can be staged by fastening the snake onto three empty spools, running on a thin black wire which extends from a short, strong stake driven into the ground at a point just outside the council ring—at a spot about four feet to one side of the chief's chair—into the fire. This wire, on which the snake glides, is about 3 inches above ground. The snake is hidden from view behind a canvas camouflage screen which is either fireproofed or dampened with water at the foot. The snake is not seen until it glides swiftly, so as not to ignite the screen, from under the cloth into the council ring. Its actions are then the same as those described above.

A little advance figuring and a few trial runs with the unlit snake before the braves assemble in council will assure a perfect performance by both the snake and those who operate the illusion.

FLAMING FEATHER FIRE

"Tonight," says the medicine man, as he stands with arms uplifted before the council fire, "a feather which flames will fall from the Thunderbird, and if it be the will of the Sky Chief, our council fire will be lit by its magic."

The warriors-in-council sit very still, and even the bravest among them fears that he may be burned by the magic flame. Suddenly a few of the warriors who have the eyes of hawks and sit close to the tribal chief's chair, think that they see fireflies dance above the council fire. Then in the silent forest a shrill, eaglelike scream shatters the silence of the night. Once again the cry is heard, and then stillness covers the land like a heavy blanket.

A sudden flash of light startles the warriors, and they see, high in the air and the height of a man distant from the council fire, a brightly flaming thing. They watch fearfully and see that the flame is a big blazing feather. The feather drops swiftly earthward. A cry goes up from the chiefs and warriors, who fear that the fall of the feather to the ground will kill the flame. But the feather does not fall. It drops swiftly, swings the length of a tall warrior toward the council fire, then rises high in air directly above the fire. The feather of flame drifts away from the fire, circles it, and hovers above it. Bright flashes of color-flame come from the feather as it dances and spins above the unlit fire. Then it drops close to the fire—so close that the warriors hold their breath as they wait to see the fire burst into flame. It does not, for the feather swiftly rises high above it.

"Give us fire, O Flaming Feather of the Thunderbird!" shouts the medicine man, and the warriors-in-council take up the prayer.

The feather hears! Slowly, spinning as it comes, the Flaming Feather drops lower and lower until it hangs only the breadth of a man's hand above the fire. The feather blazes fiercely, and the flames are colored like the fire from logs which come from the sea. Then swiftly, surely, the feather drops into the heart of the fire and is lost in the burst of fire which seems to rise to meet it.

With bowed head and uplifted arms the medicine man stands before the blazing fire. The Thunderbird has heard.

HOW TO OPERATE THE FLAMING FEATHER

This is one of the most spectacular "magic" fire-lighting devices devised by the author. The preparation is easy, and the sketch shows how it is rigged. It is one more magic fire that depends on the use of the overhead line.

If the council fire area is already equipped with an overhead line, all that is needed to complete the overhead line requirements is a black metal ring ⅜ inch in diameter, securely fastened to the line and 6 feet away from the center ring, which is *directly* above the council fire. It is necessary that this second ring be fastened to the overhead line in the *opposite* direction from that where the concealed operator will manipulate the Flaming Feather.

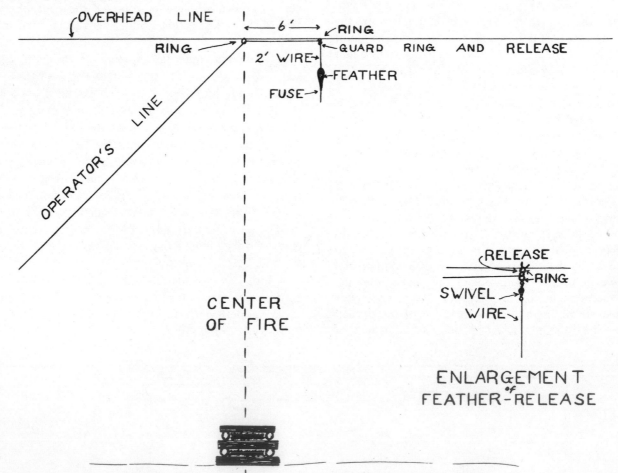

The feather is suspended in this way: The free end of the operator's 90 or 100 feet of black nylon fishline is passed through the *center* ring and then securely tied 1½ inches from its end to the top ring on a double, barrel type swivel, as described in the section on "How to Make the Flaming Feather." The remaining 1½ inch of the operator's line is firmly tied, at the very end, to the top of the bend in a strong, springy, rippled hairpin with both prongs cut off with a pair of shears 1¼ inch below the top of the bend; then a guard ring is fastened onto the operator's line as close to the hairpin as possible. As has been explained under other fire-lighting methods requiring a guard ring, the sole purpose of the ring is to prevent the Flaming Feather from being pulled too close to the overhead line and, in the case of a nylon line, destroying it.

The Flaming Feather fire lighting is easy to carry out. The two prongs of the hairpin which act as a release spring are pushed through the ring on the overhead line furthest from the council fire, and the two prongs spread sufficiently to hold the feather, which is now suspended directly underneath, by their tension. When the feather bursts into flame, the operator, from his place of concealment, gives a slight tug on his end of the line. The hairpin release-spring immediately pulls out of the ring through which it has been pushed, and the Flaming Feather, much to the surprise of the warriors-in-council, swiftly drops 6 feet toward the ground as it swings into position beneath the ring fastened directly above the council fire. From here on, the antics of the Flaming Feather are entirely under the control of the operator. He will find it a simple matter to make the feather dance and twirl, rise and fall, keeping the warriors in suspense, until at last the Flaming Feather drops into the council fire and thus accomplishes its mission. The swivel on the wire, already mentioned, greatly helps to keep the feather spinning as it moves around and above the council fire.

The Flaming Feather Fire is easy to set up, simple to operate, and spectacular to witness. Should an operator feel that his feather may prove too heavy for *one* hairpin release-spring, it is a simple matter to use *two* hairpins in making the spring described. The double hairpin spring will assure double tension in holding the feather in place.

HOW TO MAKE
THE FLAMING FEATHER

The "feather" used to light the Flaming Feather Fire is easy to make. It may be cut from a piece of thin, light wood ¼ to ½ inch thick, or be made from thick, heavy cardboard if necessary. It should have an over-all length of 16 inches, including ¾ inch for the tip of the quill, and a maximum width of 3½ inches. A small hole is bored through the center of the feather at the very tip, and another through the end of the quill. The quill end of the feather should be weighted to assure that it swings in pendulum fashion. An easy way to do this is to wind a few strips of lead, the sort used by fishermen as sinkers, around the tip of the quill. Since a wire has to be threaded through the hole in the top of the feather, and a fuse or streamer through the hole in the tip of the quill, it is well to keep a nail stuck through each of these holes, to keep them open until the feather is completely made. After the feather has been cut out and the two holes made, the feather is wrapped completely around with a 1- or 2-inch strip of black or dark porous cloth, carefully preserving the shape of the feather. A powder which burns with a bright-colored flame should be wrapped inside the strip. The feather is liberally sprinkled with kerosene a short while before council fire time, and if the delayed-action fuse method is used to add to the effect, all surplus fluid should be squeezed out, so that the fuse is not moistened by drip of the fluid. One end of a 2-foot-3-inch length of thin, black, flexible wire is threaded through the hole in the tip of the feather and securely fastened, the minimum amount of wire being used. A double, barrel type swivel about 1¼ inch in over-all length is firmly fastened to the other end of the wire.

The feather is now complete except for the addition of either a short, thick soft-string streamer about 3 inches long or the delayed-action fuse. Whichever is chosen is threaded through the hole in the quill end of the feather and tied there. The streamer is lit with the touch of a small torch, when the warriors are present. The length of the delayed-action fuse is decided by a little experimentation, so that it will burn for the necessary six or eight minutes or longer, as decided by the chief in charge of the council fire. The fuse must be lit just ahead of the arrival of the warriors at the council fire area; they must be seated and ready when the feather mysteriously bursts into flame with nobody near it. Should the fuse fail to work—which is most unlikely when it is well made and precautions are taken so that it does not become moist with flammable fluid—the feather can be lit with the touch of a torch, or even a match if no torch is ready.

To make doubly sure of the feather being ignited, it is a simple matter to use a *double fuse*. This is actually two fuses of the same length. Lit at the same moment, one of them is certain to burn until it reaches and ignites the feather. The use of the saltpeter wad and matchheads, described earlier in this chapter, is also strongly recommended at the termination point of the fuse. It is an easy matter to tie the wad onto the quill end of the feather.

around

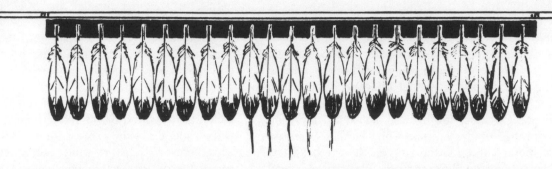

SOME COUNCIL FIRE CHIEFS need little if any guidance on basic matters concerning the organization of council fire groups. They have already established such a group or groups, based on their knowledge of American Indians and their respective ways of life. Others—perhaps the novice council fire chief forming his first Indian group, or a chief whose established group for some reason is reorganizing or changing from one habitat group to another—will need a brief introduction to the various historic Indian tribes and their main characteristics.

prior to making that important decision. Should the group-to-be live in well-wooded territory with lakes and rivers in the immediate vicinity, it is quite possible that that group will be happier and have more typical and realistic activities as a Woodland group than as one of the Plains. On the other hand, if the hearts of the embryo Indians are set on being war-bonneted braves of the Plains, there is no good reason why they should not become a group of Plains Indians who lived on the border of wooded country and spent a part of their lives hunting or living in that territory.

INDIANS OF THE PLAINS

It is because of the history and life of the Plains tribes that so many Plains groups of modern council fire Indians are established. This preference is also encouraged by the fact that, as a rule, more of the way of life of these Indians is known on account of history, story, and cinema. Much of this material, including pseudo-historical incidents, is unreliable, and considerable research and study are advisable on the part of council fire chiefs who wish to present a true picture of these tribes to their young braves-in-council. Probably another cause for the predominance of Plains tribe groups around modern council fires is the striking dress, regalia, and above all, the war bonnets worn by the Indian nations and tribes which roamed the plains. They, like most other Indians, led happy, adventurous lives before the coming of the white men.

Before deciding on a band or tribe of Plains or any other Indian group as a base for organization and council fire activities, it is recommended that a modern council fire chief consider the habitat in which their young Indians-to-be live, even for a few summer months,

INDIANS OF THE WOODLANDS

The nations and tribes of the Woodland groups compared favorably in every respect with their brothers of the Plains. They were powerful, their braves were courageous and splendidly dressed, and the nations especially set an example for wise organization that is not surpassed by any of the so-called civilized nations of the world today. Though more people know of the magnificence and power of the Five Nations—later to become the Six Nations, on the addition of the Tuscarora—there are other admirable Eastern Woodland groups, such as Woodland Cree, Ojibway, Chippewa, Sauk-Fox, Winnebago, and Cherokee.

INDIANS OF THE NORTHWEST COAST

Many campfire leaders have asked the author questions regarding the American Indians of the Northwest Pacific Coast and how to stage Northwest Coast Indian council fires. The details which follow will provide background material and ideas for those campfire chiefs who

indian council fires

wish to set up a simple Northwest Coast council fire area from time to time, in order to add variety to the regular council fire program. A visit of a clan of Indians from

the Northwest Coast to a tribe of Plains or Woodland Indians can also be easily and effectively staged. During such a council fire, challenges, magic, and coups from the tribes of the Coastal Indians can be combined with those of the Plains Indians.

The vast territory over which the Northwest Coast Indians held undisputed sway until the coming of the white men, strongly resembled Scandinavia. The rugged coastline was honeycombed with bays and countless fiord-like inlets. Into these bays and fiords swift-flowing streams and rivers poured their foaming waters. Islands, large and small, dotted the ocean and bays. They were as difficult to count as stars on a winter night. The lands of these Indians stretched from the far-northern territory of the Eskimo to far beyond the mighty Columbia River, into the states of Washington, Oregon, and California. Their domain was one of great forests of giant red and yellow cedars, spruce, hemlock, and fir, often extending from the Pacific Ocean coastline, which rose precipitously from the water in towering cliffs, up the sides of lofty mountains, to disappear on their summits. These mighty mountain ranges served as almost impassable barriers between the Coastal tribes and their inland neighbors.

The rugged land and forests proved so difficult to travel through, with the exception of a few trading trails, known as "grease trails" because valuable fish oil was carried over them, that the hardy Indian navigators had to take to canoes. In these huge, magnificent, ocean-going craft, which dwarfed the caravels of the early European explorers, they made daring voyages from Skagway, on the mouth of the Chilkat River, throughout the length and breadth of Puget Sound and far beyond. The warlike, fearless Haida often set out from their island homes to brave the wave-lashed ocean and raid the tribes as far south as California.

The powerful Tlingit, neighbors of the Eskimo, could see the Queen Charlotte Islands as they stood on the shores of their beach villages on the mainland. The Queen Charlottes cover 4,000 square miles, and were the home of the Haida. The proud Tsimshian-speaking tribes lived on the mainland to the east of the Haida.

ly accepted fact that these peoples originated in Asia and crossed from Siberia to Alaska by way of what is now known as the Bering Strait. Much of the magnificent sculpture, painting, and art work in general of these skillful artisans, as well as their slat body armor and weapons, bear witness to the strong Asiatic influence of their ancestors.

The varied peoples of the Northwest Pacific Coast were healthy, hardy, and daring. The men of the northern tribes were tall and well built. Those of the southern tribes were less tall, and stocky. The color of their skins varied from a golden light brown to darker shades of copper-brown. Their hair was generally raven-black and straight. They had the keen eyes of hunters, ranging in color from dark brown to nearly black. The majority of the people wore simple clothing woven from cedar bark, as compared to the magnificence of the dress of their chiefs, princes, and nobles, who wore garments of beautifully tanned and decorated leather and often capes of the magnificent sea otter. A distinctive mark of the Coastal Indian was his bare feet. Often the feet were conspicuous when the nobles wore their richest clothing and leggings for ceremonial potlatch feasts.

The tribes of the coastal areas called themselves Salt Water People and felt superior to the Fresh Water People, who lived inland on some of the many streams and rivers. Many of the inland people never descended the rivers to the ocean, for fear of the warlike Salt Water People.

Prior to the coming of the white men, when the strongest tribes were decimated by the evils and hitherto unknown diseases which the white men brought, the Indians of the Northwest Pacific Coast lived happy, healthy lives. Theirs was a vigorous, outdoor, adventurous life. There was an abundance of food. The ocean provided almost everything that was required to eat. Salmon and nearly every other kind of fish teemed in countless millions in the coastal waters, and shellfish and marine mammals were there in abundance. Great dead whales freshly killed by the tigers of the sea, killer whales, were often washed onto the beaches of the Indians' sea-girt villages, providing great feasts for the villagers. The country was too rocky and rugged to cultivate to any extent; but *camas,* a plant of the lily family, grew in abundance, and the natives ate the sweet roots. *Wapato,* known as Indian potatoes, was also plentiful and made fine eating when boiled or roasted. Elderberries, huckleberries, salmonberries, gooseberries, crab apples, rose hips, and the prized clover roots—which were cultivated with care in little patches of land and passed down from generation to generation—provided vegetables and fruit.

The men of the tribes were clever hunters and trappers, and added grizzly and black bears, deer, elk, mountain goats, sheep, and many smaller animals to the bountiful food supply. The bow and arrow, throwing spears, har-

Their villages, ruled by princes and nobles, extended from the ocean beaches to points far inland, bordering the swift-flowing Nass and Skena Rivers. The ocean-bordered land of the fierce Nootka provided ideal territory for these dauntless whalers, who sallied forth in their staunch canoes to hunt the humpback whale from villages set on the shores of sounds and inlets. The whale was to the Nootka and other coastal tribes what the buffalo was to the Indians of the Plains, except for the fact that they could not use the skin of the whale to cover a shelter. They did not need to; they lived in fine houses. The Kwakiutl, to the north, were the only powerful neighbors of the Nootka. The Kwakiutl were ruled by princes, chiefs, and princesses who guarded well the rights of their rich territory.

Winters were severe along the coastal region, despite the nearness of the warm Japanese current which mingled with the ice-cold waters of the North, causing heavy mists and fogs to blanket the land during many of the winter months.

There was a certain similarity of cultures and way of life among various coastal groups, which makes it possible to illustrate the mode of life of many by touching on a few. Magnificent rectangular houses, built of massive planks of red cedar, dress, food to a large extent, canoes, habits, potlatches, water travel, hunting, and fishing were similar enough to make general observations about these tribes applicable to nearly all. It is a general-

poons, clubs, and hunting knives were the weapons used by the hunters.

The winter months of these Indians were filled with splendid ceremonies. Potlatches, which were great celebration and give-away feasts, dramatics, storytelling, mystery, magic, and music provided relaxation for old and young alike.

It is of interest to note that the curtain went down on the superb culture and art of these peoples only about one hundred years ago. Their artistic work has been declared by leading experts to be the finest ever achieved by the Indians of the entire American continent.

The Indians of the Northwest Coast had many gods, as had the Indians of the Plains and Woodlands, despite the general belief that all worshiped only one god—the Great Spirit. Among the deities of the Northwest Coast peoples are found the Chief of the Sky, of the Kwakiutl; the Four Chiefs, Moon Chief, Sea Chief, Mountain Chief, and South Chief, of the Nootka. While the chief deity of the ocean-going Haida was the Sacred One Standing and Moving, who held up their islands as well as the firmament, as befitted people who lived on and by the ocean, a number of their supernatural beings were directly allied with the ocean. Such were the Devilfish People, Black Whale People, and the Ocean People. The Haida prayed to these beings and cast offerings into the ocean to pacify them. They also had other supernatural beings of importance, such as the Creek Woman and

lesser patron deities named Master Builder, Master Canoe Builder, and the Singers, who controlled not only arts and crafts but the weather. The powerful Tsimshian people had several deities, headed by the Chief of the Sky and the Evening Sky Woman.

Various tribes had lesser supernatural beings to help the principle deities. These lesser gods formed the important liaison between the gods and human beings. A number of transformers, to which group of supernatural beings the Old One or Old Man, Raven, and Coyote belonged, were beings from the supernatural world who had power to change themselves into human or animal form at will and create and recreate things.

The boys and young men of various tribes went on power quests, as did the young men of many tribes of North American Indians, in order to find guardian spirits who would give them power of different kinds. Weather power, warrior power, hunting power, wolf power, and healing power were among the many powers sought. Prayer and the strict observance of the laws of physical fitness and cleanliness played a big part in the religion of practically all tribes on the Northwest Coast.

The village sites were selected with the utmost care. Once a half-moon, sloping strip of beach was found, building commenced. Magnificent houses built of thick red cedar planks, often cut from the living trees, were as beautiful as they were weatherproof. These rectangular houses were splendid without and within. They had huge house poles in front and wonderfully carved and painted house posts and screens inside. Houses ranged from about 40 to 60 feet in width, with a length of 50 to 100 feet. There are records of enormous houses which measured as much as 500 feet in length and 75 feet in width. Such houses of the chiefs, princes, and some nobles easily held a thousand people. The massive roof of each Haida house formed a single gable, rising 20 feet or more from the ground in front. One main fire burned in the middle of the floor, often below the second terrace of beaten earth which was found in many of these dwellings.

CANOE

Canoes were almost as important as houses in the lives of the Northwest Coast Indians. The great ocean-going canoes of the Haida, built from the trunk of a huge red cedar, were often 75 feet long with an 8-foot beam, the shell thickness in the bow being about 4 inches and that in the stern from 2 to 3 inches as a rule. These craft were magnificently carved and painted, and generally the bow and stern pieces were made separately and fitted perfectly onto the main dugout section of the canoe when it was nearly ready for launching. Sometimes planks were sewn, with tough spruce or cedar-root thread, onto the sides of these canoes to heighten the gunwales. Such craft were usally manned by a crew of about forty men. They were used not only to carry war parties on long-distance raids and take chiefs and nobles to potlatches and other ceremonies but also for general transportation. Families, along with dogs and other animals, household effects, and probably two tons of baggage, were frequently carried in one of these remarkable craft in heavy seas.

The staunch whale-hunting canoes of the seafaring Nootka were ocean-going craft ranging from 30 to 40 feet in length. They had a crew of eight men, including the chief harpooner, who was also the whaler and canoe chief in charge of the hunt. The helmsman, who used his special paddle as a rudder, and the float tender were included in the crew of eight.

The Indians of the ocean and rivers of the Northwest Coast used many other types of canoes, ranging from hunting canoes 12 to 15 feet in length to spoon-type craft, shovel-nosed dugouts, and the light, swift, one-man racing craft.

INDIANS OF THE SOUTHWEST

These groups were composed of fearless warriors as well as artisans, and offer considerable scope to modern council fire groups which choose a Southwestern habitat group. In the warlike class the Apache, Yaqui, and Pima may be mentioned; among the leading artisan groups the Navaho, Hopi, and Zuni come to mind. Modern council fire groups whose habitats are close to cliffs which may be hollowed out safely into dwellings and reached without danger are well placed to live the life of the Pueblo people. The athletic achievements of the Hopi and Zuni equaled their ability as craftsmen, and both skills provide good material for modern Indians. The Navaho, though classed as shepherds, are even better known today for their artistry in other fields, such as weaving, making jewelry, and their old skill in sand painting.

INDIANS OF THE SOUTHEAST

Three interesting tribes with sufficient historical background interest to provide good material for modern council fire groups were found in the Southeast. These were the Cherokee, Shawnee, and Seminole. The Tuscarora also lived in that habitat until they became the sixth nation of the Five Nations confederacy. For council fire groups whose habitat lies on the borders of swampland or on a series of interlocking small rivers or creeks, the ways of the Seminole can be followed. This tribe of fighters held their own in the many skirmishes and battles with the United States Army and proved themselves not only warriors but also first-class exponents of jungle warfare and swampcraft.

Modern Indian groups should be more than council fire bands which meet once a week around the council fire. More than half the experience and enjoyment derived from Indian activiites should come from Indiancraft and woodcraft practised far afield from the council fire. It is at such times that exploit honors and illustrious names are earned. It is on these occasions that modern Indians learn to observe, hear, walk, and act like real Red Men. These things make them better Indians as they sit around the council fire on nights when the fragrant woodsmoke rises to form a trail joining the One Above with the Indians below.

TRIBAL ORGANIZATION AND NAMES

There are so many names of illustrious American Indian nations and tribes to select from when forming modern council fire groups that the chief difficulty will be to decide which one to choose. When there are many members in a council fire group it may be well to pick a nation to which all members will belong but divide the nation into the various tribes of which it was composed. This makes organization easier when the number of would-be braves is large. A Woodland group, for instance, may be made up of the mighty Six Nations of the Iroquois. If there are one hundred in the group, it can be divided into the five most renowned groups of that united nation. With this arrangement, twenty braves could be Mohawk, while the remaining eighty warriors could be divided equally among the Seneca, Onondaga, Oneida, and Cayuga nations. The best and most technical way to refer to these nations is given here, though one may also speak of the Mohawks, Senecas, and so on.

As a general term, the Six Nations—or Five when the Tuscarora were in the South and not yet members of the Iroquian Five Nations—were referred to as "the People of the Longhouse." A tribal name for each nation follows: Mohawk, People of Flint; Oneida, People of the Upright Stone; Onondaga, People of the Hills; Seneca, People of the Mountain; Cayuga, People of the Swamp; and the Tuscarora, Wearers of the Shirt. A little library research on the part of council fire chiefs will help to reveal further fascinating facts concerning nations and tribes of both Woodland and Plains tribes which will help in assigning authentic duties to the various groups. As an instance, the Onondaga were Keepers, or Tenders, of the Fire; the Mohawk, Keepers of the Eastern Door; and the Seneca, Keepers of the Western Door.

Under the banners of the mighty Seven Nations of the Sioux were gathered Blackfoot, Oglala; Santee, Sans Arc, Minninconjou, Two Kettles, and Hunkpapa; but no war-

rior of these nations would fail to remind you that he was first and foremost a Sioux, one of the Seven Tepees and the Seven Council Fires. Other powerful and picturesque tribes of the Plains were: Blackfoot, Comanche, Crow, Plains Ojibway, Plains Cree, Cheyenne, Assiniboine, Kiowa (Kiowa-Apache), Teton (Teton-Dakota), Omaha, Osage, Arapaho, Mandan, and the fighting Pawnee. The Menomini, Winnebago, and Sauk-Fox inhabited the Eastern Woodland area, while the Nez Perce, Shoshoni, and Snake roamed the Western plateau. The South-

eastern area was the habitat of the Shawnee, Cherokee, Chickasaw, Choctaw, and the Seminole and others, including the Tuscarora, before they became a part of the Six Nations. The Southwestern habitat is the home of the artistic Navaho, Hopi, Zuni, and Pima—to mention a few of the Pueblo people—and the Apache; but unless the modern Indian council fire groups wish to specialize in arts and crafts rather than seek the counting of coups for prowess on the warpath and in the hunt, the Apache is perhaps the outstanding tribe which appears to offer the scope and glory which the council fire braves-to-be seek. The California and Florida habitats, while they too had redoubtable warriors as well as skills and crafts, may appear to offer less to those around the modern council fire, where far too often "big names" count grand coup. Many fine tribes fall into second choice when competing against their war-bonneted brothers of the Plains.

Careful thought should be given to the choice of tribe before a council fire chief, his subchiefs, and his warriors-to-be—who should have a say in the decision—decide which illustrious nation or tribe, chosen from widely

spread habitat groups throughout the United States and Canada, they wish to become as they gather around their council fire.

The vast domain of the Northwest Coast should not be passed up when making the choice. Here is immense scope and a wide choice of arts, totem poles, and war canoes, coupled with warrior deeds. It is unfortunate that a greater study of the tribes which ruled that far-flung region has not been made by more modern council fire chiefs. The tribes and territory of the Northwest Pacific Coast offer almost unlimited scope for prowess and pageantry, dance and diversions, legend and lore! Tribes such as the warlike Haida, the whale-hunting Nootka, mighty Tsimshian, the Kwakiutl, Bella Coola, and the two Salish Groups, to mention outstanding tribes only, have much to offer. Most of these tribes, *unlike their brothers of Plains, Woodland, and Pueblo,* had totem poles and house poles, and *real* princes and princesses. The term "princess" was never used by the Indians of the Plains, Woodland, or Southwest. It is an intentional misnomer coined by publicity-seekers who, to arouse audience interest and box-office appeal, devised the make-believe term "plains princess." The Indians of the Northwest Coast also had tribal and clan chiefs, shamans with amazing powers, customs, costumes, and conservation practices which are worthy of emulation by modern council fire groups. Their way of life is especially suited for modern council fire groups whose council fires burn close to the ocean or large lakes.

NORTHWEST COAST
TRIBAL AND CLAN ORGANIZATION

Organization of camper and other groups into tribal and clan divisions is advised in order to assure interest, friendly rivalry, and keen contesting of challenges and other contests around the council fire. The term *gens* indicates that the descent of the tribe is reckoned only through the male line. *Phratry* is the subdivision of a tribe, a unit such as a clan or a group of related families. *Sept* is a tribal group, especially one which is localized and based on common descent in both male and female line. *Sib* is a unilinear, usually exogamous kin group based on traditional common descent whether patrilineal or matrilineal, usually distinguished from clan or sept. Such technical definitions have been replaced here by simpler terms, such as division, tribe, clan, kin group, and on the father's side or on the mother's side. It is interesting to note that similar divisions existed among not only the Plains Indians but also among the ancient clans of Scotland, the same technical terms being used to describe their divisions. The information which follows will help leaders to organize Northwest Coast council fire divisions in an effective yet simple manner.

The highest rank among the Northwest Coast Indian tribes was chief of tribe, the term "tribal chief" being generally used in this book. Next in rank were town chief, used among the Haida and some other tribes, clan chief, house chief, and family chief. Sometimes, in a small village, a chief was both the town chief and family chief. Another rank equal to clan, house, or family chief was that of chief harpooner, who was usually a chief of some importance, especially among the Nootka, Makah, and Haida. There were additional ranks—one might almost say titles—which could be conferred on clan members. Some were village watchman, tender of the council fire, herald, river guardian, lake guardian, message bearer, canoe chief, tallykeeper, and singer, among others.

The division of the people of most Northwest Coast tribes was chiefs and nobles, freemen or commoners, and slaves. A number of important tribes, such as the Kwakiutl, had ranks which can only be interpreted as prince and princess, and the holders of these titles were given the same respect as those of similar rank in European countries. The Haida and Nootka, among other leading tribes, used the terms first mentioned to distinguish between the peoples of the various groups which made up their tribal divisions. The term "warrior" has been used in this book instead of freeman, since any fit freeman was also a warrior when the need for warriors arose.

WOODEN HELMET

Slave was the term used to describe prisoners taken in battle. While they were literally servants, used to wait on the chiefs and nobles and their families, they were not as a rule badly treated. The highest-ranking chiefs and nobles thought nothing of working shoulder to shoulder with the slaves in order to carry out tasks, no matter how strenuous, for the good of the community, despite the fact that the leading Indian families of the Northwest Pacific Coast were as class-conscious as the leading aristocratic families of the white man of today. Slaves might escape, and during a reprisal raid chiefs and nobles who owned slaves of a certain tribe might become slaves themselves of the tribe to which their slaves formerly belonged. No doubt thoughts of this possibility eased the treatment of the slaves of most tribes. Although the title of chief was often hereditary, there is little doubt that most chiefs realized that the rights of leadership went hand in hand with the responsibility of their rank, and that they lived up to that creed.

A suitable division for council fire clans could be as follows: six or eight warriors led by a house or clan chief can constitute a clan. Another good arrangement for modern warriors who have thrown in their lot with the hardy coastal Salt Water people, such as the Nootka or Haida, is to form whaling canoe crews consisting of seven warriors, no more and no less, led by a chief harpooner or canoe chief. A larger clan, depending on the number of warriors available, could be formed by twelve or sixteen warriors and two clan or house chiefs. Twenty-four or thirty-two warriors could be led by one tribal chief, two clan chiefs, one house chief, and one canoe chief, or chief harpooner. Of course the titles of the subchiefs could be any one of those given, since all these titles carry equal rank.

Such groups could belong to any of the following clans, or people: the Bear People, Sea Lion People, and clans such as Wolf, Eagle, Whale, Killer Whale, Raven, Sea Otter, Bear, Grizzly Bear, Hawk, and Fireweed. Some of the divisions and tribes had special totem symbols and animals and birds connected with them for various reasons. They are given later to help modern chiefs in the choice of clan names. Many tribes had large communal houses which housed families and related families. Such houses had names, such as Sea Lion House, Killer Whale House, and Grizzly Bear House.

Individual names were not so numerous and are harder to interpret than those used among Plains and Woodland tribes. Some names were earned the hard way, while others were inherited, though those with proud inherited names gained little prestige or honor if they simply rested on the former laurels of their name. Names such as Little Bear, Whale Hunter, Young Eagle, Little Wolf, Killer-of-Whales, Killer-of-Bears, Seal Hunter, and similar names were often used and will serve as a base for other suitable names. Women were infrequently spoken of by individual names, though many of them had striking ones: Dawn Star, Sea Song, and Calm Woman, for instance.

There were a number of powerful secret societies among the various tribes, such as the Warrior Society, Grizzly Bear, and Wolf Society. Others can be organized, and modern council fire chiefs and warriors can be admitted to them for having attained certain achievements or for reaching certain standards of efficiency connected with the camp or organization programs.

A number of the principal Northwest Coast tribes had their homes in both the United States and Canada, though often they were known by an entirely different name when they left their usual habitat. The Haida, for example, of the Queen Charlotte Islands, also settled on Prince of Wales Island, Alaska—where they were known as Kaigani, which was the name of their summer camp. These Alaskan Haida found their new home an ideal place from which to set out in their great canoes loaded with trade goods which they exchanged for articles brought by sailing ships from Europe. The group of Nootka which left their northern shores to live in the state of Washington were given the name of Makah. Some tribes had so many subdivisions and names that there is little point in recording them here, where the tribes listed are given for the sole purpose of giving modern tribal and clan chiefs a chance to find suitable names of outstanding tribes for their council fire groups and appropriate totem symbols for their use. As a few of the tribes mentioned here had no subdivisions, with a bird or animal name for each, the suggested names in such cases have been based on the totems taken from tribal and clan traditions, or carvings on their totem poles, in order to provide a greater number of suitable clan names for the use of modern camp and council fire chiefs.

TRIBAL AND CLAN NAMES AND TOTEM SYMBOLS.

Haida	Raven Eagle	*Nootka*	Raven Wolf Eagle Killer Whale
Tlingit	Raven Wolf Eagle Sea Lion	*Makah*	Raven Wolf Eagle Killer Whale
Tsimshian	Raven Eagle Wolf Bear Fireweed Sea Otter Crane	*Kwakiutl*	Thunderbird Wolf Mink Deer Seal Sea Otter Sea Lion Whale
Coast Salish	Raven Coyote Otter Seal Sea Lion	*Bella Coola*	Lightning Snake Thunderbird Whale Eagle Beaver
Squamish	An important subdivision of the Coast Salish. The same totems and clan names may be used.		

Leaders may get further ideas for names from considering a few of the names of the Tsimshian divisions which lived in seventeen different villages: People of the Sea, People of the Canyon, Torchlight-Fishing-People, the People of the Sand, the People of the Pond, and the People of the Sea Gulls.

INDIAN PERSONAL NAMES

There are many erroneous ideas concerning the personal names of Indians. It seems to be the general belief that most Indian tribes used the same system of naming their children and braves. The methods actually differed widely. It cannot be said that all Indian children were given baby names at birth, then childhood names, and finally, perhaps after a young Indian had become seasoned on war or hunting trails, an appropriate name which was used for the rest of his life. Some tribes did just that. Others bestowed the totem names of animals, plants, or things on a child, and these names were lifelong. Some tribes observed strict rules regarding change of names. When a member of such tribes wished to change his name, certain official ceremonies had to be carried out by the candidate before the new name was recognized and used. Things were much easier for the taker-of-a-new-name in some other tribes, where all that was required was to have a herald or crier proclaim the new name throughout the village or camp. Nicknames were often used by some tribes, but whether they were flattering or the opposite, their owners had earned them. The adult name of an Indian was given respect and regarded as a badge of honor.

In order to avoid considerable research to find out which tribe did what in the giving of names, the names given to modern council fire Indians can be used season after season, but there is no reason why names should not be changed in certain cases where a more distinguished one has been earned. Personal Indian names mean more to council fire members when they are not awarded until the fourth council fire of the season. In the meantime, the tribal members are simply braves—a noble name in itself, which had to be really earned by the Indians. This arrangement gives the council fire chief and his subchiefs a chance to evaluate the braves and their behavior and award suitable names when the time comes.

Indian names given to modern council fire Indians mean more when they are awarded ceremoniously. There are many effective ways of bestowing personal names at a council fire naming ceremony. The medicine man may mark the symbols which form the name on a piece of bark with the point of an arrow, then drop the bark strip into the council fire at the moment the chief pronounces the brave's name. A short red stripe may be marked on each cheek bone of the brave who is being named immediately after the name has been spoken. The stripes can be marked by the council fire chief, a subchief, or the medicine man. Other ways can be decided on by the chiefs-in-council.

One difficulty encountered by a council fire chief is that his subchiefs and older warriors, at least, all wish to bear the unearned names of renowned chiefs, such as Crazy Horse, Sitting Bull, Handsome Lake, Yellow Shirt, and the like. As the Indian chief said, after attending a modern council fire and noting the number of chiefs and chiefs' coup feathered war bonnets, "Huhnn! Too many chiefs; not enough braves!" Actually, there are so many fine Indian names that there should be great variety and no scarcity of them even for the largest Indian bands.

PERSONAL INDIAN NAMES FOR BOYS. In the following list of suggested names, a number of names of Canadian Indian chiefs are included. Though some names may not seem to be very distinguished or complimentary, they were borne, in most cases, by illustrious chiefs.

Standing Buffalo	The Crow	Dull Knife
Crowfoot	Heavy Shield	Red Crow
Painted Face	Broad Trail	Little Pine
Little Necklace	Bear's Paw	Big Necklace
Clouded Horn	Red Dog	Old Sun
Spotted Eagle	Bear Killer	

Some of these chiefs belonged to tribes of Indians long settled in Canada, such as Assiniboine, Blackfoot, Blood, Ojibway (Chippewa), Cree, and Stony.

A general list of suggested Indian names follows:

High Wolf	White Hawk	Fisherman
Black Elk	Red Tracks	Runner
Standing Elk	Long Feather	Little Fox
Sitting Crow	Strong Bow	Yellow Fox
Yellow Hand	Tracker	Two Bears
Eagle Feather	Black Wolf	Swift Fire
White Arrow	Gray Fox	Black Hawk
Dancer	Young Eagle	Red Feather
Little Wolf	Arrow Chief	Story Teller
Little Bear	Silent Foot	Sign Talker
Running Eagle	Black Feather	

When it comes to finding appropriate names for medicine men, some care has to be exercised in selecting suitable and imposing names. Some of these can be:

Medicine Wolf	Seven Stars	Dark Moon
Fast Thunder	Red Star	Two Moons
Burning Sky	Black Sun	Rising Sun
Star Blanket	Sun Arrow	Star Watcher
Medicine Bear	Good Sky	Medicine Grass

PERSONAL INDIAN NAMES FOR GIRLS. The following may be used by girls in an Indian tribe:

Daybreak Star	Graceful Walker	Slim Girl
White Cloud	Dreamer	Soft Snow
Girl-of-the-Sun	White Bird	Sky Bird
Witch Star	Gray Dove	Blue Bird
Golden Butterfly	Echo	White Fawn
Medicine Woman	Sunflower	Evening Primrose
Little Star	Flower	White Flower
Butterfly	Flute Maid	Sings-in-the-Air
Doe Woman	Dew Drop	Yellow Bird
Evening Star	Red Duck	Song Bird

Brown Butterfly	Swan	Blue Jay
Beaver Woman	Firefly	White Doe
Honeysuckle	Wild Rose	
Green Leaf	Rose Bud	

PERSONAL NAMES IN INDIAN LANGUAGE. Though the use of names in the Indian language would seem to give an additional touch of authenticity to a name, this is not always the case. It takes a great deal of research to find the right tribal names in the Indian language for members of a band. Too often such names are selected by council fire chiefs from a general, haphazard list, or published lists, in which the name of tribe or habitat, or even the sex of the name-bearer is not stated. Without further study, research, and interpretation, the use of such ambiguous lists may cause a Blackfoot brave to bear a Sioux name, and a fighting Pawnee may be saddled with the name of a Zuni.

Let's take as an example the council fire chief of a Sioux group who has an outstanding dancer in his band. He has seen or heard the name *Namid* somewhere and learned that the name means "dancer," so he gives this apparently suitable name to his brave-who-dances. He may be embarrassed to discover later that his dancing Sioux bears a Chippewa name. The casual bestowing of names in the Indian language may lead to Woodland warriors bearing Plains names. Even when a council fire chief knows that the name is in a certain language, there may be some difficulty in discovering the exact translation of the name into English. This may lead to a not-too-handsome and quite small chief taking the Iroquian name of *On-on-tio,* because of its euphonious quality. He would not wonder why some of his older braves, who have been making a study of the Iroquian names, smile when he pronounces his name at the council fire if he knew that the translation of his name is "Beautiful Mountain." A chief of the same group, also working on the phonetic principle, may take the name *Ro-he-hon.* The fact that the chief in question is one of the least active in the group and prefers to sit rather than stand at council fires, makes the name inappropriate. To remain in character, a far more appropriate choice of name would have been *Tes-kah-hea*—"Resting on it."

AMERICAN INDIAN SPEECH

The many languages of the American Indians were far from the guttural grunts and static syllables which some people suppose, though like many unwritten languages they were perhaps best interpreted through dance, gesture, and song. Many Indians formed mind-pictures, then described what they imagined or actually saw. Some tribes, more than others, thought in terms of song, which made for lilting, musical speech. To hear an Indian in-

terpret his dreams through song is a thing long to be remembered.

Unless a council fire group has made some study of the actual language spoken by the tribe whose name it bears, it is bad medicine to try to use actual Indian phrases, which may belong to the language of a tribe whose council fire burns in an entirely different habitat. It is perhaps safest and best to use picturesque phrases in English which could easily be an interpretation of actual Indian speech. Imagination, the displacement of a few verbs in the right places, and the occasional use of blank verse will greatly add to the effectiveness and interest of council fire talks and stories. This would help to eliminate the pidgin-English sort of jargon which passes for pseudo-Indian talk at some modern council fires. A council fire chief does not make the best impression by declaiming: "Me heap big chief! Me make plenty talk! Me make braves shake with my palaver!" True, he may make the "braves shake," but the chances are that they may do so with suppressed laughter. An impressive talk given by a chief at a council fire opening, or to introduce a ceremony, is best given in natural, simple English unless some time has been spent beforehand in giving each phrase careful Indian construction. Really picturesque, suitable phrasing in English can actually give a talk an Indian-sounding eloquence and add distinction without affecting the clarity of meaning. Below are a few phrases chosen at random, which help to illustrate this point.

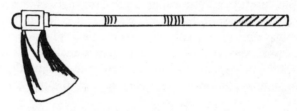

UNRELATED PHRASES. Listen well to my talk. It is good medicine to gather here in our council ring—a circle is power. Together we are strong, like many arrows held together, but one by one we are weak. Friends shall we be; in sun and storm will I point my arrow with yours. Together shall we hunt and be friends, as long as grass grows and water runs. I have only good thoughts about you in my heart. What is in your hearts? Your words are good, so my ears tell my heart to listen. Good words! You say well! So! That is well! And now that I have said what is in my heart . . . my heart sings. The sun shines strong in our hearts. Our hearts are heavy; dark thoughts are in them. It is better that wisdom come little by little. Thus I learn things. He speaks with a straight tongue. His words are false; they will lead us on false trails. He speaks with a forked tongue. He has the heart of a rabbit. Our enemies are many; as the leaves on the trees are they—yes, they are like the grass.

The sun left, to make place for the moon. The sun has gone, to let the stars come. Night was leaving to let

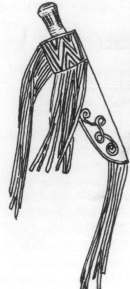

WOODLAND

morning come. When the moon is round. Till the moons have gone. So long ago that the time cannot be counted by suns or moons. He was gone three sleeps. A journey of nine suns and nine sleeps. Further than a fast pony could run from moon to moon. Fast as a war arrow travels. Tall as a pine tree. Deep as a tree is high. Three times the height of a tall brave. Twice the height of a tall man away. Twice as long as a war canoe. The length of a canoe paddle. As deep as a spear is long. It was so cold the sun built a fire. The painted leaves danced with the North Wind. Soon the keen knives of winter will cut the air. The leaves whispered. The small sounds of the forest folk. The wings of the air. The furred things. The furred and feathered ones. The forest was covered with the dark blanket of night. Covered with a blanket of sky-colors. A whisper soft as a falling leaf. Silent as a moon-shadow. Gone, silent as smoke!

THE CHINOOK JARGON

It will prove good medicine to learn a little of this simple, useful, and amusing trade language of the vast Northwest Coast Indian territory. It will come in handy at times during council fire ceremonies. The following true story, though little known, gives some idea of how the Chinook jargon was evolved and built around the Indians' interpretation of the things said by the white men.

KLA-HOW-YA! Not many who use the wide-spread Chinook greeting, *Kla-how-ya!* know how it originated.

In the early days of the white man's contact with the Indians, a Hudson's Bay Company man named Clarke lived just outside the company's fort stockade. Each morning when the gates were opened before the day's trading began, the officer in charge of the guard greeted Clarke: "Hi, Clarke, how are you?" or he shouted, "Clarke, how are you?"

In a very short time, the Indians, who sat around waiting for the gate to open started using their own versions of the greeting: *Kla-how-ya!* and *Hi-ya!* (A little further on you will learn why no R's found their way into their modified greeting.)

Today, not only is *Kla-how-ya!* heard throughout the American and Canadian Northwest, but the salutation is also frequently used by the Blackfeet and other tribes of the Plains as well.

Next time someone informs you that the Hawaiian greeting of *A-lo-ha* is the only one which is used both as a greeting and farewell, you will know that they don't know Chinook. *Kla-how-ya!* is used both as "Hello!" and "Good-by."

INTRODUCTION TO CHINOOK. This jargon has eighteen letters and grew from less than thirty words to approximately 350 generally accepted words. These words adequately perform the work of 4,000 English ones! Perhaps the first written mention of the Chinook Jargon is made in the records of the Lewis and Clark expedition. Possibly it was used to some extent by Sacagawea, "the Bird Woman," who performed the remarkable feat of "guiding" the expedition across country which she had never seen before and of which she had no knowledge!

The Chinook Jargon very soon became the accepted trade language of the entire Northwest Coast and adjoining territories. It was spoken and understood by six hundred Indian tribes and the white men who visited, invaded, and eventually took over the Indians' vast territory. Despite the primitive nature of the jargon, and the many sources drawn on to form it, Chinook proved flexible and intelligible. This strange, mixed-up trade language was to the many tribes of the Northwest Coast what the sign language was to the tribes of the Plains and Woodland Indians. The simplicity and coverage of the jargon took it far from the Indian territory of the Northwest Coast, so that it was heard, and still is, even among the Plains tribes of the United States and Canada. The jargon is so condensed that it crowds an association of ideas into a few curt words and phrases. There are imitative words, such as *tin-tin* for a bell or bell sounds and *tik-tik-tyee* for the telegraph, the word *tyee* meaning chief, or a god. Many words were taken from the English language, such as house, moon (meaning the moon and one month), s'pose for suppose, stone, salmon, sun, and wind. Other words in the jargon are of French origin: *la hache* (the hatchet), *pipe,* and *courir* (to run). The fact that you will not actually find *courir* as such in the jargon brings up a strange fact regarding native speech on the Northwest Coast. These Indians could not pronounce the letters F, R, and L; so we find that the Chinook word for run is *cooley,* not *courir.* Again, we find *piah* used for the word fire, that being the closest pronunciation the natives could achieve. This is not so very strange when we remember that their Oriental ancestors could not pronounce some of these letters either, nor can many Orientals even today. German words also crept into the trade language, such as *tanze* for dance.

The Chinook language does not accent the syllables, but it is full of faltering breath sounds, voice inflections, and explosive sounds. As spoken by the natives, the jargon contains many multiple-shaded meanings for various words, as the speaker's voice can graphically express pleasure or sorrow, belief or disbelief, agreement or disagreement, sympathy, anger, and other emotions by simple inflection of the words uttered.

PART 2

GALA GAMES
JAMBOREE

chapter 6

fast and furious campfire games

ONCE THROUGH THE PORTAL into the world of games, one is caught up in a whirl of fun, laughter, and excitement. Contesting in the spirit of fellowship which prevails in the campfire circle, friends compete in fast-moving, lusty games. There is the sincere urge to cheer a winning rival, since the fun and friendship which hold sway transcend personal desires to win. The intimate atmosphere of the campfire circle or council ring promotes friendly rivalry and lasting fire-fellowship. Whether the games are taken from far-distant lands or from the contests and challenges enjoyed by our American Indian brothers, they all provide a sense of well-being—especially when played in the charmed circle where the air is invigorating, where the fragrance of woodsmoke and the out-of-doors heighten the natural desire to contest in the games which follow.

POINTERS ON CAMPFIRE GAMES

Because the author has so often been asked, "What are some really good campfire games?" he sets down his invariable answer: Any game, preferably active, which is more or less competitive, amusing for onlookers to watch, requires at least half a dozen players or more, does not require a lot of explanation or equipment, presents no danger to the players, and can be played safely within the limits of a campfire circle.

Singing games and quiz games of general interest, in which all of those around the campfire can participate, are also worthwhile and popular additions to specialty games programs. No games should be played in the campfire circle which are likely to cause injury to a player. Many games belong in this category—WRESTLING ON HORSEBACK, for instance. In one camp, a hefty but not too mature counselor was not discouraged by the campfire director when he offered to demonstrate the game known as BULL IN THE RING. When the campers all joined hands around the campfire circle in order to make a fence to prevent the "bull" from breaking out, the hefty

counselor who played the imprisoned animal did manage to break out of the ring without personal injury. It is a pity that four campers who were taken to the camp hospital suffering from sprained arms and bruises were not so fortunate. True, there are accident-prone campers who can knock themselves out while playing a simple game of tag. Some of the games and challenges in this book are of a rough-and-tumble nature too, but the calculated risk of possible injury shows an almost negligible chance of a player being injured when the activity in carried out under competent supervision.

A smooth-surfaced campfire circle, free from all stones, pebbles, roots, and branches or other hard objects which can cause possible injury to the players, is absolutely essential for active campfire games.

ILLUMINATION FOR GAMES

Sufficient illumination is another *must,* not only in the interest of safety but also to assure good visibility for the onlookers. For special events, particularly solo ones, it is better to use a spotlight, or improvise one, rather than have the effect of an act lost in the dim light of a poorly tended campfire. A really bright fire—but not a bonfire—throughout the entire game part of the program at least is also necessary in the interest of safety and visibility for all active campfire games. Plenty of suitable and instantly available dry branches or split, dry logs, cut to the right length and thickness so that they can be dropped into a log cabin type of fire whenever necessary, or preferably just before, will assure the bright lighting necessary for a successful games program.

ORIGINAL CAMPFIRE GAMES

No attempt is made in this book to retell or rehash any of the games with which many leaders are already familiar. All the games given here have been devised or

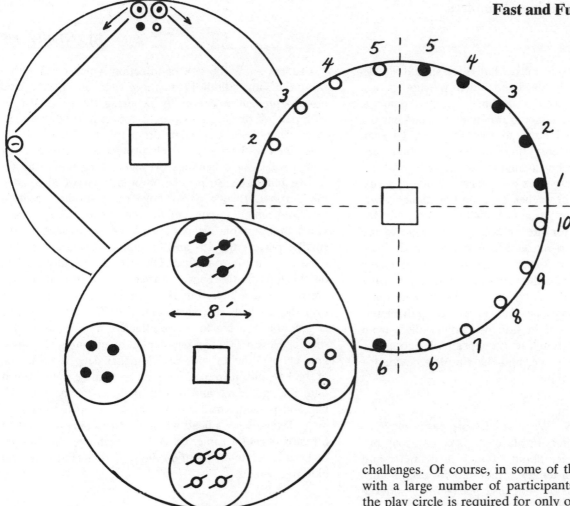

evolved to provide something brand-new, exciting, and acceptable to campers of all ages. Twenty-eight of the thirty-eight campfire games, and twenty of the forty-six challenges for the council ring, have never before appeared in print. All these games and challenges have been successfully played and contested at many campfires. The original novelty games such as SWITCHBACK, BARREL BALANCE BOUT, MERRY-GO-ROUND, BOP!-OUT!, HAYFOOT, STRAWFOOT, BRIDGES AHEAD!, HIGH STEPPERS, PUPPY IN THE DARK, BULL FLIGHT!, CIRCLING THE CIRCLE, and DIAMOND OBSTACLE RACE were devised especially for this book and have been extensively tested by campfire groups of all ages. The games here have been developed with the thought of providing fun for the spectators as well as for participants.

QUADRUPLING CAMPFIRE FUN

Too many campfire directors forget that there are *four* sides to a campfire. Making good use of this feature can double, triple, or quadruple the campfire fun, not only for the onlookers but also for the many additional players who can thus take part in the activities. *At least two sides of the fire* should be utilized when staging games and

challenges. Of course, in some of the more active games with a large number of participants, the entire space of the play circle is required for only one set of players. But the great majority of games and challenges can be carried out successfully with four teams or contestants using all four sides of the campfire. With a leader directing the activity on each side of the fire, the campfire circle can be turned into a four-ring circus for the benefit of all concerned.

BOUNDARIES

Definite boundaries should be plainly marked for all games which require them. A start and finish line are most often needed; but in some cases side lines are also necessary in order to keep players within bounds, or markers have to be used to prevent players from taking unfair short cuts. The layout of campfire and council fire areas makes it tempting for players to take short cuts without intention to cheat. Markers are important, since they usually affect the rules of a game or challenge and let the players know when they are playing the game fairly. Without conspicuous, correctly placed markers games become haphazard and are often open to argument, unfair practices, and wrong decisions. Players who purposely ignore clearly marked boundaries should be ruled out of a game after they have broken boundary rules twice.

MARKERS

Markers are so easy to make that there should always be an adequate supply on hand when playing games. Starting lines, finish and side lines, circles, oblongs, squares, and other markings are difficult to mark on the ground with a pointed stick so that they can be seen easily by firelight. White liquid marking solutions are effective but not always available, so good substitutes must be used. The best ones are perhaps made of strips of tough cardboard 12 inches long and 3 inches wide, painted white or yellow to assure visibility, not only for the players but also for the onlookers who wish to see what is going on. Strip markers can also be made from short lengths of 2- or 3-inch gauze bandage or heavy white cotton. Other excellent markers are stout white paper plates and saucers, which can be bought quite cheaply in sizes ranging from 4 to 12 inches in diameter. Markers can also be cut in 6-inch-diameter discs from heavy white cotton or tough white paper. All such markers should be held in place, and the simplest device for this is a camp-made staple.

MARKER STAPLES. Wire staples are easily made to hold all types of markers in place. A piece of strong but fairly pliable heavy wire about ¼ inch in diameter and from 8 to 12 inches in length is required for each home-made staple. It should be bent in 2 places at the middle to make a flat top about 2 or 3 inches long. Such a flat bend will give each staple 2 legs from 3 to 5 inches long. The best length for the staples' legs is decided by the hardness of the ground in the campfire and council fire areas. These staples are pushed down through the paper plates, strips, or discs into the ground. Two holes the correct distance apart, based on the length of the staple top, may be made in the plates and other markers before use, to help get them moored in place more rapidly. *The staple must always be pushed down flush with the top of the marker.*

BLINDFOLDS

Leaders know the risk of infection which comes from using the same blindfold on more than one player, and how to prevent infection by covering the players' eyes with pads of sterilized absorbent cotton or other pads, or even clean tissue paper, before applying the blindfold. Once the eyes have been safely protected, a strip of 2- or 3-inch-wide gauze bandage 30 inches long makes an effective blindfold. Strips of cotton or scarves also serve the purpose. Brown paper bags offer another form of blindfold which is convenient and speedy to use, provided that suitable clean paper bags are available. For smaller players the 16- and 18-pound sizes are best, but these are often hard to find. The sizes are usually marked on the tops of the bags. Fourteen- and 20-pound bags are usually available, but the 14-pound bag will only fit over the heads of very small children. The 20-pound size is generally too big to prove effective as a blindfold for smaller players, but can be adapted by cutting a U-shaped hole about 3 inches wide and 5 inches deep in each side of the bag, not in front. The bag can then be pulled down onto the shoulders, and a fold made in the back of the bag and pinned with a safety pin will keep it from slipping off the player's head when he is creeping or bending forward during a game. Of course, each bag should only be used once, unless worn by the same players for several blindfold games.

PREPARING TOY BALLOONS FOR GAMES PROGRAMS

Inflating and tying balloons for use in games can present some technical difficulties not always appreciated by novice leaders. A balloon which is blown up to almost maximum size will usually burst when exposed to hot sunlight for a while. It will also burst very easily when crushed a little too hard or struck too forcibly. New balloons, the larger ones, should be inflated fairly fully

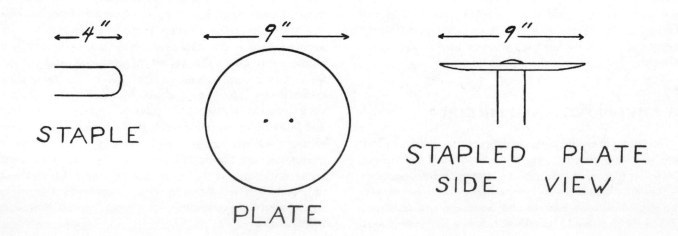

←4″→

STAPLE

←——9″——→

PLATE

←——9″——→

STAPLED PLATE
SIDE VIEW

the day before they are going to be used, left inflated overnight, and the necks untied the next morning so that the air escapes. Balloons treated this way will inflate much more easily and be considerably larger when blown up again just before the games are played. Fastening the necks of balloons so that they hold the air throughout the entire play periods presents no problem when any one of the three following methods is used. (1) Fairly heavy wool may be used to tie the necks of balloons after they have been blown up. If a clove hitch knot is used and the wool ends pulled tightly before making a square knot to hold the hitch in place, this method is sure-fire. (2) Another good way to get a balloon ready in a hurry with the certainty that it will not deflate is to wind a very small rubber band around the neck a number of times until all of the slack is used up. (3) The best method of all, for small balloons which will be used time and again for many games, is to inflate them fairly fully and then tie a single knot in the neck. The very end of the neck is held in the fingers of one hand after the knot is made and the balloon pulled gently but firmly away from the end of the neck, using the other hand, by pulling on the knot. The end of the neck is then snipped off, and the balloon is ready for action.

Care should be taken, when ordering balloons in quantity, to specify "round" ones—since the long and pear-shaped balloons are little used in games. The No. 4 and No. 5 round balloons are quite small and good for many games where the balloons are propelled with wands or blown along the ground. A partially inflated balloon is much stronger than a fully inflated one and will take far more punishment during games in which the balloons are roughly used. The safety margin must be small, though, as players get less fun from playing with balloons which are not firm enough to bounce or respond quickly to a sharp tap with the hand.

On days when there is a very slight breeze blowing it is sometimes possible to use big balloons after dropping two or three dried round peas into them before blowing them up. Weighted balloons also provide more fun when used for certain games.

MERRY-GO-ROUND

This is a tricky form of relay race played around the campfire circle by two teams with four players on each team. The equipment for each team consists of: a volleyball, basketball, or soccer ball, white or whitened for the occasion so that it will show up better by campfire light; two white paper plates 9 inches in diameter, and a smaller paper plate or saucer 6 inches in diameter, as markers. Two of the four large paper plates, the 9-inch-in-diameter ones, are stapled side by side on the ground toward the outer edge on one side of the campfire circle. The two other large plates are stapled in the same man-

ner directly opposite the first two on the other side of the campfire circle. The two 6-inch plates are stapled to the ground as markers at each end of the center of the outer edge of the campfire circle at opposite ends from the two pairs of large plates. The diagram shows the simple arrangement of players and plate markers.

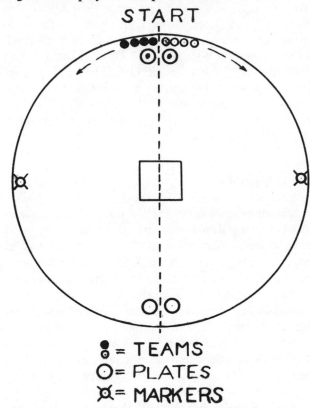

A volleyball is placed on each of the two plates at the starting side of the circle. A relay team of two to four players lines up beside each starting plate. The players on each team face and run in opposite directions around the circle.

When the leader calls "Go!" the first player on each team snatches up the ball, races around the half-circle, touching the marker with the ball on passing, and continues around to the plate on the opposite side of the circle from which he started. There he puts the ball into the plate on his team's side of the circle, shouting "Ready!" when the ball is actually in the plate.

The word "Ready!" is the signal for the second player on the team to race around the half-circle, touching the plate marker with *both* hands, on the way to pick up the ball. He then races back to the starting plate, touching the marker with the ball on the way. Each of the remaining players on the team runs the half-circle, the odd numbers following the motions made by the first player on the team and the even numbers making the motions of the second player—the odd number players calling out "Ready!" only when the ball is actually in the plate on the opposite side of the campfire circle. It will be noted that the first and third players on each team only race halfway around the circle, while the second and fourth players race two half-circles. The last player on a team who is the first to race the ball back to the starting plate decides the winning team.

What makes this a tricky and exciting game is the fact that the marker must be touched by each player with the ball, or with hands and ball, according to his place on the team. Sometimes players forget to touch the marker in the correct way, and those who do so must return to the starting point and try again. When a runner awaiting the "Ready!" call takes off before the call is given by the player ahead of him, he must return to the starting point and start again. Such unforseen happenings make the final result of this race uncertain right up to the last lap of the relay.

GLADIATORS

In this attempt to bring the lighter side of the Colosseum of ancient Rome into the campfire circle, everybody gets hurt—and likes it! The chief sufferers are rightly the gladiators, although onlookers frequently claim that they get hurt more than the players—or at least their sides do—from laughing.

Two would-be gladiators are selected from unwary volunteers, because of their matching size and weight. Once in the arena, one is given 15 feet of soft ½-inch or heavier rope and the other contestant a large double blanket, preferably one that has already had quite a lot of wear and tear. The two gladiators face each other and await the signal to begin. First of all, the leader of campfire games tells them of the rules, or rather the lack of rules, for the coming titanic struggle. Worse still, the leader breaks the news that there are practically *no* rules, at least none which he, the referee, knows about. This apparently makes things extremely simple for the gladiators. All they have to do is try to render each other helpless through the use of the primitive "weapons" which have been thrust into their unwilling hands. One or two husky counselors should stand between the combatants and the campfire in case the struggle should surge in that direction.

When one of the gladiators has been so muffled up in the blanket or tied up with the rope that he cannot even give the "thumbs up" signal on his own behalf, he is the loser.

Rarely will the gladiators offer to exchange weapons and renew the struggle!

HAYFOOT–STRAWFOOT

This amusing coed participation race is based on the footwork of the recruit who had difficulty in putting the right foot forward. The only equipment required includes four paper-plate markers 9 inches in diameter stapled around the campfire circle, 5 feet from the outside edge of the circle, with an equal distance between each marker. The recruits in this race stand in line, about 3 feet apart, with their toes touching a mark on the ground at the starting point. A girl "helper," wearing slacks or jeans, kneels or crouches behind each boy and grips an ankle firmly in each hand. On the word "Go!" the boy, with the assistance of his helper, puts one foot at a time forward, his assistant shouting "Hayfoot!" when he has to move his left foot forward and "Strawfoot!" when he advances the right foot. The boy may take small or big steps, as decided in a conference with his helper just before the take-off, but the team should take care to work together so that the helper does not lose her grip on an ankle. When she does, the team must go back two steps and then carry on from there. The helper may travel on her knees or in a crouching position, pushing each leg forward in unison with her shout and the boy should not move a foot forward until the shove and shout are given by his assistant. Too hard a shove may bring the runner down, but good teamwork will help both members of the team to keep their balance and move forward at a good pace. The first team to complete the circle correctly and return to the starting line is the winner.

As in a number of the races given in this chapter, this race can be made more amusing and exciting by having six teams start in two groups of three teams in each group. The groups stand back to back at the starting line and travel in opposite directions around the campfire circle, though each team tries to beat all the other teams. What happens when the teams meet and try to be the first to pass between the markers and the outside of the campfire circle has to be seen to be appreciated.

Racing teams in opposite directions around the circle usually adds to the fun, difficulty, and excitement of many events and gives each onlooker in the audience a grandstand seat.

DELUGE!

This is an amusing and exciting stunt-game, to be played only on hot nights and with older campers who can catch fairly well. They should wear old shorts and shirts for the event—just in case! The only gear needed is three round balloons about 5 or 6 inches in diameter when inflated; but the catch lies in the fact that they are not blown up—they are filled with tepid water instead. The balloons should be blown up once or twice before being filled with water. They should be yellow, orange, or white, a different color for each of two teams, since these colors show up best in the firelight.

Two teams, with three players on each, face each other in two straight lines 6 feet apart. There should be 2 feet between the players on each team. The leader gives each player on either team a water-filled balloon. When the game leader says "Catch!" the players holding the balloons throw them, *underhand* style only, to the members of the other team who stand directly opposite them. After the first toss, each player throws and catches independently of the other players on the team. After about a minute or so of play, the leader stops the game and has one of the lines of three players step back 4 feet, so that the teams are 10 feet apart. The game continues at that range for a short time, and then the leader moves a line of players back 8 feet. At that range, 18 feet, there is almost certain to be a casualty or two among the balloons. The balloons are replaced, and the players who caused the casualties are out of the game. The leader extends the range to what he considers a maximum distance, say about 25 feet, but such increase in distance should not get the throwers or catchers too close ·to the spectators! At this range the winning team will soon be decided.

The rules for this stunt-game are simple. Any player who bursts a balloon is out of the game. Any player who dodges or avoids catching a balloon purposely is out of the game and given a forfeit. A suitable one is to have him throw a water-filled balloon higher and higher into the air, catching it each time it comes down. The forfeit should be considered paid in full if and when the balloon ascends to a height of 30 feet.

This game can also be played with much smaller balloons, and appropriately called RAINDROP!

PUPPY IN THE DARK

This coed game provides fun for the older campers who play it and amusement for the spectators. An 8-foot line is marked on the ground on one side of the campfire circle, extending inward from the outer edge of the circle toward the campfire. A length of white tape or a gauze bandage stapled to the ground will indicate the line which is the starting point. Three white paper-plate markers are stapled to the ground around the campfire at equal distances apart, each marker being placed 4 feet from the outer edge of the circle. Half a dozen strips of opaque cloth, or the same number of brown paper bags, to serve as blindfolds, are required to complete the simple equipment.

To begin the game, four boys kneel directly behind the starting line, all facing in the same direction. Four girls are chosen as trainers, and each is put in charge of one of the kneeling "puppies." The trainers are told that they must make a strange-sounding noise or invent a special whistle signal which their puppy will recognize easily as it races, on hands and knees, around the campfire circle. Each puppy must try to follow its trainer around the circle, and the trainer must not touch her puppy either to stop or guide him; nor must she talk to him. The trainer moves directly in front of her puppy,

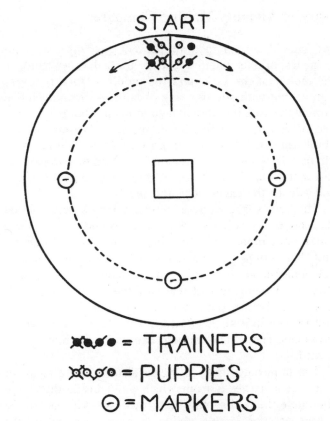

x'x'o o = TRAINERS
x'x'o o = PUPPIES
⊖ = MARKERS

making her special signal noise so that her puppy will follow her around the circle, passing between the plate markers and the outside edge of the campfire circle. The first puppy who returns with its trainer to the starting line is the winner, provided he has circled the course correctly.

When, on special occasions, a campfire director wishes to add additional chaos to fun and excitement, he should try staging PUPPY IN THE DARK in this way: Race six or eight puppies, with the same number of trainers, from the starting line as before, but with one half of them traveling around the campfire circle in one direction and the other half moving in the opposite one! What happens when the puppies meet and try to pass, perhaps at the markers? That is a problem for the trainers to solve, but they have the assurance that it can be and has been done.

BULL FLIGHT!

This stunt-game is even more exciting for the campfire circle onlookers than the brawny contestants! The only equipment required is a big clean potato sack, or a sack equally large, stuffed full of dried grass, straw, or large newspaper sheets rolled into fairly tight balls. A piece of stout soft rope, about ¾ or 1 inch in diameter and 2½ feet long, is also needed. The sack should not be filled with rags, cloth, or excelsior, since these fillings may make it too heavy to provide good fun. A big knot, made by tying two or three knots on top of each other, and pulling them all tight, is tied in one end of the rope. The other end should be whipped to prevent raveling. Three or 4 inches of this knotted end is pushed down through the mouth of the sack, and the mouth is then tied very tightly shut with strong string or cord. A clove hitch tied around the sack mouth will help to assure that the knotted end of the rope remains inside the sack. We now have a "bull" and his "tail," or at least a safe substitute. Now all that is required are six older or senior campers, to throw the bull. The choice of three boys and three girls will add to the excitement and fun.

The bull is thrown by a camper taking a firm hold on the end of its tail, swinging clear around two or three times—not more—with the bull flying above his head, and then letting go. When the tail is suddenly released, one understands why this game is called BULL FLIGHT! The art of swinging and releasing the bull is done in almost exactly the same way as the hammer is swung and thrown in athletic contests. The clever use of wrists, shoulders, and follow-through can make the bull fly like a bird.

The important thing to be decided by the director of campfire activities is from which point inside the campfire circle the bull should be thrown. He will have to be a seer of considerable ability to even guess where the bull will land, no matter from where it is thrown! This is what makes the stunt so exciting for the onlookers. The author has found that the best throwing point is from fairly close to the campfire, but not close enough to knock the logs off. This point of departure assures that the bull will not land on the fire. Once the throwing point is settled and marked by a white cardboard disc or white paper-plate marker stapled to the ground, a leader volunteers to stand somewhere on the outside edge of the campfire circle in order to retrieve the bull after it lands. The ability to duck in a split second will prove of considerable advantage to him, as he also marks the direction in which the bull must be thrown.

One by one, the six campers who are to do the throwing take turns at trying to heave the bull as far as possible. Four complete swings around is the maximum number allowed, but a camper may throw on the second swing if he wishes. The winner is the one who throws the bull the greatest distance, provided it travels in the right direction; the distances are measured by the campfire director or a counselor. According to the skill of the contestants, the bull will either sail swiftly over the heads of the onlookers, traveling in the correct direction, or will land with a soft but scary thud in the laps of the spectators, after traveling in the wrong direction. All this adds up to fun, which should make BULL FLIGHT! a popular campfire stunt-game.

Note for leaders. The fun-secret in BULL FLIGHT! lies in the fact that it is surprisingly difficult for the average person who is swinging the bull to release it at the mo-

ment desired. The swingers only realize this when they try, in vain, to release their grip on the tail. The author has seen a girl counselor swing the bull six times, at which point the bull took over and swung her! After a few more swings, the counselor was overcome with laughter and fell on top of the bull.

With this release difficulty in mind, the games leader can ask that the bull be released on the fourth, or even fifth or sixth swing.

TAG ALONG!

The simple equipment required for this amusing race is four white paper-plate markers and a 4-foot length of white tape or strip of cotton, to be used as a starting line. The four plate markers are stapled to the ground 4 feet from the outer edge of the campfire circle, one on each of the four sides of the campfire. The starting strip is stapled to the ground halfway between any two markers, running from the outer edge of the circle toward the fire.

Two teams, with a boy and girl of about the same size in each, stand side by side just behind the starting line, with the boys on the right of their partners. Each pair joins hands, the right hand of the girl being held by the left hand of the boy. Four teams can race simultaneously by having two teams start from opposite ends of the campfire and run in the *same* direction.

When the leader calls "Go!" each boy leaps in front of his partner and runs ahead of her, pulling her along behind him. In a moment or two the leader calls "Change!" whereupon the girl jumps ahead, pulling the boy behind her. The partners never run side by side except at the moment when they pass each other as they change positions. Partners who run alongside each other can be disqualified. A partner team may also be ruled out of the game for releasing hands during the race. Each couple must pass between the four markers and the outside edge of the campfire circle. A couple which passes on the inside of a marker while circling the circle is sent back one marker as a forfeit.

To make the game more amusing and difficult, the leader can call "Change!" four or five times during one circuit of the campfire. The race can be run once or twice around the circle, as announced by the leader before the start.

To complicate things a little and add to the fun, two teams may start the race facing in the opposite direction from the other team—or teams, if there are four teams in the race. The complications arise when the teams try to be the first to pass between the markers and the outside edge of the circle as they race around to the starting point, where the race may finish or continue for another round, as decided by the leader prior to starting.

HIGH STEPPERS

This is an amusing game to play and watch, and one which is not so easy to play as it may seem. It gives older campers a chance to display their combination of high stepping, rhythm, and co-ordination. The only gear required is five paper-plate markers. One is stapled on each of three sides of the campfire circle 6 feet from its outer edge, as shown in the drawing. The two remaining markers are stapled 2 feet apart at one end of the campfire circle, to mark the starting point of the race.

Teams consist of two players, each about the same height. The best and most amusing arrangement is to have a boy and girl on each team. The game is made still more amusing and a little more involved by having four teams contest at the same time, each set of two teams standing back to back at the starting-plate markers, the width of the markers separating the two pairs of teams. The partners on each team stand side by side with elbows linked.

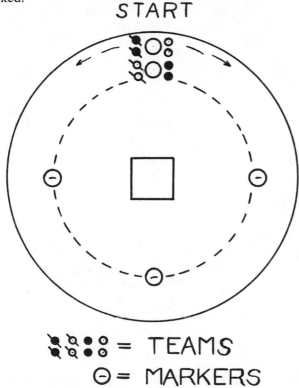

On the word "Step!" the partners step off quickly and together. The partner on the right of the team steps off raising the *right* foot, with the leg stiff, to a position in which the right foot is slightly above the level of the left knee. He repeats this step with the *left* foot and continues to march, right, left, right, left, as fast and evenly as possible, keeping time with his partner as closely as possible, until the circle has been circled and the team arrives back at the starting plates. The partner on the left of the team performs exactly the same step, but starting with the *left* foot. The first difficulty lies in the fact that

it is rather tricky for the two partners to keep in exact step, using the correct leg each step, as each partner is using the opposite leg. The steps should be long, high, and in unison. Using the wrong leg or exhibiting too noticeable a difficulty in keeping in step and in line, can lose points for or disqualify a team, as decided by the leader in charge of the game. Should a team practice together between contests, it is surprising how the speed, style, and rhythm can be improved. Of course, all teams must keep *inside* the markers, passing between the markers and the outside of the campfire circle. This brings about the hardest and most amusing part of the race— the meeting at the markers. Two teams, moving in either direction, have room to pass gracefully at the same time between the markers and the outside edge of the campfire circle. But it is evident that the arrival of three teams simultaneously at any marker can cause confusion. To overcome it, markers must be passed in the sequence of arrival, so that only two teams, sharing the space as fairly as possible, pass through at the same time. The third team must mark time, using the high-stepping action, clear of the passage until there is space for it to march through and continue the race.

The first team to finish, provided it has marched in good style throughout, is the number one winner, but the outcome of the race can also be judged so that the first *two* teams which started in line and marched in the same direction are the dual winners. This, of course, applies whether they both arrive at the same time or not, provided they both finish before both of the opposing teams do.

TANDEM PEDAL RACE

This game requires neither bicycle nor equipment, with the exception of a few plate markers, but it does provide exercise for the contestants and amusement for the spectators. A line is marked on the ground at one end of the campfire circle, and three paper-plate markers are stapled one on each of three sides of the campfire circle 6 feet from its outer edge, as shown in the drawing for the preceding game. There are two players to a team, and they stand one behind the other, with approximately 2 feet between them and a 3-foot lane between each tandem team. The best race arrangement is to have four tandem teams, two on each side of the starting line, each two tandem teams facing in opposite directions around the campfire circle. Boy-and-girl teams assure the most fun, the boy pedaling ahead of the girl.

On the word "Go!" each team starts off and pedals as fast as possible around the campfire circle, each player holding his arms and hands as though grasping the handlebar of a bicycle, while the knees are raised alternately to about waist level as the tandem advances.

This imaginary form of cycling is not easy to accomplish, one difficulty lying in the fact that it is tricky to advance quickly, while even greater trouble is caused the players on each team by the fact that one must remain directly behind the other and hold the same distance, approximately 2 feet, between them while pedaling around the circle, keeping always between the markers and the outside of the circle.

A relay version of this race can be carried out with four or six riders in each team, each tandem team starting out in sequence after the team ahead of it has finished the run at the starting point.

The leader of the game, who acts as referee, will have his hands full trying to keep the two players on each tandem team the proper distance apart and seeing that each team advances while pedaling, *not running,* around the campfire circle.

For younger campers this race can be contested by lone riders, riding single imaginary bicycles. The individual racers cannot then say that their partners slowed them down.

An extra fun feature can be introduced into TANDEM PEDAL RACE by having one girl and one boy compete on single bicycles against two tandem teams, each composed of a boy and girl, racing around the campfire circle at the same time.

KANGAROO BOXING

This is an amusing form of SACK BOXING which the author improvised at a campfire in France when no sacks were available. The only equipment needed is a set of 16-ounce boxing gloves—or at least big, well-padded gloves—and a strip of strong cloth about 3 inches wide and 5 or 6 feet long for each "kangaroo." These strips are to bind the ankles securely together; the contestants' legs should be held closely together, the toes pointing straight ahead, while the strip is wound tightly around the ankles. The two ends are tied together with a reef (square) knot.

The ground on which this game is played should be flat and carefully cleared of all stones, and even little pebbles and sticks. The two contestants should be fairly equally matched, and they are placed opposite each other about 6 feet apart. Once the "Go!" signal is given, the usual rules of boxing—not too strictly applied—are observed.

Whether a kangaroo sits down inadvertently without help from his opponent or is knocked down, each fall counts against him. A player can greatly help his chance of winning by dodging, feinting, and ducking insofar as possible, as his opponent will nearly always overbalance in the face of such tactics. The winner is best decided on a two-out-of-three falls basis.

HALF-MOON BALL PASS

The only gear needed for this fast-moving game is two balls of about volleyball size. Balls should be white or yellow in color, to increase visibility by campfire light. Two teams of equal size, of from ten to twenty players on a team, stand in the half-circle formation shown in the drawing. One half of each team stands on each side of the campfire, close to the outside edge of the campfire circle. The diagram clearly shows how a team of ten players is numbered and what positions the team members hold on different sides of the fire. The end players on each team, Numbers 1 and 10 in the positions furthest from the fire, make sure that the players on their half of the team know their numbers and to whom they should pass the ball, before the game begins.

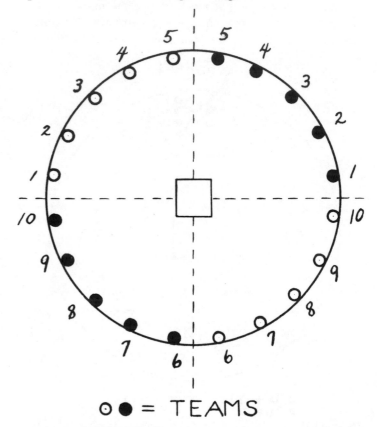

○● = TEAMS

The passing is done in this way. Number 1 on each team tosses to Number 10, who passes to Number 2. Number 2 passes to Number 9, and so on in this order until the ball reaches player Number 5. He must instantly toss the ball to Number 1 to complete the round. The team wins whose Number 1 player is first to hold the ball at the end of the round. Excitement and uncertainty are added to this game because of the chance of balls colliding as they cross the campfire circle. The game leader will do well to have a couple of fielders in the campfire circle to pass dropped balls back to the team to which they belong and also see that no dropped ball accidently rolls into the fire.

HEAVE HO!

This is an amusing game for the spectators, most of whom wish to become active participants whenever they get the chance. Two fairly evenly matched campers are blindfolded and tied together with a 12-foot length of rope fastened around each waist. A bowline will be found the best knot for the purpose, since it cannot slip and tighten the loop around the body. Each player is given a pillowcase stuffed with straw. The leader tells the combatants to stretch the rope taut by stepping backward. On the word "Go!" each player tries to hit the other with his pillow by hauling in the rope and letting fly when he thinks his opponent is within range. The contestants pay out rope in order to get out of range.

The leader acts as referee; at the end of each round, which may be based on time or activity, he lets the players rest for a moment or two before starting another round. The new round must always begin from the taut-rope position. The winner is the one who gets in the most hits in a bout of three rounds.

Some campers become quite expert and manage to manipulate the rope with the left hand while the right is always ready to flash into action when they think the time is ripe. The hardest thing is to estimate distance accurately, as it is difficult to figure out how much rope the opponent has managed to gather in.

SWITCHBACK

This is an amusing race for three teams with two campers on each team. The only gear needed is one volleyball or similar large ball for each team, and five white paper-plate markers 9 inches in diameter—one to mark the start and finish point of the race, and the other four to indicate the boundary lines.

Four of the paper plates are stapled to the ground around the campfire circle, 2 paces away from the fire, each plate marking ¼ of the distance around the circle. The starting-plate marker is placed on the ground halfway between any of the four markers, fairly close to the outside edge of the campfire circle. The teams line up alongside the marker, the players of each team standing back to back. The campfire director now gives each team of two a volleyball. He tells the teams that on the word "Go!" each pair on each team will place the ball between them, just below the shoulders, and hold it there by the pressure of their backs while running around the circle, one player running forward and the other backward. He indicates the direction in which the race will be run and points out that no team must run between the four markers and the fire.

On the "Go!" signal, the players run to the *second* plate from the starting one, where the switch part of the game comes into effect. The boy who was running backward now leads and runs forward. Should the ball fall to the ground during any part of the race, the team must always go back one marker before continuing the race. The winning team is the one which first arrives back at the starting marker after having circled the campfire correctly.

The futile attempts of the runners to make speed and still keep the ball in place prove amusing to the onlookers. SWITCHBACK can also be run as a relay race, with two or three pairs of players on each team, the first pair touching off the second pair after completing the circle, and so on until each pair has circled the circle.

BRIDGES AHEAD!

The campfire director or leader of campfire games asks twenty or thirty campers to form a big circle around the campfire, standing in a comfortable feet-astride position with about 1 long pace between players. Girls as well as boys can play, if they are wearing slacks or jeans. All campers in the circle face inward toward the fire. The leader staples a paper-plate marker to the ground between any two players, 3 feet inside the circle of players. This is the start and finish marker.

Two of the bigger boys open the game, or a girl and boy may contest. They kneel facing each other, one on either side of the starting marker. The leader explains the rules of the race. Each player must circle the circle on hands and knees in the following way. He starts with the player nearest to him and crawls head first through the bridge formed by that player's legs. He crawls completely around the next player in the circle and crawls *backward* between the legs of the third player. The contestant now returns to the head-first, under-bridge crawl and starts the progression sequence all over again. In this manner the two contestants, moving in opposite directions, circle the circle by using the three methods described. The games leader must be on the lookout to see that the correct method of progression is carried out by both contestants. There will, of course, be some difficulty should the players meet directly at a bridge, but perhaps if a girl and boy are competing he will be gallant enough to give her right of way—however, there is no rule that necessitates this! The first player to arrive back at the starting marker after circling the circle correctly is the winner.

This amusing race can also be contested in relay race fashion, with two or three racers on each team. The first player on each team to make the bridge circuit correctly, touches off the next player on his team, and the race continues until each member of the team has circled the circle. With older players, the leader can send a player who uses the wrong sequence at a bridge back one bridge as a forfeit, but as a rule·players may only be asked to get the sequence straightened out without being further penalized.

DIAMOND OBSTACLE RACE

This amusing race is contested in a diamond pattern. The *obstacles* in the race, very real ones, are the players themselves, as each tries to be the first to reach a marker and continue on to the next marker.

The only equipment required is five large paper-plate markers 9 inches in diameter and two white volleyballs or basketballs. When dark-colored balls are used, they should be temporarily whitened to increase their visibility for the benefit of the onlookers. The camp-made staples described at the beginning of this chapter should be used to hold the markers in place during the race. The drawing shows the position of both players and plates.

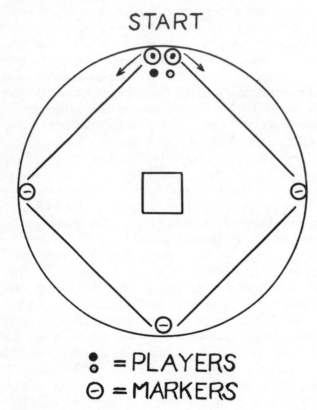

START

● = PLAYERS
⊖ = MARKERS

Two players stand back to back beside the two starting plates. A ball is laid on each of these plates. On the word "Go!" each player picks up the ball beside him. The runners race in opposite directions to the nearest of the first three plate markers. There each player stoops and bounces the ball, catches it, and continues to the second plate marker, where he again bounces and catches the ball. He does this again at the third, last marker and continues on to the starting plate, into which he puts the ball. The first player to place the ball back into the plate at the starting point is the winner.

The fun and excitement in this game center on the fact that the players are quite likely to meet at one of the markers on their way around the circle, which adds a handicap to the race.

This game can also be played as a relay race with two teams of two or four players on each team. Each player on a team begins the race only when the ball has been placed in the starting plate by the player ahead of him.

CIRCLING THE CIRCLE

From twenty to thirty of the bigger campers who are wearing slacks or jeans stand in a circle around the campfire, with 1 long pace between them. They should stand 1 long pace from the outer edge of the campfire circle. All these players face in the same direction around the circle and stand in a comfortable feet-astride position. A white paper-plate marker 6 inches in diameter is stapled to the ground between any two players, on the campfire side and 1 long pace away, as the start and finish point for the race. A girl and boy of about the same size are chosen by the campfire games leader. They stand facing each other alongside the marker. Each is given a volleyball or basketball, and the game is ready to start.

When the leader calls "Circle!" all the players in the circle raise their arms to form a circle above their heads, with the fingers interlaced. The leader then calls "Go!" and the girl and boy race around the circle in opposite directions, passing the ball through the hoops formed by the arms of the players in the circle. The runners start with the players closest to the markers and continue around the circle, putting the ball through each "hoop" as they go. Should a ball fall to the ground, it must be picked up and the player who dropped it must go back two hoops as a forfeit before continuing the race. Of course, it is a little difficult when boy and girl meet at the same hoop on the way around the circle—but that is all a part of the fun. When *both* arrive back at the marker from which they started, the other players in the circle drop their arms to their sides, and the two opponents who have circled the circle start around it again, this time driving the ball along the ground—with one hand only—under the bridges formed by the legs of the players, who still stand in the feet-astride position. The first contestant to arrive back at the starting marker after completing the first round of the circle starts at once to drive the ball under the bridges, without worrying about where the rival player is. When the ball fails to go under a bridge, it must be driven back to the bridge it missed and driven through it before the player goes on to the next bridge. The player who first circles the circle for the second time is the winner.

This amusing obstacle race can be carried out as a relay, with three girls competing against three boys. All the players line up at the starting marker, and each member of each relay team is touched off by the player ahead who completes the circle for the second time. In this form of the race, as in the first, the leader decides whether the runners run inside or outside the circle of players. The inside track is, of course, a little shorter. The leader may also decide to let the girls run on the inside track and the boys outside the circle. Even if both run on the same track, there is no collision to be feared when the players meet, as the speed of movement is not fast enough to cause the players to bump each other.

As this relay version is a longer-period race, it may prove difficult for some of the players in the circle to keep their arms above their heads throughout the race. The leader may avoid arm fatigue by telling the players that they may rest their arms if they feel tired, by placing their hands, with the fingers interlaced, on their heads until the players moving around the circle arrive about two players away. The leader reminds them that a player will come from both directions and that it is most unfair not to have a good round hoop ready for both of them when they arrive. Naturally, as this game is played from time to time, the leader will give the players who formed the circle the chance to be runners on some other occasion.

TWIN HAZARD RACE

This amusing event requires skillful timing on the part of the two players forming a team. Four paper-plate markers or cardboard disks about 8 inches in diameter are stapled to the ground, equally spaced around the campfire circle about 4 feet from the outer edge, as shown in the diagram. The players should wear jeans for this race. A starting line is marked on the ground, or two paper-plate markers are stapled 4 feet apart, at one end of the campfire circle. Two teams, facing in opposite directions, go down on hands and knees with their feet touching the line.

The player on the left in each team places his right arm over his partner's shoulders and holds his partner's right shoulder with his right hand. The player on the right puts his left arm across his partner's shoulders, holding the left shoulder with his left hand. The leader of the game now securely fastens together the partners' knees and ankles which are alongside each other. The ties are best made from strips of strong cloth 2 or 3 inches wide and about a yard long. One tie should encircle the ankles, and the other should be fastened just below the knees. The race can now start.

On the word "Go!" the teams set off to circle the campfire circle and return to the starting point. Were circling the circle the only stunt, in addition to moving in unison to assure speed, the race would be easy. Other hazards arise, however, such as crawling completely around each marker en route, and having the two teams meet head on and continue without bumping into each other. This is doubly upsetting when teams meet almost at a marker, since the team which arrives first must be given right of way and be allowed to circle the marker

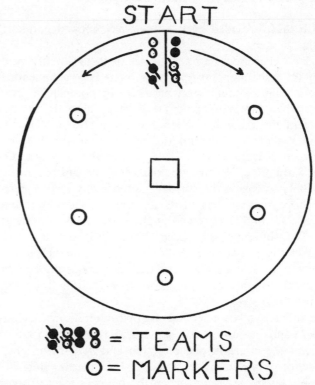

START

🏃🏃🏃🏃 = TEAMS
O = MARKERS

undisturbed. The first team to circle the circle and all markers correctly is the winner. Should more than two hands be used for support at any point in the race, the team doing so is disqualified and the rival team wins. If partners lose their grip on each other's shoulders at any time during the race, that team must stop and the correct hold be regained before the race continues.

Additional fun can be provided, when there is enough space, by having four teams compete at the same time, two teams racing together in each direction around the circle.

ZIGZAG FROG RACE

This amusing race requires no equipment. It is contested around the campfire circle in this way. The players line up behind a line at one end of the campfire circle. They stand 4 feet apart and face around the circle, two contestants at a time being all that there is room for in the average campfire circle. On the word "Hop!" the players race around the circle in this hop sequence: The first hop is forward but angled to the *right,* the second hop is forward but angled to the *left,* and the third hop is straight forward. This form of advancing is repeated in the correct sequence until both hoppers have circled the circle, establishing first and second place. A hopper who hops in the wrong direction or in the wrong sequence drops out of the game.

ZIGZAG FROG RACE can be contested as a relay race with three campers, standing one behind the other, on each team. Each player hops in turn, starting when the player ahead returns to the starting point. The team to finish first, provided each hopper has hopped correctly, is the winner.

For a real laugh, a PRECISION ZIGZAG FROG RACE with two or three hoppers on each team is recommended. The hoppers should wear sneakers or compete in bare feet, when the campfire circle is really smooth, for this form of the race. The teams form in a straight line, the team players one behind the other, with about 3 feet between players and a 4-foot lane between teams. On the word "Go!" team members hop in unison, trying not only to follow the correct sequence but also to gauge the hops so that they cross the finish line in the same precise formation observed at the start of the race. Both precision-hopping and speed should influence the decision of the leader of campfire games. In all such games it is wise to post a couple of older campers as fire guards, in order to prevent contestants from getting too close to the fire.

Laughter takes over the campfire circle when four older campers contest this game, with two of them racing around the circle in one direction and two in the other direction. They start back to back at the starting line, and the big laughs are heard when the hoppers meet at some point on their way around the circle. Four paper-plate markers stapled about 8 feet from the outer edge of the circle and equally spaced around the circle, marking the lane inside which hoppers must travel, add to the fun.

BOP!—OUT!

This is an amusing game based on the trial by ordeal used by witch doctors of some African tribes to find out whether a man was guilty of some mumbo-jumbo to which he would not confess. This game is similar to the "trial" method—except that volleyballs or any other big soft rubber balls are used instead of hunting spears. One advantage of this game is that it can be played on all four sides of the campfire circle at the same time, and the onlookers have almost as much excitement as the players, since balls frequently fly in their direction. The only gear required is two or four balls of the type mentioned and about twelve or fourteen paper-plate markers, if circles are not marked on the ground. In this case, the players stand inside 8-foot squares, marked by paper plates at each corner.

A circle 8 feet in diameter is marked on the ground,

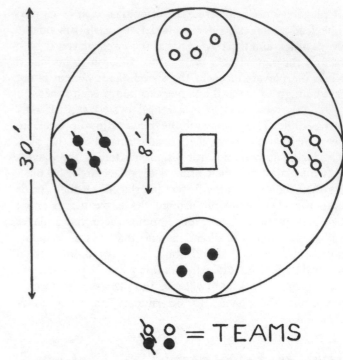

= TEAMS

or outlined by markers, on each of the four sides of the campfire circle, as shown in the drawing. Three or four players, one team, stand anywhere inside each of these four circles. A ball is given to the teams in any two adjacent circles, and these teams throw at their opponents directly across the circle.

On the shout of "Throw!" given by the counselor in charge of the game, the players throw the balls to and fro, aiming—below the waist only, when younger players participate—at any player in the *opposite* circle. Any player hit by a ball is out of the game and leaves the circle at once. A player struck by a ball which rebounds from the player first hit, is not out. The team with the most remaining players after the first few minutes of play is the winner.

Games leaders can, of course, reduce the number of players in each circle when older campers contest, and two or three good shots can challenge an equal number of crack shots to a bout. In such games, players hit by rebounds can be counted out, and strikes between waist and shoulders can also be considered in order.

Further fun can be introduced into BOP!—OUT! by providing *each* of the four teams with a ball. If heavier, somewhat harder balls such as soccer or basketballs are used, they should not be fully inflated.

chapter 7

breathing-spell campfire games

MOST OF THE GAMES in this chapter are quiet, compared with the rough-and-tumble ones that have preceded. They are especially adapted for campfire play, and many of them are competitive. They provide interest for the campfire circle spectators while they regain their breath after more strenuous activities. Leaders of games know how much a change of pace is appreciated and advisable.

If games are staged simultaneously on two or on all four sides of the campfire, a greater number of campers can participate in each game, and all the onlookers have ringside seats throughout the program.

DIZZY TRIO RACE

This amusing race requires no gear. Each team consists of three players, and a coed team of two girls and one boy forms a fun-provoking trio. The players on a team should be of about equal size, though a team of pint-size players may easily defeat a team of much larger players. Starting lines are marked on the ground at each end or side of the campfire circle and directly opposite each other. A team lines up behind each of the two lines, a boy in the center and a girl on each side of him. The

boy stiffly extends both arms sideways, and each girl grips one arm above and below the elbow, the boy and one girl facing one direction and the other girl on the team facing the opposite way. Both teams move around the campfire circle in the *same direction*. A fire guard posted on each side of the fire is a useful precaution.

On the word "Go!" the girls start turning the boy around by pushing on his outstretched arms and moving around him while advancing as quickly as possible around the campfire circle. The boy spins obligingly around as the girls push, advancing as fast as he can in that manner, and in the circumstances! The team which returns to its starting line first is the winner, provided it carries out the race as set down.

Another way to contest this game is for each team to twirl only as far as the halfway line and then return, turning the boy in the opposite direction, back to the starting line from which it began. The movement of the teams can be either clockwise or counterclockwise throughout the entire race, or the direction may be changed at the halfway lines, but both teams must carry out the leader's instructions regarding mode of progression.

The leader of the game should see that each team really advances by *turning* and that they do not work in a few straight forward steps between turns. The team which uses the best, smoothest twirling style throughout the race, though coming in second, may be judged the winner.

The boys can be given their chance to do the pushing, a girl taking the central position in each trio from time to time.

TRICK TUG OF WAR

This is an amusing contest which can be staged on all four sides of the campfire circle at the same time. The only gear required is a 15-foot length of stout rope, not less than ½ inch in diameter, and two paper-plate markers 6 inches in diameter, for each pair of contestants. The rope should be marked 3 feet from each end with indelible ink or pencil or by a piece of colored twine securely tied around it.

Each pair of contestants squats directly opposite one another and 9 feet apart on one side of the campfire. A counselor gives each player one end of the length of rope and staples a plate marker beside each tugger to assure that they remain the correct distance, 9 feet apart. Each player must remain beside his mark throughout the entire contest. With the distance established, each player will have 3 feet of "spare" rope. This length of apparently surplus rope plays a major part in the strategy of the game, since it is with this that each player tries to trick his rival and win the tug of war.

When the two tuggers squat in the ready-to-pull position, they hold the rope with one hand just in front of the 3-foot mark and the other hand somewhere behind it. On the word "Ready!" each player takes the strain lightly on his end of the rope so that it is held taut between them. On the command "Pull!" they tighten up on the rope, and each player tries to throw the other off balance so that he is forced to fall backward or place a hand on the ground for support. This is accomplished by a player tugging hard, then suddenly releasing unexpectedly a foot or two of the reserve rope. A little practice helps to develop this strategy. The player who is thrown off balance so that he either falls forward or backward or uses a hand for support is the one who loses the match. It is best to let three pulls decide the winner of the contest.

Invariably, the clever use of the spare rope decides the champion.

INTERNATIONAL QUIZ

This game can be made to embrace the entire world, its geography and peoples, its authors and artists, and many other global features, at the will of the campfire director or play leader.

The leader stands near the campfire. He holds a white volleyball, or one that has been whitened for the occasion. He tells the campers that he is going to ask for the names of rivers all over the world. This is better than saying in Scotland or France, for instance, as it widens the scope too much for players to be prepared in advance. He then throws the ball in a slow, easy-catch style to any camper on any side of the fire. As the ball leaves his hands, he says, "Canada" or "Switzerland" or any other country in which he wishes a river named. As soon as the player catches the ball, he throws it back to the leader, naming a river in the designated country as he does so. If he takes too long to think about it, the leader may count to ten. If the player has not thought of a name by that time, he is out of that round and the ball is not thrown to him again until a new round is started. The name of a river, or other places or objects used in the game, cannot be used twice in the same round. Players doing so are out of the game until another round starts.

The leader should give all sides of the campfire circle a chance, and caution players not to grab for a ball unless it is coming straight at them. This prevents players from leaning over or reaching up to grab a ball which is not intended for them. Naturally, more difficult questions are asked when the ball is tossed to the sections where the senior division of the camp is seated.

The game may include cities, capitals, mountains, seas, kings or other rulers, and may branch out into still other fields. The leader may say, "Who wrote *Treasure Island?*" or *"Ivanhoe?"* naming the book just at the moment of throwing the ball. He may also ask, "What is the name of the book written by Daniel Defoe?" For the youngest group at the campfire, the leader may draw on a Who's Who in Fairy Tales and Story Book Land, asking for characters and happenings from stories for younger children.

Played briskly for not more than five minutes at a time, this game will open up new fields of knowledge for many campers, but in such an unobtrusive way that frequent "repeats" of the game may be asked for in the course of the camping season.

SQUAT ROPE PULL

The leader of campfire games chooses two, four, or six boys and has them stand 6 feet apart facing each other, in pairs. Each is given the knotted end of a 6-foot length of rope, which is held in one hand. When the leader says "Ready!" the players squat on their heels, holding the rope taut between them—but not straining on it. On the word "Go!" each pulls on the rope, trying to unbalance the other. The pull may be steady or in the form of sharp tugs. The winner is the one who succeeds in upsetting his opponent most often, on a two-out-of-three-wins basis.

The length of the rope may be increased, up to 10 feet, but in each case there must be no slack allowed on the rope. This means that two contestants pulling on a 10-foot rope squat 10 feet apart.

FOUR-WAY TUG

The leader selects four boys of about the same size and weight. They stand back to back in the form of a small open square. An 8- or 10-foot length of about ¾-inch rope is joined by knotting the two ends together. With his back to the rope, each boy holds the rope loosely with one hand, either the right or left.

Gradually they pull on the rope until it forms a square with a boy, facing outward, holding each corner. When the rope is taut, a paper drinking cup or a small square of white cloth about 3 inches in diameter is placed 3 feet in front of each player. The leader says, "Take the strain—tug!" Each player then strains forward in an effort to pick up the paper cup or other marker. The first one to do so is the winner.

BARREL BALANCE BOUT

This is a rugged game for older campers, though there is no reason why younger campers, playing under supervision, should not enjoy its thrills and fun. This sport is a modified form of the lumberjacks' game of BIRLING, without logs and water.

The necessary equipment includes two light empty barrels about the size of apple barrels, in good condition. As apple barrels are scarce these days, very strong large cylinders of papier-maché or reinforced cardboard, such as some foodstuffs are packed in, can be used. Light barrels should be strengthened by either nailing the tops on or cutting and fitting improvised tops to replace lost ones. No nail points or rough places where splinters can be picked up should be left on the outside of the barrel. A hammer and some sandpaper, or sand, will soon remove such rough spots. A white line 1 inch wide should be painted along the middle of the barrel, running from

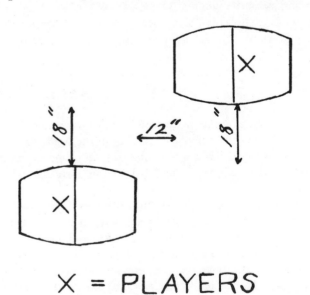

X = PLAYERS

end to end on both sides. In addition to the two barrels, two lightweight pillows, or pillowcases loosely stuffed with straw or grass, are needed. Two volunteers are secured for the first bout. They should wear sneakers.

The barrels are placed as shown in the diagram. A counselor takes charge of each gladiator and holds the barrel steadily in place while the contestant mounts and seats himself securely on top of the barrel. He may brace his feet anywhere on the barrel *except* below the white line on each side. When both boys are ready, they are each given a pillow. The campfire director shouts "Go!" This is the signal to attack and the boys swing their pillows in an effort to knock each other from the barrels. A player whose foot is placed on the ground for balance, even for a second, after the bout has begun, is either ruled out of the game or allowed to continue with the loss of two or three points. Each boy tries to knock the other off balance by striking him anywhere with the pillow. The slight rolling motion of the barrel does not help the players to keep their balance, and a too lusty swipe with a pillow is just as likely to unseat its wielder as his opponent. The barrels can, with a little skill on the part of the riders, be jockeyed into position if they roll too far apart for combat. Provided the ground is quite flat, as it should be in a campfire circle, the barrels should not roll too far apart; but if the sharp movements of the riders do roll them out of effective pillow range and they cannot be rolled by their riders into favorable positions again, the bout is stopped and the counselors move the barrels back into position before the combat recommences. The campfire director should keep a sharp lookout to see that no mishap, other than a gladiator being knocked from his barrel during the bout, occurs.

FORWARD BACKWARD

The only equipment needed for this game is a white or whitened volleyball and four white paper-plate markers 9 inches in diameter for each player or team. A white ball is best for campfire games, as it is more easily seen by the onlookers. The plate markers are stapled to the ground in a crescent formation 10 feet apart, with a distance of 6 feet forming a lane between each row of markers. In this way two crescent-shaped lines of markers can be set out on each of two sides of the campfire. It is well to mention here that large, light-colored balloons, about 10 inches in diameter when inflated, are fine substitutes for volleyballs, except on a breezy night.

The leader in charge of the game places a ball 2 feet in front of each starting marker, and a player stands with his back turned toward the line of markers, his legs spread apart and the ball just between his feet.

On the word "Go!" each player bends well forward and moves backward toward the first marker, driving the ball forward by striking it between his legs with the palms of *both* hands. Should a player strike the ball with only one hand, he must drive the ball back to the marker which he just passed and start from that point as a penalty. When the ball is squarely on the first marker, he continues on to the second one and so on until the final marker is reached and the ball patted onto it. The first player to place the ball on his last marker is the winner. For older campers the distance may be doubled by having the players turn and race back to the starting point, driving the ball in the same manner as before.

FORWARD BACKWARD makes a good team game with only two players on each team. One player begins the race from the starting point; when he has placed the ball on the fourth marker, his teammate, who has been waiting at that marker, takes over and drives the ball back again to the starting point. The first team to finish is the winner.

This game also makes a good relay race, with from two to four players stationed on each end marker position. When the ball is driven up to one end of the lane, the first player in line at that end drives it back to the other end, touching off the next player, and so on until every player on the team has driven the ball, always using *both* hands, from one end marker to the other end marker. The team to finish first is the winner.

JUMP-THROW BALL

This is an amusing campfire game which can be contested by both boys and girls. Two boys competing against two girls always makes an amusing race. Four players start from a back-to-back position at one end of the campfire circle, with two players facing in one direction and the other two in the opposite direction. The players should stand 2 feet apart, at the start, with a distance of 2 feet between the back-to-back players. Four white paper plates are stapled to the ground at equal distance apart, 6 feet from the outer edge of the campfire circle. Each player is given a ball about the size of a volleyball or a smaller soft rubber ball. The ball is placed on the ground directly in front of each player.

On the word "Go!" each player straddles the ball, picks it up between his feet, jumps straight up into the air, and throws the ball as far as possible by a kicking motion while off the ground. The player then hops on both feet to where the ball has landed, picks it up with his feet as before, and continues to throw it in this manner around the entire campfire circle, always keeping the ball between the outer edge of the circle and the plate markers. Should the ball roll outside the circle, the nearest camper should pick it up and place it a few feet inside the circle, in line with where it rolled before it left the circle. Each player continues to jump-throw the ball until he has made the circuit of the circle and ar-

rives back at the starting point. The first player to circle the circle correctly is the winner.

This game can be played on a team basis, each team consisting of the two players facing in the same direction. Each player is given a ball, and the game is played as in the individual version. The team whose two players finish first wins. In case of a tie the two teams contest again.

HANDICAP TWIRL

This game is played by grownups as well as young people in some parts of the Orient, and many of these players develop considerable skill in spinning as well as getting lots of fun out of the game. No equipment is required other than a few paper-plate markers or circular white cardboard disks about 6 inches in diameter. This game is best played within a 3-foot circle; but when there is no white liquid substance for marking play patterns, the twirling can take place within a 3-foot square. The square is marked at each corner with a plate marker stapled to the ground, and the players whirl around within the markers. Several squares can be marked out, closer to the edge of the campfire circle than the fire, and contestants take their places, each one inside a square. A fire guard posted on each side of the fire is a useful precaution for this and similar games. Each player in the square crosses his arms in front of him, the fingers of the left hand firmly grasping the right ear, while the fingers of the right hand hold the left ear.

On the word "Twirl!" each player spins around clockwise or counterclockwise, as decided by the leader of the game, keeping inside the square and whirling as quickly as possible. A player who releases his hold on an ear or puts either foot outside of the circle, is out of the game. The player who twirls longest and best inside his square is the winner. The leader should see that each player actually spins within the square, and those who slow down too much should be ruled out of the game.

BALL DUEL

This is an exciting game which requires some practice to develop skill. So that all campers in the audience may have a box seat, this contest, like so many others, can be carried out on all four sides of the campfire circle at the same time.

The equipment required for each two duelists is a 10-foot length of thin rope about ¼ inch in diameter, a white volleyball or one whitened for the occasion, a 16-inch length of heavy string or cord, a metal ring about 1½ inches in diameter, and seven white paper-plate markers 6 inches in diameter. One end of the 16-inch length of cord is tied securely to the laces of the volleyball, the other end is tied to the ring, and the length of rope is passed through the ring. The exact middle of the rope should be plainly marked with indelible ink or paint. The ring is placed on this mark at the start of the duel and also when the counselor who is acting as referee for each pair of duelists has to stop the match because the duelists have gone outside the boundary markers. When they are in position again the ring is placed on the mark before the duel is recommenced.

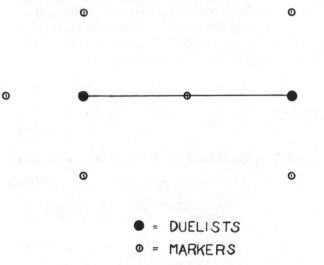

● = DUELISTS

◍ = MARKERS

Each two duelists stand halfway between the fire and the outer edge of the campfire circle and stretch the rope between them as they back toward the ends of the circle, so that there is a distance of 10 feet between them. A plate marker is then stapled to the ground directly beneath the center mark on the rope, from which point the volleyball hangs. Three plate markers are stapled to the ground, one on each side of and directly in line with each duelist, each marker 4 feet away from him, and another directly behind each duelist, also 4 feet distant, as shown in the diagram. This gives the duelists a lane 8 feet wide in which to duel; and the other markers, one stapled 4 feet behind each duelist, mark the total length of the dueling ground.

When the counselor in charge says "Ready!" the duelists tighten the rope between them so that the ball hangs down from the center of the rope, over the plate. The rope must be held by the very end and with only one hand throughout the duel. On the word "Duel!" each duelist tries to hit his opponent with the volleyball by swinging it violently on the rope so that the ring slides the ball along the rope to within easy striking distance. The player attacked tries to avoid being hit by raising his end of the rope and advancing or retreating, not only to avoid contact with the ball but also to maneuver into the best position from which to launch a counterattack.

All duelists must keep within the boundaries, and it is best to have a counselor act as referee for each pair of duelists. When a player goes out of bounds, the referee stops the duel and starts it from the original position

again. When the same duelist goes out of bounds more than twice in succession or jumps over a boundary in order to avoid being struck by the ball, his opponent is declared the winner. The best out of three rounds decides the champion.

POSSUM RACE

This amusing and original game is best contested in jeans, after the leader of campfire games has assured himself that there are neither pebbles nor twigs in the campfire circle. Two 6-foot straight lines are marked opposite each other on each of two sides of the campfire circle, toward the outer edge. Teams with two players in each line up directly behind each of the starting lines. As a rule, the average campfire circle can accommodate only two teams contesting side by side on each side of the circle, since there should be about 3 feet between teams at the start of the race. The players on each team go down on hands and knees, side by side, with one player directly alongside the other.

When the leader of the game says "Go!" the player on the left of the team crawls completely around his teammate as closely and as quickly as possible, without touching him as he circles. He must then continue to crawl until he is directly in front of, and at a distance of about 3 feet ahead of, his partner. When the player behind can just reach and touch *both* heels of the "possum" ahead, he calls "Stop!" and then in his turn circles the player in front of him, also trying to stop with his feet about 3 feet in front of the rear player. The player in the rear can stretch forward from the all-fours position, in order to be able to touch the heels of the player in front of him, but the player ahead must not stretch a leg backward in order to make it easy for his partner to reach it. However, the leading player may back up so that he is not out of reach. The race continues as described until the player in the lead of each team crosses the finish line, and the first player to do so decides the winning team.

The leader who referees this game should keep an alert eye open to see that no player crawls in too large a circle and that no legs are stretched back in order to make it easier for a player to touch his partner's heels.

With older, hardier players, the leader may decide that the race should include a complete circle of the campfire area, and ask the team to race back from the halfway lines to the original starting point. First team carrying out the race correctly wins.

TWO-ROPE TRICK PULL

This amusing game lives up to its name. It is quite different from TRICK TUG OF WAR, to the extent that a champion of this game may not rank top rating in the other. The only gear required is four lengths of rope each 25 feet long and about ½ inch thick. Each rope should be marked 3½ feet from each end. India ink or a piece of colored string tied around the ends will do the trick. Two lines are marked on the ground 18 feet apart and directly opposite each other, on two sides of the campfire circle. Now the leader of the campfire games chooses two pairs of contestants, each pair being of about the same size and weight—though, strangely enough, the tuggers being evenly matched in appearance does not matter too much in this contest. Brains and wiles count for at least as much as brawn. The contesting pairs squat directly opposite each other just behind the lines marked on the ground. The leader places each pair on the lines which he assigns to them and gives each tugger one end of each of the two ropes, pointing out that each has 3½ feet of slack rope with which to win or lose the match and that only one rope end must be held in each hand throughout the tug of war.

On the word "Tug!" each tries to pull or maneuver the other off balance so that he is forced to touch the ground with his hand, lose control of his squat position, or release the end of a rope. Any of these moves will disqualify either contestant, as will holding one rope in two hands. The leader should explain that the trick is to try to throw an opponent off balance by suddenly and unexpectedly giving him slack rope and using similar strategies which the additional length of rope allows. The winner from each side of the fire can tug for the championship.

This is an amusing game for the campers to watch, as the winner is uncertain right up to the time his opponent topples. The leader allows some leeway in the match, and no contestant need be disqualified because he is forced to sway backward and forward. The author has staged many matches in which quite a little fellow, who was good at rope work and a quick thinker, repeatedly defeated older and much heavier rivals. There is no reason why girls should not compete in this match as well as boys, and even challenge the boys to a campfire match.

ROW BALL

This is one of the many games which can be played on both sides of the campfire at the same time, giving the entire campfire audience a good view at close quarters. The only equipment needed is two balls of volleyball size, either white or whitened for the occasion to increase their visibility by campfire light. This is how the contest is staged on each side of the circle: Two teams of eight to ten players in each sit in two parallel lines 4 feet apart, each team facing in opposite directions

and each pair of rival players directly opposite each other. The lines can be curved slightly, provided the same distance is kept between all parts of the lines. The feet of each player should just touch the seat of the jeans of the teammate directly in front of him. The first player in each line keeps his legs fully extended in front of him. The two teams sit directly opposite each other, as shown in the diagram, with the right hands in the 4-foot lane between the teams. The other hand must be kept on the left-hand side throughout the entire game. The leader of the game staples a small, stout circular cardboard marker to the ground in the middle of the lane and exactly halfway from each end.

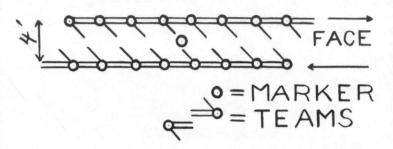

The leader places the white volleyball or basketball on the center marker. When he shouts "Row!" (pronounced as in row a boat) the two players opposite each other and who are closest to the ball begin to drive it *along the ground,* down the row between the two teams, toward the end of the line. Each team drives the ball in the direction in which that team is facing. *Only the right hand* may be used, and the ball must not be struck or pushed higher than a few inches above ground level, except to force it over the hands of the players on the rival team. When the game is played well by evenly matched teams, almost every player has a chance to push or strike the ball, with the palm of the hand, as it moves up and down the lane. When the leader who acts as referee sees that the ball has been lofted or knocked out of the lane, he calls "Hold!" stops the game and places the ball back in the lane at the point from where it was lofted or driven out. The team which first drives the ball to the end of the row and out is declared winner of that round. The team which first scores three goals is winner of the game.

This exciting and somewhat strenuous game requires some strength and skill. A player who may not have sufficient strength to force his opponent's hand back can often maneuver the ball so that it passes either close to himself or close to his rival, thus assuring less pressure on the ball.

For a variation, to exercise the players' left arms and to make the game a little more difficult, the positions of the teams can be changed so that the players strike the ball with their left hands. The same width lane is kept between the two rival teams, and the only change in the game is the position of the players.

BACK-TO-BACK BALLOON RACE

A round balloon from 6 to 8 inches in diameter when fairly fully inflated, and a few spare balloons, are required for this game. The players—either boys or girls, or both —form two to four teams of two and stand back to back behind a starting line marked on the ground, with the player nearest the line facing it. Another line is marked on the ground 30 feet distant. A balloon is placed just below the shoulder blades of the two players on each team, and they hold it in place by exerting enough pressure to hold it in position but not sufficient to cause it to burst.

On the word "Go!" each team runs forward as fast as possible to the second line, the second member of the team running backward in time with the player in the lead. Between them they try to keep the balloon in one piece and at the same time prevent it from falling to the ground. Should it do so, the team must stop immediately while one player replaces the balloon in the correct position, after which the race is continued. When the second line is reached and crossed by both players, the team races back to the starting line. The player who ran backward is now leading. The first team to cross the line with the balloon in the correct position wins.

Considerable co-operation on the part of both players is required in order to carry out this event smoothly and in quick time. A sudden stop by the player in the lead, because he thinks the balloon is slipping, will cause the second player to put such pressure on the balloon that it will burst. With spare balloons available, the leading player may run to the starting line and return to where the balloon burst, with another balloon. When it has been placed in the correct position, the race continues.

INFORMER!

This breathing-spell type of game requires no equipment. It is evolved from a game played in the Philippines. Two teams of equal size line up behind two lines marked on the ground, one at either end of the campfire circle. A campfire games leader stands close to the fire, halfway between the two teams. (He takes the place of two captains, one for each team, and the "chief of police," as used in the Philippines, since a leader's triple role simplifies the game and speeds it up.)

The leader, known as the "inspector," points to any player on either team. That player runs to him, whispers the name of any player on the opposing team, and returns quickly to his place. The inspector then points toward the other team and calls "Advance!" *Any* member of that team walks toward the inspector. If by sheer chance that player is the one whose name has been given to the inspector, he lets the player come up to him, informs him that he is a prisoner, and asks him to name a player on the opposing team. When the prisoner has whispered that name he sits down in line with the inspector on the edge of the campfire circle, and the area in which he sits becomes the prison. Should the first player to advance *after* the inspector has been given a name not be the one named, he goes to the inspector and whispers the name of any player on the opposite side. He then runs back to his team and falls in line, and the inspector, facing the other team, calls "Advance!" and *any* member of that team goes quickly toward him. The game continues in this way, teams being pointed at alternately, until one team has lost all or most of its players and the opposing team therefore wins the game.

Should no member of the team pointed to go toward the inspector quickly, he counts loudly up to six, and if nobody starts toward him before the end of the count, he declares the other team the winner. Of course, no player advances for a second time until each player on his team has advanced once.

Surprising things sometimes happen during this game. Sometimes, by chance, players whose names have been whispered go to the inspector one after the other, so that soon there are practically no players left on either team. At other times, by luck, there are almost no prisoners taken during the first five minutes or so of play, so that there is practically no reduction in the number of players on either team. In such cases, the inspector can stop the game after five or ten minutes of play, and declare the team with the greatest number of players in line the winner.

Another good way to speed up this game is to have the players advance—once an impasse has been reached—in twos, so that there is more chance of one of them becoming a prisoner.

ANCHORED HOOP PASS

The equipment required for this exciting game is two lengths of rope, each 40 feet long, and four strong, smooth wooden hoops, or metal ones, about 18 to 20 inches in diameter. Two of these hoops must be 1 or 2 inches in diameter smaller than the other two. The leader of this game should see that each hoop is perfectly smooth on all sides. Sandpapering wooden hoops or winding adhesive tape around metal ones will assure this. For the first form of this game, a rival team of five to nine players contests against a team of the same size. Each team stands in a half-circle formation on one side of the campfire circle, as shown in the drawing. The players must not change their feet position more than one step in either direction throughout the game. A rope is given to each team, and the players hold it almost taut between them, using both hands held in front of them. Now a hoop is

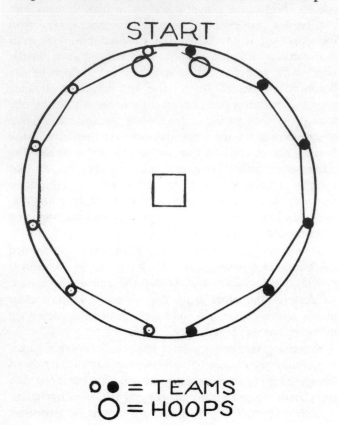

START

o ● = TEAMS
○ = HOOPS

strung on each rope and held by the end player on each team, as illustrated.

When the leader of the game shouts "Pass!" the end player, with the hoop, lets the foot of it rest on the ground and wriggles through it in the way he thinks fastest, while keeping the hoop strung on the rope. As soon as he is through, and still holding the end of the rope, he slides the hoop quickly along it to the next player. He and the rest of the players all pass through the hoop as it moves along the rope, until the last player passes through. The game can end here when younger players are participating, but in the case of older players the hoop is started instantly back along the rope, after the end man has gone through the hoop for the second time. The first team to finish, after each player in it has passed through the hoop twice, wins.

The two extra hoops are used in another form of this game. A hoop is started from each end of each team's rope, one hoop measuring about 1 or 2 inches less in diameter than the other. Each player passes through each hoop only once, and through only one hoop at a time, in this version. However, somewhere along the rope some player will have not only the job of wriggling through two hoops but also the task of putting one hoop through the other, so that it may continue along the rope to the next player. The fact that each player must remain, insofar as possible, in his original position throughout the game means that patience as well as speed is needed to win this game.

rain on the roof—

chapter 8
campfire's off

T HE CHEERLESS CRY of "Campfire's Off!" which follows a sudden rainstorm or other happening which makes it necessary to postpone the eagerly awaited event, need not bring disappointment to the campers if some worthwhile entertainment has been worked out in advance to meet such a contingency. After supper, a program using some shows, stunts, skits, and games can be given in the recreation hall. When the hall is not available, which can happen occasionally in the best-organized camps, more impromptu cabin programs can be carried out on rainy nights when the campfire cannot be held—especially for younger campers, as the senior campers can usually dance and find other ways to amuse themselves despite the sudden forced change in plans.

The size of the average camp cabin does not allow for any fast-and-furious games, but some of the breathing-spell games in Chapter 7 can be used. Guessing games are generally popular in cabin activities, provided they are not too trite and the answers are not too far-fetched or obvious. PYGMY HUNT, with the 2- or 3-inch square "pygmy" conjured up in the imagination, awaiting discovery behind any unlikely object in plain view, or LOST TREASURE—which is a one-cent piece or a silver piece "concealed" openly somewhere in the cabin—are still

popular in the guessing-game category. A *colored disc* about 2 inches in diameter can be substituted for the hidden coin, and it gives much more chance for using protective coloring concealment methods than the coin. Sticking a suitably colored disc onto a colored picture or poster on the wall of a cabin is one sure way to keep the hunters busy for some time. When a player discovers the coin or hidden disc, he should move around a little afterwards, to throw the other players off the scent, and then tell the counselor in charge of the games just where he believes the object is hidden. In this way players can be given first, second, and third scores for discovery. The camper group is always told that the object sought is visible without anything in the cabin having to be moved. Such an advance statement will prevent a general upheaval by the searchers as they move about during the search. The simple guessing game which follows also allows all of the group to guess at the same time.

GIANT OR PYGMY?

The players form as large a circle as they can in the cabin, or they can form a square, and the counselor or a player stands in the middle. The players are told to turn their backs to whoever is in the middle of the group and then close their eyes. Each has to guess whether the one in the middle of the circle is a pygmy or giant. It is explained that the one who plays the part of both pygmy and giant will either stoop down, when he plays pygmy, or stand very tall when he plays giant. He will tap on the floor when he is ready for the players to guess which he is. Each player will make up his mind, and if he thinks that the central figure is a giant he will raise his right hand above his head. Should he believe that a pygmy is being impersonated, he will raise his left arm. After a moment or so the leader calls out "Turn!" and the players in the circle swing around to see whether their guess was right or wrong. This game can also be played with two players at a time. One guesses and is blindfolded; the other does the impersonation. After three guesses, these players change places.

The leader can give this game a twist by introducing a third mysterious person. The newcomer is a "halfling" from outer space, and he is neither small nor tall. He is an "inbetweener," as his name suggests. When the halfling makes his appearance, the impersonator simply remains his natural height. This stance makes it easier for the one playing the triple role. The addition of the third person makes it considerably more difficult for the guessers to make up their minds, and those who decide that it is a halfling fold their arms. The author knows one little player who was so bright—perhaps psychic is a better word—that he always guessed correctly when playing this game. When asked how he managed it, the player assumed the look of Sherlock Holmes explaining an obvious point to Dr. Watson. It appeared that anyone playing the triple role always made some mysterious noise, rustle or creak of joints, perhaps, which betrayed his position to the deductive and astute ears of that juvenile sleuth. When the impersonator plays the halfling there is no noise occasioned by a change in position. "Of course," the young player explained, "when the player stoops down to pretend he is going to be a pygmy and then changes his mind and becomes a giant, I can always hear him come up." Simple!

OBJECT LESSON

This is a little visual quiz game which can be good fun but requires some advance preparation on the part of the leader. Too much work should not be done, since the objects serve only once to advantage with the same group. The objects used can be cut from cardboard and colored or left plain. They can represent a key or kite (Benjamin Franklin), a footprint of a bare foot (Robinson Crusoe), a hatchet (George Washington), a lamp (Aladdin), and a score of other suitable things. For older players, the drawing of two or three "dancing men" will sug-

gest the author of *Sherlock Holmes,* while a small slipper will be linked to Cinderella by a younger player.

Another way to play this game is easier for the leader. Instead of using cutouts, the leader may simply say, "I am thinking of a famous lantern. Whom does it suggest?" Diogenes, will be the likely answer. This form of play provides greater scope, without too much advance preparation.

WOMAN—TRAP—MOUSE

This amusing little game is played all over the world, in various ways and under different names. In England, players call a similar game HUNTER, GUN, RABBIT, while in Argentina youngsters and grownups too know the game as MAN, GUN, TIGER. This version, which uses different subjects and signs from any other version, is called WOMAN—TRAP—MOUSE.

No equipment is needed, and there can be almost any number of players. They stand in pairs, one player directly opposite the other and 2 paces apart. When playing the individual form of this game, each player secretly decides whether to give the hand sign for the woman, the trap, or the mouse. The signs are as follows: woman, closed hand, except for the raised index finger; the trap, hand held open and flat, palm upward; the mouse, thumb and index finger touching and pointing forward, as shown in the drawing. All three signs are made with one hand only. The scoring is simple and decides the winner in this way:

The woman controls the trap, and wins.
The trap catches the mouse, and wins.
The mouse scares the woman, and wins.

To begin the first of a series of three tries, the players turn their backs to each other. One player says "Ready" —slowly, so that his opponent has time to decide and get his hand sign ready. On the word "Go!" both players swing completely around so they face each other, with the hand making the sign held out at about waist level. Should both players make the same sign, which happens fairly frequently, that try is considered a tie and neither player scores. If the players wish, instead of turning

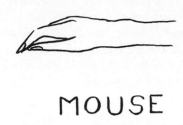

WOMAN　　　　TRAP　　　　MOUSE

around to make the sign each time, they can face each other and bring the hand, with the sign made, from behind the back on the word "Go!"

This makes a good team game, with four to ten players on each side. The two teams stand back to back, with 2 paces between teams. One player on each team is chosen as the leader for the first three tries. Each leader secretly shows the sign chosen to the other members of the team and on the word "Show!" each team wheels about, giving the sign decided on by their leader. After each set of three tries, a new leader is chosen.

FOUR IN A ROW

Each player draws a big oblong and marks it off into sixteen smaller oblongs, as shown in the diagram. The leader gives the players a sixteen-word sentence, such as HIKING AND EXPLORING ARE FINE OUTDOOR ACTIVITIES FOR OLDER BOYS OR GIRLS DURING THE CAMPING MONTHS—or HIKING, CLIMBING, SWIMMING, BOATING, PROVIDE FUN AND ADVENTURE WHICH THRILL CAMPERS DURING SUMMER MONTHS AT CAMP. Each player writes any word in any oblong. The leader can write the words on slips of paper, mix them in a box or paper bag, then draw them. Actually, there is no need to do so, unless for the purpose of showmanship or to increase suspense, because he will have no idea in which oblong any player has written any word, so he can call

out words at random as he glances at the sentence. The words should be marked off in the sequence called, however, in case a check-back is necessary. Players check off each word as it is called, and the first player to have any four words in a row crossed out vertically, horizontally, or diagonally is the winner. The game should continue until second- and third-place winners have been discovered.

The leader can introduce suspense by hesitating now and then before calling out a word. When composing new sixteen-word sentences for this game, the leader will need to avoid using linking words, such as a, the, and, or other common ones twice in the same sentence, since this makes the game too easy.

THREE OR OUT

This quiet game helps to develop quick thinking, in addition to providing opportunity for audience participation. The leader points to any player, then says and spells out any three-letter word, counts silently or softly up to 10, not too fast, and ends by saying "Out!" when required. For instance: "Man, M-A-N, 1-2-3-4-5-6-7-8-9-10-OUT!" Before the leader reaches the word "Out," the player pointed to must name three words, each beginning with one of the letters of the word given. The words must be in proper sequence, and proper names must not be used. If the word is W-A-Y, for instance, the words can be waltz, about, yonder—or any other ac-

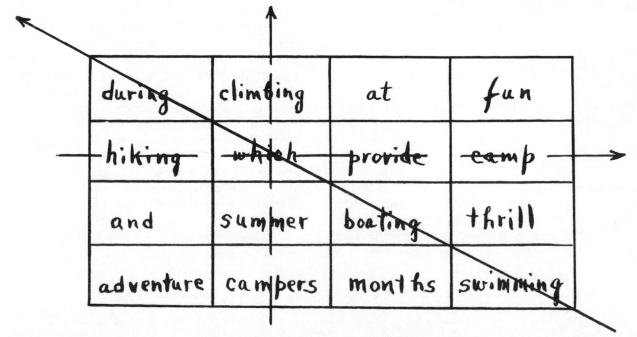

ceptable words given in the correct order. This is not so easy as it seems, since it is difficult to think fast when working against time. Words of four or five letters may be used with older players, which makes this game really hard. In the case of four- or five-letter words, a little extra time may be allowed.

OUT OF REACH

The leader asks a camper to place one hand where the other cannot possibly touch it.

Solution. When either hand is placed on an elbow, the other cannot possibly touch it.

PYRAMID BUILDER

The leader places ten white paper plates or foot-square pieces of white cardboard or paper on the ground, in the form of a pyramid. The squares should be arranged in rows about 6 inches apart. Four squares, about 4 inches apart, are placed in the bottom row. Three squares are then placed in the next row, two in the next, and one on the top row. The pyramid will now look like a V upside down. The leader asks for a volunteer who has no previous knowledge of how the puzzle is done but believes he has worked out the solution, to reform the pyramid with its top facing in a different direction by moving *only* three squares, or plates.

When a volunteer fails to do so correctly, the plates which he has moved are replaced in their original positions and another camper tries his skill.

Solution. The diagram shows how the pyramid may be most easily reformed in three moves.

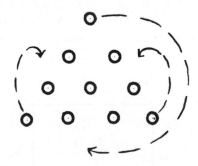

KNOT-TO-BE

The leader places a 2-foot strip of 2-inch bandage or white cloth on the ground and calls for a camper who does not know how the stunt is done to make a knot in the center of the strip while holding one end in each hand.

Solution. The only way to make the knot is to fold the arms before taking an end of the bandage in each hand. When the arms are unfolded, the knot forms on the bandage.

CHECKERBOARD PUZZLE

The counselor either puts a checkboard on the cabin table, or uses a facsimile drawn on a sheet of cardboard or heavy paper. He places eight checkers, or eight pieces of heavy cardboard cut out to look like checkers, on the table beside the checkerboard. He then asks for a volunteer who is good at figuring things out to come to the table and arrange the eight checkers on the squares of the checkerboard so that *none of them is in line* with any of the others—either *vertically, horizontally, or diagonally*. He can, if necessary, draw lines on a sheet of paper to show the direction in which each of these lines runs. When players contest by this one-by-one method, it is best to eliminate each would-be solver as soon as he has inadvertently lined up any two checkers in a manner which does not meet the puzzle requirements. This speeds up the game considerably. Several checkerboards and sets of checkers make it possible for several contestants to compete at the same time.

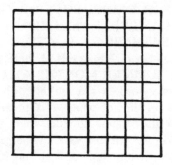

Another way to avoid making eager would-be contestants wait is to provide each person in the group with a small sheet of paper with squares on it, as illustrated, and a pencil. Large sheets of paper with squares of almost any size printed on them can be cut into the smaller sheets required for this game. Once the object and rules of the puzzle are explained and the "Go!" signal is given, each camper begins to mark dots on the squares in a way which he thinks will solve the problem. Of course, these dots may be rubbed out and the places of dots changed at will by each player, since it is the one who first completes the puzzle correctly who wins.

Solution. The drawing gives one solution to the puzzle; there are others.

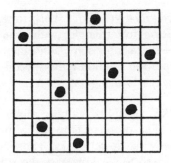

NUMBER PUZZLES

There are many simple number puzzles, some of which are very ancient, which stimulate thought and are not beyond the ability of the average camper. Three of them follow, including the well-known FERRARIS SQUARE. The first two puzzles, to which there are several correct solutions, can be best worked out by giving each camper a square of paper measuring about 4 inches, which he divides into nine smaller squares, in order to be able to add more easily. A way to make it even easier for the campers to work out this puzzle is to give each camper nine squares of white paper, each about 2 inches square, so that he can put a number on each and move them about in the form of a big square, in order to more easily arrange the numbers to form the correct totals. The drawing shows nine detached squares.

NINE-SQUARE PUZZLE (A). Each camper participating in this puzzle is asked to take the numbers 1 through 9 and mark *one* number in *each* small square, so that the total in the big square will be 15, whether the numbers are totaled *vertically, horizontally,* or *diagonally.* This makes a total of eight different ways, as indicated by the broken lines in the drawing.

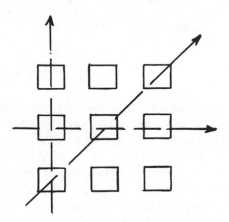

NINE-SQUARE PUZZLE (B). In this puzzle the number of squares is the same, but the numbers used are from 2 through 10 inclusive, omitting the number 1; and the total, in all directions, must be 18.

THE FERRARIS SQUARE. To work out this number puzzle, a square of paper is divided into sixteen equally sized squares, as illustrated. The players have to use the numbers 1 to 15 in this puzzle, and the answer is that all squares must add up to a *total of 34,* whether the addition is done horizontally, vertically, or diagonally. The numbers used to arrive at this total are marked in each square in each contestant's final solution.

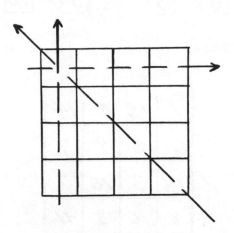

THE PERFECT CROSS. By connecting with straight lines twelve of the dots shown in the drawing, a perfect cross can be formed. As a helpful clue toward solving this puzzle, it can be said that when the cross is completed it will have five dots inside it and eight dots outside it.

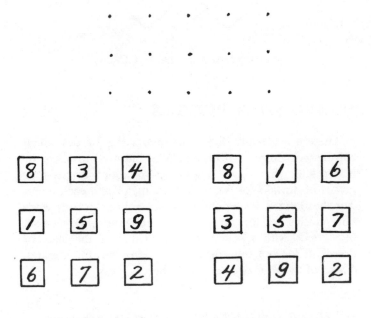

SOLUTION TO NINE-SQUARE PUZZLE (A)

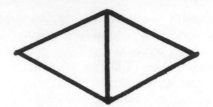

SOLUTION TO NINE-SQUARE PUZZLE (B)

QUINTUPLE TRIANGLES. This time, the players are asked to form five triangles with nine dowel sticks. This is not an easy task for some contestants, though others will figure out the solution quite speedily.

TRICK STICKS. This is really a tricky puzzle, as its name suggests. The problem is to make three and a half dozen, using only six dowel sticks. Those who fail to do so will be surprised to see how easy the solution is, once the dowel sticks are arranged by another player.

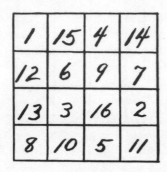

SOLUTION TO THE FERRARIS SQUARE

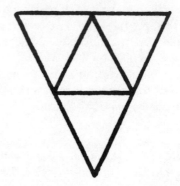

SOLUTION TO DUAL TRIANGLES

SOLUTION TO QUINTUPLE TRIANGLES

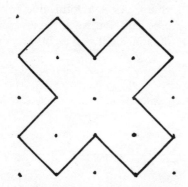

SOLUTION TO THE PERFECT CROSS

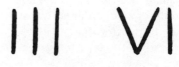

SOLUTION TO TRICK STICKS

DOWEL STICK PUZZLES

There are literally dozens of interesting puzzles which can be worked out with the help of big used matches, or better still, thin dowel sticks. With about twenty-four pieces of dowel stick ¼ inch in diameter and each about 3 inches long, a leader can have several contestants work out puzzles on the tabletop simultaneously. Of course, lines made with a pencil on paper can take the place of dowel sticks, but this form of play provides far less fun. Three of these puzzles are given here.

DUAL TRIANGLES. The contestants are asked to form two triangles with five dowel sticks.

STATE EMBLEMS

This is an interesting quiz game for older campers or precocious younger ones. The group divides into two teams of equal size, and the leader asks the following type of questions. "Who can name the state flower of Washington?" he asks, pointing toward one of the teams. The first player on that team to raise his hand is asked to name the flower (rhododendron). If the camper is correct, points are awarded his team and the next question is asked of the other team. The leader may then ask for the name of the tree chosen by that state (western hemlock), and finally for the name of the state bird (willow goldfinch.)

When one state has been covered, another is introduced. When the group is composed of younger players, the leader may ask only for the name of the flower or bird for each state.

The players' knowledge can be well tried by states such as Hawaii, which claims hibiscus for its state flower, the *nene* (Hawaiian goose) for its bird emblem, and the coconut as its state tree. A "catch" occurs in such states as Alabama, which has a flower, a tree, a bird, and *a fish* (tarpon) as emblems.

The leader of the game can also ask the state "nickname," such as Empire State for New York and Lone Star State for Texas.

Five points can be awarded for each emblem correctly named, and the winning team can be decided either after three or six states have been covered; or a score can be kept, and the points for each team totaled after five or ten minutes of play.

Lists of state emblems are given in most almanacs and similar publications.

TONGUE TWISTERS

The faster you try to say them, the harder they are to say. A number of these samples are original. Some, dealing with woodchucks, peppers, thistles, and "tooters," are too well known to merit repetition.

> *She sells sea shells on the seashore*
> *So the shells she sells are sea shells, she's sure;*
> *She sells sea shells on the seashore*
> *So she's sure she sells seashore shells.*

> *She sighs, shyly seeking shoal sea shells on the seashore.*
> *Seesaws she said she saw, she said she saw seesaws.*
> *A fine field of wheat and a fine wheat field.*
> *Does your shirt shop stock short spotted shirts?*
> *Swift streams sail short swift ships, short swift ships sail swift streams.*
> *Six thick thistle sticks.*
> *Ten thin tin things.*
> *Six short slim sycamore sticks.*
> *A cup of coffee in a copper coffee cup.*
> *Three thrifty trippers saved seven shiny silver shillings.*
> *A glowing gleam growing green.*

STORY RIDDLES

Campers always like stories in which they can take part, and the solution of story riddles always has an appeal for the many amateur sleuths. THE KNIGHT'S SHIELD is not an easy one to solve, but at least every camper taking part will be able to cut and fit and try if each participant is given a piece of thick paper and a pencil, and is able to share a ruler and a pair of blunt-ended scissors. As a rule, only a bright older camper works out the correct solution after considerable time and thought. ROUNDUP REWARD, MEDIEVAL MATHEMATICS, and BOY TREAT GIRL? are not too difficult for the average camper.

MEDIEVAL MATHEMATICS. A counselor tells the campers that he is going to ask them to work out a very simple problem in mathematics. He then marks a square on a table or wall, with chalk, and tells them it is one yard square. The counselor then relates the following story.

"In medieval times, people in an English town called Lancelot were taxed on the size of their windows. One knight, who had more courage than cash, had a window which was exactly one yard square, the same as the one I have just drawn. He could not afford to pay the tax on a window of that size. He would have bricked one half of it up, but he did not want to do that because he needed a window one yard high and one yard wide so that he would have sufficient light for his work. After much thinking, and consulting a wizard, he hit on a way to brick up one-half of his window so that he still had a *square window, one yard high and one yard wide.*

"How did he do it? Better still, how would any one of you do it? Here is a piece of chalk, so that you can illustrate just how the knight solved his problem."

Of course, any campers who may know how it is accomplished should be asked not to tell how it is done until other campers, who have no previous knowledge of the simple solution, have a chance to try.

Solution. How the knight solved his window problem is best shown by this sketch.

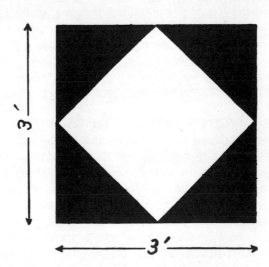

ROUNDUP REWARD. The fall roundup was over, and the cowboys of the Bar B Q Ranch gathered at the corral for the pay-off. The owner had told the boys that cash was scarce, so many of the boys had agreed to take their back pay in horses. Things went smoothly, and the cowboys drove off their share of the ponies as the chief wrangler had the animals hazed into bunches of the required size. Then trouble came along!

Three brothers rode up to drive off their combined share—35 ponies. The chief wrangler of the Bar B Q would gladly have had these three cowboys drive off all of the horses in one bunch, but the boys asked that the division be made by him at the corral.

"We all have a different share of hosses comin'," the eldest brother explained, "and we can't figure as easy as we can ride." As he spoke, he sheepishly held out a slip to the chief wrangler.

"Well I'll be doggoned!" the foreman exclaimed as he looked at the pay-off slip from the ranch owner. Red was to be given one-half of the herd, Pete was to have one-third, while the youngest brother, Bud, was to have one-ninth of the bunch.

No wonder the chief wrangler had shown surprise. You try to divide 35 ponies into *two* equal halves! Continue the division by one third and one ninth and the task does not become any easier.

Fortunately the chief wrangler had not neglected mathematics at school. "I'm going to give you a break, fellows," he said. "Each of you will get a little more hoss than he is entitled to according to the boss's order, and there will be a little bonus for me for my risk and my figurin'."

How do *you* think the clever foreman managed to keep his promise? Put yourself in his place. What would *you* have done to solve the problem?

Solution. The clever foreman added his pony to the brothers' herd of 35, making a total of 36 ponies. He then gave Red his half share (18) and Steve his one-third share (12). Then he gave Bud his ninth share (4). Though this only used 34 ponies, the brothers figured each had had a better deal than if the foreman had tried to divide the 35 ponies. The foreman got his pony back, and none of the brothers grudged him the "extra" pony which his clever division of the herd had netted him.

THE KNIGHT'S SHIELD. Sir Kay of Kent was a brave and gallant knight. He went with King Richard the Lion Hearted to fight against the Saracens in the Holy Land. One day of battle, Sir Kay was surrounded by many fierce tribesmen. After a great battle, the knight was overpowered and taken before Saladin.

Although the great Saladin was leading the fighting against the Crusaders, he admired bravery and skill at arms. His chiefs asked that Sir Kay be put to death because he had slain many of Saladin's warriors. Saladin did not wish to harm Sir Kay, whom he knew as a brave and fearless Crusader, so he had him taken to a tent and a guard posted outside. Then Saladin thought how he

could best save Sir Kay's life and still not displease his chieftains. As he pondered, his eyes fell on the knight's shield which stood against the wall of the tent. The fine, battle-dented shield was shaped like a triangle. It was dark blue in color and on it a gold cross gleamed.

Suddenly a smile brightened Saladin's face. Then he sent for three of his chiefs and told them of his plan. They too were brave fighters and approved Saladin's plan to give Sir Kay a chance to save his life. Then they asked what that chance was going to be. Saladin cut three triangles from a piece of stiff paper and handed one to each chieftain. Each triangle was shaped exactly like the knight's shield, with three equal sides.

Saladin asked each leader to cut his paper shield into four pieces, any way he liked, *but* the pieces when put together must form a perfect square, and all of the triangle must be used. At first this seemed to be a puzzle which could be solved by a little thought; but as each chieftain failed on the first attempt and cut up more and more little shields in fruitless efforts to form a perfect square, they all gave up the attempt and told Saladin that they did not believe it could be done. Saladin assured them that it could—otherwise he would not give the problem to the knight—but that the Crusader would only be given *one* triangle of paper, instead of the many which the chieftains had used in trying to solve the puzzle.

The chieftains readily approved the test. Saladin then sent for Sir Kay, gave him a triangle, and told him that if he could make a perfect square from it before daylight the next day, his life would be spared.

Sir Kay thanked Saladin for this chance to save his life and told him that the task set should not be too difficult. He promised that within an hour he would bring Saladin the perfect square formed by using all of the triangle. The chieftains remained in Saladin's tent and used up many more little triangles in their efforts to make a square from them. Two of the wisest chieftains did manage to make a hollow square inside the paper, but the solid pieces of the triangle did not then form a square. None of them could make what Saladin had demanded. At the end of an hour, Sir Kay was brought to Saladin's tent, and he presented the Saracen leader with a perfect square, cut from the triangle which Saladin had given him.

The leader and his chieftains were amazed. The square which Saladin held was proof of the knight's skill. Sir Kay was given many rich presents and sent back to King Richard's lines with an escort of honor.

How do you think the knight cut his triangle to form the square? Do you think that you can do it? Cut three cardboard triangles, each side 3 inches long, and take three tries. There is no trick about it, as pieces can be cut from the triangle which form a perfect square when they are placed one against the other. All of the triangle must be used. By the way, this sort of triangle, with all sides equal, is called an equilateral triangle. Perhaps it is fair, after giving you such a big word, to give you an equally big hint. The knight cut his triangle into only *four* pieces to make the perfect square. The diagram shows the solution.

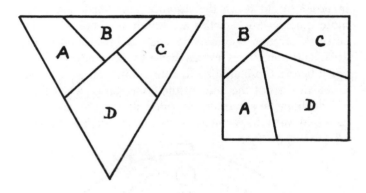

BOY TREAT GIRL? Five boy campers had planned to go to the canteen by themselves to feast on ice cream, but were unexpectedly met by five girl campers, who were home-town friends. The girls wished to join in whatever activities the boys had decided on. This, the boys knew, would mean treating the girls to ice cream; but the boys' financial situation did not permit this. Each boy had his mind firmly set on ice cream. What could be done to make this possible? One of the older boys had a bright idea. He was a clever amateur mathematician, and after a brief mental calculation—and a few whispered words to each of the other four boys—he suggested that the group of ten form a circle, all facing inward, to play a game of "chance," which would decide their program. He explained that it was a sort of "counting-out" game

which would divide the group into two equal halves, after which they would go off together and enjoy themselves during the free period, which the camp bugler had just sounded.

The girls thought the idea a thrilling one, and each of them looked forward to pairing off with a boy chosen by chance. It sounded kind of mysterious! They formed a circle, apparently in a haphazard way, and the boy who had suggested the counting-out idea said that in order to let chance and the girls take over, a girl should do the counting out. This, he said, would assure the division being made fairly. He pointed to a girl at what he called "the top of the circle" and suggested that she count all around the circle, clockwise, beginning with the camper on her left, who would be *one*. Every eleventh camper would be counted out, step from the circle, and form a second group.

How did the campers stand in the circle so that only girls were counted out and the boys alone remained in the circle? Campers can best work out the solution on paper by drawing a circle and marking the ten players, with different signs for boys and girls, who stand around it. The girl chosen at the "top" of the circle to do the counting out should be exactly in the center of the top half of the circle.

Solution. The girl at the "top of the circle" started counting clockwise around the circle, beginning with the camper on her left, indicated by the arrow in the diagram. White circles indicate the girls, all of whom were eliminated from the circle, and black circles the boys, all of whom remained.

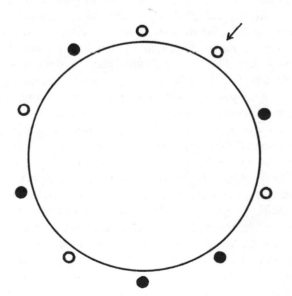

indian tribal

ALL THE CHALLENGES WHICH FOLLOW, the majority of which are of Northwest Coast origin, can be contested with equal success by camp council fire groups and organizations which now use Plains, Woodland, or other tribal programs at their council fires. In practically all challenges, the mere change of the name of the tribe or individual challenger is all that is required to make the challenge suitable for *any* Indian council fire. The activities and ideas derived from the Northwest Coast Indians require but slight change, if any, for adaptation to the existing Plains, Woodland, or Pueblo Indian programs. In cases where the present council fire programs of the latter Indian groups have lost some of their original freshness and appeal over the years, an entire Northwest Coast Indian program—with its pomp, pageantry, ceremony, complete newness, and many surprises—can be staged for a season, or longer, to add fresh fuel and excitement to council fire activities.

After lengthy visits with various tribes of the Northwest Pacific Coast and much time spent in counsel with their old chiefs, shamans, and older representative Indians, one realizes that there is a wealth of brand-new, thrilling—and educational—material in their way of life. Their comparatively modern and magnificently developed arts, culture, challenges, games, sense of humor, council fires, and magic can provide exciting new material to help modern council fire chiefs widen the present horizons of their Indian programs and activities.

HOW TO MARK COUNCIL FIRE CHALLENGE BOUNDARIES

Many council fire contests and races are not so successful as they should be, because too often distinct boundaries are not marked at all or are not visibly marked. Without some sort of guiding markers in events, for instance, which are supposed to circle the outer edge of the council fire area, some of the warriors and teams may keep as close to the council fire as possible in order to cut down the distance and finish the event more quickly. Such tactics are unfair to those who race correctly around the outside edge of the council fire area, and sometimes events have to be contested over again before those entitled to count coup can be decided. Often this is not the fault of the contestants, when there are no boundary markers to guide them. The sure way to avoid such happenings is to place suitable markers

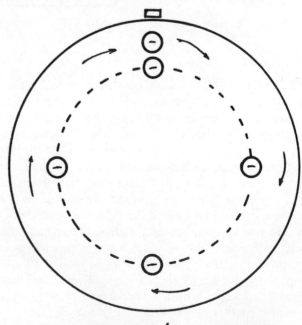

□ = CHIEF'S CHAIR
⊖ = MARKERS

and clan challenges

from 2 to 4 feet away from the outer edge of the council fire area at three or four points situated at equal distances apart. The runners are warned that in certain events they must keep outside of these markers in order to count coup. How to make and place such markers, and hold them securely in place, is given in Chapter 6.

CHALLENGES AND CHALLENGE PAGEANTS

Council fire chiefs who direct various challenges know that a certain spirit of friendly rivalry is helpful in having all challenges contested keenly. It is for this reason that all challenges in this book suggest that warriors from different clans contest in the varied events. It is also important that the contestants be fairly evenly matched, in order to add fairness and increased excitement to the events. Matching evenly does not always mean the consideration of size and weight only; very often smaller warriors outrun and outfox the bigger ones, to the amusement of the warriors-in-council.

WARPATH

For excitement and pageantry, WARPATH is a unique tribal challenge. It provides thrills and action for the contesting braves and almost constant suspense for all the spectator braves-in-council. The very fact that twenty warriors compete at the same time fills the entire council ring with unusual activity. Another good feature is that five braves from four different tribes contest at the same time, so that most spectator braves are represented in the *mêlée,* unless many tribes attend the council fire. This rather rough challenge is especially recommended for older braves, with two mature chiefs assisted by four "dog soldiers" supervising; with alert supervision, even younger warriors can safely participate.

The diagram gives a clear picture of the warpath territory, the peace strips where the warriors gather in front of their villages, the villages, and their boundary lines. It is important that the lines shown in the drawing be *clearly* marked in the council ring. White tape can be used to mark the lines, but liquid lime or chalk is best,

as it remains in place more easily than tape, even though the tape is fastened to the ground with long staples made from heavy wire. The circle is a natural one, formed by the first row of benches or logs used as seats in the council ring. The diagram shows the manner in which the braves and dog soldiers enter the council ring and indicates the posts of the two chiefs, the four dog soldiers, and the warring braves at the start of the attack. The chiefs, who should if possible be from neutral tribes, change their positions at will in order to follow the movement of the *mêlée* more closely.

Each band of five whooping warriors is led into the council ring by a dog soldier, who carries a short lighted torch (how to make these torches is described in Chapter 1). The four dog soldiers bark and bay as they circle the council ring. This was always the call and rallying cry of these brave volunteer Indian police. All bands of braves enter the ring at the same time and trot around the circle in Indian file in the following order. The Sioux are followed by the Apache; they trot twice round the ring clockwise, nearest to the spectators. They take up their respective positions in front of their villages the third time they circle. The Crow and Arapaho, in that order, enter the ring at the same time as the first two bands, but they trot three times counterclockwise around the circle on the inside, nearer to the fire. They take up their positions in front of their villages on the fourth time around. This simple entry can be most easily accomplished by making the dog soldiers responsible for the good order and timing. They should keep count of the number of times that the ring is circled and lead each band to its village at the right moment. This is not difficult, because a dog soldier leads each band of whooping braves into and around the council ring. (Of course, the braves taking part in this challenge can be from any of the tribes participating in the council fire, and the names of the tribes used in this description are merely given as examples.)

When each band is in fighting formation, the four dog soldiers take up their positions, as shown in the diagram, around the fire and as close to it as proves comfortable. It is the duty of these dog soldiers to prevent the struggling braves from getting too close to the fire. The chief on either side of the council ring sees that the warriors keep on the correct sides of the fire and also

WARPATH

ENTRY INTO COUNCIL RING

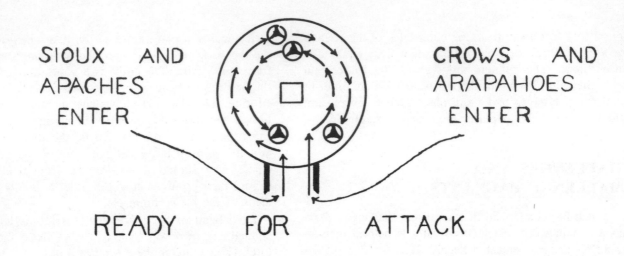

SIOUX AND APACHES ENTER

CROWS AND ARAPAHOES ENTER

READY FOR ATTACK

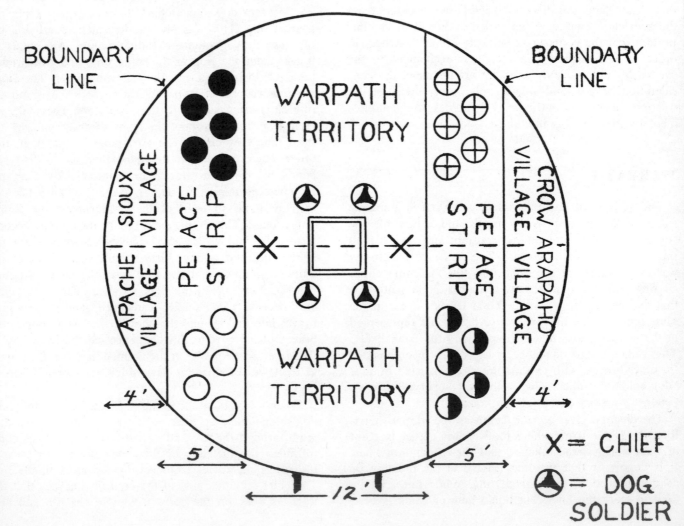

BOUNDARY LINE

BOUNDARY LINE

APACHE VILLAGE | SIOUX VILLAGE

PEACE STRIP

WARPATH TERRITORY

WARPATH TERRITORY

PEACE STRIP

CROW VILLAGE | ARAPAHO VILLAGE

4'   5'   12'   5'   4'

X = CHIEF

◉ = DOG SOLDIER

observes that they do not contest too roughly. The Sioux fight the Crow, and the Apache the Arapaho, as the diagram indicates. Needless to say, the braves are not armed in any way, and they must not strike each other at any time—only catch, hold, push, or pull in order to take prisoners. It is best that no headdresses be worn; neither should the contestants wear their best regalia, necklaces, or other ornaments.

When the chief in charge shouts "Attack!" any or all warriors may go on the warpath by entering the warpath territory. The warring tribes take prisoners in this area and pull, drag, or carry them into their respective villages, from which they must not escape or be rescued once they have been taken across the village boundary line. The captives may try to break loose from their captors only up to this line; and the warriors of the captives' bands, themselves risking capture, may try to rescue those taken prisoner up to this boundary line, but not over it. Those trying to rescue captives on the enemy's peace strip may be captured while doing so but must not take prisoners on the peace strip. This applies to all bands. Any fainthearted brave who is captured may save himself from some discomfort at the hands of his captors, or from too painful a grip on his arm or leg, by shouting, "I surrender!" He must then stop struggling, and one warrior from the band which captured him may conduct him to the captors' village. Once the brave has surrendered, he must make no attempt to escape, and he may not be rescued on the way to the village. He must tell any would-be rescuer that he has surrendered.

A band is defeated as soon as all its members have been taken prisoner. The entire battle ends when stopped by the chief in charge—at the end of about five minutes, for instance. He shouts "Hey-a-a-a-hey!" to attract the attention of all warriors and then raises his right arm as a signal for the struggle to cease. The two bands with the most prisoners are then declared the winners. They may contest against each other at the next council fire, should the chief so decide. After such a strenuous struggle, even the bravest warriors are often glad to "let down their ponies' tails"—leave the warpath. The chiefs may decide to award coup feathers to the warriors who fought best throughout the challenge. To end the event, the bands march twice around the council ring, the two victorious bands leading and the four dog soldiers bringing up the rear, as all contestants leave the ring at the end of the challenge. They return shortly for the remainder of the program.

MEDICINE LODGE

A square measuring 10 feet in diameter is marked by placing one round white cardboard marker 6 inches in diameter at each corner of the square. Each marker

should be pegged to the ground with a strong piece of stiff wire about 12 inches long, bent to form a staple, the two legs being forced into the ground through the cardboard to hold it in place. This square is the medicine lodge. A lodge may be set up on either two or four sides of the council fire, according to the number of contestants.

A clan chief or warrior, playing the role of a medicine man, stands in the center of each lodge. He guards six rolls of "birch bark," which can be made of strong white paper or lightweight cardboard, each 10 inches long by 2 inches in diameter. These rolls are laid separately in a circle around the medicine man, each roll 2 feet away from him. Six warriors surround the medicine lodge. When the tribal chief gives the signal "Attack!" each warrior tries to seize a birch-bark roll without being touched by the medicine man. Only one roll at a time may be taken, and the warrior taking it is not safe until he has escaped without being touched, to outside the boundary of the medicine lodge. Warriors trying to take the rolls should not use a rush-and-grab method but must secure the rolls through a series of stealthy approaches and feints which mislead the medicine man and are good to watch.

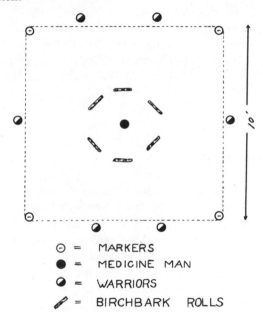

⊖ = MARKERS
● = MEDICINE MAN
◔ = WARRIORS
⟋ = BIRCHBARK ROLLS

With an alert tribal chief judging the contest, an exciting addition may be made. Should three warriors succeed in touching the medicine man at the same instant, before being touched by him, the medicine man is their prisoner and the attackers count coup. Fast action makes it difficult for the chief to decide who touched whom at times.

The warrior who captures the greatest number of rolls without being touched counts coup and wins.

Rivalry may be increased by having a medicine man from one clan guard the birth-bark rolls against six warriors from another clan, or clans. Two, four, or six warriors may contest against a medicine man, as decided by the tribal chief.

MEDICINE DRUM

This is an interesting contest suitable for ceremonial council fires. It is carried out with exactly the same lodge, marked out in the same way, as in MEDICINE LODGE. Instead of using birch-bark rolls, a camp-made drum is used. It is placed in the center of the medicine lodge, with a drumstick laid on top of it. The skin side is uppermost, and a medicine man stands with his toes touching the drum. He is blindfolded, but the blindfold must not cover his ears. Three warriors stand 3 paces away from the medicine lodge, on different sides. When the tribal chief says, "Attack!" the three attackers approach the medicine lodge as silently as possible and try to pick up the beater and strike the medicine drum once before the medicine man can hear and touch them. A warrior who is touched is out of the contest; he leaves the council fire area, and the contest does not commence until he is clear of the area.

The tribal chief may have the warriors attack one at a time, signaling to the one whom he wishes to start the attack. Each warrior who beats the drum without being touched counts coup. Stealth, silent approach, and timing, not wild rushes, mark the skillful warrior in this challenge.

LANCE HOLD

For this challenge a "lance" is made from a straight hardwood pole. It can be from 6 to 9 feet in length and about 1 inch in diameter, quite smooth and rounded at both ends. Two lines, each ½ inch wide, are painted in dark red or black around the lance, so that each line is 4½ inches from the center. Two other lines are marked in the same way 10 inches from each end of the lance. These distances are suggested for two teams with six braves in each. Longer lances can be used, and the stripes marked further from the ends and center, when the contesting teams are larger. This is worked out proportionately in order to give the increased number of players a chance to have a hand in the game. Instead of paint stripes, strips of colored adhesive tape can be used for the lance markings—which allows the distances to

be increased or decreased easily. The challenge is carried out in the following way.

Two teams of six to nine players face each other in two straight lines 30 feet apart. A chief stands exactly halfway between the two lines, in line with the last players on either end. He holds the lance upright with one hand on one end of the lance; the other end of the lance rests on the ground. The top of the lance is held so that it can be released instantly. The chief tells the contestants that when he lets the lance fall on the ground between the two lines, the moment it touches the ground but not a second before, they may rush forward. From either side they are to try to grasp the lance with the *left* hand only, anywhere between its two ends; *but* the center section of the lance, between the two stripes, counts grand coup and equals two hands in the scoring. The section marked at each end counts coup and equals one and a-half hands when the scoring is done at the end of the challenge. A left hand on all other parts of the lance counts one hand. The lance must not be carried more than 6 feet away from where it fell when dropped by the chief, and it must not be raised more than shoulder high at any time during the challenge. This is a safety measure. Actually the lance is best held about waist level throughout the struggle. Right hands must not be used for any purpose at any time throughout the challenge, and the players should be cautioned before the rush begins that they must not try to shoulder each other out of position. The challengers who fail to grasp the lance in any of the three places which count coup should still try to get a handhold with the left hand somewhere else on the lance.

The chief in charge of the challenge, as soon as the rush begins, starts counting loudly and fairly slowly up to 60 and then shouts, "Hold!" All players must "freeze" instantly on this command; those who grab or move their hands after it has been given are disqualified. The chief counts the left hands on the lance, and the band wins which has the highest score made by the left hands squarely on the lance. A hand on top of another hand or partially on top of another hand does not score.

Another version of this challenge is to count *only* the left hands on the grand coup and coup sections of the lance—center and end only. Other versions will suggest themselves to modern chiefs, such as having the challengers grasp the lance with *both* hands, placed separately only or together only, or barring the hold on the lance in the middle, grand coup section.

Big rival groups of Indians used to contest this challenge on a 10- or 12-foot lance, with no sections marked —and no holds barred!

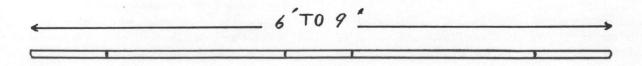

TETHER FOOT

This is a challenge game which Indian boys play on the Canadian Northwest Coast. It can be played equally well by modern Indians at the council fire, and it is certain to cause amusement to the chiefs and warriors-in-council. This is how the challenge is carried out.

Two lines are marked on the ground, one exactly opposite the other, 30 feet apart, and these lines can continue directly across the council fire area, with warriors contesting on two sides of the fire. The players, in groups of two from each clan, line up at one of these lines. One player kneels facing the line, on hands and knees, with finger tips resting on the line. His racing partner also goes down on hands and knees, a little way behind, facing in the opposite direction. When each team of two is in the correct position, a chief ties one ankle of each two contestants together with a strong strip of cloth about 30 inches long and 1½ inches wide. Each team of two partners in the race is secured together in this way, with a distance of 3 or 4 feet between teams.

When the chief shouts, "Go!" each team "races" away from the starting line toward the second line, the boy with finger tips on the starting line advancing head first toward the second line, while his unfortunate partner has to race backward. Each pair of partners tries to coordinate their movements in order to advance as swiftly as possible. This is easy to write about but hard to do! When the racer advancing head first toward the line is able to touch it with his finger tips, he shouts "Back!" whereupon his partner, who now has the pleasure of facing forward as he crawls, sets off at top speed toward the starting line, his wrong-way-round partner following as best he can. The first team to return to the starting line, with both partners crawling on their knees, counts coup just as soon as the leading partner touches the line with the finger tips of both hands.

A second version of this challenge is for the pairs of warriors to race with *both* ankles tied to those of their partners, which is not easy.

KICK STICK

This lively challenge race is contested by Indian men and boys from the Northwest Coast to the Southwest, sometimes over distances of ten miles. The Zuni and most of the tribes used straight sticks ranging from 2½ to 5 inches in length and from ¾ to 1½ inches in diameter. In order to add difficulty and amusement to this challenge, a stick similar to one used by Woodland Indian boys takes the place of the straight kick stick.

These sticks are made in the form of a crescent by cutting willow wands about 1 inch thick into 10-inch lengths. The two ends of each unpeeled stick are then tied together with strong twine so that the two ends are about 3 inches apart. After drying in the sun for a day or two, the sticks straighten out a little when the twine is removed but usually retain the correct crescent shape required for the challenge. These sticks look better, and show up clearly when the challenge is being contested by council fire light, when they are painted, without removing the bark. Light colors such as white or yellow should be used at each end, with a 2- or 3-inch stripe of red, black, orange, or green in the middle of the stick so that each warrior or pair of warriors can identify the sticks. These color bands take the place of carved ownership marks.

To contest the challenge, two pairs of warriors, representing two different clans, stand side by side in front of the chair of the tribal chief. Each pair of warriors stands beside a strip of cloth or cardboard about 12 inches long and 2 inches wide, stapled to the ground. Four circles of cloth or cardboard 6 inches in diameter are stapled 1 long pace from the outer edge of the council fire area and at equal distance apart, as markers. These markers may be painted a light shade of yellow to represent "buckskin."

When the four warriors are in line and ready, the chief places a kick stick, each with a similar curve but different-colored stripe, before each warrior. He then shouts, "Kick!" and each warrior tries to kick his stick as quickly as possible around the outside edge of the council fire area, making his stick pass between each marker and the outer edge of the council fire area as he races around to the starting point. The curved stick is very difficult to kick in a straight line, and some of the sticks will have to be retrieved from under the feet of the warriors-in-council who sit in the front row, before the challengers can continue the race. Another amusing thing about this challenge is the difficulties the contestants run into as they meet at the various markers and each tries to be the first to kick his stick between the marker and the outside of the area, so that he may pass correctly and continue to the winning marker in front of the chief's chair. The first warrior to finish the race, still kicking his own stick, counts coup.

Another way to carry out this challenge when it is contested by two warriors from each of two clans is for the tribal chief to give only one stick to each pair of warriors, so that they have to kick and pass it between them around the area. The team which finishes first counts coup.

The author has seen KICK STICK turned into a warlike but amusing *mêlée* by six Indian boys who stood in three's, back to back, at one starting mark on one side of the council fire area. A chief gave each boy a differently marked stick. Markers were placed at four points around the area, fairly close to the outer edge;

then the chief gave the signal to start. The efforts made by these young Indians to be the first to run around the markers and the errors resulting from players kicking the wrong sticks caused much fun. The first boy to circle the area correctly won, but any player ending the challenge with a stick which was not his own was disqualified. This method of play can lead to much fun and excitement at a modern council fire.

Another and simple way to dispute this challenge when younger warriors are contestants is to have four or six warriors from four or six different clans start at a line marked on the ground at one end of the council fire area. Another line is plainly marked on the ground at the opposite end of the area. Three warriors stand on each of two sides of the council fire, and each has a stick placed directly in front of him. On the word "Kick!" each young warrior tries to kick his stick as quickly as possible to the line marked on the ground at the other end of the council fire area. The first warrior to finish the race with his own stick counts coup.

SIT POLE PULL

This game was played by men and boys of some of the Northwest Coast tribes, and a similar game is played by some Woodland tribes. As usual when a game is played in far-spread sections of the country, there are some variations in the form of play. However, amusement and challenge will be found in contesting it in any one of the following ways.

A stout, smooth pole 8 to 16 feet long and about 1½ inches in diameter is the only equipment needed. The length of the pole should be based on the number of contestants taking part. The pole is placed on the ground, and from three to six players sit along either side of it, at the opposite ends and as close to their end as possible. The clan team sit partly inside each other's legs, with the legs spread out for balance. The pole is held only with the right hand, and when in pulling position it is held at or just above waist level.

When the council fire chief cries, "Ready!" each team raises the pole into pull position and takes a firm grip on it, ready for the command to go into action. On the word "Pull!" each team tries to pull the other one toward it, without themselves giving ground. The game should be played on smooth ground when played outdoors, so that there is nothing to brace the feet against.

Various versions of this challenge can be carried out. The pulling may be done with only the left hands or with both hands, for example.

As a man-to-man challenge, two players, one on each end and on opposite sides of the pole, can contest SIT POLE PULL as an individual challenge.

CHALLENGE KICK BALL

Four warriors are chosen, two from each of two clans. They stand together at the chief's chair. The rival teams stand back to back at a strip of "buckskin" or a line marked on the ground. A blunt-top red-colored stake 15 inches long and 2 inches in diameter is driven into the ground at the center of the buckskin strip. Seven blunt-topped stakes painted light yellow, and also 15 inches long and 2 inches in diameter, are driven 3 inches into the ground around the council fire area 2 feet from the outer edge at the points shown in the drawing.

The tribal chief gives each team of two warriors a round blown-up bladder or a volleyball. He explains that when he says, "Kick!" each team, going in opposite direction to the team facing it, will kick the ball on or close to the ground, around each stake. The ball must be kept close to the stake, which must be touched once by the ball while being encircled. The seven stakes are circled in turn, each nearest stake being circled before a team goes on to the next one. The team whose ball is first kicked against the red stake beside the chief's chair, after it has correctly circled all of the other stakes, counts coup. Five stakes may be used in this challenge instead of seven when younger warriors contest.

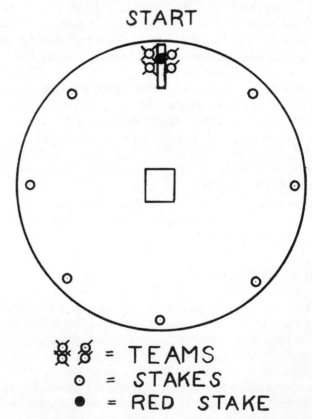

CHALLENGE KICK BALL is a challenge of some skill and some luck, but the team which passes and dribbles the ball best will most likely be the one to count coup. There will be moments of excitement and fun if the two teams meet at the same stake, or even when they pass each other between two stakes. Should one team's ball knock the other team's ball out of the council fire area during such encounters, no points are deducted from the team's score whose ball first bumped the one belonging to the other team. No warrior is allowed to kick or stop the ball belonging to the other team or to touch the ball of any team, including his own, with his hands.

An equally exciting and amusing way to carry out this challenge is to have both teams circle the council fire area in the same direction, from the red stake around the other stakes and back to the red stake, where the first team to arrive counts coup. Three warriors instead of two may play on each team if the chief so decides.

Cloth or cardboard markers may be used instead of stakes.

CRAB RUN

This is a challenge which will make even the wise men of the tribes smile. All that is required before the challengers are called to the council fire can be borrowed from the white campers' chief. Four volleyballs or balls of similar size are needed. Should such balls not be available, any sort of rubber balls about 4 or 5 inches in diameter can be used instead. Four paper plates or cardboard circles 6 inches in diameter, to be stapled to the ground as markers, complete the gear. The markers are placed at equal distance around the council fire area, each one being stapled 1 long pace away from the outer edge of the area. A line is marked on the ground for the start and finish point, or the place can be indicated by a strip of white cloth 6 feet long, placed halfway between any of the four markers and running from the outer edge of the council fire area toward the fire.

The chief calls on eight warriors, two from each of four rival clans. They are paired, and the pairs who race together are from the same clans. Two pairs stand on one side of the starting strip, facing two other pairs who stand on the opposite side of the strip. When the chief tells the warriors to prepare to run, they turn sideways, ready to run around the area sideways in opposite directions. Each pair of runners is given a well-inflated ball by the chief and told that they must race with it held between their shoulders, with only the pressure of their backs to hold it in place. Each two pairs run in opposite directions and must pass between the four markers and the outer edge of the area as they run around the circle.

On the command "Run!" which is given after the balls are in position, the pairs start out, crab fashion. When they reach the second marker, each pair will turn around, still holding the ball between their shoulders, so that the warriors who were on the inside of the area will be on the outside of the area, and the race will continue from the second marker in that manner. Should a ball fall at

any time during the race, it must be picked up and replaced in the shoulder position before the race is continued by the pair who dropped it.

When older warriors challenge, the chief asks the warriors to crab-run once completely around the circle in the first position described and turn, when the circle has been completed, to race for the second time around the area in the changed positions already described. This amusing challenge becomes even funnier as the challenging pairs meet at the various markers and try to be the first to pass between them and the outer rim of the council fire area.

This challenge can also be carried out in relay race fashion, with two to four pairs from each clan contesting. The second pair of warriors is touched off by the first pair, after they have completed the circle and turned the ball over to the next pair of crabs.

HOBBLED!

For this clan challenge, from one to three warriors from different clans line up in a straight line at one end of the council fire area. They face another line marked on the ground about 30 feet distant. When the chief says, "Ready!" each challenger bends forward and clasps the fingers of both hands behind his left thigh. Before starting this hobbled race, the chief tells the runners that they must run, or hobble, as fast as possible to the line opposite them, turn quickly, and then return from it with the fingers of both hands clasped behind both thighs. On the command "Go!" all the challengers set out for the second line, and the first one to arrive back at the starting point without having unclasped his fingers except when changing position, and without having stumbled or fallen during the double run, counts coup and wins.

This challenge can also be carried out as a clan relay race with three or six warriors on each team. Each warrior, as he finishes the double run, touches off the next, and this continues until each member of each team has completed the double run. The first clan team to finish correctly counts coup.

TUMBLEWEED

This an exciting challenge, which requires some skill on the part of the warriors who succeed in counting coup. The game from which this one was devised was played by the Indians of the Northwest Coast, who used the blown-up, round intestines of ocean mammals instead of balls. Adapted for a modern council fire challenge, the equipment required to play TUMBLEWEED includes eight round markers 9 inches in diameter, made of cloth or cardboard —for two or more clan teams—and three balls the size of volleyballs (the lighter in weight the better), one white and two brown, for each contesting clan. One marker is painted red, one yellow, and the rest white.

The start and finish point of this challenge is directly in front of the tribal chief's chair. The red marker is stapled in place 1 long pace (4 feet) opposite the chair. The yellow marker, which marks the halfway point, is stapled to the ground on the opposite side of the council fire area, directly facing the red marker, 1 long pace from the outer edge of the area. The six white markers are stapled to the ground at equal distance around the council fire area, between the red and yellow markers, also 1 long pace from the outer edge of the area. The diagram shows how these markers are laid out.

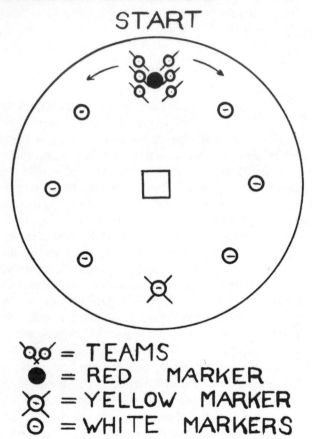

START

ᗐᗝ = TEAMS
● = RED MARKER
ᗐ = YELLOW MARKER
⊖ = WHITE MARKERS

At the start of this challenge, three warriors from one clan stand side by side 1 foot away from and directly in front of the red marker, facing away from it. Three warriors from a rival clan stand in the same positions on the opposite side of the red marker, also facing away from it. The two outside-position warriors of each clan are given a brown ball. Directly in front of each group of three warriors and 1 short pace away, a white or whitened ball is placed on the ground.

When the chief in charge of the challenge shouts, "Throw!" the warriors of each clan throw the brown balls, from a position between waist and chin level only, at the white ball, trying to drive it forward. It must be driven between the outside edge of the council fire area and the white markers, toward the finishing point, the

red marker. The balls must not be kicked in this challenge, and any warrior who does so causes his clan to be sent back one or two markers as a penalty, as decided by the chief. When a white ball passes between a boundary marker and the council fire, the clan to which it belongs must drive it back one white marker and start again from there as a penalty.

There is always excitement when the rival clans meet close to a marker as they travel around the council fire area in different directions. The clan which first drives its white ball onto the red marker counts coup.

Another way to carry out this challenge which is both amusing and confusing is for both clan teams to circle the council fire area in the same direction.

The warriors-in-council often get a chance to take part in TUMBLEWEED without leaving their places, because the brown balls often bounce out of the council fire area into the hands of the onlookers. A ball which goes among the warriors in this way should be thrown back into play *at once.*

Though the Indians use wooden stakes for most games such as TUMBLEWEED, cloth or cardboard markers are recommended here for maximum safety. While these markers are quite satisfactory, those chiefs who wish to duplicate Indian ways as closely as possible can substitute smooth, round stakes 15 inches long and tapering from 2 inches at the top to a point at the other end, which is driven about 8 inches into the ground. The risk in using stakes is that a warrior in the heat of a challenge might fall on one, or that a stake might be left in the ground after a challenge and become a menace later on, perhaps when a race is being run.

TUMBLEWEED DRIVE

This is a somewhat difficult but exciting challenge for older warriors. It is contested with the markers or stakes in exactly the same positions as for TUMBLEWEED, but there are two great differences in the way in which the challenge is contested. Only one brown ball is used by the three players from each contesting clan, and only one white ball is used for the two rival clans. At the start of this challenge, the two clans face each other at the starting point, standing just outside the red stake or marker, as shown in the diagram. The three warriors of each clan stand side by side and 1 long pace away from the three rival contestants. The white ball is placed on the ground directly between the rival groups, as shown in the diagram. The center warrior of each clan holds the brown ball belonging to his group. It can be made identifiable by pasting or painting a light-colored circle or square on it.

When the tribal chief shouts, "Throw!" each clan tries to drive the white ball by striking it with the brown ball, as each clan travels in *different directions* around the council fire area. The white ball must always be driven between the white markers and the outer edge of the area. It is the fact that each group is trying to drive the white ball in a different direction which adds greatly to the thrill and difficulty of this challenge. Skill, sharp-shooting, and split-second timing are required for one clan to drive the white ball against the red stake first. Since even with identifying patches it is difficult to tell in the heat of the contest which brown ball belongs to which three contestants, it is a good rule to let either clan use either ball, but neither clan must ever have two brown balls in its possession at the same time. The tribal chief should keep an alert eye on both clans to see that

START

◐◑ = TEAMS
● = RED MARKER
⊗ = YELLOW MARKER
⊖ = WHITE MARKERS
⊙ = WHITE BALL

this rule is carried out, and he may penalize the group which uses both brown balls at the same time.

In such a fast-moving challenge, a few rules are needed to assure the progress of the contest and fair play for both clans. The feet must not be used to *kick* any one of the three balls used, and feet must never be used to stop a rival clan's ball from striking the white ball. Feet may be used when necessary by either clan to stop its ball from going out of the council fire area. One of the most exciting features of this challenge is that either clan may throw its ball directly at the brown ball of the opposing clan, in order to drive it away from the white ball. This

may be tried even while the ball of the rival is in the air. Such tactics may backfire, even when the thrower is a good shot, and more harm than good may come from the overuse of such attempted sharpshooting. It does add to the excitement, however. Any clan warrior kicking, or even accidentally displacing, the white ball with his foot causes his clan to be sent back one or two white stakes, as decided by the chief, before returning to the attack. The chief replaces the ball in the position in which it lay before it was kicked or displaced. Since the clan which was not penalized may continue the throwing while the rival clan is going back to and returning from the stake to which it was sent as a penalty, the few seconds of un-opposed play may decide which clan counts coup and wins.

PUFF BALL KICK

This challenge is played somewhat in the manner of TUMBLEWEED, but the fact that the ball is *kicked* instead of thrown makes it an entirely different sort of contest. The markers or stakes are put in the same positions as for TUMBLEWEED DRIVE, and as in that challenge, only one brown ball is used by each group of three challengers; but each clan has also a white ball. Each clan drives its white ball around the markers in the opposite direction from that taken by the rival clan, and each clan must work out its own strategy so that a kicked ball does not get out of control by going too far after missing the white ball. The three warriors in each clan must also decide when a pass is best, instead of an attempted kick at the brown ball so that it will drive the white ball forward. This move is made when one of the three warriors, to whom the ball is passed, is in a better position to kick directly than the warrior who had the ball. The use of hands is not permitted in this challenge, and a warrior who touches the ball intentionally with a hand or hands should be ruled out of the challenge for a brief time as a penalty. When a warrior, in the excitement of the challenge, kicks the white ball in error, the chief returns it to where it was before being kicked, and the clan who kicked it must kick their brown ball back either one or two white stakes, as ruled by the tribal chief, before aiming for the white ball again.

With a little practice this challenge can be contested very skillfully, and one clan may even count coup at the red marker before the other clan has passed more than two white stakes on the way toward its goal.

TRIPLE BALL DRIVE

For this challenge three small balls about the size of tennis balls are placed in a triangle, 18 inches apart, inside a 30-inch circle which is marked on the ground.

These three balls should be colored white to assure their easy visibility. Two teams of three players in each, chosen from rival clans, contest in the following way.

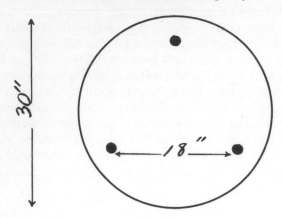

Each team stands directly behind a line marked on the ground directly opposite the 2-foot circle and from 10 to 15 feet distant from it. The chief gives each team a large ball, such as a volleyball or basketball; when he shouts, "Throw!" each team, using only the overhead toss, tries to drive the small balls out of the circle. Displacing a ball does not score unless the ball displaced is knocked or rolls outside the circle. The contestants on each team take turns at throwing the ball, and each team uses either of the two balls which comes close enough to them to be picked up easily. The clan team which drives the most balls out of the circle first counts coup and wins, but the challenge does not end until all three balls have been driven from the circle. This challenge should be decided on a best-out-of-three-tries basis. The chief may decide that all warriors must toss the ball from an in-front-of-the-face position instead of from the overhead position, as a variation, either for all three tries or for one or more of them.

just above either ankle. He is blindfolded and, from the tribal chief's chair, starts his silent circling of the council fire area. Three warriors from a rival clan are posted an equal distance apart around the outer edge of the council fire area, facing the fire. They are blindfolded and told that the belled warrior is going to try to steal past them without being caught. They are not told the direction in which he will travel. They should be able to detect his approach by the tinkle of the bells. Each warrior in ambush must try to make the capture alone and counts coup only if he manages to catch the belled warrior in his quarter of the circle. The diagram shows just how the circle is divided into four quarter segments, and the positions of the warriors at the start of the challenge. If the belled warrior can return safety to any part of his quarter of the circle he is safe and counts coup.

The chief starts the challenge with the shout of "On trail!" and the warriors-in-council should remain as quiet as possible while the belled warrior circles the circle. It is important that the warriors be told just before the challenge begins that all of them must stop moving *immediately* when the chief shouts "Stop!" This prevents a warrior from going too close to the council fire or walking into the warriors-in-council if he loses sense of direction. This should not happen when the challenge is contested by older warriors or those having some trail-craft skills, as the sound and heat from the council fire and even a slight movement or whisper from a warrior-in-council should indicate his position with fair accuracy. When the chief calls, "Stop!" another chief, who can move silently in soft-soled moccasins, steers the warrior or warriors out of possible danger, after which the chief recommences the challenge with the shout of "On trail!"

The warrior chosen to circle the council fire area unmolested should be sufficiently experienced to be able to sense his way around by the sound and warmth of the

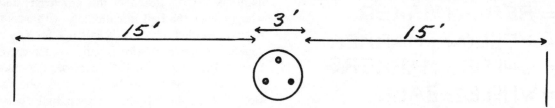

TRIPLE BALL DRIVE can be contested on both sides of the council fire simultaneously, and the winning team from each side of the council fire competes for the championship. This challenge is a simple form of TUMBLE-WEED DRIVE but requires less skill, so it can be contested by younger warriors without difficulty.

DANCE BELL AMBUSH

The warrior chosen to try to evade ambush wears one or two dance bells suspended from a thong or cord tied

council fire and the slight noises made by the warriors watching. He should be told to try to keep a safe distance between the fire and himself but, of course, cannot be asked to travel around the circle in any fixed line, since there would be no elements of surprise and suspense when the challenge is carried out a second time. The warriors who try to ambush and catch the belled warrior must be told not to start their stalk to cut him off and catch him until they *actually hear* the bells as he draws near. Naturally, the warrior trying to evade ambush is listening keenly for the slightest sound which will betray the approach of an ambusher, who is not wearing bells to betray him. With a clean council fire area, only Fenimore Cooper could conjure up the ubiquitous twig to betray either the hunted or the hunters! The chief in charge of the challenge should be certain, by advance trials, that the bell or bells worn are neither too loud nor too soft-

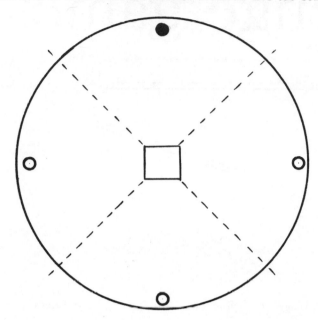

● = BELLED-WARRIOR
○ = STALKERS

toned, as either characteristic can spoil an otherwise thrilling challenge. The contestants should be taught to rely on stealth of movement and the ability to outthink their rival while contesting this challenge. Sudden rushes should be discouraged, because of the danger of collision; quick, silent advances should be suggested as a substitute.

DANCE BELL AMBUSH is a thrilling, suspenseful challenge when it is cleverly contested. On one occasion, there was wonder and enthusiasm when a group of teenage warriors-in-council watched a full-blooded, blindfolded Seneca *twice* circle the council fire area, avoiding capture in what appeared to be an almost superhuman manner, as six white "chiefs" posted around the council fire area at points unknown to the Seneca failed to intercept him. The Indian wore an anklet on each leg with four dewclaws suspended from each. These deer-hoof rattles made a pleasant ringing-tinkling sound as he lithely moved around the council fire area. His evasion tactics differed to meet each critical situation. When he heard, or more likely sensed, a would-be interceptor silently stalking him, he would "freeze" instantly, sometimes in a crouching position. When the hunter had

passed, often with a hand and arm fanning the air directly above the head of the motionless Indian, the Seneca would steal forward on noiseless feet, apparently leaving the sound of the dew claws rattling behind him. At another point, judging exactly his opponent's position, the Seneca stopped. One leg was lifted and extended noiselessly with the foot far behind him. Suddenly, the foot quivered and shook. A rattling sound, magnified many times by the absolute silence of the chiefs and warriors-in-council, came from the tinkling dewclaws. The ambusher sprang in the direction of the evasive sound. Instantly it was gone—so was the Seneca!

FIRE TENDER

A brave, representing the tender of the fire, sits cross-legged on the ground close to the chief's chair. Directly in front of him are three sticks, painted white so that they will be more visible, 12 inches long and about 1½ inches thick. The ends do not quite touch his crossed legs, and the sticks point away from him, as in the sketch. The wood gatherer stands five paces in front of him behind a marker, such as a white feather placed on the ground.

The chief blindfolds the fire tender, leaving his ears uncovered, and gives the signal "Guard!" At once the wood gatherer advances as silently as possible, either erect or on hands and knees, in an attempt to take one stick without being caught. The fire tender must sit with his hands on his legs. He reaches out swiftly only when a noise close at hand warns him that his sticks are in danger of being taken, and he can grope above the sticks while he believes they are still being reached for by the wood gatherer. In order to be caught and lose the coup, the wood gatherer must be seized and held by the hand or arm, not just tagged.

The wood gatherer may use any ruse he wishes, such as creeping past the fire tender and trying to snatch a stick from over his shoulder. He may strike the ground on one side of the sticks with his hand to distract the fire tender's attention and then seize a stick from the opposite side. He must not use a stick or throw anything in order to deceive the fire tender. The sticks must be taken one at a time only. After each coup in which a stick is taken, it must be carried back to the wood gatherer's marker before he tries to secure another stick.

As a tribal challenge this makes an interesting contest. Three different braves, each in the role of wood gatherer, may take one turn each at taking a stick from the fire tender, who belongs to another tribe. In turn, three braves from the fire tender's tribe have a chance at trying to take the sticks from a rival fire tender. The tribe which has made the best showing counts coup.

chapter 10
indian challenge games

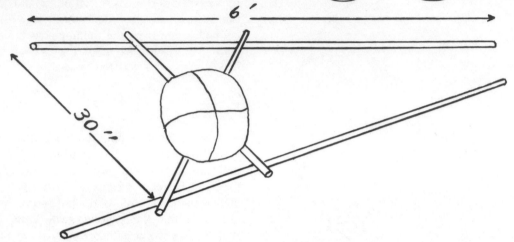

THE LIGHTER SIDE of Indian challenges and games is stressed in this chapter. Indians of all ages are quite willing to be amused, and even the oldest and most reserved chief will enjoy a laugh as the challengers meet in some of the amusing contests which follow.

BEAR CAVE CHIEF

This is an amusing rough-and-tumble challenge which should be contested by warriors of about the same weight. The only equipment required is four wooden hoops about 2 feet in diameter. The hoops may be 2 inches less in diameter but not more than 2 inches larger.

This challenge is adapted from one contested by Indian boys on the Northwest Coast, enacting a race between two or more bears to take possession of a cave. The four hoops represent four caves. Two warriors, from different clans, contest each challenge. The four hoops are held upright with one side on the ground, each hoop being held in place by a warrior or clan chief. One hoop is held on each of four sides of the council fire, halfway between the fire and the first row of warriors-in-council. One rim of the hoop faces the fire, and the other rim faces the onlookers. These four hoops should be placed approximately the same distance apart. A marker, which can be a white paper plate, is placed halfway between any two hoops as the starting point. The two warriors, on all fours, wait for the signal to start. They both face in the same direction, one warrior on each side of the marker.

When the tribal chief shouts, "Search!" both bears crawl as fast as they can toward the first hoop. Should both bears reach the hoop—which represents a cave entrance—at the same time, then the fun begins. Each bear should try to shoulder the other one out of the way in order to crawl through the hoop first. Once a bear has his head inside the hoop, he is permitted to creep through it without being bothered further by his opponent. The other bear follows after him as quickly as possible and tries to reach the second hoop ahead of his rival, or at least at the same time. The contest continues until the warrior-bear who will be the winner is the first to crawl through the fourth and last cave entrance and up to the marker from which he started. There he counts coup.

Three or four bears, instead of two, can race in the same way over the same course, causing more fun and much more shouldering. Each bear is on his own.

When four bears, on two teams, contest this challenge in relay fashion, the second bear of a team starts for the first hoop just as soon as his bear teammate returns to the starting marker. In this way each bear on the team touches off his teammate until every bear has gone through all four hoops and returned to the starting point.

Another fun-provoking way to carry out this challenge is to have two rival bears start from the marker on the command "Search!"—each bear traveling in the *opposite* direction. Not only speed but also the points where the bears meet as they circle the council fire area and pass each other en route, will decide which bear finally counts coup. If the bears pass each other between cave entrances, there will be no clash at the cave, and speed may decide the race; but if the bears meet head on at a hoop, they may push head on to see which can force the right of way. The bear who first gets his head through the hoop wins right of way, and his rival must withdraw and let him crawl through first.

Of course, bears in search of caves are often not too even-tempered, and there is no rule which keeps one bear from going after the other and shouldering him around a bit, in order to slow him down, when they meet at any point between the hoops. The clan chiefs who hold the hoops should see that neither bear uses hands or feet in the scuffles at any point. All pushing must be done with the shoulders except where there is a head-on meeting in the mouth of a cave.

No rules prohibit growling as the bears clash, and this can add considerably to the fun.

KIWA TRAIL

Kiwa means "crooked," and warriors will find that this challenge is built around a trail which is "crooked" in any language! Required for this contest are five round markers of white cardboard, 6 inches in diameter, for each individual challenger or clan. A trail is laid by placing these markers about 1 pace apart in a straight line from one end of the council fire area to the other. The challenge can be carried out on one or two sides of the council fire. There is a separate line of markers for each individual player or clan, and the lines should be about 1 pace apart. There should be a space of about the same width outside the line closest to the council fire, and also outside the line nearest the onlookers. There should be ample space for two or three lanes of markers on each of two sides of the council fire.

One of the simplest ways of carrying out this challenge is as follows. A warrior from each contesting clan stands behind the first marker in each line, when the tribal chief has decided which is the starting end. On the word "Go!" each warrior must run completely around the first marker, in any direction but keeping as close to it as possible without touching it, and then continue around each of the other four markers to the end. Should a warrior touch any marker with a foot, he is sent back one marker. He need not circle it, but continues from it. The challenger who first circles all the markers correctly, counts coup.

Another version of this contest is to have two warriors from the same clan posted, one behind each end marker of a lane. Challengers from other clans take up similar positions in the other lanes of markers. When the tribal chief says, "Go!" each warrior behind the starting marker circles it, then continues on around each marker until he reaches and circles the last marker in the lane. Here the second warrior starts up the line, circling each marker until he stands behind the last one, which

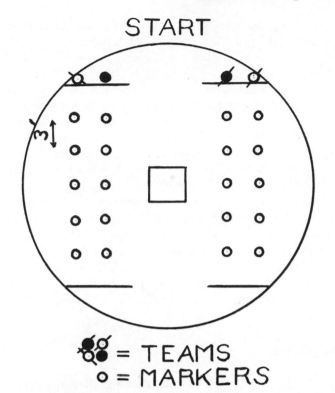

START

$\bigcirc\!\!\bigcirc$ = TEAMS

$\circ$ = MARKERS

was originally the starting marker. The team of two warriors which finishes first counts coup for its team and clan.

The most exciting way of all of contesting this challenge is to have three or four warriors from the same clan stationed in single file, one behind the other, facing the line of markers. Warriors from other clans take up similar positions on the other lanes of markers. When the tribal chief commands, "Go!" the first warrior in each line circles the first marker and continues to circle the other markers, going around in any direction he likes, until he circles the last marker. Then, and only then, the second warrior in line begins to follow the "crooked trail." When he has completed its windings, the next warrior in line starts, and the challenge continues until each warrior has covered the trail. The group of warriors which finishes first, counts coup for its clan.

Tribal chiefs can turn this challenge into a riot of fun by ordering all warriors to circle all markers in the same direction. Many warriors will become so giddy that it will be difficult for them to reach the end of the trail. While staggering warriors will provide laughs for the onlookers, it is a wise precaution to post a husky clan chief on each side of the council fire when the challenge is carried out in this way.

SEA LION SLAP

This is an amusing challenge, to be contested by six to ten warriors from different clans or by several warriors from the same clan. Those taking part lie flat on their stomachs on the ground, facing the warriors-in-council. There should be several contestants on each side of the fire, so that all in council may have a clear view. When the chief in charge says, "Ready!" all those contesting immediately take up the position of hands and toes resting squarely on the ground, with the body bridged and rigid, as though they were going to do push-ups. On the word "Go!" each warrior touches his head with his right hand, returns the right hand to the ground, touches his head with his left hand, replaces the left hand on the ground, and finally slaps both hands together as loudly as possible, replacing them most speedily on the ground, to avoid collapse of the bridge! Each contestant who can, tries to carry out these three movements as fast as possible while the chief counts, fairly fast, up to 20. The warrior most often carrying out this difficult feat correctly counts coup. Perhaps some chiefs will have to leave the slap part out!

SCALPS

This is a fast, skillful, and exciting challenge which can be contested by two to eight braves at the same time, either with one brave pitted against another or as a tribal challenge. In the latter case, three or four braves from one tribe contest against the same number from another tribe. The competing warriors are chosen either by the chief in charge or by one brave, clan, or tribe challenging members of another group.

At the start of the challenge, each pair of opponents face each other 6 feet apart. A strip of cloth or crepe paper about 12 inches long and 2 or 3 inches wide is tucked under the belt or breechclout so that it hangs down about 9 inches. These "scalps" can also be pinned on with small safety pins. They should all hang down the same distance; the strips can be of varying colors, or a different color can be used for each clan.

When the chief shouts, "Attack!" each brave tries to snatch the other's scalp. This should be done by the speedy circling of an opponent, clever footwork, and deceptive feinting, which generally decide the outcome of the challenge. Braves may spar as in boxing, but with open hands only, in order to hold an opponent off; but they must not hold, strike, push, or trip during the contest or they are immediately disqualified. This challenge is best decided on a two-out-of-three-wins basis.

Individuals and groups can contest inside a circle, the size of which is based on the number participating in the challenge at the same time.

Size or weight is not very important in this contest, and amusing results are usually derived from the most unevenly assorted pairs—such as when a three-and-a-half-foot-high challenger defeats his five-foot-ten opponent.

SCALPS makes an exciting free-for-all challenge when four or six members of one clan contest against the same number from another clan. In such a mêlée, each side wears differently colored scalps, and the members of each clan are not paired one against another but are free to snatch any scalp of any member of the opposing clan. The first clan to capture all of the scalps of the rival clan is the winner and counts coup. When the challenge is carried out in this way, it should be well supervised by at least two chiefs, in order to eliminate rough tactics.

COUP STROKE

This is a fast and exciting challenge game which is best played by older braves. Dodging, strategy, and speed are necessary in order to count coup, and it is an interesting game to watch when good players are in action. The only equipment required is two or three fully inflated volleyballs or basketballs and four white circular disks to be stapled to the ground as markers. Six or nine braves can take part in the challenge at the same time. The drawing shows the line-up when the game is contested by nine braves, but the setup is unchanged when only six braves take part. The three braves stand *on* the starting line facing in either direction, as they can run in either direction around the council fire area, all going one way or two running one way and the other in the opposite direction in order to throw their opponents off balance. The three attackers on each of two sides of the council fire can move anywhere between the two markers shown in the drawing, but if they go outside the lane shown by dotted lines in the diagram they are disqualified and must leave the council ring. They may attack as a trio or individually. The latter form of attack usually gets the best results. The ball carriers too have, perhaps, more chance when they work as lone braves instead of bunching together. Before the challenge begins, the chief warns the players to be on a constant alert in order to avoid possible collision.

At the start of the challenge the braves take up their positions as shown in the drawing, and the three ball bearers on the starting line are each given a volleyball. They hold it tightly between the *palms* of their hands, one hand on either side of the ball, arms half extended in front, and the hands held about waist level. During the challenge the ball bearers may turn, twist, and dodge; the ball may be moved to either side, extended, or lowered, in order to protect it from attack, but it must not be raised above shoulder level at any time.

To start the challenge the chief shouts, "Attack!" and the ball bearers start out in an endeavor to circle the council ring and pass safely through the two sets of attackers without having the ball struck from between

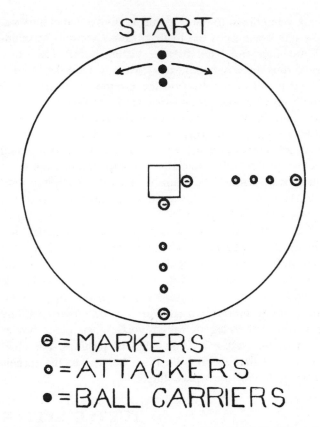

START

⊖ = MARKERS
◦ = ATTACKERS
● = BALL CARRIERS

their hands. The attackers must strike the ball only with the palm of either hand, with either a downward or upward stroke. Only one hand at a time must be used to strike the ball. If an attacker strikes a ball bearer on an arm at any point above the wrist, he is ruled out of the game. When a ball has been correctly driven from between the hands of a brave, he leaves the ring at once and his attacker counts coup. Should two ball bearers avoid attack and arrive back at the starting point, they count coup, but if only one arrives back without mishap the attackers count coup. Grand coup can only be counted when all ball carriers return safely to the starting point, and the attackers can count grand coup when they succeed in striking all balls from the hands of the ball bearers.

The chief may modify this challenge in various ways, especially to suit younger braves. One way to do so is to make the area of attack only between the two markers at the opposite end from the start, thus eliminating the second attack; or only two attackers can be used to oppose three ball bearers. Attackers and ball bearers should be fairly evenly matched both in size and weight to assure a fast, tricky challenge of interest to both participants and onlookers.

GRIZZLY GUARDIAN

This is a challenge where a warrior, aided by a "grizzly bear," guards six feathers against raids by four warriors

of another clan. The warrior who is chosen to guard the feathers stands a few feet away from the council fire with his back toward it. The warrior who plays the part of the grizzly squats close beside him. One end of a white rope leash 15 feet long is attached to the back of a belt around the grizzly's waist, and the warrior holds the other end. The feathers used in this challenge should be about 7 inches long. Two paces in front of the warrior the six feathers are laid side by side about 8 inches apart, in a semicircle. The feathers are placed so that the quill ends point toward the warrior.

The four warriors chosen to carry off the feathers may start from any point of the council fire area and attack singly or in pairs. A raiding warrior may pick up as many feathers as he can but must secure each one singly in a separate attack. The warrior with the bear remains on the same spot throughout the entire challenge, but he may warn and direct his bear when he thinks it will prove helpful in protecting the feathers. The bear puts the attacking warriors out of the challenge by striking them with the palm of either hand. The grizzly may charge the warriors at any time when they are within reach, whether they are approaching the feathers or in the act of picking them up. Any warrior struck by the bear leaves the council fire area, and if he has been hit just as he has picked up or is picking up a feather he must replace it before leaving the circle.

The attacking warriors win if they manage to get all six feathers, even though only one warrior is still in action at the end of the challenge. The defending warrior and grizzly win when all attacking warriors are put out of commission before they can carry off all the feathers.

This challenge may be carried out in various ways. Two or three warriors, instead of four, may do the raiding. The warrior with the bear may also be allowed to put attacking warriors out of the challenge by touching them only with the hand which is not holding the leash of the bear.

MAMOOK KOPET (STOP!)

This dance challenge is a high-stepping, jumping dance game which is contested around some council fires on the Northwest Coast. A drummer is seated just outside of the council fire area or behind a blanket rigged up beside the chief's chair. With hardwood sticks, he beats a skin-topped drum or a small hardwood board. From two to six dancers of each clan stand in a wide circle around the council fire, about a long pace apart. They all face in the same direction. When the tribal chief shouts, "Dance!" the drummer begins to beat out a fairly fast time and the dancers step or jump, or do both alternately, clockwise around the council fire. They try to keep in time with the rhythm and are supposed to stop instantly when the drum stops abruptly. The drummer tries to trick the dancers into stopping at the wrong time, by slowing down and then increasing the tempo, or by sudden and unexpected stops. He must keep in mind that even a slight pause may rightly be considered a stop by the dancers, and the tribal chief considers this while judging the contest. All dancers who do not "freeze" instantly when the drum stops, leave the council fire area immediately.

The tribal chief, with whatever help he needs from one or two clan chiefs whose warriors are not contesting, must be constantly on the alert to see that the dancers observe the rules of the challenge. He may start the dancers again after each *Stop!* with the command "Dance!" or may leave that to the judgment of the drummer, if the latter is stationed so that he can see the dancers without being seen. Some tribes are careful to have the drummer play out of sight of the dancers, while others carry out the contest with the drummer in full view, seated near the chief's chair. It makes little difference in the end result of the challenge.

TRAVOIS RACE

This amusing and exciting race teaches contesting braves something about travois construction and knot tying, while providing fun for the onlookers. The equipment required includes: two straight poles about 7 feet long and 2 inches in diameter at the butt end; two straight sticks about 30 inches long and 1 inch thick; a blanket stuffed with grass or leaves and tied into a roundish bundle; and five lengths of thick cord or thin rope, four of them about 16 inches long and the fifth 5 feet long. This gear is needed for each team of two braves.

A straight line is marked on the ground directly opposite the chief's seat, and the gear for each team is placed in a separate pile, one on each side of the line. A team stands on each side of the line beside its gear. Once the travois is assembled and the gear fastened to the crosspieces, each team will race around the council fire ring back to the starting point.

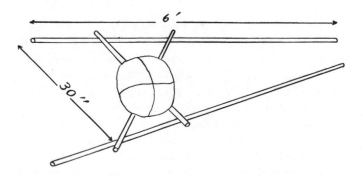

On the "Go!" signal, both braves on each team start building the simple travois, as illustrated, then tie the blanket-bundle onto the crosspieces. Once that is finished, only one brave pulls the loaded travois around the council fire area and back to the starting point. The other brave runs directly behind the travois to retie the bundle, should it fall off or drag on the ground. The moment a bundle touches the ground or slips from the crosspieces, the brave in the rear must seize the travois and hold it back, calling to the travois puller to stop. The travois must not move forward while the bundle is being tied back in place. Only when this is completed can the team run forward again. The team to reach the finish line first, with the bundle firmly lashed to and riding on top of the crosspieces, counts coup.

The chief warns both teams before the race starts that they must take great care when passing each other at some point during the circuit of the council fire area. It is well to staple four circular white markers, one on each side of the council fire area and 3 feet from the fire, to indicate a safety margin which must not be entered by any brave nor either leg of the travois. When older braves compete, who have a knowledge of lashings, the chief may decide that the bundle must be tied to the travois crosspieces with the squaw hitch.

TURTLE KEEPER

This is an amusing clan challenge which is carried out by four warriors of one clan contesting against a senior warrior or chief of a different clan. Two clans may challenge at the same time, each using one side of the council fire area. Each group of four turtles and a turtle keeper takes up a spread-out position on one side of the council fire, the turtle keeper standing 3 paces away from the nearest turtle in his group.

When the tribal chief calls, "Catch!" the turtle keeper must try to touch all four turtles on his side of the fire as quickly as possible. This is not too easily done, as any turtle in danger of being touched may avoid capture by dropping to the ground, turning on his back and raising his arms and legs in the air. He is safe while in this position but must not remain in it longer than for a slow count up to 6, which each turtle makes for himself. Should the turtle keeper decide not to chase another turtle after the one he is chasing has turned on his back, he can stop 3 strides away from the upturned turtle, count up to 6 slowly, and then resume the chase. All turtles touched must leave the area just as soon as they are touched. The clan counts coup which has even one turtle remaining after all the turtles of the opposing clan have been caught. A variety of this challenge, which is especially useful for small council fire areas where the turtles have not much space for running and dodging, is for the turtle keeper to be told to hop on one or both legs while chasing.

An even harder version, for the turtle keeper, is for the

turtles to be able to free a brother turtle who has been caught by touching him before he can leave the council fire area. The turtle who has been touched must not run toward a free turtle in order to be touched and freed but must proceed out of the council fire area trusting that a keen-eyed and speedy turtle will touch him on the way out.

This challenge may be carried out with as few as two and as many as five turtles in each clan's group. In order to assure as much space as possible, each group can use one entire side and half of each end of the council fire area.

TWIN FROG RACE

This is an amusing challenge contested by teams of two or more braves from rival clans. A starting line, or a starting point indicated by two markers, is drawn on the ground directly in front of the chief's chair. Four large paper-plate markers should be stapled to the ground an equal distance apart around the council ring, each marker 4 feet from the outer edge. A finish line is marked on the ground directly opposite the starting point, on the other side of the ring.

Each team of two braves stands one behind the other, the toes of the leading player just touching the starting line. Two teams contest the event, and they stand 3 feet apart. When the chief in charge of the race says, "Get Ready!" each team squats, and the warrior in the rear places his hands firmly on the shoulders of the brave in front. When the chief shouts, "Go!" each team hops off in the squat position, which must be maintained throughout the race, to the line or marker at the opposite end of the council ring, keeping *between* the markers and the outer edge of the council fire circle en route. When the second line is reached, the brave in front makes a "back," as for leapfrog, and the teammate behind, resting his hands on the back, leapfrogs over him. Then both turn around quickly and change places, squatting as before, *except* that the boy who was behind now hops in front of his partner, leading the hop back to the starting point in the tandem hop-squat position. The first pair to finish correctly counts coup.

For added fun, two or four rival teams can start back to back at the starting line and race *entirely around* the council ring, changing places as before at the halfway mark and continuing around to the starting point. The most amusing moments—especially with four teams racing, two in opposite directions—occur when the rival teams racing around the circle meet at the markers on the way.

TRIPLE FROG RACE

To greatly increase the difficulty and add to the merriment of the preceding race, it is only necessary to add a third frog! The difficulty arises as the three team members try to hop and advance in unison. In this form of the race it is better to have the teams hop completely around the circle, without changing positions at the halfway mark. Of course, style as well as speed should count.

BEAVER BALL

This is an amusing game, which can be played on two sides of the council fire simultaneously, as the braves seated in council often become participants. The name is taken from the fact that Indian youngsters used to bounce soft rawhide balls off beaver and wolf pelts when they

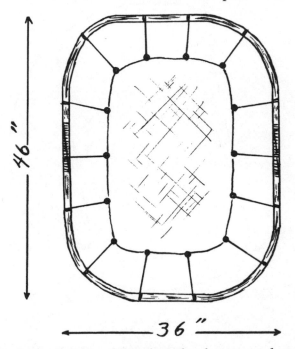

were hung up on oval or triangular frames to dry. The players tried to catch the ball on the rebound or see how far the ball could be made to bounce after striking the pelt. The latter form of play is not recommended for council fires. A little typical Indiancraft work is required in order to make the necessary equipment, and the following things are needed: an oval of strong canvas measuring about 30 by 20 inches; and a stout oval or oblong frame, 46 by 36 inches. This frame can be made from two stout, supple saplings, each about 8 feet long and approximately 1¼ inches in diameter, bent, overlapped, and lashed in the center, as shown in the drawing. The finished oval should be large enough to allow a space of 8 inches all around between the canvas oval and the frame when the canvas is strung in place. The necessary gear will include: two stout, straight poles each about 4 feet long; two strong, pointed stakes each 10 inches long; fourteen pieces of strong cord each about 24 inches long; and fourteen strong metal rings about ¾ or 1 inch in diameter. A well-inflated volleyball is the best sort of ball for council ring use, though the Indians used balls of about the size of tennis balls. Once the frame is made, the rings are sewn strongly around the canvas oval at the fourteen points shown in the drawing. One end of a piece of cord is then passed through each ring, and the two ends are tightened and tied fast around the frame directly opposite each ring. Shallow notches can be cut into the frame to assure these cords remaining in place if the clove hitch or a similar knot is not used. These cords must be loosened or tightened a little, as required, while stringing the canvas in place, in order to hold it taut and at about the same distance from the frame all around. The frame is now ready to be set up.

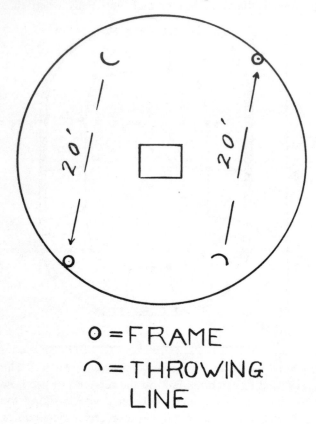

O = FRAME

∩ = THROWING LINE

A frame, with the oval of canvas in place, can be set up on any one side of the council ring, as illustrated. When the frame is in position, close to the edge of the council ring, each of the two sharpened stakes is driven firmly into the ground just behind and on each side of the frame. The frame is then firmly attached by a strong cord to each stake. The two poles are tightly lashed, one on either side of the frame, at the top with the long ends pointing backward. These poles balance and steady the frame, holding it in place like the legs of an easel, and they are set further back or further forward to increase or decrease the slant of the frame, in order to secure the best angle of bounce when the ball strikes the canvas oval. The ends of these poles may be sharpened and pushed slightly into the ground, both at the same angle, in order to hold the frame perfectly steady. The slant of the canvas, once the poles are in place, decides how the ball will rebound, and it is interesting to experiment with various angles to assure the exact type of rebound desired. The ball will bounce fairly directly back or rebound high into the air, according to the angle at which the frame is set. Balls thrown to hit the center of the canvas bounce best. A semicircular throwing line is marked 20 feet from each target, as illustrated.

Two or three players from each tribe contest, a player from the rival team throwing the ball against the canvas target from just behind and between two players, either or both of whom attempt to catch it on the rebound. The thrower must throw the ball as accurately and fairly as possible or, as often happened, an impartial chief throws the ball for each of the two rival teams. The ball must rebound to or over the throwing line before it may be caught. As the throwing distance is rather limited in a smaller council ring, where a 20-foot throw is about the limit, the ball can be bounced on the target by an overhead or face level two-handed toss. Another method of play is to have each member of each team take turns at throwing the ball. There is room for two teams with two braves in each to contest from just behind the slightly curved throwing line, each brave bouncing the ball in turn; or older players can play one against another using a one-bounce-each method, each trying to catch the ball on each rebound.

This challenge can be decided either by letting the members of each team strive to catch the rebounds or by having each team do the catching separately, the team making the highest number of consecutive catches up to twenty, for example, counting coup. The non-participating braves seated in council frequently have the chance of making catches in this game, when balls that bounce too hard fly out of the ring or when an occasional ball misses the target. Two complete sets of equipment in use simultaneously in the ring add to the fun.

chapter 11

I challenge!
indian man-to-man
challenges

INDIANS APPRECIATED INDIVIDUAL SKILL, speed, and dexterity as well as the clan and tribal contests which displayed mass skills. That is why old and young alike were always ready to match their ability in individual challenges and why an interested group of spectators was always on hand to encourage the braves in action.

OVER

This is a wrestle challenge which Indian boys often contested when they found the simple equipment required —a suitable piece of stick.

The two contestants lie flat on the ground on their stomachs facing each other, with their legs stretched out behind them, points of toes resting on the ground, and their elbows supporting the upper parts of their bodies. The left elbow of one warrior and the left elbow of his opponent should touch. The chief gives each pair of braves a strong, straight stick 24 inches long and from 1 to 1½ inches thick. The stick is held quite close to one end by the right hand of each warrior, while his left hand also grasps the stick firmly just beyond the center, as shown in the drawing. The left hand being close to the middle of the stick helps each warrior to exert the required pressure to turn his opponent over onto his side, if he can, which is the object of the challenge. Each brave sees the backs of his own hands.

The chief says, "Ready!" in order to allow the warriors to get the correct hold on the stick and brace themselves for instant action. On the command "Attack!" each brave, without changing his position and while keeping his elbows bent, tries by leverage on the stick to turn his rival over onto his side. This is not too easy a feat to perform, as the other brave exerts pressure not only to offset his opponent's efforts but also to turn him over on his side if he can.

A little practice will help the contestants to develop the fine points of this challenge, in which wiles and bluff are more important than strength at times. For instance, a brave pretends to be exerting all his efforts in an endeavor to force his rival onto his *left* side, and then swiftly and unexpectedly changes his push or pull so that his opponent is easily forced onto the *right* side, partly because of his rival's resistance to the pressure which was forcing him toward the left.

This challenge may be made more difficult by allowing the contestants to spread out on the ground with the toes pointing outward and heels almost touching, as in this position each warrior can exert a greater strength of resistance. Challenges such as this can be contested on four sides of the council fire at the same time.

SKUNK!

For this challenge, the chief has the braves prepare four "skunk skins." These are actually four pieces of strong white cloth cut to look like skunk pelts. These dummy skins should be about 20 inches long and 7 inches wide, without tail or legs. Black paint or stain should be used to give these "skins" the characteristic skunk markings.

One skin is placed on each side of the council ring, halfway between the fire and the first row of braves. The chief chooses four braves. One stands in front of each skunk, facing the warriors in the council ring. One of these braves challenges for all four. He shouts, "If there are four warriors in council who fear not to tread on a skunk, let them come forth. Should these braves be very strong, it is we of the Blackfeet who will return to our lodges holding our noses. Then our women will smile and say, 'Our men have been in the violet patch playing with the Silver Spots (butterflies).' "

When four braves who are willing to risk the laughter of their women have been found, the chief pairs them off with the four challengers. He places each pair four feet away from a skunk skin. He tells them that each brave must try to force or wrestle the other onto a skunk. Each brave who touches a skunk with any part of his arm, leg, or body loses the coup. The chief then gives the signal "Attack."

This challenge may be fought out in a less strenuous way by having each pair of braves place his hands on the other's shoulders. They then try to push each other onto a skunk, always using the shoulder grip. But the free-for-all wrestle method, so dear to the hearts of the young men of the Six Nations, provides more excitement.

SLIP STICK

This challenge was contested by the boys and men of some of the tribes of the Northwest Coast. It required a strong wrist and fingers, but a little know-how helped. Each two challengers required a round, entirely smooth stick about 18 inches long and 1½ to 2 inches in diameter, but a stick 1 inch in diameter will prove thick enough for council fire challenges, provided it is of hard wood. The stick must be perfectly smooth, so that there are no splinters to injure the hands of the contestants. Once the Indians of the Northwest Coast had secured the right sort of stick, they used whale blubber or seal oil to make the stick really slip. Modern council fire chiefs can rub the

stick thoroughly, after it has been sandpapered smooth, with talcum powder instead of whale blubber. This challenge can be contested within a circle ranging from 12 to 16 feet in diameter when there are only two challengers; when there are more, the circle can be increased in size.

When two challengers of about the same size and weight stand ready within the marked-off space, the chief tells them which hand can be used, left or right only, then throws the stick gently straight up into the air, shouting "Go!" as he does so. The challengers try to catch the stick as is falls or when it reaches the ground, and each one tries to snatch it from the hand which first secured it. The chief must warn the two warriors that the stick must *never* be held above chest level during the contest and that only *one* hand, designated by the chief before the challenge begins, is used throughout the challenge. The hand which is not engaged in trying to secure and hold the stick must not be used in any way, and the chief should see that the contest does not become a wrestling match. The contestant who holds the stick after the chief has counted to 60 or 100, counts coup. In this version, instead of the chief throwing the stick into the air at the beginning of the challenge, each challenger may be given one end of the stick, and the pulling commences on the word "Go!"

In a clan challenge, when anywhere from four to eight contestants participate with only one slip stick, the challenge becomes more of a rough-and-tumble one, and it sometimes requires two or three alert chiefs to supervise the bout in a larger circle.

LOG CHIEF

The equipment needed for this challenge is best found in the woods or forest. Two good logs from 30 to 40 inches long and 11 to 12 inches in diameter are required. These logs should be fairly free from bumps and of the same thickness from one end to the other. The logs are peeled and any bumps removed, so that the logs will roll evenly and easily.

A finish line is plainly marked on the ground in front of the chief's chair, running from the chair to within 4 feet of the council fire. Fifteen feet away from this line and on each side of it, another line is marked on the ground. It is from just behind these two lines that the would-be log chiefs start the challenge. A log is placed immediately behind each line, and a warrior—each from a rival clan—stands directly behind it.

When the chief shouts, "Roll!" each warrior gets on top of his log and tries to roll it with his feet, while remaining balanced on top, to the finish line in front of the chief's chair. The warrior who manages to reach this line without having had to step down from his log counts coup and wins, even if his opponent, who was forced to leave his log one or more times, arrives a little ahead of him. When a warrior is forced to get down from his log, he must not change its position in any way before mounting it again. Sneakers or bare feet are recommended for this contest, but the bare feet should be kept out from under the log. As the log rollers become more expert through a little practice, the distance is increased by having the contestants start at equal distance from points on the opposite side of the council fire and finishing at the chief's chair line. It is surprising how adept warriors can become in log rolling with a little practice. All that is required, apart from practice, is a good log and a smooth surface on which to roll it. As a rule softwood logs are the easiest to obtain, and they are the lightest. Before a log-rolling contest all twigs, little branches, and small stones, which should never be found on the council fire area in any case, must be swept clear. In order to assure perfect safety, a chief should follow closely behind novice log rollers who have not acquired the knack of jumping clear of the log when suddenly thrown off balance.

Another amusing form of this type of contest is what the lumberjacks call "birling." This is how challengers may birl. The two logs used in LOG CHIEF are placed opposite each other and 8 feet apart in the vicinity of the chief's chair. A warrior mounts each log, and when the chief shouts, "Go!" the two rivals try to revolve the log under their feet as quickly as possible, while remaining on top of it, for as long a time as possible. The last warrior on a rolling log, who has also shown good rolling speed, counts coup.

Still another amusing way to carry out a birling challenge is for two warriors to stand on top of each log, a contestant toward each end, and try to unbalance their rival by revolving the log under their feet. The two contestants may face either in the same or opposite directions. Here again, a chief should be close enough to the birlers to help in case of necessity—though, apart from a fall from the log, there is no danger involved in such contests.

FEET CAST BALL

This is an amusing challenge based on an inflated bladder contest of the Indians of the Northwest Coast. Two warriors from different clans lie down at one end of the council fire area, one on either side of the fire. They should be exactly opposite each other, in order that the contest can be judged fairly. Bare feet or soft moccasins are best for this challenge. For the first ball cast, their feet point toward the far end of the council fire area. When they are in position, a chief gives each contestant a volleyball or basketball, to take the place of the inflated round intestine of a sea mammal used by the In-

dians. Each contestant places the ball carefully between his ankles and heels.

When the chief in charge of the challenge shouts, "Ready!" each challenger, with his back flat on the ground, raises his legs quickly upward so that his feet, holding the ball, are above his head. When the chief shouts, "Throw!" each warrior throws the ball from the between-the-feet position as far toward the other end of the council fire area as possible. The ball which travels furthest without touching the ground en route enables the warrior who threw it to count coup. The distance is counted from where the ball first hits the ground. Some really powerful ball casters may throw the ball among the warriors-in-council at the far end of the council fire area. This only adds to the fun and will not likely happen very often except when older warriors are contesting. This is still less likely to happen during the second ball cast! Here is how that is done.

The warriors change their positions so that their heads, instead of their feet, point toward the far end of the council fire area and their backs are flat on the ground. They should be in line as for the first part of the challenge. When the chief hands each warrior a ball, it is placed between the feet as before. On the word "Ready!" the legs are stretched out, ready to throw the ball over the head toward the far end of the council fire area. When the chief shouts, "Throw!" each warrior throws the ball as far as possible from this not-too-easy position. Each throw is measured as before. This challenge is best contested by letting each contestant throw the ball three times from each position, the total distance covered in each three throws deciding which warrior wins the right to count coup.

If the chief of the paleface campers will lend the council fire Indian chiefs volleyballs or basketballs for this challenge, it can be carried out by four warriors, two throwing from each end of the council fire area. This adds greatly to the fun, as there is always the chance of balls colliding or a contestant being struck with a flying ball from the other end of the area. This, of course, can only happen when all four warriors carry out the command to "Throw!" in unison.

ELBOW GUARD BALL

This is a man-to-man challenge which can be contested on two sides of the council fire at the same time by pairs of opponents, when four basketballs or volleyballs can be borrowed for the occasion.

Each pair of warriors stands opposite the council fire in the middle of the area on one side of the fire. They are placed 8 feet apart and face each other. Each warrior is given a volleyball, which he balances on the angle made by raising his left arm to chest level, with hand closed and resting against the chest. The ball is placed on top of this angle formed by the upper and lower arm. The ball must not be locked in position by pressure of the arm at any time throughout the duration of the challenge. The right hand and arm are used to defend the ball, so that it cannot easily be knocked off by the opponent, and also for trying to dislodge the balanced ball of the opponent. This is a challenge requiring balance, good judgment, steadiness, smooth quickness of movement, and concentration. When the chief in charge of the challenge sees that each warrior has the ball correctly balanced in position, he gives the command "Attack!" whereupon each warrior tries to knock off his opponent's ball while at the same time protecting his own. The two warriors can move about on any part of their side of the council fire, unless the chief decides to mark off a set area about 20 feet long and the width of the area from the fire to the outside edge of the council fire area on that side of the fire. This challenge requires considerable skill and balance, as each contestant has not only to avoid or ward off the attacks of his rival but also avoid dislodging the ball which he has balanced on his arm. The best way to decide the winner of this contest is on a basis of two-out-of-three wins.

When four balls of the same size are available, two warriors from one clan can contest against two warriors from a rival clan. This is an exciting method of carrying out this challenge, and often co-ordinated team play between warriors of the same clan will lead to the speedy defeat of the rival clan's contestants. More scope can be given for this challenge, should the chief so decide.

A very simple challenge on the above order can be contested by younger warriors by having them race around the council fire area, two or three warriors at a time, with each ball balanced on the angle of the left arm, as described above, without interference from other contestants.

When no suitable balls are available for these challenges, a paper plate 6 or 8 inches in diameter may be issued to each contesting warrior instead of a ball. This switch does not simplify the challenge, as the plate is quite as difficult as the ball to balance and still more difficult to dislodge. The challenge can also be carried out, on still nights, with balloons measuring about 6 or 8 inches in diameter when inflated, instead of either balls or plates. Warriors will find that balloons are hard things to balance on the arm, and they may contribute to their own defeat almost as much as the attacks of their rivals.

STRONG BADGER

Two braves of about the same weight face each other on hands and knees, with a dividing line exactly between them. Several pairs of braves may compete at the same time. The dividing line may be marked with a piece of white tape or a straight branch or pole long enough to allow room for each pair of contestants.

A strip of strong webbing 2½ inches wide and 60 inches long, strongly sewn together at the ends, is required for each pair of braves. It is placed over their heads when they are on their hands and knees. The center of this headband is directly over the dividing line on the ground. When the chief says "Get ready!" the braves adjust the bands to where they are most comfortable, usually just above the neck and below the ears. The braves keep this band taut without actually pulling, by holding their heads back. When the chief sees that the headbands of all contestants are centered above the ground marker, he calls "Pull!" Each brave then crawls steadily backwards, keeping his head well back and trying to pull his opponent over the dividing line in the center. Any warrior who lowers his head so that the band slips off loses that coup, whether his action is forced by the pull of his opponent or is involuntary. The brave who drags his opponent about 3 feet over the center line wins. It is fairest for the chief to judge this challenge on a two-wins-out-of-three basis.

DEER STALK

Two braves wearing soft-soled moccasins—or sneakers, which can easily be camouflaged to look like moccasins—stand some distance from the fire. The chief blindfolds one of them, the stalker, taking care not to cover his ears. The stalker is then placed four feet behind the brave who is to play the part of the deer. The deer is not blindfolded.

When the chief calls, "Stalk!" the deer circles in any direction, moving around the council ring in a zigzag pattern. He moves on silent feet, or at least as silent as he can make them. The stalker follows, keeping as close as possible without touching the deer, in an endeavor not to lose his quarry. The deer uses every ruse in his noiseless efforts to throw off his pursuer. He doubles in his tracks when possible and "freezes" (stands completely still without movement), but always keeps at a safe distance from the fire, since the stalker is blindfolded. It is understood before the contest starts that the stalker is to stand still immediately when the chief calls, "Stop!" After two or three minutes of stalking, the chief decides in favor of the brave who has played his part better, since either the deer or the stalker may win. The deer always wins when he is able to throw the stalker off his track.

Additional excitement is provided by having the winner challenge a brave from another tribe. The braves in the council ring should keep as quiet as possible while the stalker stalks the deer.

STRONG HAND

This is a man-to-man challenge in which two warriors from rival clans contest. Each warrior kneels directly opposite his opponent, and they lock fingers, palm to palm, holding the hands just above shoulder level. From three to nine pairs can contest at the same time, with a space of 4 feet between each pair of contestants. When the chief shouts, "Now!" each warrior tries to force either of his opponent's shoulders to the ground, by forcing his hands and arms to incline in either direction. Usually when a warrior gives in to superior force, he will drop suddenly sideways; but the one who was first forced to the ground knows that he gave in, even if this is not always apparent to the chief who acts as judge. The warrior who has the honor to count grand coup may be decided at a later council fire by having the winners of the first contest pair off with the other winners.

PUSH!

This is another challenge in which warriors from rival clans pair off. From four to eight pairs can contest at the same time, standing back to back with arms folded, in line with the chief's chair. When there are only three or four pairs, they form a single line on a line marked on the ground; but in the case of more than four pairs, they form two lines, one line forming on the opposite side of the council fire but also in line with the chief's chair. When the chief shouts, "Push!" each warrior tries to push the other around the council fire area back to the starting point. With two lines, there will be some difficulty about right of way when the pushing pairs meet, but that is a matter which will have to be decided by the contestants, and it will not make the contest less amusing. There will be so much forward and backward movement in this challenge that even the seasoned chiefs will be unable to guess, until close to the end of the contest, which warrior will count coup. Any warrior of the pair who purposely moves to one side to avoid pressure from his opponent's back is disqualified, and his opponent wins. Chiefs should be stationed at one or two points around the council fire area to see that the challenge is carried out properly. This challenge can be carried out by each pair of contestants locking arms at the elbow, but it is more difficult and better fun when the arms of the contestants are folded in front.

BACK!

This is one of the push-pull challenges which the Indians of the Northwest Coast liked to contest. Two warriors of about the same height and weight stand chest to chest, each one looking over a shoulder of the other, with both arms outstretched to the sides. A line is marked on the ground about 2 long paces behind each contestant. When the chief calls, "Ready!" the two contestants push firmly against each other, bending slightly forward but without trying to move the other.

On the word "Back!" each one leans against the other and tries to push his rival backward to the line behind him. Both challengers keep their arms fully stretched out to the sides as they push, chest to chest. The one who succeeds in pushing his rival up to and over the mark is the winner and counts coup. The fairest way to decide the winner is on a three-tries basis.

The winner of each pair contesting can challenge the winner of the next pair, and this can continue until the warrior with the right to claim grand coup has been decided.

FOOT PULL

This amusing challenge provided the Indians, who had a fine sense of humor, with the opportunity to pull each other's legs. An old Tlingit shaman informed the author that he believed this amusing contest was a "gift" from their Eskimo neighbors to the north, who contested it sitting on the ice.

The contestants sat face to face in pairs on smooth ground, with legs outstretched and slightly apart. One foot of each contestant just touched his opponent's knee. When the chief shouted, "Ready!" each man seized the ankle of his rival's near leg. On the cry of "Pull!" each contestant exerted a strong, steady pull on his rival's ankle in an endeavor to pull his opponent's feet *along the ground* until they were in line with his own waist, without slipping forward himself. Many merry contestants owed their defeat to lusty laughter rather than the strength and skill of their opponents.

Modern Indians contesting this challenge must be careful to avoid the natural impulse to raise the opponent's leg when giving the first hard tug, since this might cause the opponent to strike his head forcibly on the ground. The leg being pulled should *not* be raised from the ground at any time during the challenge. The best result in three tries will generally decide the warrior entitled to count coup. The chief conducting this challenge must see that it is contested on smooth ground, so that neither contestant has a place to brace either the leg being pulled or the other one. Usually this challenge "proves a slip" when the challengers are seated on groundsheets, pegged to the ground.

This contest may also be carried out as a clan challenge with three or four challengers from different clans sitting alongside each other, with about 4 feet between each pair. They sit in a straight line facing their opponents, as described above. Another way to contest FOOT PULL is to have three or four warriors from the same clan

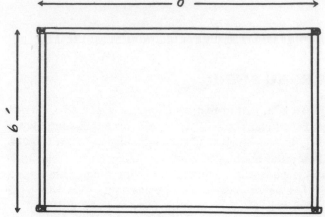

sit in one line, while the rivals from another clan sit facing them. The winning clan, in this case, is the one which drags the greatest number of opponents forward, as described above in the man-to-man challenge.

TRAPPED!

This is an amusing challenge which the Indians of the Canadian Northwest very likely learned from the Eskimo, who were a merry, game-loving people. It is played in the following way.

Two warriors of about equal weight go down on their hands and knees facing away from each other, with the soles of their moccasins touching. A chief securely fastens the right ankle of each challenger together, using a stout piece of cloth about 30 inches long and 1½ inches wide. On the word "Pull!" each contestant tries to drag the other backward for at least 12 feet, to decide the winner. The chief can mark a line on the ground in front of each contestant at a distance ranging from 10 to 20 feet. This challenge is best conducted on a two-wins-out-of-three basis.

Carried out as a clan challenge, from two to four warriors from each of two clans carry out this challenge as described above.

As in all such challenges, chiefs can devise variations, such as joining the two contestants by the left ankles or tying *both* feet together. This last method increases the difficulty for the challengers and adds to the amusement of the onlookers.

POLECAT HUNT

This amusing challenge is contested by two warriors from rival clans. The only equipment needed includes: two stout, straight poles each about 8 feet long and from 2 to 3 inches in diameter; two shorter, straight poles each 6 feet long and also 2 to 3 inches in diameter; and two blindfolds, one yellow and the other red. The four poles are lashed securely together, as shown in the drawing, and laid flat on the ground on one side of the council fire. This frame may be attached to a peg driven into the ground at each corner to hold it firmly in place, if desired. This makes it easier for the contestants, as their positions are not so easily betrayed by vibration or movement of the poles. With two such frames, a contest may be carried out on two sides of the council fire at the same time.

The two contesting warriors crouch on hands and knees, one brave at each end of the oblong, with the fingers of one hand touching the shorter poles, as indicated in the drawing. The chief directing the challenge tells the warrior who is blindfolded with the yellow band that he plays the part of the wily polecat, while the one blindfolded with the red band is the hunter. Each contestant must always touch one of the poles throughout the challenge with the finger tips of the right or left hand, though a quick change of hands may be made during the challenge at any time. The contestants are blindfolded, care being taken not to cover the ears.

When the chief commands, "Hunt!" both the polecat and the hunter begin to move cautiously and silently in a crawling position around the pole oblong. They can move in any direction they like, keeping either inside or outside the poles, but must always move on hands and knees. The object of the game is for the hunter to catch the polecat, while the polecat tries to avoid capture by stealthy changes in position and the good use of his ears. Each warrior listens keenly for the slightest sound made by the other, so that the polecat knows in which direction to move to avoid capture while the hunter knows in which direction to crawl in order to capture the cat. A slight vibration on a pole can reveal the position of a rival to an alert contestant.

This is an exciting challenge, and the warriors-in-council should be warned in advance to remain as silent and stoic as possible throughout the contest, so that the challengers will not be guided or warned by exclamations from the warriors-in-council. Even seasoned chiefs may find it hard to restrain themselves when the polecat and hunter are on the verge of a head-on encounter!

This challenge can be set up in a different way. The oblong pole structure can be lashed securely at the four corners to the tops of four stout poles driven into the ground, with the top of each pole 2 feet 6 inches above ground. With this arrangement, both hunter and hunted can move freely from the inside to the outside under the poles forming the oblong. The chief should warn the contestants from time to time that only the *finger tips* of one hand must touch the poles. This can add greatly to the excitement of the challenge, as the polecat, moving silently forward inside the oblong with his finger tips touching the *bottom* of the pole, and the hunter, crawling silently outside the oblong with his finger tips touching the *top* of the pole, may pass each other without suspecting one another's presence! Such suspenseful moments, which occur from time to time during this challenge, keep even the older and wiser chiefs on edge; so the younger, untried warrior-in-council cannot be blamed too greatly for giving an involuntary whoop from time to time.

PART 3

CONJURING
THE STORY SPELL

chapter **12**

campfire storytelling

Unleash The Imagination, settle down in the spirit of the glowing campfire and its cheerful camaraderie, and soon the storyteller will carry you along with him to distant places, far beyond the everyday world. The adventure and mystery surrounding our brother man when the world was young; the glint of moonlight on the armor of gallant knights riding forth on quests of chivalry; the dull thunder of unshod hooves as Indian ponies are urged forward on the trail of adventure—we share the suspense and delights of all these experiences, as a cunning weaver of tales unwinds them from his multifaceted magic loom. Relaxing around a fire—where stories are forged in the flames—we explore together the fabulous treasures of storyland.

STORYTELLING AROUND THE CAMPFIRE

This activity, with good storytellers and worthwhile, suitable stories, can be made one of the most popular, thrilling, and unobtrusively educational features of the campfire program. Really worthwhile stories with scope, suspense, and action stir and stimulate the imagination, put the world on parade, and serve as stepping stones to more advanced literature. A good story well told is worth a dozen good stories well read. The book held between the reader and his audience presents a tangible handicap. No degree of careful inflection, planned pauses, knowing glances, meaning smiles, and similar tricks of the story reader between paragraphs—while he or she loses the place in the meantime—can entirely dissipate the physical barrier of the printed page. Yet a well-read, suitable story can be more effective than a story told in a halting, bumbling manner.

The storyteller should look and feel relaxed. He can either stand close to the campfire, turning slowly and easily to face all points of the circle of listeners as he unwinds his story, or he can stand at a central point in the spectator circle where he faces at least three-quarters of his listeners and can be seen at close range by the remaining quarter. In addition to the illumination provided by the campfire, a pole may be driven into the ground near where the storyteller stands and a torch fastened to the end in order to provide additional light for the audience to follow his various expressions as his tale unfolds.

HIGHLIGHTING CAMPFIRE STORIES

When a storyteller lacks confidence, a youthful audience can almost invariably sense the lack of certainty generated by the storyteller. Such an audience is also quick to detect inaccuracies, often magnified by attempts to explain them or cover them up. One whose knowledge of American Indians goes no deeper than the paint on a cigar store Indian should not presume to tell a story about Indians, whether on the warpath or spending a peaceful evening with their peace pipes in their tepees. A teller of tales who does not know the difference between being close-hauled and keel-hauled should steer clear of stories of the sea. One will fare best when he sticks to subjects which he likes and of which he has a fairly intimate knowledge.

The campfire audience can also feel the lack of enthusiasm which the teller of tales may have for the story he is relating, should he be unwise enough to embark on a story for which he has little sympathy. Should he, for example, have no real interest in nature and no deep sympathy for nature's wildthings, he should never at-

tempt to tell a nature story to a discerning audience, or any other. Sometimes lack of fervor on the part of a narrator is not only the result of disinterest or not knowing a story well; unfortunately, it can come from knowing the story too well and having told it too often. When a teller of tales has reached the conclusion that he no longer needs to take pains to stress or shade the subtle tracery of the highlights of his story, he is riding for a fall. When he feels that he can "tell the story with his eyes shut," so to speak, he may finish his tale only to find that the audience too has its eyes shut! When a weaver of tales is discerning enough to realize that his once-favorite stories seem to have lost a good deal of their lustre, and the telling of them its spontaneity, his wisest course is to focus on a new group of stories.

A good storyteller invariably has the framework of his story set up in his mind's eye. He knows that there must be a definite *beginning,* a *middle,* and an *end* to all good tales. Sequenced highlights should be like islands in a chain of islands, and a storyteller must swim straight from one island to the next without turning back or getting off course en route. When he has explored and developed the last island satisfactorily, the story stops.

PITFALLS TO AVOID IN STORYTELLING

What are some of the general storytelling faults and those which are likely to be resented by campfire audiences? Let's look at a few of them. Old favorites, much *too* old; unsuitable stories; overly sentimental stories; inaudibility of the narrator; "talking down" to the audience; "preciousness," certain gestures and mannerisms which the storyteller often believes inimitable; stories in dialect, which only the storyteller seems able to understand and enjoy.

Any story loses interest for the listeners if the storyteller permits the pattern to become blurred. Three things at least must be perfectly clear in a good story: the things that happen; the characters they happen to; and the setting of the happenings, where and when they occur.

Characters in a story should not have names so similar that the listeners have difficulty in deciding whether things are happening to Ross or Russ, Jean or Joan, Bart or Burt, Colette or Claudette. Unless the teller of tales can create from the beginning a sympathy and interest in his listeners' minds for his heroes and heroines, there is little point in telling the tale. In stories "made up" by the storyteller, too often coincidence is overplayed to offset lack of imagination on the storyteller's part. Too much coincidence crowded into an otherwise good story kills the listeners' interest. Another cause for audience complaint is the disruption of the listeners' attempts to concentrate by too sudden shifts in narration, without preparation in advance for these shifts.

At times, storytellers fail to differentiate between simplicity and the commonplace in storytelling, despite the gulf which divides them. Even major points and highlights suffer greatly from overelaboration. Overdescription of the chief characters will also bore most listeners. They usually prefer to visualize the characters to their own satisfaction, without too much descriptive detail being given. It is far more effective to say, "Burt Bryson was as hard as nails," than to enter into a lengthy description of how he got that way. Frequently narrators lump most of their description in one place. This usually disrupts the smooth flow of the story. Description is best when spread rather thinly throughout the action and dialogue. Overemphasis can be as hurtful as underemphasis in putting a story across successfully, and any story which necessitates the effect-spoiling anticlimax of an "explanation" at the end of it can be safely dropped from a storyteller's repertoire.

Mystery and high adventure stories often lose a great deal of their effectiveness because suspense is not introduced early enough.

Many stories told to junior audiences of varying age groups suffer because the teller of tales gives the characters definite ages. The listeners almost invariably prefer to decide for themselves the ages of the hero or heroine—as a rule it is the same as their own!

Where the campfire audiences consist of both boys and girls, it is well to remember that girls will frequently listen with interest to a story of adventure in which a boy is the hero, but most boys dislike almost any girls' story of adventure, especially when the heroine is a girl. This can be circumvented by telling brother and sister adventure stories or stories where both a boy and a girl are protagonists.

Dialect is best left out of storytelling unless one is an expert dialectician who uses brief dialectical dialogue with finesse. Dialect should always be avoided when there is the slightest chance that some of the listeners will be hurt or misled by its use. Another good reason why a story requiring a lot of dialect is best left out of the average storyteller's repertoire, especially where younger listeners are concerned, is the fact that a great number of the listeners will be unable to follow the parts of the story told in dialect, and many or all of the highlights of the story will therefore be lost to them.

STORY MATERIAL TO AVOID

Opinion is divided regarding the sort of stories which should be told to youthful audiences. The author, after years of study and experiment with many groups of all sizes and widely varying ages, has come to some definite conclusions regarding stories which should and should not be told. No off-color, discriminatory, sarcastic, satirical, oversentimental, ghost, horror, or other type of really "scary" story is suitable or advisable for a younger or even teen-age camper to carry off in his highly imaginative mind as he returns to his cabin in the darkness after the campfire. Most alert leaders realize that there can be danger in such stories. Why burden young minds with morbid stories such as Rudyard Kipling's "Morrowbie Jukes" or "The Mark of the Beast" when one can choose other, and far more appropriate, stories from the wonderful repertoire of Kipling? If one must tell one of Poe's highly imaginative tales at a campfire, why not relate "The Gold Bug," playing down Jupiter's dialect, rather than tell "The Pit and the Pendulum"? Why build a sense of horror and unrest into the surroundings of a camp or an outpost by telling one of Algernon Blackwood's clever atmospheric masterpices, such as "The Willows," when one of a hundred thrilling stories which do not arouse the spirit of fear can take its place?

Once, during the telling of W. W. Jacob's harrowing tale of "The Monkey's Paw," when the paw wriggled after being produced at the crucial moment, several girls shrieked—"It moved! It moved!" Further on in the story, when the dead son arrived at the front door, after opening the squeaky gate, the storyteller suddenly knocked sharply and loudly under the table top. Nearly all of the group screamed, one girl was sick, and another actually fainted. On another occasion, the story of "The Beast with Five Fingers" was told to adults, complete with a white, natural-looking plaster hand in a half-clenched position climbing its eerie way up a wall. One woman sprang to her feet, shrieked loudly, "The hand, the hand!" and then collapsed. Such experiences are a warning against telling "atmospheric" stories more exciting than the fine yarn entitled "The Sire de Malétroit's Door" even to the most sophisticated adult audiences.

The efforts of some storytellers fall flat because they fail to take into consideration the fact that mass taste rather than individual taste must be the rule when meeting the age-old cry of "Tell us a story!"

Most campfires can get along very well without "tall tales." The counselors will hear sufficient tall stories during the camping season to satisfy any personal predilection for this sort of thing. The tall stories about Ol' Paul, Pecos Bill, Baron Manchausen, and the other yarns are best told around the campfires of fishermen and hunters.

When searching for authentic material to be used in telling stories of the American Indians, it is best to give James Fenimore Cooper's most implausible yarns a wide berth. This is especially true of *The Deerslayer*. Analysis of his stories clearly proves that Cooper painted an ignoble picture of the "noble Red Man" in general, and his pseudo-woodcraft and tracking incidents are only worthy of a comic strip.

EFFECTIVE STORYTELLING

Narration made visible should be the storyteller's prime objective. The story should be brightened and made vivid by the introduction of visual and sensory experiences: *see* the flowers; *hear* the wind howl; *smell* the pine needles made fragrant by the warmth of the afternoon sun. Substitute action for adjectives, and make the action *vivid*. The listeners should be made to feel that they are participants rather than listeners as the adventure unrolls before them and they are drawn into it. Don't *tell* them—*show* them! When telling a story about a savage dog, there is little point in telling your listeners how very, very fierce the dog is. Have the dog rip the trousers of some objectionable character in the story and then tear them into shreds in fury, as their owner escapes over a wall.

Try to catch the listeners' attention with the first few words. A pause until there is complete quiet on the part of the listeners is a good way to open. Plato must have had storytelling in mind when he said, "The beginning is half of the whole business." Don't feel that all the best "good old" stories have been told to death. Remember the frank admission of the greatest English writer of all times—"And all my best is making old things new." They must really be made new, though!

Old and young audiences alike appreciate the fine art of implication. They will usually draw their own conclusions and have mental exercise and fun in doing so.

Keats was one of the many masters of implication. Volumes of adventure could be built around two brief lines of his: "Charm'd magic casements, opening on the foam of perilous seas, in faery lands forlorn."

Repetition can be helpful in the art of storytelling, though it is most appreciated by younger groups. It can be used in a subtle and effective way to increase the interest of young listeners. One good instance of direct repetition is found in the repetitious tale of *The Three Bears*. Its theme is so effective that quite often the young folk will instinctively join in, without invitation, when the story is well told. Some modern tellers of tales may not be aware that this little story was originally written by no less a storyteller than Robert Southey. When it was first published, in 1835, the heroine was not Goldilocks but a quaint little old woman who took on the three bears singlehanded. Somewhere down the line, in the course of the last hundred years, the little old lady was ousted by Goldilocks, who apparently has come to stay.

Condensation is a valuable art in storytelling. Short stories, even short short stories, can be quite as striking as longer stories. Modern storytellers who condense longer stories to make them campfire-fit must bear in mind that cutting should not affect clarity. Successful treatment assures a good and striking opening, highlights with impact throughout the condensation, a middle, and a satisfying ending.

Many long stories can easily be divided into a series of short stories, each one a worthwhile adventure and complete in itself. Some books are better adapted to this treatment than others. In *Campfire Adventure Stories*[1] "Moose Boy" is divided into nine one-telling sections, and the girls' adventure story "A Loon Laughs" is divided into seven adventures. Almost any one of these sections can be made into a short, complete story by following the suggestions given above.

RIGHT WORDS IN THE RIGHT PLACE

A storyteller should be able to find the right word quickly and, when necessary, coin original phrases to meet the needs of the story being told. When telling an outdoor story, with or without Indians, phrases such as "lightning fast," "quick as a falling star," "swift as a loon dives," "cat quick," "arrow fast," help the tale along and make it more picturesque. When the teller of tales wishes to introduce a frightened Indian, the brave will seem even more scared if the storyteller trails along in an Indian vein and says, "Fear came on fast feet!" The effect of many old stories of the American Indians is frequently spoiled by modern storytellers failing to reword and rephrase them, without losing the Indian

[1] By Allan A. Macfarlan (New York: Association Press, 1952).

flavor. This especially applies to ancient myths and legends. Even they need new modes of expression. To supply these is not a difficult task, as the framework is already there.

When you are the hero of your own story, which is always a ticklish thing to be, you will get far more sympathy and laughs from your listeners by telling how you got lost in the woods, were scared by an owl, and bumped your shins on every branch across the path than if you told them how fearless you were, how completely at home in the inky darkness, and how your keen eyes invariably spotted the many obstacles that would have made the path impassable for anybody else.

After the storyteller finds a story which impresses him as a suitable one for narrating at the campfire, he will discover that it takes a lot of rereading and study until the plot and characters are firmly established in his mind. In thinking up words other than those used by the author, he will find that pictorial ones are most effective when not overworked. In order that his new-found story may prove successful, he must try to keep the story action rolling like a ball. A taut, well-told story will make the listeners forget the presence of the storyteller. An old story such as *20,000 Leagues Under the Sea,* by Jules Verne—which used to be classed in the fantastic story category—is a good book to use excerpts from, since the farseeing author gave such an intimate description of scientific gadgets, events, underseas craft, and background that a modern storyteller can feel quite at home either in the Nautilus or on the sea floor exploration expeditions. With such things firmly established in his mind, the teller of tales is ready for his debut in the fitful flicker of the firelight.

CREATING ATMOSPHERE

By the use of simple props and off-stage noises, atmosphere can be created to help a story along in fine style. A "shot" in the dark, somewhere in that mysterious land of night which lies just outside the safety and warmth of the campfire, can vitalize a story. Off-scene music, a bugle call as the gallant Legionnaires gallop to the rescue of a beleaguered fort, the call of a bird or beast, the whoop of an Indian, the sound of distant bells—all add greatly to the story, provided there is perfect timing in the combination of words and effects. Some ways of co-ordinating off-stage effects with storytelling are described under "Bell Effects" and "Bell Tower Fire" in Chapter 3.

SURE-FIRE CAMPFIRE STORY MATERIAL

A vital point in successful campfire storytelling is the building of a really worthwhile repertoire of stories of all sorts, suitable for all occasions and for mixed and varied age groups. The verdict of the youthful listeners should prove the final factor in the establishment of the storyteller's repertoire. Parents, teachers, and storytellers may introduce children to literature, but it is the children who make the final decisions regarding the books they like best and the stories they enjoy hearing most.

There are hundreds of first-class stories of high adventure which unroll in the forest, on the prairie, in the air, on sea, on the trail, in the saddle, in foreign countries, and in outer space. There are clever detective stories, and inspiring, imaginative, humorous, cloak-and-dagger, romantic, knights-and-chivalry, campfire, cowboy, science fiction, American Indian, nature, and aviation tales from which to draw. Today, many such stories can be found in paper cover anthologies which can be bought for prices ranging from 35 cents to a dollar each. Even one well-chosen anthology may contain suitable material for storytelling at half a dozen campfires. Stories of high adventure and high horror may keep company in one paperback. There should be no doubt in the mind of a good storyteller as to which ones he will select for his youthful audiences. The plot and action of "derring do" stories should be made as plausible as possible, in order to make them worth telling.

Usually, fast-moving stories which can be told at one campfire in a period ranging from five to fifteen minutes are best. In exceptional cases, as when an expert storyteller holds his listeners spellbound, the storytelling time for one story can be lengthened to thirty minutes or so. Long stories which have to be told in serial form and continue to another campfire night often lose their interest and appeal before the second installment is well under way and are, as a rule, best avoided.

The following advice was given by the late Joseph Pulitzer, writer, journalist, and newspaper owner, to his story writers. It is equally applicable to storytellers if one simply changes the word "read" to "listen to."

Put it before them:
Briefly, so they will read it,
Clearly, so they will understand it,
Forcibly, so they will appreciate it,
Picturesquely, so they will remember it, and above all,
Accurately, so they will be guided by its light.

SUGGESTED MATERIAL FOR CAMPFIRE STORIES

A complete catalogue of material to draw on for campfire storytelling would fill dozens of pages. The idea here is merely to suggest some sources of material suitable for the *average* storyteller to use at the *average* campfire. Expert storytellers can frequently hold their campfire listeners spellbound while telling even uninspired stories of little general interest, which less gifted tellers of tales do well to shun. A school principal or English teacher may proudly perform the none-too-easy task of apparently holding a campfire audience's polite attention while relating something from Chaucer or Shakespeare. But such fare is not usually the sort of material that suggests the experience of having lived through high adventure, to the average campfire audience of mixed age groups.

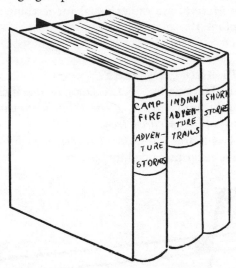

The list which follows steers clear of most myths, legends, fables, and historical tales which are best told in the classroom—although quite a few of these make suitable reading, when accompanied by the necessary explanations, to cabin groups of mixed ages on rainy days or evenings.

Most of the list consists of material chosen because it will not suffer greatly by being told in the simple, graphic words of the average teller of tales. Such a choice makes it unnecessary for storytellers to memorize long stretches of stories which are effective only when told in the inimitable words of the authors. A few suggestions, mostly for younger listeners, are listed under the cabin reading list; others may be taken from the selected suggestions for campfire storytelling.

FOR READING ALOUD TO CABIN GROUPS

Andersen, Hans Christian   *Fairy Tales.*

Carroll, Lewis   *Alice's Adventures in Wonderland* and *Through the Looking Glass.* Though these masterpieces from the mathematical mind of Professor Charles Lutwidge Dodgson rank high among the classics for children, many modern children consider them dated and show little interest in Alice's adventures. The reader will be wise to try these books out with different age groups, by reading a few selections, in order to see how the children react to them.

Grahame, Kenneth   *The Wind in the Willows.* An all-time masterpiece which will be taken to the hearts of listeners, from ten-year-olds to understanding grownups, once they have heard the mystic Pipes of Pan in Chapter 7.

Kipling, Rudyard   *Just So Stories*—one or two at a time.

Lang, Andrew (editor)   The Fairy Book Series. These books of all colors offer great scope and choice, as does *Arabian Nights.*

Macdonald, George   *At the Back of the Northwind,* and other fairy tales.

Nesbit, Edith Bland   *The Treasure Seekers; Five Children and It; The Phoenix and the Carpet; The Story of the Amulet.*

Pyle, Howard   *The Wonder Clock.*

Tolkien, John Ronald R.   *The Hobbit.* A remarkable yarn by a learned professor. It deals in a most realistic way with goblins and dwarves, elves and hobbits. The fight with the spiders may have to be played down for younger listeners. Time has burnished, not tarnished, this story.

POETRY

De la Mare, Walter   *Peacock Pie,* a book of rhymes. Also selections from his other books of juvenile verse.

Milne, A. A.   Selections from his verse and stories. (*When We Were Very Young; Winnie the Pooh;* etc.)

Stevenson, Robert Louis   *A Child's Garden of Verse,* and other rhymes.

ANTHOLOGIES

Hubbard and Babbit (editors)   *The Golden Flute*

Stevenson, Burton K.   *The Home Book of Verse for Young Folks*

Thompson, Blanche J.   *Silver Pennies*

FOR THE CAMPFIRE

ADVENTURE THROUGHOUT THE WORLD

Ballantyne, Robert Michael   *The Coral Island* (1858); *The Dog Crusoe* (1861); *The Wild Man of the West;* among others. The fact that the first two books listed are recently available in popular price editions, after the lapse of one hundred years, speaks for itself!

Best, Herbert   *Garram the Hunter.* African boy and dog story. Selections.

Bishop, Claire Huchet   *Twenty and Ten.* Children outwit Nazis.

Buchan, Sir John   *The Adventures of Richard Hannay.* Three novels in one volume: *The Thirty-Nine Steps; Green Mantle;* and *Mr. Standfast*—secret agent stories by a former governor general of Canada.

Chesterton, G. K.   *The Father Brown Omnibus.* Detective stories.

Davis, Robert   *Pepperfoot of Thursday Market.* The adventures of a boy and donkey of the Berbers; the French Foreign Legion takes a hand.

Doyle, Sir Arthur Conan   *The Boys' Sherlock Holmes* (compiled by Howard Haycraft) and *The Lost World.*

Driggs, Howard R.   *The Pony Express Goes Through.* Selections.

Du Soe, Robert C.   *Three Without Fear*

Gatti, Attilio   *Saranga, the Pygmy.* Adventure in Equatorial Africa.

Haggard, Sir Henry Rider   *Allan Quatermain; King Solomon's Mines;* and others. Selections.

Household, Geoffrey   *The Spanish Cave.*

Kipling, Rudyard   *The Jungle Book.* See also his short stories at the end of this list.

Meader, Stephen W.   *Shadow in the Pines.*

Orczy, Baroness Emmuska   *The Scarlet Pimpernel.* The adventures of that elusive character, during the French revolution, who also plays the lead in some of her other stories. Selections.

Nordhoff, Charles, and Hall, James N.   *Falcons of France.* Aviation, Lafayette Squadron.

Pyle, Howard   *The Merry Adventures of Robin Hood; The Story of King Arthur and His Knights; Men of Iron.* Selections.

Ransome, Arthur   *Swallows and Amazons* (1931). An intriguing story of the camping and sailing adventures of a very-much-alive group of six youngsters.

Sperry, Armstrong   *Call it Courage.* Boy and dog adventures in the south seas. Selections.

Stevens, Alden Gifford   *Lion Boy.* A tale of East Africa.

Stevenson, Robert Louis   *Treasure Island.* Selections.

Streatfield, Noel   *The Stranger in Primrose Lane.* Mystery.

Verne, Jules   *Twenty Thousand Leagues Under the Sea.* Selections. One hundred years ago this was science fiction. Today it is reality. Also, *The Mysterious Island.*

Waldeck, Theodore   *Lions on the Hunt; On Safari.*

Wheeler, Post   *Hathoo of the Elephants.* Selections.

Wilder, Laura, Ingalls   *Little House in the Big Wood; By the Shore of Silver Lake.* Pioneering.

Wren, Percival Christopher   *Beau Geste.* The Foreign Legion. Selections.

ADVENTURE ON THE HIGH SEAS
Pease, Howard   *The Tattooed Man.*

ANTHOLOGIES
The Argosy Book of Sea Stories (1953).
Best Sea Stories from Blue Book Magazine (1954).
Treasury of Sea Stories (edited by Aymar).
(Most of the older classics by authors such as Captain Frederick Marryat are rather dated for retelling at modern campfires.)

KNIGHTS AND CHIVALRY
De Angeli, Marguerite   *The Door in the Wall.*
Doyle, Sir Arthur Conan   *The White Company.*
Pyle, Howard   *Men of Iron.*
Tappan, Eva March   *When Knights Were Bold.* Good details regarding knightly customs.

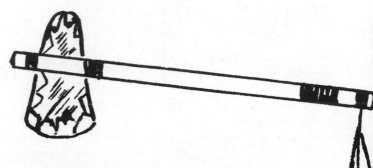

AMERICAN INDIANS
Eastman, Charles   *Wigwam Evenings.*
LaFarge, Oliver   *Laughing Boy.* Selections from this Navajo country story of Laughing Boy and Slim Girl will prove a treat for a discriminating campfire audience of older boys and girls.
Long Lance, Buffalo Child   *Long Lance.*
Macfarlan, Allan A.   *Indian Adventure Trails.*
Parker, Arthur C.   *Skunny Wundy;* and other Indian tales.
Schultz, James W.   *Sinopah, the Indian Boy; With the Indians in the Rockies.* Blackfoot stories. Selections.

NATURAL HISTORY
Anthology   *The Book of Naturalists* (edited by William Beebe).

DOGS AND HORSES
Bulla, Clyde   *Star of Wild Horse Canyon.*
James, Will   *Smoky, the Cowhorse.* Selections.
Rounds, Glen   *The Blind Colt.*
Terhune, Albert Payson   Selections from some of his best dog stories.
See also anthologies of dog stories.

*FANTASY, SCIENCE FICTION, AND
PSEUDO-SCIENCE FICTION*

Hawthorne, Nathaniel   *The Wonder Book*. Selections. Somewhat dated.

Wells, Herbert George   Selections from some of his science fiction books are good for older groups. Three books in one volume are obtainable at most libraries.

ANTHOLOGIES

There are hundreds of inexpensive paperbacks available in the field of science fiction from which to make a choice of suitable material.

SHORT STORIES

Benet, Stephen Vincent   "By the Waters of Babylon."

Connell, Richard Edward   "The Most Deadly Game." Thrilling for older groups, but the Trophy Room part can be played down or eliminated.

de Maupassant, Guy   "The Diamond Necklace." For Girls' groups.

Kipling, Rudyard   "Mowgli's Brothers"; "Rikki-Tik-ki-Tavi"; "Toomai of the Elephants"; "Wee Willie Winkie" (perhaps best with the least understandable baby talk eliminated) . "The Mark of the Beast" is *not* recommended for campfire story telling.

Macfarlan, Allan A.   *Campfire Adventure Stories*. Selections.

Poe, Edgar Allan   "The Gold Bug." This story is better for listeners when Jupiter's dialect is played down. (His other short tales, such as "The Pit and the Pendulum" and "The Cask of Amontillado," are best omitted from campfire story programs.)

Stevenson, Robert Louis   "The Sire de Malétroit's Door." For older groups.

West, Jessamyn   "The Pacing Goose." Selection from *The Gentle Persuasion*.

White, Stewart Edward   "The Long Rifle." A selection from the novel of the same name.

chapter 13

original campfire

The Few Original Short Stories selected for this chapter are set down to show that a variety of subjects which do not involve high adventure can still be suitable for campfire storytelling purposes. Each tale can be told in a few minutes, and they are all appropriate for an average campfire coeducational audience of mixed ages.

THE OWLS FLY SOUTH

Norman McLeod, the factor of a Hudson's Bay post in the far Canadian Northwest, looked anxiously at the sky. There were signs of neither storm nor snow clouds in the clear blue overhead, yet the post manager frowned as his keen eyes swept the skies.

"Yes," he said aloud, in the way that some outdoor people who lead lonely lives have of speaking to themselves, "these are Snowy Owls. They are heading South. Too bad! Now I must send to headquarters in Winnipeg for money and supplies to lend my Indian and Esquimaux trappers. They'll need help now, to tide them over the hard winter months that are close at hand."

"It's a great pity," he sighed as more and more big Snowy Owls flew high overhead on noiseless wings. "This is one of those years when our trappers will have to tighten their belts and hope for better luck next winter."

A tenderfoot in that northern region might wonder what hard times, luck, and Snowy Owls had to do with each other. Surely nobody trapped or ate these birds?

Could it be because some of the natives regarded all owls as bad-luck birds? Better listen in as the factor continues to talk aloud. Perhaps we may learn something from his words.

"Well, there goes my chance to send my Toronto friends the Arctic Fox skins which I promised them when they visited here this summer," he mutters regretfully as he watches flock after flock of the great white owls fly overheard in their strange gliding and jerky flight. "There won't be many Arctic Foxes left anyway, when the win-

stories

ter snows fly for a month or so. Those which are still alive will have lean bodies and almost worthless skins."

As McLeod walked back to the post, two Indian trappers passed him. They stopped to point to the owls in the sky. "Bad," they said, "bad, bad." They shook their heads, and both of them drew the side of their right hands across their stomachs as though cutting themselves in two. The sign spoke of HUNGER, even to one who did not know the Indian sign language.

As McLeod cooked his supper that night, he still muttered to himself: "Where do the little beggars go? There were hundreds of thousands of them last winter. The snow-clad Arctic barrens were covered with their tiny, furry-feet tracks, and sometimes there were moving patches of them which looked as though dozens of our big, buff trade blankets were being pulled across the snow by invisible hands. Now there are likely only a few left in all the thousands of burrows."

What do you campers think the furry-footed "little beggars" mentioned by the Hudson's Bay Company man were? Certainly, by his description, they were not Snowy Owls, nor were they Arctic Foxes. No, the little animals which the factor was thinking about were Lemmings, little rat-like rodents not much larger than big mice. They almost disappear every three or four years. At these times they sometimes swim out in huge droves into great lakes or the sea, swimming on and on until all are drowned. Why?

Nobody really knows, except Mother Nature. Since these Lemmings are the chief food of not only the Snowy Owls but also the Arctic Foxes, these birds and beasts must either go South to seek other food or die of starvation when the Lemmings are gone. It is hard to believe that the fate of these little Lemmings can decide whether other bigger animals and birds will live or die. Imagine such small creatures deciding whether men shall have money and good food, or little or no money and poor food. Yes, it seems almost impossible, but it is perfectly true.

You will learn something about the wonderful thing which men call the "balance of nature" while you are here in camp, during the summer. You may be surprised to learn that insects, flowers, animals, trees, and man all need each other in order to be healthy and happy. There is a regular chain reaction and interrelationship here, of which we campers are an important part. If there were not friendly, useful insects working for us every minute of the day and night we could hardly exist.

The Creator who made all things, including ourselves and the tiniest insect, has created a marvelous balance of things which we can easily upset in camp if we are not careful. We can upset it by the careless use of a match, a hatchet, a stick, or a hand which pulls wildflowers or kills frogs or dragon flies, which are really our good friends. Ask your counselor about these things, so that one sad day we may not be left in a world which has lost much of its beauty and wildlife through our own fault.

THE VISIT OF IT

The campers at Camp Clearwater were excited. The head counselor had told them that he expected a mysterious visitor during the next three days. The visitor was so mysterious, the campers were told, that it could not be spoken of as "he" or "she," so it was best to call the visitor IT. There were many reasons why IT

was so much of a mystery, the head counselor went on to explain. It was often very difficult to tell when IT was around. IT kept no fixed hours and might come at any time. Very often IT was invisible, though that was not always so. One never knew for certain where to find IT, because quite often IT was not where people expected it to be. IT traveled fast, and one had to be quick to act and prepared to act when it came along. IT had to be caught as it approached, for once it had passed, there was little or no chance of catching it again. IT could not be sensed or seen by some people, but others could sense it, see it, hear it, or smell it quite well at times. Very wise men in Greece were believed to have seen IT from time to time, and the fact that they could describe IT, and had sculptors make statues of IT, seemed to prove that they really had seen it.

The head counselor told the campers that he had discovered what the Greek wise men knew about IT and that he was going to tell the secret to four counselors. These counselors were going to help him decide at the end of the three days which of the campers had really discovered the mysterious IT. Those who did, the head counselor promised them, would most likely be rewarded and learn something which would prove helpful to them for the rest of their lives.

Some of the older campers said that they thought it would be difficult to tell which of them had met IT, and wanted to know how it could be proved or disproved. The head counselor assured them that at the end of three

days he would have the campers who had met IT— even though they might not have seen IT, or even known that IT was around—tell of their experiences at the campfire on the night of the third day. At that time, if he and the four counselors who knew about IT were quite sure that at least one of the campers had met the mysterious visitor, they would relate what the Greek wise men knew about IT and tell the campers the name of the mysterious stranger. When the campers learned the secret, all of them would be prepared and better able to make use of IT's powers when they met up with IT again, because they would be on the lookout for IT and less likely to let it get away from them.

As the exciting three "Days of the Visitor" passed, the counselors spoke each night with all of the campers who imagined that they had seen, heard, or been helped by IT. A few campers, both girls and boys, felt that in some mysterious way they had been in contact with IT. When the head counselor had heard all of their breathless stories, he asked them to promise to say nothing until campfire time on the third night. At that time, those selected by him and the four counselors as the most certain to have met up with IT in some way, were to tell of their experiences.

On the night of the third day, the Clearwater Campers were more excited than ever, though most of them were disappointed because they thought that they had neither detected any signs of IT nor been helped in any way by the mysterious visitor. As the campfire blazed bright that night, the head counselor called on two of the older boys, Jack and Howard, to tell of their experience with IT. Both of them showed surprise at being called to the fire and declared that they had neither seen nor heard IT at any time during the past three days.

The campers wondered why the head counselor wore a broad smile as the two boys returned to their seats. "Now we shall hear from Tom Ware," the head counselor said.

There were cries of "Yea, Tom!" as Ware went over to the campfire.

"I don't know what IT has got to do with it; I thought it was luck," Tom declared, "but when I told my counselor what I'm going to tell you, he told me to tell the head counselor what had happened to me. He asked me to say nothing about it in camp until now. Here's what happened: This afternoon, after Jack, Howard, and I had fished at the dam for rock bass and carp, we passed the big pool in the stream on the way back to camp. In the pool we saw the big trout that we call Big Bill. Most of the fellows have seen him and perhaps tried to catch him during the past few weeks. For a few moments, Big Bill rested above a whitish rock where we could see him quite plainly; then he either swam under the big rock or lay on the sand where it was very difficult to see him. Howard and Jack went back to their bunks, because they had only worms with them. They wanted to fetch some special flies which they thought would make Big Bill strike. I had only a few worms left but did not go back to camp with Jack and Howard, though they told me that Big Bill probably would not even look at a worm on a hook. I decided that it would be better to make the most of my chance, and try to persuade Big Bill to hitch into one of my worms, than to make the long hike back to the bunks and find him gone when I got back to the pool. I could see Bill moving lazily around, which seemed to show that he had not been scared by us. I stayed back in the shadow of the trees and used a trick that my dad taught me. I took a little piece of clay from the stream back of the pool, put a nice fat worm on my hook, and made a little clay ball around him, so that he was in the middle. I lowered the ball gently into the pool, close to where I could just see Big Bill's head. Down the clay ball went. It did not wash away until it lay on a bluish rock. Then there was no clay ball, only a wriggling worm. Then came a flash, a splash, and a strike that nearly jerked my arm off. Big Bill was fast on my hook! It must have taken me about twenty minutes to get him tired enough and close enough to slip my landing net over his head and body and lift him out onto the bank. Jack and Howard had come back with their dry flies just as I was landing my prize. They both told me what a lucky guy I was. I was even more certain of my luck when cook weighed Big Bill. He was all of three pounds."

down in front of his forehead, but the rest of his head was completely bald. In order to catch him, one had to be prepared, resourceful, ready, and quick enough to grab him by the forelock of hair, because once he had passed, he was gone and could neither be grasped nor caught up with until he was good and ready to pass by again. He might come again, or he might not. The Greeks called him by the name we still use—OPPORTUNITY."

THE QUITTER

Last summer, two little fat frogs lived under a farmhouse, not far from here. They caught flies with their long, sticky tongues, took sunbaths, and sang as they splashed and swam in the farmer's duck pond. Of course, there were no ducks on the pond or they would not have gone there, because frogs are scared of ducks. One of these little frogs was happy and brave, but his little friend was not a bit cheerful and not at all brave, though he was boastful and liked to pretend that he was fearless.

One day the two little frogs saw a big black bull in a field. The not-very-happy frog said, "I'm sure that if I puff myself up as big as I can, I'll be just as big as that big black thing."

He started to puff himself up, but his little fat friend smacked him real hard on the back and "de-puffed" him.

Tom sat down, while the other campers gave him a loud cheer.

"No," said the head counselor with a smile. "Big Bill was not IT, but I want to tell you how I know that Tom met the real IT. Jack and Howard really met IT at the same time as Tom, but as they did not recognize IT; we must leave them out. The Greeks described IT as an athletic young man with wings on his heels, who dodged as he ran and wore only the close-fitting shorts of a Marathon runner. He had a short lock of hair hanging

"Why did you do that?" gasped the boastful little frog.

"Don't you know what happened to the other frog who tried to blow himself up until he was as big as an ox?" asked the cheerful little frog.

"No. What?" questioned the gloomy little frog.

"He blew up and burst," explained the cheerful little frog, sadly.

One sunny morning, as the two little friends froghopped along past the farm dairy, they saw a big pan of cream sitting on the ground under an apple tree.

133

"What a funny yellow pond," piped the sad little frog, who had to jump high into the air to see over the edge of the pan.

"Let's swim in it," chirped the cheerful little frog, after taking a look. "It will be fun."

Together, the two frogs sprang high over the brim of the bowl and landed smack in the cream. They started to swim across the pan but found it difficult to swim in the thick cream. After swimming around for a while, they reached the other side of the dish. Then they became scared, because they found that they could neither climb up the edge of the slippery pan nor jump out of it.

They started to swim again but became more and more tired with each stroke. They had nearly reached the other side of the dish again when the gloomy little frog became discouraged. "I'm tired," he gasped, "there's no use trying to swim any longer. We'll never get out of this awful sticky pond anyway."

"Keep on trying," urged his determined little friend. "If we keep on trying we're sure to get out."

They swam some more, and then the doleful little frog quit. He stopped swimming, struggled for a moment, and then with a little frightened croak he sank beneath the surface.

The brave little frog swam, and swam, and swam. Just as he thought that he would have to give up, because he could hardly force his legs to move, he found himself sitting on a little yellow island. At least, he thought that it must be an island, because he did not need to swim any more—and still he did not sink. He was really sitting on a little lump of butter which he had churned with his brave efforts to keep afloat. He panted a little, puffed a little, rested a little and then jumped from the little "island" which had saved his life. His leap took him sailing over the edge of the pan, and he landed safely on the soft grass.

WHY WOLFE WON

Of course, all of you campers know who Wolfe was? (A brief pause for exhibition of knowledge is advised at this point.) Yes, that's right! James Wolfe was the famous

British general who defeated the French general, Montcalm, on the Plains of Abraham at Quebec, Canada, a long time ago—in 1759 to be exact.

You campers seem to know so much about history that perhaps there is no point in my trying to tell you how and why he won such an important victory before he died for his country on that fateful day in September. But perhaps you don't know about the French washerwoman who helped Wolfe win.

You all know that generals have aides-de-camp, assistants who help them with their plans. Now General Wolfe had some very strange aides-de-camp who helped him win the battle on the heights. They were so very strange, these silent helpers, that they deserve a very special place in history, which they rarely get. Who, and what, do you think these helpers were? Things helped almost as much as people in Montcalm's failure to keep the Wolfe away from his door. Like to guess? (A pause for campers' guesses.)

Well, its not surprising that you cannot guess correctly. General Wolfe's greatest helpers to victory were a pair of red drawers, a pink nightgown, a washerwoman, and—this is important—a bright young army scout with sharp eyes and a keen mind, which he put to good use. It was this unusual combination of people and things that brought victory to Wolfe on the heights. Let me tell you about them.

One bright morning, way back in September 1759, a quick-thinking young scout serving with the army of General Wolfe lay hidden in the bushes on the south shore of the wide Saint Lawrence River, directly opposite the towering cliffs on top of which lay the Plains of Abraham. "I say," he said softly to himself, "the General's going to have a hard time getting his troops up onto those high cliffs. I know that I'd hate to have to hang onto a ladder under them while the Frenchies took pot shots and heaved rocks on top of me. My captain says that if the General has to go all the way around behind the Plains, the enemy will not be taken by surprise and we'll likely never get onto the Plains to fight a deciding battle. So the Captain says to me, he says, in his friendly, off-parade manner, 'Barlow me boy, go and take a good look at those cliffs. Don't try to swim across the river. It's too wide, and the French sentries are sure to take a shot at you if you try to land on the opposite bank, but look well at the cliffs and tell us how to get on top of them when you come back.'"

"He does like his joke, does the Captain. 'Come back and tell us how to get up on top of those cliffs,' he said, with a straight face. Why, a mountain goat couldn't do that unless it had wings. I'd like a nice swim now, but that's not in my orders. No, I've only got to find a way to get the General and his men on top of the precipice. Perhaps the men had better ride on sea gulls, with ducks for the officers; that seems the likeliest way of doing it." While the young scout talked to himself, one of his keen eyes was sweeping the cliffs and the opposite bank of the great river through a telescope. "Blimey! I wish that woman washing clothes on the other side could wash my shirt. It could do with a good wash. Fancy wash she has there! Just look at that pink nightgown, and those red drawers! The old girl must be getting ready for winter. Hope I'm back home before snow flies. Better eat hearty now, old son, before you report to the Captain that the General will have to fly his troops to the objective."

The young soldier ate his cold rations, then decided to scout thoroughly up and down stream and take a good look at different parts of the towering cliffs of the opposite side of the great river before returning to headquarters. He did not want to report failure. He wished that one of the intelligence officers had gone along with him, but he reasoned that they were busy looking for a more likely place to attack than up the face of a steep cliff. After he had finished his thorough survey of the cliffs, the young scout decided that he would have to report that there was no way to tackle the steep cliffs without plenty of long ladders—and plenty of men!

One last keen look through his telescope showed him that the washerwoman must have finished her wash. There was no sign of her on the opposite bank. "She was quick," he told himself. "Wonder where she came from? There's no house nearby." Then slowly he scanned the heights once more with a steady telescope. "Blimey!" he shouted excitedly to himself, "there's the red drawers and the pink nightgown hanging up to dry on top of the cliffs. If the washerwoman got up the cliff, so can we," he reasoned.

The breathless report of the young scout caused his Captain to exclaim, "Barlow, me boy, I'll lose a good scout when they make you a sergeant!" Intelligence officers at once followed up the discovery of the observant scout. A narrow, almost invisible path was discovered which wound up the face of the cliff from the river, where the young soldier had watched the washerwoman, to the top of the Plains of Abraham.

Luck was with General Wolfe's army a night or two later when his advance guard, led by a French-speaking officer, surprised and overpowered the few sentries who were on duty at the top of the path. Before morning, General Wolfe's army was drawn up in battle positions on the Plains of Abraham.

Barlow, who always tried to make his eyes and brain work together, lived through the battle and later on became an intelligence officer.

HOW FIRE CAME TO THE FIVE NATIONS

Often around the fire in the long house of the Iroquois during the Moon of the Long Nights, this American Indian legend is told.

Three Arrows was a boy of the Mohawk tribe. Although he had not yet seen fourteen winters, he was already known among the Iroquois for his skill and daring. His arrows sped true to their mark. His name had been given him when, with three bone-tipped arrows, he brought down three flying wild geese from the same flock. He could move through the forest as softly as the south wind, and though he was a skillful hunter, he never killed a bird or animal unless his clan needed food. Three Arrows was well versed in woodcraft, fleet of foot, and fearless. His people said, "Soon he will be a chief like his father." The sun shone strong in the heart of Three Arrows, because soon he would have to meet the test of strength and endurance through which the boys of his clan attained manhood. He had no fear of the outcome of the Dream Fast which he was so soon to take.

When the grass was knee-high, Three Arrows left his village with his father. They climbed to a sacred place in the mountains. Here they found a narrow cave at the back of a little plateau. Three Arrows decided to live in it during his few days of prayer and vigil. He was not permitted to eat anything during the days and nights of his Dream Fast. He had no weapons, and his only clothing was a breechclout and moccasins. His father left, and the boy's ordeal began.

Three Arrows prayed to the Great Spirit. He begged that soon his clan spirit would appear in a dream and tell him what his guardian animal or bird was to be. When he knew this, he would adopt that bird or animal

as his special guardian for the rest of his life. After such a dream he would be free to return to his people, his Dream Fast achieved.

For five suns Three Arrows spent his days and nights on the rocky plateau, only climbing down to a little spring for water after each sunset. The boy's heart was filled with a dark cloud, because he knew that the next day, the sixth sun, he must return to his village, even if no dream came to him that night. This meant returning to his people with a heavy heart and little or no chance of undergoing another Dream Fast.

That night, weak from hunger and weary from ceaseless vigil, Three Arrows cried out to the Great Mystery: "O Great Spirit, have pity on him who stands humbly before Thee. Let his clan spirit or a sign from beyond the thunderbird come to him before tomorrow's sunrise, if it be thy will." Even as he prayed, the wind suddenly veered from east to north. This cheered Three Arrows, because the wind was now the wind of the Great Bear and the bear was the totem of his clan. It was dark when he entered the cave, and as he did so he smelled, for the first time, the unmistakable odor of a bear. This was strong medicine! He crouched at the opening of the cave, too excited even to lie down. As he gazed out into the night, he heard the rumble of thunder, saw the lightning flash, and felt the fierce breath of the wind from the north. Suddenly a vision came to him. A great bear stood behind him in the cave. Three Arrows heard it say, "Listen well, Mohawk. Your clan spirit has heard your prayer. Tonight you will learn of a great mystery which will bring help and gladness to your people." A crash of thunder brought the dazed boy to his feet as the bear disappeared. He looked from the cave just as a streak of lightning in the shape of a blazing arrow flashed across the sky.

Suddenly the air was filled with a fearful sound. A shrill shrieking came from the ledge just above his cave. It sounded as though mountain lions fought in the storm. Three Arrows felt no fear as he climbed toward the ledge. As his keen eyes grew accustomed to the dim light, he saw that the force of the wind was causing two young balsam trees to rub violently against each other. The strange noise was caused by friction. As the boy listened and watched, fear filled his heart, for from where the two trees rubbed together a flash of lightning showed smoke curling skyward. Motionless, Three Arrows gazed until flickers of flame followed the smoke. He had never seen fire of any kind at close range, nor had any of his people. He scrambled down into the cave again in dread of this strange magic. Then he smelled bear again. He thought of his vision, of the bear and its strange message. Maybe this was the mystery which he was to take back to his people. Yes, the flaming arrow in the sky was to be his totem, and his new name—Flaming Arrow.

When the sun came, Flaming Arrow climbed onto the ledge and broke two dried sticks from what remained of one of the balsams. He rubbed them violently together. Nothing hapened! "This magic is too powerful for me," he thought. Then a mind picture of his clan and his village came to him, and he commenced rubbing the hot sticks together again. Again nothing happened, but his will power took the place of his tired muscles. After a long, tiring time, a faint wisp of smoke greeted his renewed efforts. Then a bright spark was born on one of the sticks. Flaming Arrow waved it as he had seen the fiery arrow wave in the night sky. A resinous blister on the stick glowed, then flamed! Fire had come to the Five Nations!

THE FIRST MAGIC MOCCASINS

A great Plains Indian chief had very tender feet. Other mighty chiefs laughed openly, lesser chiefs smiled secret smiles, and the rest of the people enjoyed the big chief's discomfort in smileless silence. They were all in the same canoe—all of them had bare feet and no horses, but few of them had tender feet. The unhappy medicine man who was the Chief-of-the-Tender-Feet's adviser was greatly troubled, because each time he was summoned by the chief he was sternly asked, "What are you going to do about it?" The "it" referred to the tender feet of the chief.

Driven to desperation, the medicine man hit upon a plan which he knew was not the final solution to the problem but was nevertheless a fine makeshift. He had some women of the tribe weave a long, narrow mat of reeds, and when the big chief had to go anywhere, six braves unrolled the mat in front of him so that he walked in comfort. One day the braves, who were worn out from seeing that the big chief's feet were not worn out, carelessly unrolled the mat over a place where flint arrowheads had been chipped. The arrowheads had long since taken flight, but needlelike chips remained. When the chief's tender feet were cut by these splinters, he let out a series of whoops which made the nearby aspens quiver so hard that they have been doing so ever since.

That night the medicine man was given an impossible task by the enraged chief: "Cover the entire earth with mats so thick that my feet will not suffer, or you will die when the moon is round."

This was an order which the frightened medicine man knew he could never carry out, even if he had been commanded to do so before five snows had come and gone. When he returned to his lodge, he saw the hide of an elk which he had killed pegged out on the ground, with two women busily scraping the hair from the skin. An idea flashed into his groping mind. He sent out many hunters, many women were busy for many days, many braves with hunting knives cut, and women sewed with rawhide sinews.

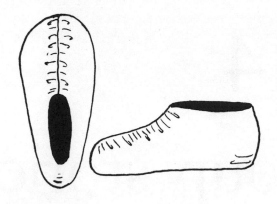

Just before the moon was round, the medicine man appeared before his chief and told him that he had covered as much of the earth as possible in so short a time. When the chief looked from the door of his lodge, he saw many paths of skin stretching as far as the eye could see. Long strips, which could be moved from place to place, connected the main leather paths, and even the chief thought that this time the magic of the medicine man had solved tenderfoot transportation for all time—but this was not to be!

One day, as the big chief was walking fast along one of his tough, smooth, leather paths, he saw a beauteous maiden of the tribe gliding ahead of him. She glanced back when she heard his feet patter on the elkhide path and lighted his heart with an encouraging smile. She was going in the same direction as he, and she was so lithe and agile that she seemed to float rather than walk, though her trim bare feet trod Mother Earth. The chief set off on the run to catch up with her. His eager eyes were fixed on the back of She-Who-Smiled, and so his tender feet strayed from the narrow path—and landed in a bunch of cacti! The maiden ran for her life when she heard the hideous howls of the chief, and Indians in the distant village rushed outdoors, fearing the worst.

Two suns later, when the chief was able to speak again, he sent for his medicine man and told him that when the sun was high, next day, he would be sent with all possible ceremony and speed to the Land of Shadows. The chief was still so upset that he could not be spoken to, even in sign language.

That night, the medicine man went to a high hilltop on a Power Quest. He waited for a dream-vision which would help him to solve immediately the only problem that would save his life: how to cover the entire earth with leather. In a flash of lightning, the answer was shown to him, soon after his vigil had begun. He sped down the hillside, out-howling the big chief at times, as jagged rocks connected with his big feet, but not stopping until he was within his lodge. He worked all night and until those who were to send him on the Shadow Trail came for him just before noon the next day. He accompanied the war-club-armed guards, clutching to his heart something tightly rolled in a piece of deerskin. His cheerful smile surprised the onlookers.

"He is brave!" said the braves who watched his coming. "He is very brave!" said the women of the tribe. The big chief was waiting just outside his lodge, and he gave the guards swift, stern orders. Before the maker-of-magic could be led away, he asked leave to say a few words to the chief. "Speak!" said the chief, who was sorry to lose an able medicine man who was very good at all minor magic—for even the chief knew that covering the entire earth with leather was an impossible task.

The medicine man quickly knelt beside the chief, unrolled the objects from his bundle and slipped one of them on each foot of the chief. The chief appeared to be wearing a bear's hairless feet, instead of bare feet, and he was puzzled as he looked at the elkhide handcraft of the medicine man. "Big chief," the medicine man exclaimed joyfully, "I have found the way to cover the earth with leather. For you, O chief, from now on the earth will always be covered with leather." And so it was!

chapter 14

council fire coup stories

UNLESS THEY ARE STAGING a Northwest Coast Indian night, council fire chiefs who are using the Plains, Woodland, or Pueblo Indian organization at their council fires will of course use the tribal and individual Indian names of their own tribes and braves, instead of the Northwest Coast names used throughout this chapter. The Northwest Coast Indian names given will prove useful when Plains or Woodland tribes receive a "visit" from a clan of the brothers from the Coast.

ADAPTING THE COUP STORY

In this chapter, there are only a few coup stories in which minor changes have to be made in order to keep the story in Plains or Woodland character. In the first story, "The Circle of Life and Death," the Nootka chief speaks of his hunters killing many whales. This can be changed so that a Plains chief named Star Blanket states that his hunters have killed many buffalo. Whales were to the Northwest Coast Indians what buffalo were to the Indians of the Plains. This is why whales crop up from time to time in most Northwest Coast stories and legends.

In the second coup story, "The Quick Thought," the medicine man Future Teller speaks of whales. A white buffalo or herd of buffalo, a strange cloud in the sky, or a white deer or elk may be mentioned instead. Later in the story, instead of referring to a chief being drowned while hunting seals, one can say that the chief was killed while bear hunting.

In the next story, "The Accusing Finger," the theft of six sea otter skins can be changed to the theft of beaver or marten skins.

Finally, the scene of "The Missing Warrior" can take place on the shore of a big lake partially surrounded by cliffs and huge rocks, so that the cove described is on the shore of the lake instead of the ocean shore.

In the remaining stories, a change of individual names and locale is all that is required to make the stories applicable for either a Plains or Woodland council fire.

NARRATING THE COUP STORY

Leaving out even a small part of a story may rob listeners of the clue which makes it possible for them to solve the problem. Naturally, the clear, detailed, and simple way in which all of these stories must be told and the stressing and timing of the principle points and leads are of the utmost importance to the listeners.

THE UNSEEN NARRATOR. Should a council fire chief wish to tell these following coup stories exactly as they are set down, there is an effective and easy way to do so. Let the storyteller of the tribe, or a clan chief with good clear diction, read these stories either from behind a screen directly behind the chief's chair or from immediately behind the backdrop, when a backdrop is used. This is much better than the council fire chief trying to read and rule the council fire area at the same time. Some section of a council fire audience may show restlessness while a council fire chief reads, but this is rarely the case when they are listening to an unseen narrator.

With the council fire chief in his chair to govern the warriors-in-council, his eyes and thoughts on the warriors instead of on a book or paper, there is no reason why the council fire program should not proceed in the usual ceremonious manner while the narrator reads.

THE VISIBLE NARRATOR. Should the chief in charge prefer, he can use a visible narrator, a storyteller

in regalia. This narrator stands near the chief and relates the stories.

THE CIRCLE OF LIFE AND DEATH

A silence broken only by the murmur of waves on the sandy beach fell over three groups of Indians who stood at the edge of the great cedar forest. Two groups of prisoners, with their arms bound behind their backs, were surrounded by a band of warriors of the powerful Nootka tribe. There were fifteen warriors in each band of prisoners, one group of Cowichan and the other of Coast Salish. Both groups had been taken prisoners by the warlike Nootka when they had landed on Nootka territory during a great storm. Now the Nootka chief was about to decide their fate.

"These days have been good ones for us," he began. "Many whales have been killed by our hunters. Now, in thanks to the moon, I offer the lives of fifteen of our captives, who will be set free. The others must die. Let all our prisoners stand in a circle. Every ninth prisoner shall be taken from it to die, but those who remain in the circle when the fifteenth brave of those who will die has been pointed out, will be given food and their weapons and will be set free. I have spoken."

As soon as the chief stopped speaking, a very wise old medicine man, one of the Coast Salish group of prisoners, spoke swiftly and softly to his fourteen fellow captives. He had stood directly behind them, as his guiding medicine power had directed him, while the Nootka spoke. He told each Salish warrior which number to take in the circle, counting clockwise from himself, and he would make magic so that he would be Number 1 in the circle and could be used as a marker by the members of his band. His wisdom told the medicine man that the Nootka chief would count clockwise. The Nootka people danced in that direction and so, reasoned the wise man, the chief would follow the same direction as he counted around the circle.

The Nootka gave the thirty captives time to sing their songs and talk with each other, before ordering them to form a circle. The downcast Cowichan braves did not care when the Salish slipped in among them. Perhaps the Cowichan thought that they might have a better chance to escape being the fatal ninth, as the Nootka Chief counted, if some of the Salish stood among them. They suspected nothing of the Salish medicine man's plan, and they believed that nobody but the Nootka chief would decide where the counting would begin. Even the puzzled Salish warriors had no idea of how their medicine man would trick the Nootka chief into counting him Number 1.

When the Nootka chief stepped into the center of the circle to begin the counting which meant life or death to those in the circle, the Salish medicine man cried, "Choose me as the first to die, O Chief. I am old and ready to take the trail to the Shadow World. Choose me for death," he begged.

"No, Wise One," replied the chief. "You shall have your chance to live, but because you are brave enough to ask to be the first chosen for death, you will be honored by being counted first among the chiefs and warriors in the circle." With these words the chief pointed at the medicine man and said, "One!" He then continued counting, clockwise, around the circle. He pointed directly at a brave each time he called a number. Each time he said "Nine!" the warrior indicated by the chief's finger was led from the circle under guard.

Yes, the magic of the wise old medicine man must have been very powerful, for when the Nootka chief's finger had traveled round the circle for the last time, and the last of the fifteen victims had been led away, the fifteen Salish warriors alone remained in the circle. They were freed, as the Nootka had promised. As they paddled away in their two great cedar canoes, they left behind a puzzled band of Nootka, the most puzzled of all being the Nootka chief.

How would you here in council have numbered the warriors you wished freed, had you been that wise old medicine man? Do not decide now, but when our council fire burns low and you return to your houses, put down the numbers which you would have given to your band so that all fifteen would go free.

The clan whose runner first brings the correct numbers to my house will be honored at our next council fire. I have spoken.

One way to honor the winning clan would be for the tribal chief to present it with a replica of a "copper," a wooden plaque of the usual copper size, from 30 to 40 inches in height and 10 to 20 inches in width, in the shape shown in the illustrations in Chapter 23. This copper can be suitably painted and displayed before the house of the winning clan for one week following the council fire, when the coup story was first told.

An interesting display can be staged by letting the winning clan act out "The Circle of Life and Death" around the fire at the next council, following the telling and solution of the coup story. The winning clan would take the fifteen "safe" numbers, and the tribal chief would select the additional fifteen warriors, co-operative ones. The remaining warriors-in-council would play the part of the Nootka, with a clan chief acting as the Nootka chief and doing the counting. A practice or two before council fire time is wise, to assure the fifteen Salish warriors finding their correct places as quickly and as surely as possible.

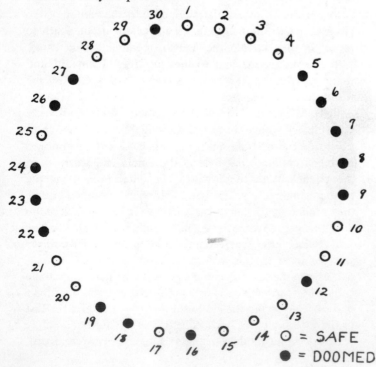

O = SAFE
● = DOOMED

Solution. The Salish medicine man, feeling certain that he could trick the Nootka chief into counting him as Number 1 in the circle, gave each of his warriors a number and ordered him to take up that position in the circle, counting their medicine man Number 1 and facing inward so that the numbering would be done clockwise from the medicine man's left. The "safe" numbers are shown in the diagram.

THE QUICK THOUGHT

"Tonight," began the tribal chief, "you warriors who stand before me have been chosen by your clans because you are said to think fast. Thinking fast can save lives, perhaps your own. Listen while you hear of a wise man who thought fast, and what came of it. Listen well, because you will be asked what you would have said had you stood on the dangerous ground on which the medicine man Future Teller stood, after he had angered the tribal chief many times.

"He-Whose-Harpoon-Is-Sure was a tribal chief of the fearless whale-hunting Nootka. He was praised and admired yet feared by his people, who rarely knew fear. When he was very angry, no man could stand before him and live. You will learn of a night when he was very angry, and why. Future Teller was a powerful medicine man. He had gained much power in the councils of his tribe, because he could see far into the future. He told the chiefs and the people what would happen when they went fishing and whale hunting. He even told the chiefs when dead whales would be washed up onto the beach. When he said, 'In two suns a whale will be found on the beach,' the whale was always found, and on that very day.

"One morning, when the tribal chief had his whalers ready for a whale hunt, Future Teller told the chief that he had chosen an unfavorable day to start on a whale hunt. 'No whale will you get,' the medicine man told the chief. But the day seemed a good one to the tribal chief. All signs pointed to the killing of a whale, so the chief set out in one of the great ocean-going canoes on a quest for whales. His seven strong paddlers drove the huge canoe through the water for one whole day of sun and one night of darkness, but no whale did they see. When he returned, the chief was angry, but no fault could he find with Future Teller. He had only told the truth when he said that the whale hunters would not bring back a whale.

"Things such as this happened too often to please He-Whose-Harpoon-Is-Sure. In time, his words might prove less powerful in council than those of the medicine man. Soon after the whale hunt which brought no whale to the village, another thing came which made He-Whose-Harpoon-Is-Sure very angry. Early one morning, when the tribal chief was ready to take a raiding party to kill or capture a chief of clan of a neighboring tribe who had said hard words about the Nootka, Future Teller spoke. 'It is too late to set out on your raid, O Chief. He whom you seek was drowned as the sun rose this morning, while hunting seals.'

" 'How know you this, O Wise One?' angrily demanded the tribal chief. He knew that the village where the clan chief lived was almost a day distant, even by swift canoe, and he could not understand how even one as wise as Future Teller could know such a thing.

" 'A Raven told me, O Chief,' Future Teller answered with a little smile.

" 'I go to learn if your words are true or false,' declared He-Whose-Harpoon-Is-Sure, as he signaled his paddlers to carry the big canoe across the beach and out to where it floated easily in the ocean. The tribal chief was gone for three suns. When he returned he was very angry. He was angry, not because the medicine man had spoken falsely, but because he had spoken truly. He had learned of the drowning of the clan chief, on the morning when the medicine man had told of it.

"That night, when the village was asleep, warriors seized Future Teller as he slept and hurried him bound before the tribal chief. When Future Teller entered the tribal chief's house, he saw that there was nobody there except the chief, who sat on his chair, and two tall warriors—each armed with a great club—standing beside him. When Future Teller faced He-Whose-Harpoon-Is-Sure, he saw a cruel smile on the face of the tribal chief and noticed that the chief signaled to the two club bearers to stand behind the medicine man.

" 'I have learned that you see truly into the future, Medicine Man, sometimes too truly for your own good' exclaimed the tribal chief angrily. 'Now tell me, if you can, when are you going to die?'

"For only a heartbeat the medicine man hesitated; then he looked knowingly into the tribal chief's eyes and said a sentence of only four short, wise words. Instantly, the tribal chief released Future Teller and gave him many rich gifts.

"What do you think these words were, O warriors of your clans? He who first steps forward with these four correct words, or those closest to them, will count coup for his clan, which will wear a coup shell on its copper because their warrior has thought fast. I have spoken."

Solution. Future Teller saved his life by swiftly answering the Tribal Chief in these four words: "Four days before you." Legend states that from then on the tribal chief showed great concern regarding Future Teller's health. When He-Whose-Harpoon-Is-Sure greeted the medicine man each morning with an anxious, "I hope you are strong?" Future Teller knew that the words came directly from the tribal chief's heart.

MEDICINE MAN MAGIC

"Listen well, O Warriors of the Beaver, Hawk, Whale, and Sea Lion clans who sit by my chair," said the tribal chief. You too, when you have heard this story, will be given the chance to tell how you would have done the thing of which the story tells. Many who hear my words will say, 'Here is a thing which cannot be done.'

"Even today, none of the wise men of the Nootka knows whether Whale Hunter, the chief harpooner of the tribe, hoped to have their medicine man lose face or whether he wished to see if the wise one possessed such powerful medicine that he could do that which seemed impossible. This thing happened at the great potlatch given by Whale Hunter at the time when his towering totem pole was set up.

"There was a blanket of silence covering those in the great house of Whale Hunter. He sat on his beautifully carved and painted chief's chair, close to the bright fire. In front of him, behind him, and on both sides of him were piles of treasures which he would give away at this big ceremonial potlatch. Clan chiefs, helpers, and slaves stood close at hand ready to help at a sign from the chief harpooner. The night was almost gone, and chiefs who had come far on the invitation of Whale Hunter were loaded with rich gifts. Ocean-going canoes, sea otter skins, slaves, long strings of dentalium shells, rich robes, and beautiful blankets had he given with pride and generous hands. Splendid, richly carved cedar boxes, harpoons, and other fine weapons lay among other gifts ready to be given by Whale Hunter at this great give-away.

"This tribal chief, as was fitting a great harpooner and warrior, showed that no tiredness had touched him, but the lesser chiefs and his other helpers were weary.

" 'Here have I some Tsimshian blankets to give to my three sons,' said Whale Hunter. 'Because of the great worth of these blankets, they will be given away in this way. My oldest son will receive half of the blankets, my next oldest son must receive one-third, while my youngest son shall have his rightful share, one-ninth. The strain of giving—and I have much more to give—has been heavy, but so that the pleasure and honor of giving may go on without stop, I now ask our tribal medicine man to take my place in the giving of these blankets to my three sons.'

"As the chief stopped talking, he sat down and gestured toward a pile of splendid blankets. The medicine man came forward to take the chief's place. The wise man was glad because of the honor which the tribal chief had done him, but he was puzzled by an action which rarely happened at such a potlatch. Nearly always were the family gifts given to the relatives by the chief who gave the potlatch.

" 'Honor has come to me, O Chief,' declared the medicine man, saluting Whale Hunter and bending over the pile of blankets.

"The medicine man's own magnificent blanket touched the floor as he stooped over the wonderfully woven Tsimshian ones. He folded his blanket carefully, placed it on a guest seat beside him, then counted the blankets in the pile which lay before him. The chiefs and people saw that he was startled. He counted the blankets again, carefully. 'There are seventeen, O Chief!' he exclaimed, but his words were those of question.

"Since Whale Hunter smiled without replying, the medicine man continued: 'It is your wish that I give *one-half* of these blankets to your oldest son, *one-third* to the next oldest, and *one-ninth* to your youngest son. Do I speak truly?'

" 'Your words speak my wishes,' Whale Hunter replied.

"The medicine man looked puzzled for a heartbeat. You too would have been puzzled had you stood in his place. Could *you* divide *seventeen* blankets into *two* equal parts without tearing a blanket in two, something which no one there would dare do except the tribal chief?

"A wise smile chased the frown from the face of the medicine man after he had stood in deep thought for a heartbeat or two. He then divided the blankets exactly as Whale Hunter had ordered. When those at the potlatch saw how he did it, they murmured and marveled. Then the medicine man threw his blanket over his shoulders and strode to his place of honor, while Whale Hunter —whose turn it now was to wear the puzzled look—continued the great give-away.

"Now, I ask the question of each of you four warriors. How would *you* have divided the blankets so that Whale Hunter's wishes were obeyed? Tell me softly, one by one, that I may know which warrior thinks fastest and best. He shall be rewarded, and his correct answer will count coup for his clan. I Have spoken."

Solution. The fast-thinking medicine man was only thrown off balance for a few moments by the startling fact that there were seventeen blankets, which apparently made the division ordered by the tribal chief impossible. After a brief and wise thought, the medicine man added his own blanket to the pile, which gave him eighteen blankets for distribution. He was then able to give the oldest son nine blankets (one-half). To the next oldest he gave six (one-third), and to the youngest son he gave two blankets (one-ninth). Then, as the story tells, he threw his own blanket, which he never had any intention to give away, over his shoulders and strode to the seat of honor to which his wisdom rightly entitled him.

WISE WORDS RIGHT A WRONG

Chief Twisted Foot was old and ill. Two sons had he. The elder was called Killer of Bears. He loved power

and riches and was crooked in his thoughts. The younger son, known as Fireweed by his tribe, was as straight in his thoughts as the arrows which sped from his powerful bow, and he was brave and a good hunter.

While his younger brother was hunting the sea otter, Killer of Bears went to his sick father. The old man was so ill that he could hardly speak, but he managed to tell his son that before he took the trail to the Spirit World he was going to declare his will. Next day, before the chiefs of the tribe and the medicine man he would say that he was leaving his houses, rights to the beach, canoes, coppers, weapons, blankets, furs, and many other rich possessions to be divided equally between his two sons.

"I am the elder, father," said Killer of Bears, "and I do not ask for more than my share. But as the elder son, I ask that you allow me to make the division of property which you believe right, one-half to each son, and that no chief or others of the tribe will have words to say about the division."

The father did not trust his elder son and would not have granted his wish; but the old man was worn and weary, so he gave in. "Yes," he whispered, "it will be as you wish."

The next day, because Twisted Foot was about to take the last trail, his two sons, the three clan chiefs, and the medicine man gathered in the old chief's house. Many of his friends were also there, as Twisted Foot was respected and liked by the people.

"Hear me, chiefs and people of the tribe," Twisted Foot began in a voice so faint that those furthest from him gathered around his bed of furs. "It is my last wish that all I possess be divided equally between my two sons. Half will go to Bear Killer and the other half to Fireweed. I have promised by elder son that he alone will make the division of all my possessions and that the dividing done by him will be agreed to without question."

There was a murmur of surprise from those who were gathered in the great house, and the medicine man's eyes showed surprise, because they knew Bear Killer.

"What must I do to make things straight for my younger son," Twisted Foot whispered in a voice so low that only the medicine man heard. "I know that my unwise decision will prove most unfair to him."

The medicine man was not considered very wise by the people without good reason. His eyes were no longer troubled, for he had quickly thought of a few wise words to right a wrong. He whispered in the dying chief's ear.

The old chief looked surprised for an instant; then he smiled a tired, contented smile. "You have heard my wish that Bear Killer make the division of my property," he said. "I feel that he will do so fairly, but I also want you to remember this last wish. When the division is made - - - - -," and here the old chief repeated the five words which the medicine man had whispered to him.

These five simple words made everything straight and right. The chiefs and people murmured again, but this time it was caused by wonder at the old chief's wisdom.

What five words do *you* think Twisted Foot said?

Solution. The five words uttered by the dying chief were, "Fireweed must have first choice." (The tribal chief can accept as the correct answer any similar five words which express the same statement.)

DEATH ON BIRCH BARK

"O Warriors four who sit by my chair," said the tribal chief, "you are free, not like the young chief who lay in a guarded house awaiting death. Listen well, that you may hear his story. But in hearing it you must decide what you would have done had you been that young man. You too will be given the chance to save yourselves. To do so you must think quickly, and well. The first among you to do so will count coup and be rewarded, but the fate of those who fail to do so will be decided by a council of clan chiefs."

"This is the story: Clan Chief Sea Otter of the powerful Squamish was young and strong and brave. He had been noticed by his people, yes even by his tribal chief. This had caused his trouble and was the reason why he was a prisoner, under guard of his enemies in the tribe, in the tribal chief's house. The young chief had hunted so well, fished so well, and given such a great potlatch that the heart of the chief of the tribe was black with jealousy. He feared that the words of Sea Otter in council would have more weight than those of the tribal chief. Even a greater fear darkened the tribal chief's thoughts; he feared that Sea Otter might be chosen by the Squamish to be their tribal chief. True, that could not happen while the present chief lived, but death was never far from the tribal chief as he hunted bear and sought the seal in his light canoe. He felt that death drew closer and closer as Sea Otter became more and more noticed by the people, so one day he had the young chief put into prison, accusing him of doing things harmful to the tribe. Enemies who were jealous of the young chief declared that the tribal chief spoke truly, so Sea Otter was to die when the sun came again.

"Because some chiefs and many of the people had murmured against the tribal chief's treatment of Sea Otter, it was decided at a council of chiefs that the young chief was to be given one chance. The tribal chief agreed to put two birch bark strips into a basket which was to be kept in his house. On one strip was the drawing of a ceremonial kill-club, which meant death. On the other strip was the drawing of an eagle, meaning freedom. It was agreed that when Sea Otter was taken to the place

of death in the forest, he would be allowed to put his hand into the covered basket and take out one slip. The drawing on the slip was to decide his fate, Freedom—or Death.

"The clan chiefs and people thought this would give Sea Otter a fair chance to escape death. The good spirits should help a young man who lived a good life, they thought. But they hoped without knowing how black was the heart of the tribal chief. In the dark, on what might be the last night of Sea Otter on earth, the young chief's keen ears heard a noise, as though someone had stumbled over something at one end of the great house. The moon was high and, without moving, Sea Otter saw the tribal chief. Sea Otter thought at first that the tribal chief, knowing he was without weapons, had come to kill him while he slept. But no, the tribal chief was too cunning to give the young chief's friends the chance to say that he killed Sea Otter to make sure that he died. In the moonlight which came into the house through holes in the roof high above, Sea Otter saw his enemy go to one corner of the house where splendidly carved boxes and beautifully woven baskets stood on the floor and on shelves. He moved some of the boxes, took something down from a shelf which he could just reach, and after a moment put it back again. What had been done, Sea Otter could not tell.

"When the tribal chief had gone, Sea Otter, making no noise in his bare feet, went to the corner where the chief had been and tried to see what had been moved by the chief. He could only see dimly some baskets in the moonlight. He decided to wait until the very first ray of light of day shone into the house and then look again. Sea Otter believed that the guards outside would not come into the house so early; so when the light came, he stole softly down to the baskets and looked at those on the higher shelves. They were small, covered baskets, and the thought suddenly came to Sea Otter that the strips of death and freedom might be in one of them.

"There were many boxes, far too many to open and close, but the young chief shook all within reach, hoping that his keen ears would hear the little rustle made by birch bark, if the strips were inside. He heard nothing. He was about to give up the search but decided to say a prayer to the Great Chief Above and then look once more. He raised his arms high in prayer, lowered them a little and then opened his eyes. His hands pointed to a beautiful ceremonial basket on a corner shelf. He took it down and raised the lid. Inside, there was a small, round, wonderfully decorated basket. He took it out quickly, shook it, then opened it. Yes, two strips of birch bark lay inside. He could see a drawing on the strip that faced upward; it was that of a kill-club. He shook the little basket so that the other strip turned over. When it did so the young chief looked at it in amazement. Fear filled his eyes for a heartbeat,—for it too bore the drawing of a kill-club!

"Sea Otter then knew that the tribal chief had made sure that he would have no chance to escape the death that had been so cunningly planned for him. Stunned by the treachery of the tribal chief, Sea Otter could not think clearly at first. He knew that the guards outside of the house were picked from among his enemies. If he called them they would only tell the tribal chief, who would perhaps have him killed at once by the guards, and then tell the people that Sea Otter had been trying to escape when killed. No doubt his enemy would find some sure way to outwit him.

"Then a thought came to him, a bright thought which put his heart at ease. He knew a sure way to defeat the plans of his enemy. He went back to the other end of the house and was asleep on the skins when the guards came to take him to the place of death. He saw some of the councilors of the tribe come in with the tribal chief and carry away the basket in which was the little basket, in which were the strips of death on birch bark.

"The chiefs and people crowded around the place of death but were held back by guards so that they could not approach the young chief or the warriors who surrounded him armed with heavy ceremonial clubs which they would be ordered to use if Sea Otter took the death strip from the basket.

"The tribal chief spoke to the people. He told them of the fairness of the trial of Sea Otter and the wisdom of the judgment which declared he must die. In spite of this, they had given Sea Otter a chance to save his life by means of the birch bark strips. The people murmured but decided to leave things to chance. Surely the good spirits would help a young man who was fair and good, they thought.

"As Sea Otter looked calmly around, he smiled on his friends and enemies. Yes, he felt sure that he had decided on the only sure way to save himself from death.

"Now, warriors of the clans, here is the same sort of basket which stood before Sea Otter on that fateful day. Tell us what you would have done had you been that young chief in deadly danger. The first of you to tell me how he tried to outwit his enemies will count

coup for himself and clan. Tell me softly, that the warriors of the other clans cannot hear. The fate of those who cannot tell may be decided by a Council of Clan Chiefs."

Solution. At the place of execution, Sea Otter drew a "Death" slip from the basket. He smiled happily and exclaimed, "The Eagle of Freedom! I love freedom! It is a part of me. See, I eat it, to prove my words! I thank you, Chief, for having given me the chance to be free again." Since the second slip, still in the basket, bore the same symbol of death as the one which Sea Otter had partially concealed in his hand and then eaten, the tribal chief dared not admit, even to his closest friends, that he had acted so dishonorably as to put two death slips into the basket. A chief who dared to do so would meet swift justice at the hands of the other chiefs. So when the chief of the guards took the death slip from the basket and held it up for inspection, the tribal chief could only join in the shouts of the people—"Justice is done!"

THE ACCUSING FINGER

Listen well, warriors, that the wise ones among you may count coup when I have finished this story of the shaman High Cloud, whose wise words bring a warning to all of us.

When this wise old medicine man was asked by the tribal chief to decide which of two warriors was guilty of the theft of six sea otter skins from the house of a hunter, he promised that he would use his shaman power to make the decision.

When the council met in solemn silence around the council fire, as we do tonight, two warriors faced the shaman in the bright light of the fire.

High Cloud the shaman first spoke to Swift Paddle, who had been accused of the theft of the sea otter pelts by Winding Trail, the warrior who now stood beside him before the council fire.

"You have declared that you are not guilty, Swift Paddle, yet you have been accused by Winding Trail of having taken the skins from the house of the hunter while he was on the mountain trail and the rest of the clan worked with the salmon catch. Tell me, remembering that my mind searches in your heart, if *you* did not take the skins, who did? Only Winding Trail and you were on guard in the village. I know that between you and Winding Trail there is often a dark cloud, that you do not point your arrows together as friends do. Still I ask you, do you think that he took the pelts? Speak with a straight tongue and tell me whom you accuse of the theft."

"I accuse none, O Wise One," answered Swift Paddle in a low, troubled voice. "I only know that I am not guilty."

The shaman looked searchingly at Swift Paddle, then turned his keen eyes on Winding Trail. "Speak, O warrior," High Cloud commanded. "Name the one whom you accuse, and know that as you do so your heart will tell me the name of the stealer of the skins."

No sound came from the lips of Winding Trail, but he raised a hand and pointed his forefinger directly at Swift Paddle. The shaman stared hard at the hand of the accuser. Suddenly it shook like the leaves of an aspen tree. "Winding Trail, you point at Swift Paddle as the one who is guilty, but your pointing hand accuses *you* of the theft," said the shaman sternly. "Even if your hand trembled not, it still tells me that you are the thief and not Swift Paddle. Admit the wrong that you do Swift Paddle in blaming him for a theft which you yourself have committed. Speak now with a straight tongue, Winding Trail, while there may still be pity in the heart of our tribal chief," ordered High Cloud.

Winding Trail dropped his accusing hand, bowed his head, and stretched out his arms to his tribal chief in a silent appeal for mercy, as he said in a hoarse whisper "I am the guilty one."

After the embers of the council fire were black, the tribal chief walked in the forest with the shaman. As they neared the village, the chief asked a question in order to find the answer to a thing which had surprised and troubled him. "Will you tell me, O Wise One, how the hand of Winding Trail, while pointing to Swift Paddle, accused not Swift Paddle but himself?"

The darkness of night hid the shaman's smile as he told in one sentence the secret of the hand pointed to accuse one who was innocent.

Can a warrior in council tell me what he thinks the shaman told the chief. Who will do so and count coup?

Solution. This is what the shaman told the tribal chief: "Often the accusing forefinger points to an innocent person, but the other three fingers point to the guilty one!"

THE MISSING WARRIOR

Silently the chief led his little party through the great cedar forest toward the ocean. Swiftly and surely, though it was near dark and no trail could be seen, he brought his band to a steep and narrow gorge which opened onto a small rock-strewn beach. The sixteen warriors and three chiefs who made up the party were armed with light clubs. Carefully the chief posted his warriors be-behind big rocks which were scattered some distance from the water's edge around the almost circular beach. There was no need for him to put a guard on the high cliffs which completely surrounded the cove; they towered straight up from the beach and offered neither handhold, foothold, nor hiding place. The only openings were the little beach on the ocean side of the cove and the entry to the narrow gorge which cut through the cliff wall. The small bay was like a trap, and the only way out of it on the land side lay through the slitlike pass in the cliffs.

After the leader had put his men in position, he returned with his three chiefs to the mouth of the ravine which led onto the beach. They melted into the darkness as they hid themselves behind boulders at the narrow entrance. They were silent as the night as they lay with their war clubs held ready for use. The chief had learned from one of the tribal scouts that another coastal tribe planned to send four of its best scouts to spy out the land before sending a powerful raiding party to attack the village which lay a short distance from the beach where the ambush was prepared. The small scouting party was to travel by canoe, and the raiders knew that the little cove was the easiest, perhaps the only, spot on the rough and rocky coast where a safe, unobserved landing could be made.

The chief who had set the trap felt sure that the little rocky cove, now surrounded by his warriors, would be chosen by the enemy scouts as the landing place. The peace had not been broken for many moons on that part of the coastal strip, and for that reason the little bay had long lain unguarded.

Only the soft ripple of the waves could be heard by the tense warriors in ambush. For long they lay without movement, peering oceanward into the darkness. Suddenly, a long dark shadow outlined against the phosphorescent ocean appeared close at hand. It was a hunting canoe which had approached almost noiselessly. Silent paddles urged the craft cautiously toward the rock-strewn beach. There was a soft splashing noise as the bow of the canoe came close to the shore. Four shadowy figures disembarked and carried the canoe silently onto the beach. Then, spears in hand, the invaders separated and the men who had come from the ocean moved like ghosts in the direction of the mouth of the gorge. Though the night was dark, they moved easily among the rocks. Then the shrill cry of an alarmed sea bird shattered the silence, and the warriors in ambush struck. In a moment, three of the raiders had been clubbed or seized before they had time to use their spears. Those in ambush had been given the order not to kill but to capture. The fourth raider must have moved lightning-fast under the cover of darkness, for the searchers could not find him.

They peered behind rocks and felt cautiously in fissures, but the missing warrior could not be found. The three prisoners were dragged to the mouth of the gorge, where a chief tied their hands and feet, while the other two chiefs kept their constant lookout toward the ocean. The prisoners spoke the same language as their captors, since they were members of the same linguistic and tribal group. They were questioned about the missing spy, but they would not even admit that there was a fourth man in their party.

The leader ordered the searchers to spread out, and he joined in the search. No movement was heard either on the beach or in the water. Warriors searched in the shallows and swam out to look in the shadows of rocks which rose up out of the ocean. The leader peered into the darkness around the beached canoe. He felt cautiously inside the craft as his men once again searched every part of the beach from the water's edge to the mouth of the gorge. The missing warrior had vanished without leaving a trace. There could only be one explanation, the chief thought—magic! Useless to fight against such a powerful thing he reasoned. No, he would stop the search and lead his warriors back to the village.

He was about to give the order when a second thought flashed into his mind. Such magic could only be beaten by still more powerful magic! He went up the beach to the chiefs who kept guard at the entrance to the ravine. "Return quickly to the village," he told one of them, "and bring back the medicine man."

Soon the medicine man stood beside the chief and listened to the story of the missing warrior. Darkness hid his smile as he glanced for a moment toward the almost invisible searchers, dim moving figures which still combed the beach like tired shadows. Three words only did the medicine man speak to the chief. There may have been strong magic in them, because the leader repeated them to two of his chiefs. Then, before a swift runner could have run around the cove, the warrior who had vanished was dragged before the astonished leader.

What, O warriors, were the three wise words of the medicine man? Who will be the first to tell them to me that he may count coup?

Solution. The medicine man said: "Count the searchers."

YOUNG-MEN-AFRAID-OF-THEIR-HORSES

A legend of how two fast horses became slow and two slow horses became fast

When Chief Wise Wolf was very old, he sent for his two sons, both warriors of his tribe, and spoke these words:

"Not many moons away your father will journey to the Land of the Red Sunrise. I have horses, fine robes, and many possessions. I have decided to leave them to one of you. Last night in a dream a Wise One told me that instead of dividing my goods between you, I must leave all to my wisest son. He told me how this must be decided—so listen well. Outside my tepee stand my two *fastest* horses. Both, as you know, are equally swift. The medicine man will give one to each of you as a present. You will both ride away from our village, and all my possessions will be given to one of you—to him whose horse returns *last* to my tepee. I have spoken."

Two puzzled sons rode sadly away from their father's village. Each would have preferred a race. Both knew well what to do with swift horses, but neither knew what to do with slow ones. They both loved the wild "Hooka-hey" as braves swung onto the backs of swift ponies and raced for a coup. For many moons they rode from friendly village to friendly village. Each sought advice but they found no one wise enough to give them good counsel. Each brave kept close on the trail of his brother, since he did not wish to be the first to return to his father's lodge.

One day both brothers rode up to the tepee of a wise medicine man. They knew of him as the one who had warned the Red Men that the buffalo herds would run from the beat of their drums. Now here he was, an old man playing softly on his eagle-bone whistle and living only a few bowshots from their father's village.

"A dream has told me that the two braves now known to the tribes as the Young-Men-Afraid-of-Their-Horses would come to me for counsel," he said gravely as he greeted them. He told them that if they would tell him their difficulties, one at a time, he would give them both a straight answer at the same moment. After each son had told the medicine man almost the same story, he called them back to his tepee. His advice was brief, but it set both braves rushing out to the horses.

The wise medicine man watched the two brothers race toward their village. Their quirts urged the willing horses forward.

What had he told them, my braves? What could he have said that thus changed their entire course of action after so many moons? He said *only four words!* What were they?

Solution. The four words of advice which the wise medicine man gave were: "Ride your brother's horse." This occasioned the rush for the horses, since each brother knew that if he could race his brother's horse home first, his own would come in last and he would be his father's sole heir.

PART 4

WHEN THE SPIRIT SOARS

chapter 15

variety campfire

IN ORDER TO INCREASE THE VARIETY and scope of weekly campfire nights, about half the season's usual eight campfires can be devoted to special nights, when memorable events or places unfold by campfire light. A few suggestions for such activities follow.

INTERNATIONAL NIGHTS

One campfire in the season can be given over to the picturization of a night in some foreign country, such as France, Italy, India, Japan, Holland, Switzerland, South America, or some other country with distinctive landscape or building, costumes, customs, and music. In transporting a part of one of these distant lands to the campfire circle, instrumental music, appropriate songs, and colorful improvised costumes will play a major part in helping to create the right atmosphere. Most campers, with a little help from the arts and crafts people, will be able to wear a costume which, even though made of strong crepe paper, will be more or less typical of the clothing worn in the country chosen for portrayal at the campfire. A well-known landmark of a city in the country represented can be painted a heroic size on a piece of canvas or cloth and hung up at one side of the campfire circle as a backdrop to heighten the effect. The painted background need only give a rough general outline of a building or an object typical of the country represented. The Arc de Triomphe or the Eiffel Tower for France, a Torii or Fujiyama for Japan, the Taj Mahal for India, a windmill in front of a length of the famous dike for Holland; the Leaning Tower or part of the Grand Canal, with a gondola in plain view, is unmistakably Italy. A close-up of a chalet with bright painted flowers in window boxes, or a little chalet on a mountain with a goat or two in the foreground, can portray Switzerland as well as, or probably better than, a painted backdrop of the Covered Bridge in Lucerne or one of the Matterhorn. These backdrops should strike a light, colorful note rather than a somber one.

Imagination can· result in devising outstanding stunts which may be introduced as surprises on some of these special events nights. Here are a few dramatic effects which the author has devised and uses with considerable success, aided by arts and crafts and a few specially detailed leaders who provide the behind-the-backdrop effect.

EIFFEL TOWER OR ARC DE TRIOMPHE FINALE

As a grand finale, when one of these backdrops is used, a torch is made from a number of non-flammable firework sparklers and set off by a leader mounted on a strong chair behind the backdrop, with the flare rising from just above the center of the painted structure. When such an effect is used, the top of the tower or arch must, of course, be level with the top of the backdrop.

FUJIYAMA FINALE

When a Fuji backdrop is used, a metal pail with a length of heavy chain or several rather heavy round stones in it, and a metal or tin can with a few teaspoonfuls of the powder which makes red-colored fire when lit, can be used to advantage. At the end of the "Campfire in Japan" night, a counselor behind the backdrop rattles the chain inside the pail for a moment or two, then lights the powder in the tin can. The red fire flames upward with a realistic volcano-in-action effect as the red fire reflects from the snow on the mountaintop.

nights

Lighted Japanese lanterns can be strung across the campfire circle throughout the campfire to heighten the Japanese effect.

DUTCH DIKE OR WINDMILL FINALE

Two sensational effects can be introduced as a finishing touch to the "Night in Holland" campfire. The first is achieved by having the sails of the windmill painted and mounted so that they turn easily when the top sail, which rises for at least a foot above the canvas top of the backdrop, is pushed in either direction by the hand of a leader stationed behind the backdrop. The sails of the windmill lie close to the canvas, almost touching it, the two arms being held in place by a big bolt which goes through the center where they meet and is fastened in place—after passing through a supporting plank driven into the ground—by a nut in the rear of the backdrop. One or two large washers between the head of the bolt and the backdrop will assure that the sails revolve easily and smoothly. Nobody except the few briefed in advance will suspect that the sails turn; and when they start to revolve toward the end of the campfire, the campers are surprised. Just in case some of the campers try to push the sails around in advance, it is well to fasten one of the windmill arms securely in place by passing a strong piece of wire or strong cord, staple fashion, through it and then fastening the wire or cord securely at the back of the backdrop. The leader whose job it is to make the sails turn as a finale must be certain to remove this restraining wire or cord, by pulling it out from behind the backdrop, before starting the sails in motion.

The dike finale requires a little preparation, but the result is both startling and amusing. Somewhere in the dike, which is painted on the canvas behind the windmill and runs the entire length of the backdrop, a small round hole—not larger than ⅜th of an inch in diameter—is cut about 3 feet above the ground and to one side of the windmill. This hole can easily be covered by fastening a small circle of canvas, painted the same color as the dike, on the front of the backdrop. It should be fastened only at the top. A big garden type of syringe, which holds a lot of water and has a pointed nozzle, is concealed close to the rear side of the backdrop in readiness. If the campfire circle is situated so that a hose can be used instead of a one- or two-gallon squirt, so much the better; but the stream of water which comes from the hose must be so regulated that when it is turned on, the water will not go through the hole in the canvas for more than 10 or 12 inches. The same precaution should be observed when using the syringe. Should the hose not prove practical because of the situation of the nearest faucet, and should no syringe be available, a working substitute may be made from a large watering can used without the spray nozzle.

A leader or two should be unobtrusively stationed behind the backdrop just before the time when the windmill sails will turn and, a few moments later, the dike spring a leak. After the turning sails have been admired for a little while by the campers the leader takes care of starting the leak in the dike. The stream's arrival can be signaled by a low whistle from the leader behind the backdrop. This is to warn an assistant who has taken up a position a few feet away from where the water will spurt through, inside the campfire circle. As soon as the assistant sees the water coming through the hole in the dike he shouts, points, and shoos the campers away from the immediate vicinity of the "leak in the dike." He pantomimes panic, then apparently tries to stop the flow of water by putting his hand over the leak. The only result is that he manages to get rather wet in his gallant attempt to hold back the sea. At this moment, a very small camper clad in traditional Dutch costume or a good facsimile walks into the campfire circle. Slowly he approaches the circle of campers surrounding the leak. He walks calmly up to it and covers it with his finger. The flow of water stops almost instantly, "instantly" being decided by how soon the leader behind the scenes can direct the water away from the hole, through which he sees a finger appear. While the campers sing "Taps" and leave the campfire circle, the little hero remains steadfastly at his post. He is the last thing the campers see as they look back on their way to the cabins. As in all other stunts, showmanship is required to put this one across effectively. The campfire director must call attention to what is going on. He must point out in an unobtrusive way the arrival of the small Dutch boy at the campfire circle and see that space is cleared for him and around the dike so that as many campers as possible have a good view of his actions as he plugs the dike. Finally, he calls for three cheers for the little hero, after the flow of water has ceased.

Neither Dutch people nor Dutch campers will take offense at this little skit. They are the people who know best that no boy, nor anyone else, ever performed the impossible task of saving any part of Holland by plugging a leaky dike with his finger. With a commendable sense of humor, and tongue in cheek, the Dutch are now, because of the tourists' positive belief in the story and their insistent demands that the heroic feat be fittingly commemorated, erecting a monument to the unknown "hero" of the dike!

AFRICAN SAFARI CAMPFIRE

This can be made an eventful night which will prove both interesting and amusing, by the judicious use of colorful costumes—at least enough of them to keep the campers from catching colds—drums, interpreters, and various jungle effects and props. Additional humor can be supplied by staging a skit in which two or three "explorers" loaded with the most unsuitable hunting equipment, such as butterfly nets, and accompanied by a native "interpreter," meet a group of natives who have never seen strangers before. The back-and-forth conversation, which should be written and learned in advance, is interpreted by the interpreter and can be made very funny. The old gag of having the very longest sentences translated from the "Africanese" by one brief word in English can be used as a part of the skit. For instance, the leader of the safari tells the interpreter to ask the native chief if there is drinking water nearby. The interpreter singsongs a funny-sounding paragraph in the native dialect. The native chief answers, with much gesticulation and waving of a formidable-looking spear, by a much longer series of phrases.

"What did he say?" the safari leader asks.

The interpreter replies, "He said 'Yes.'"

"Ask him how far away it is and whereabouts it is," orders the leader impatiently.

"Dagomba?" questions the interpreter curtly.

"Dinka!" answers the native chief.

"What did he say?" the safari leader asks anxiously.

"He says that there is a small spring beyond the high blue mountain, on the other side of the crocodile river, about nine miles to the northwest of this place," the interpreter explains blandly.

"I can take care of this interpreting business myself," the safari leader says angrily. "I will get some chickens for our supper." He takes a long, large, and fancy necklace from a big bag carried by a native bearer and dangles it before the amazed native chief. "Me to you—you to me," he shouts, then clucks loudly imitating a chicken. The chief looks blank. The leader clucks some more and flaps his arms like wings. A big smile lights up the face of the native chief. He dashes out of the campfire circle and disappears for a moment.

"See!" says the safari leader proudly looking at his fellow explorers.

A moment later the chief rushes back into the council fire. He stops before the safari leader and holds out on the palm of his open hand a hen's egg.

This safari campfire can end with drumming, suitable songs, and "native" dances by the belles of the tribe.

GYPSY CAMPFIRE NIGHT

This can be especially gay and colorful. A caravan can be painted for a backdrop, and gypsy music and dancing built into the program. Picturesque gypsy costumes can be improvised without much difficulty. A soulful violin, playing the accompaniment for gypsy songs, can help the act immensely, and such a night offers a fine opportunity for solo gypsy dances.

CIRCUS CAMPFIRE NIGHT

Such a night can bring the big top to the campfire circle without too much effort on the part of the organizers. At times, blaring circus music—which can be supplied by an off-stage gramophone—will heighten the effect as tumblers, jugglers, performers on the *low* tightrope, clowns, and a lady lion-tamer perform in the spotlight under the watchful eye of a ringmaster. Comedy animals can be improvised without too much effort, and add greatly to the fun.

AMERICAN CAMPFIRE NIGHT

There are many places in the United States where colorful events take place which can be staged in the campfire circle. The theme can be the Mardi Gras in New Orleans; a sparkling fiesta of the Southwest; a night in the Wild West, with cowboys, cowgirls, pioneers, and Indians to add variety to the costumes; or early days in America. At an "Early Settlers" night, familiar figures such as Davy Crockett, Johnny Appleseed, Daniel Boone —without a coonskin cap, as he disliked and never wore one at any time—and other celebrities of this period can be featured. As an "extra added attraction," a square dance can be put on. Such an American night can be brought to an end with a campfire corn roast, with the corn properly prepared for roasting beforehand. While it is roasting, old-time songs can be sung and suitable stories told.

STORYBOOK CAMPFIRE NIGHT

This can be not only a striking campfire but—unobtrusively, of course—an educational one also. Campers of all ages can participate, in the dress of their favorite storybook hero or heroine. Long John Silver can rub shoulders with Alice, from Wonderland. Robinson Crusoe can pay compliment to Little Nell. William Shakespeare can exchange luminous words with Rob Roy. And Uncle Tom can indulge in witticisms with Brer Rabbit, though he may not know what Brer is talking about, if he uses the same sort of talk he used in the book dealing with his life and adventures. There is a limitless choice of stunning characters for campers of all ages and, above all, the thrill of being able to impersonate a hero or heroine who has been the object of much admiration since the day he or she stepped from between the covers of a book to become the ideal of the reader. The most erudite of the older campers can introduce any remembered phrases of the characters which they represent into the conversation with the other characters. To make this event even more interesting and instructive, all of the older groups of campers can be asked to make a list of all characters recognized and spoken to during the campfire. A prize, or prizes, may be given for those campers who are able to list the greatest number of characters recognized.

FAIRYLAND CAMPFIRE NIGHT

For the younger campers in particular this can be, with some help from the dramatic arts leader and the arts and crafts people, a thrilling and kaleidoscopic event. Cinderella and the awakened Sleeping Beauty can meet fairy princes, Aladdin with or without his wonderful lamp, Humpty Dumpty, the Red Queen, Snow White with or without the dwarves, and a host of other fairyland characters. Once after the event was staged for younger campers, the older ones decided to put on a "Fairyland Campfire" night of their own. It is difficult, and certainly would be indiscreet, to state which group got the biggest bang out of the affair! The Rumpelstiltskin of the older group apparently got his foot stuck firmly in the ground, as in the fairy tale, and was only rescued from his delightful dilemma by the individual and massed aid of a bevy of beauties who might easily have stepped from the pages of any one of the better fairy tale books.

In the younger groups' activities, Aladdin has brought his wonderful lamp and performed conjuring feats with its magical assistance; the *real* princess proved her upbringing by being the only princess among a group of five who was irritated by the pea concealed under the sixth mattress. The handsome prince and his mother played their part in the little sketch, and there was much burlesquing as the mother's handmaidens carried in the apparently very heavy mattresses, one by one. The manner in which the *real* princess emoted after her sleepless night, stole the show. There are many other stunts that can be pulled off on such a charmed night; thinking up *original* ones and staging them is fun which leaders and their assistants will not want to miss.

MISCELLANEOUS CAMPFIRE NIGHTS

Among the very many memorable nights to be conjured up are ones such as "When Knights Were Bold," *Robin Hood, The Arabian Nights, Peter Pan and Wendy* with the Pirates in the Never Never Land, and "A Night in Outer Space," where unleashed imaginations can create fantastic creatures and effects!

Much experience in these things has taught that, while fantasy and originality should be encouraged, no campers should be allowed to wear fantastic costumes where one hand must be used to hold on a golden crown while the other holds up a pair of baggy breeches. Comfort as well as dramatic effect should be strongly encouraged when the costumes worn cannot be cast off lightly after ten or twenty minutes, as in a brief skit or play. Clothing worn should be of the sort that will still be in place, and in the original number of pieces, at the end of one and one-half hours of campfire activity, and should be non-flammable.

THE CAMP ECHO

Just after the first campfire of the season has been lit, with appropriate fanfare, the director of campfire activities tells the campers a story about the wonderful echo which their camp has. He then tells the campers that he is going to try to let them listen to the echo—if it works in the evening as well as it does in the early morning.

It should be revealed here that just before the campers gather around the campfire a male leader, a boy, and a girl are hidden somewhere about twenty yards from the campfire circle. They may be concealed behind trees, bushes, or any other good natural cover which the area offers. The place has been chosen by the director of campfire activities prior to the campfire, and he knows exactly the direction from which the "echos" will return to him.

After pointing out the best spot, close to the campfire, from which to try to coax the echo to reply, the director stands there, cups his hands to his mouth, and calls loudly—"Hi!" After a suitable pause of a few seconds in order to promote suspense, a manly voice which sounds very much like that of the director answers "Hi!" in rather an eerie, somewhat muffled tone which produces a ventriloquial effect. The director then tries, "Good evening!" "How are you?" and other sentences of about the same length. Always his voice comes back in exact repetition.

The director then tells the campers that he believes the echo, which seems to be in unusually good form that evening, will perform for a camper. A boy is chosen or voted for by the campers and he stands where the director stood. He is warned not to use too long a sentence or the echo may not reply or may only send back a part of the sentence. The director suggests that he try "How do you like Camp _____?" The boy tries that question, but the boyish echo which replies only says "How do you l-i-k-e—," trailing off without finishing the last two words. A girl is next called, and to the surprise of many campers a girlish echo repeats her words exactly.

Now the director takes over the "echo spot" and addresses a brief but flattering word of thanks to the echo for co-operating so well. "You must be very wise, Echo," he concludes, "and so I call you seer and await your echoing reply as I say, 'Good night, seer.'" He stands perfectly still, as though listening intently. To the surprise and amusement of the campers, a high-pitched, girlish voice replies loudly—"Good night, *dear*. Sleep well!"

This stunt can be repeated successfully when new campers join the camp or on Visitors' Day.

THE VANISHING ROMAN

This can be a very mystifying disappearance act when it is carried out smoothly, after a little practice when nobody is around. The fact that it may be simply staged and requires few props does not detract from its effectiveness. For older campers, whose sleep would not be disturbed by thoughts of ghosts, this stunt can be staged as The Ghostly Visitor. In a camp where the audience is made up of older and younger campers, it is better to stage it as The Vanishing Roman. This eliminates the spooky business and causes wonder and amusement instead of a "creepy" feeling in the younger campers.

This is how the stunt looks to the watchers in the campfire circle. A bearded figure, dressed in a flowing white Roman toga, stalks suddenly into the campfire circle. He is carrying a white three-panel screen folded under one bare arm. His bare feet and legs can be seen under the toga, which reaches to below his knees.

"He looks like an ancient Roman!" the campfire director exclaims aloud. The "Roman" walks slowly around the campfire, sometimes walking fairly close to the edge of the campfire circle, but apparently without seeing the spectators. Rather hesitantly the campfire director goes toward the Roman, but the strange visitor appears neither to see nor hear him. The director goes into rather loud consultation with a leader about what should be done. The visitor sets up his three-paneled folding screen at one or two points in the campfire circle but seems to be dissatisfied with them. Finally he chooses a spot about eight feet away from the campfire, where he sets up the screen. He steps inside and closes the two outside panels of the screen tightly, so that he is invisible.

After a minute or so the campfire director cautiously approaches the screen and pretends to peer inside. He steps back hastily. "The fellow is asleep," he calls to the leader. "Let's get some help. We'll surround and catch him!"

The leader hurriedly rounds up some seven or eight assistants who, although the audience does not know it, have been awaiting the summons. The campfire director, by elaborate hand signals, spreads the assistants out in a circle surrounding the Roman's hideout. The circle becomes smaller and smaller as the assistants advance slowly toward the screen. When the circle has been closed so that the assistants are only about four feet away from the screen, and fairly well shoulder to shoulder, the director yells "Get him!" The assistants make a swift rush for the screen. They reach it and knock it over in the scrimmage. The screen lies flat on the ground, but—the mysterious visitor has vanished. After some excited shouting and a hurried search of the campfire circle the puzzled assistants give up and run in different directions out of the campfire circle. The leader picks up the screen and carries it, folded, under one arm to a point just outside the campfire circle. The assistants rejoin the onlookers around the campfire circle.

The program continues through the last number or two, but the topic of conversation is, "Where did he go?" —"Who was it?"—"Did you see him disappear?" and the like.

SOLUTION FOR THE VANISHING ROMAN. The simple solution to this "disappearing" act has no doubt been guessed by the reader, so the following is merely and explanation of how the stunt can most easily be carried out.

The leader who poses as the "Roman" must be of the same average height and build as that of the assistants who set out to capture him. The Roman wears a pair of loose-fitting slacks and and a long-sleeved dark shirt, very much the same shade as the shirts and trousers of the assistants who charge his frail hideout. All wear sneakers, unless the Roman wears low shoes, in which case all participants should wear low shoes too.

The only disguise worn by the Roman is a very effective one and consists of a bushy, arts-and-crafts-made black wig and a beard which is held in place by an elastic and slips off easily when it has to be hurriedly removed. To complete the costume, a "toga" made from a big white bed sheet covers the Roman from just below the knees to the neck. The toga must be fastened lightly but securely at the neck and held by one hand at the waist in such a way that it can be slipped off at a moment's notice and with little movement. The trouser legs and shirt sleeves are rolled up out of sight, and the bare feet will soon be covered with sneakers or low shoes, like the feet of the other counselors in the stunt.

The framework of the screen which the Roman carries under one bare arm is made from light pieces of flat wood. The six uprights are 7 or 8 feet long, 3 inches wide, and 1 inch thick. The crosspieces, ten of them, are attached to the uprights in the places shown in the diagram. They are each 3 feet long, 3 inches wide, and from ½ to ¾ inch thick. The three panels, made with the lumber mentioned, are covered with heavy white cotton. Old sheets will do the job very well. They should be securely fastened with tacks or thumbtacks on the outside of the panels, each panel being covered separately. The three panels are hinged, outside, at the top and bottom so that they fold together easily and closely. The panels form a triangle when set up, and the screen must stand steadily and balance well. Where the two outside panels meet when the screen is closed, they are held tightly together at the center by a latch such as is used on a screen door. Inside the center panel of the screen, on the second and top crosspiece, two strong white tape ties, each about 14 inches long, are securely fastened to the crosspieces 6 inches apart. To these ties are fastened the pair of sneakers or easy-fitting low shoes. They should be tied in place securely but in such a way that they can be untied speedily. It will be noted from the drawing that the crosspiece on which they are hung is so arranged to let them hang down without causing a bulge in the screen. The crosspiece directly under it on the inside panel is the one that the Roman can lean on slightly for support when slipping on his footwear.

When the Roman finally sets up the screen on level ground, so that it stands firmly, he goes inside, closes the three panels, and hooks the latch. Inside, where he is invisible from the onlookers, he removes his beard. He slips off his toga, wraps wig and beard securely inside it, and ties it firmly in place with the ties—in place of the footwear, which he now holds between his knees. He puts on the sneakers or low shoes, which should fit him so easily that he can slip them onto his feet even if the laces are loosely tied in advance. If he cannot manage

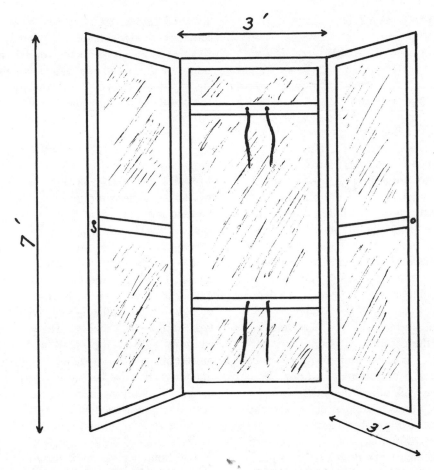

this, he holds the crosspiece of the inside panel tightly with one hand, so that the keeps his balance, while he eases on the footwear with his free hand. If the laces are not tied in advance he may find that tucking the ends down inside the sneakers or shoes will be enough to hold them in place. He rolls down his trouser legs and the sleeves of his long-sleeved shirt, provided the assistants are wearing long-sleeved shirts too. He stands slightly bent forward, facing the middle panel of the screen, with the other two panels tightly closed directly behind his back. He can reach behind him and hold them together with his hands if necessary, while awaiting the finale of the disappearing act. The Roman must take great care throughout not to upset the screen either while changing his clothing or while awaiting the rush of the assistants to complete the "escape," *and he must not fail to unhook the latch holding the panels shut.*

When the assistants rush the screen in a tight circle, at least three of them should completely block the view from both sides and the closed ends of the two panels—which allows the Roman to instantly merge with, and vanish in, the circle of searchers without being seen when the two side panels are jerked open and the screen is thrown forward onto the ground. The screen must be pushed forward onto the ground so that it immediately closes, with the toga folded inside out of sight. The one-time Roman joins the assistants in the brief search for

himself. The suddenness of the gathering of assistants, the swift circling of the screen, and quick charge on the Roman's hideout take the watchers completely by surprise. Only a budding Sherlock Holmes may note that there is one assistant more in the search party after the screen falls than there was prior to the rush on the screen —especially when, immediately after the disappearance, the group makes a quick exit in different directions. In a large camp there can, of course, be more assistants in the search party, up to a dozen not being too many if there are that number available.

Naturally, the leader who takes the part of the Roman must not be on duty with a group of campers, since his absence would be noticed. Again, a leader must not be chosen to play the Roman who is considerably smaller or taller than those of the search party, nor must he have a distinctive walk or any other easily identifiable mannerism. Someone who does not take part in the campfire except in the role of the Roman is a good man for the part.

The Vanishing Roman stunt is an easy one to stage, and with very little practice it can be carried out so smoothly and deceptively that even in daylight it would take a very keen observer to note the sudden switch when the former Roman becomes a member of the search party.

THOUGHT READING MAGIC

The only paraphernalia needed for this puzzling stunt is two empty boxes of any sort, covered with fancy paper to dress them up a bit; two small sheets of paper; and a piece of pencil. What happens is this:

The campfire leader announces that he will give a demonstration of thought reading without either the help of an accomplice or any other trickery. He then asks any senior camper—chosen by the others, to avoid any chance of conspiracy—to join him in the campfire circle. He calls for two assistants as a double check on the genuineness of the feat, gives the chosen camper the two sheets of paper and the piece of pencil, and asks the camper to write the name of his camp on one of the slips of paper. He then asks that the camper write the name of any other camp, preferably an invented name, on the other slip of paper. The leader in charge then says:

"As we all know that Camp _____" (mentioning the name of his camp at the campfire) "is ten times better than any other camp, I request that the number 10 be written on the slip which bears the name of our camp. By stretching a point, we will allow the other camp 1 point, and I ask that this number be written on the slip bearing the name of that camp. Here are two empty boxes. They need not be examined, since I will neither touch them nor go near them. I ask the camper to place one of these boxes on the ground just to the left of him and the other box on the ground just to the right of him. He now stands between these two boxes while I go to the opposite side of the campfire circle and turn my back to him." (He does so.) "Now I ask the camper to hold a slip in each hand and *triple* the figure in his *right* hand and *double* the number on the slip in his *left* hand. He will now add these two figures together and tell me whether the result is odd or even. Now the camper will put the slip which he holds in his right hand into the box on his right and the slip which he holds in his left hand into the box on his left. I will now tell you in which box the judges will find the slip on which is written the name of our camp."

The leader then solemnly announces that that slip is in the box on the right, or left, side of the camper. This statement proves to be correct, and the leader should perform the feat once again to prove the infallability of his magic. This stunt will probably puzzle the majority of those around the campfire, though the method of arriving at the correct answer each time is very simple. The leader who is staging the stunt should, of course, read the solution before trying the trick.

SOLUTION FOR THOUGHT READING MAGIC. When the camper with the slips has *tripled* the number on the slip in his *right* hand and *doubled* the amount of the number on the slip in his *left* hand and told the amateur thought reader what the two amounts total, the rest is easy. When the total is an *even* number, the name of the amateur magician's camp will always be in the *right-hand* box. When the total is an *odd* number, the name of the magician's camp will always be in the *left-hand* box.

PHANTOM SLAM-BANG

While this stunt can only be staged once in a camp where the same campers spend the entire summer, it can be used any number of times in camps where the campers spend only ten days or so prior to the arrival of a new contingent. This is how it is staged.

Two fairly evenly matched boys enter the campfire circle. They are volunteers for a blindfold pillow fight. The leader, who gives them each a well-stuffed pillowcase, will referee throughout the match. He is the athletic type and wears sneakers. He gives them the usual ref's cautions against foul play and warns them that they must both stop immediately when he shouts "Stop!" as that cry will only be given when either contestant is in danger of bumping into the audience or the fire. When both are blindfolded in a sanitary and efficient manner, a leader slips a pillow to the referee. Yes, that is why he wears sneakers!

The bout begins. As it progresses, each pillow fighter receives a bang from the referee's pillow whenever the chance comes along. Most of the blows which either of these doughty battlers-in-the-dark receives, come from the referee. While the boxers hear the onlookers laughing, they imagine that the laughs are because they are coming very close to each other or have just missed the chance of landing a beaut at close quarters. A referee who carries out his double role cleverly will cause a great deal of amusement by his wily tactics, as neither of the legitimate contestants suspects what is going on when the bonus blows are slyly given. Other duties of the referee are to separate the pillow fighters should they come to grips, keep them from bumping into anything, and give "helpful" advice, which seems to come from one place while the slam of the pillow appears to come from another. A really good referee will bring the bout to an end, having got rid of his pillow first, by declaring that honors are even and the match ends in a draw, which seems a fair decision to each unsuspecting fighter.

DAVID AND GOLIATH

This amusing stunt, when well staged, is an excellent take-off on pantomime and mimes. This is how the show appears to the onlookers.

After the campfire director makes a brief comment on how some artists can impersonate a hundred different persons and how their task is often made easier by effective make-up and sufficient time to apply it, he comes to the point of introducing the coming sketch, David and Goliath. Here, he points out, there is little time, hardly any, for make-up or padding; and the mime who can play the dual role successfully must be good, very good! He has a gigantic task! This opening keys the onlooker to what is coming. From behind a big screen, with a flap on each side if necessary, so that the audience cannot see behind it, a small figure appears. It is a small, bright camper simply dressed in white shorts and a white shirt. He moves around the screen area in a sprightly manner. He disappears behind the screen for a few moments. Then a figure about 6 inches taller than the shepherd lad appears. He is clad in a sort of Roman toga which envelopes him fairly thoroughly. His face, most of it, is hidden behind a big, bushy beard, and he carries a huge club. He stalks heavily around the screen, stopping from time to time to shade his eyes and peer into the distance as though searching for someone.

Several moments after Goliath has vanished behind the screen, David reappears and performs more or less as he did the first time, then goes behind the screen. After a lapse of about a minute, Goliath reappears, but this time he is a good foot taller than David. The giant walks around with heavy step, looks into the distance toward the direction in which David will make his reappearance, and waves his big club menacingly before retiring behind the shelter of the screen. About another minute elapses, and then David prances out again, looking smaller than ever after the appearance of the giant. He circles the screen, and looks a trifle scared as he glances toward it. Again he goes behind the screen. About a minute—which seems a long time to an audience—elapses, and then a really *big* giant stalks from behind the screen. He is at least two feet taller than the shepherd lad, and he carries an enormous club. He is dressed and walks exactly like the two previous giants. He mugs, appears to make a vehement speech as he faces the screen, whirls, shakes his fist, and swings his mighty club before returning behind the screen. David appears, for the last time, about a minute later. He appears to be in a hurry, without covering much ground, and looks back over his shoulder once or twice. Suddenly he stops and stares toward the screen. He whirls an imaginary strip of cloth in the direction of the screen and lets one end go. His eyes follow keenly the flight of the imaginary pebble as it flies toward its mark. There is a very loud *pop* behind the screen, and the now smiling shepherd lad skips to, and behind, the screen. Mission accomplished!

SOLUTION FOR DAVID AND GOLIATH. Of course, there are actually three Goliaths. Each one is made up and costumed in exactly the same way and con-cealed behind the screen, along with David, prior to the arrival of the campfire audience. It is impossible to tell one bearded giant from the other except by the difference in size. Except for that difference, they should be as alike as three peas. They endeavor to accentuate the likeness by using the same style of walk, movements, and mannerisms. The club is easily made from brown paper wrapped around a stick, so that three clubs of different size do not take long to make. The loud *pop,* coming a second after David slings his trusty pebble, is caused by the bursting of a big strong paper bag behind the screen, at exactly the right moment. The type of slingshot from which David fires the pebble is, though invisible, important. If the leader staging the skit feels that the campers imagine that David used the modern slingshot, a forked stick with elastic bands and a small pocket for the pebble, then David must pretend to use such a sling to liquidate Goliath. If all campers know that David used the usual narrow strip of cloth sling of his times, winding the pebble into it, swinging the strip around and above his head before releasing one end to send the pebble on its way, then that is the sort of sling that the modern David should use.

For an older audience, this skit can be lengthened to advantage by having each of the three giants appear twice, always following David as described. Each appearance must be made after a sufficient time lapse for David's supposedly donning Goliath's sheet and beard. Many campers believe that David has really done a surprisingly quick change and a fine job as a mime, until the third giant appears. When the giants appear twice, they can try to appear bigger on their second appearance, which is not a hard feat once they get the hang of it. Of course, when each Goliath makes two appearances, the third giant must not be deflated until after his second disappearance behind the screen.

CITY MAGIC

This little "magic" stunt can be carried out effectively by the director of campfire programs, aided by a small, bright camper. The director asks any section of the campfire circle to decide secretly on the name of a city, town, or village anywhere in the world, write the name on a slip of paper, and bring it to him. While a choice is being made, he calls for his little assistant and asks him or her to stand on the opposite side of the campfire, with back turned toward the director. When the director receives the slip, he reads the name and hands the paper back to the bearer. He then starts to name aloud villages, towns, and cities in America and elsewhere. By choosing real places with funny names he can make the stunt amusing. "Portland, Boston, Podunk, Los Angeles, Bombay, Madrid. . . ." "That's it, Madrid!" shouts the mediumistic camper. The answer is right too! Another name is chosen by a different section of the campfire audience. This time they're sure that their choice will not be discovered. "Rangoon, Oskaloosa, Norfolk, Chicago, New Orleans, London, Paris, Bordeaux. . . ." "That's the place!" shouts the bright camper.

By this time, some thoughtful camper may imagine that he has discovered how the trick works, and will volunteer to be the "medium." Unless sheer luck guides his choice, or he is unusually observant, he will not be able to name the place selected by the campers. When he has given up—and he should be encouraged to do so fairly soon—the little camper once again rings the bell, to the astonishment of the campfire audience. The third correct guess ends the stunt for that time, though popular request may cause the test to be renewed at a later date. Here is how the stunt works, and why a bright camper is needed for a the role of medium.

On the first "guess" the city, town, or village selected will be the *second* place named by the director *after* he names *any* place with a *double* name, such as San Francisco, New Haven, Los Angeles, New Orleans, and so on, being careful never to name a place with a single name which *sounds* like a double-named place. The second round ends with the name of the *third* place named after any double-barreled place name, while the third and last round will disclose the chosen place *four* places after the place with a double name. This change of position in the place selected after each correct guess makes it almost impossible to figure out how the stunt is worked.

RECORDING STUNT

This is a spoof playback number which can cause a lot of fun and, when well done, amazement in camp. All that is required is a big, gramophone type cabinet made from either a few strong cardboard cartons or a large wooden case. This cabinet should be large enough to hold either a large girl or boy quite comfortably. One side or the back of the case should be made to swing outward, so that the performer can get in and out of the cabinet easily. The cabinet is best when made without a bottom, so that the performer inside can help those moving the cabinet in and out of the campfire circle. The boy or girl inside can do this quite easily by simply shuffling along on hands and knees in the direction in which the case is being moved. The top of the cabinet, which can be the upturned bottom, is equipped with a large horn made from cardboard and painted, or a big megaphone, the thin end of which must go down inside the cabinet a little way, so that the performer in the case can speak or sing through it easily. The case may be covered with strong paper painted a dark or light brown, and the entire mock-up should be made to look as much like a real outsize gramophone as possible. There must be enough small hidden holes toward the top of the case to provide ample ventilation.

Just before the campfire begins, and when nobody is around except the leader who helps with the stunt, the hidden artist especially chosen to fit the coming act enters the gramophone cabinet. When the performer takes up his position in advance, the stunt is best put on shortly after the opening of the campfire. When the performer takes up his place outside of the campfire circle, slipping into the cabinet unseen by the campers around the fire, the act can go on at any time. It may be carried out as a "straight" act or spoofed, or both.

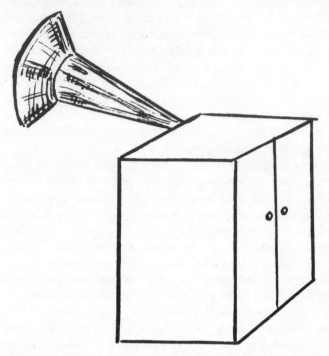

The campfire master of ceremonies announces that the camp has been lent a recording machine, which plays back songs, poetry, and other recordings. When a girl singer is concealed in the cabinet, a call is made for a girl who would like to have one of her favorite songs played back. Of course, she has been chosen privately in advance, and the girl inside the machine should be able to match the recording artist's voice fairly exactly. As the artist prepares to sing, the director in charge of the recording machine does some business with a big cardboard record or a real one, or he can adjust a length of outsize recording tape. The artist then sings a verse or two of a popular, easy-to-sing number. The director adjusts a knob or two then says "You shall now hear the playback of Miss ____'s delightful selection." Sure enough, out of the horn of the gramophone comes the song just "recorded." The closer the resemblance and rendition of the song, the better. Some secret rehearsals and practices in preparation for the event are, of course, necessary. When the playback ends, the director can apologize for the fact that the machine sounds a little mechanical and that some of the beauty of the song has been lost in the recording. A recitation or speech can be played back equally well. Two older campers with similar untrained voices can put a song across so well that it is very difficult to detect that the second solo is not a genuine playback.

Special stunts, such as a drum or tom-tom solo, or harmonica number, can be played back very realistically, as with two players of equal skill there is very little difference between the original solo and the duplicate one. The director can have the tom-tom beater stop after a few distinctive bars, tinker with the machine knobs a little for effect, and then play back what has been played.

As a grand finale a "translation" act goes over very well with audiences of all ages. The director announces that the machine on exhibition is a most unusual one, as it not only plays back but translates from *any* language into English. Work is going on, the director continues, to have the machine translate English into any other language, but the task is proving very difficult, and it may be five years or so before the "translatory" mechanism is perfected. In the meantime, the wonder of the invention will be demonstrated by having an Indian chief address the campers in Sioux, Cree, or Choctaw, whereon the recorder will play back the address in English. The director explains that for translatory recording the machine takes a great deal of adjustment. To demonstrate his point, he struggles realistically with the machine's mechanism from all sides and angles. The hidden performer, inside the cabinet, adds considerably to the effect at this point by letting an alarm clock ring loudly, banging on a metal rod, or clashing two metal rods or hardwood sticks together, and so on. The director can make his melodramatic adjustment antics one of the program highlights.

When the adjustments have been made, a blanketed, painted Indian warrior moves majestically into the campfire circle. The director, exhibiting some nervousness, leads the chief toward the recording machine. The director speaks rapidly in English to the chief who replies with a few loud, monosyllabic grunts. The chief shows some distrust as he approaches the recording cabinet, and draws and flourishes a realistic tomahawk. The director backs away in pretended fear, but soon musters up enough courage to have the chief give his brief but dynamic address. He need not speak directly into the horn, but moves around and declaims from either side of it for the benefit of the campfire audience. When he has finished his oration, he stands with his arms folded in front of the machine. The director touches a knob, which serves as a signal to the performer inside the machine. At once the speech plays back in the original language spoken. The chief draws his tomahawk and pretends to make a savage war-whoop-punctuated attack on the priceless machine. The director, after struggling with the chief for a few moments, shouts for help, and

four volunteers come on and lead the struggling chief from the campfire circle.

The director rushes to the still-orating machine. The speech can be begun all over again if necessary. He shuts it off, tinkers with it a bit, and says aloud, "Now I think it will work." It does. Back comes the translation of the chief's oration in somewhat broken and garbled English. As the speech has been carefully prepared in advance, it can be a serious one, recommending conservation or dealing with woodcraft. Should a goofy speech have been decided on, it can prove a real show-stopper, especially when it deals with "The Place of the Squaw in the Tepee."

For a fine finish to the translation act, a girl or boy can sing a simple song in French, Italian, or German, which is played back beautifully in English. The machine is then "rolled" out of the campfire circle by four husky counselors. The weight is only a few pounds, as the concealed operator creeps out on his own steam.

FORFEIT QUIZ

To make quizzes of any sort more competitive and exciting, one camper or more can be chosen to represent each of the four sides of the campfire circle. Each of these four sides contests as a team. The campers from each team stand beside the campfire, and the questions are asked aloud—so that the onlookers can hear—by the director of the campfire activities or a leader. When any one of the campers on a team believes that he or she knows the correct answer to the question asked, he or she raises a hand. The leader takes the campers who raise a hand aside, one by one, the first one to raise a hand being questioned first. The leader checks the answer, and each camper who has the correct answer counts 5 points for that team.

When any one of the campers gives a wrong answer, that camper may be asked to carry out some forfeit following the quiz, unless he can be saved from doing so by his team, which is seated in the campfire circle. In order to save him, his team must send another camper from that team with what it believes to be the correct answer to the question. If the answer sent proves to be right, the camper who failed to answer the question returns to his team without forfeit, and the one sent to save him takes his place. If the answer sent by the team is wrong, however, then both campers have to pay the penalty by carrying out some amusing forfeit, dual or individual, after the quiz is finished. It is a good plan to change the campers representing the teams after two or three quiz questions have been asked and answered.

Here are a few suggested riddles and catch questions to be added to the many others which counselors will be able to contribute.

Treasury of Memory-Making Campfires

RIDDLES

The pet. What little animal do children like, whose name is spelled the same forward and backward?

The rabbit. What four letters would scare a rabbit if it understood English?

The bootblack. Why should a farmer's son be a bootblack?

The oceans. If all the oceans dried up suddenly, what would people say?

Watchdogs. What two breeds of dogs make the best watchdogs on space ships?

No cat. What looks like a cat, has a tail and feet like a cat, but isn't a cat?

The parrot. What syllables are easiest for a talking parrot?

Relationship. What relation is a doormat to a doorstep?

Double time. What will be yesterday although it was tomorrow?

Flood-free France. Why is France in no danger from floods?

Star dog. The Dog Star is most likely of what breed?

Minus two. What is the most suitable word to remove two letters from so that six will remain?

Talkative. On what day of the year do campers talk least.

Three-footed. What has three feet: one in the middle and one at each end?

Yardage. What is bought by the yard and used by the foot?

Etiquette. How would you speak of a tailor if you forgot his name?

Garden scene. What is the difference between a gardener and an actor?

Hold on! What can you hold in your right hand that you can't hold in your left hand?

Language. Is there a word in the English language which contains all of the vowels?

Knightly. A knight in armor had a pain. If you know when it was, you know where it was. Where was it?

Help! Why is it difficult for a brother to help his sister with her homework?

Figuratively speaking. Why is there no difference between 100 and 1000?

(It will be noted that these riddles are suited for varied age groups.)

QUIZ QUESTIONS

What color is the stripe at the top of the American flag: red, white, or blue?

What did President Lincoln see by the millions that the present President has never seen at all?

What was *Excalibur?*

What does one call a baby kangaroo?

Name some of the colors on the brilliant discs, known as "eyes," which beautify a peacock's tail.

What is a simpler name for the *aurora borealis?*

What is the name of the most southerly city in the United States?

Does it take longer to raise the flag to half-mast or full-mast? Why?

How are the stars arranged in the American Flag?

What are the names of the members of a swan family used in speaking of father, mother, and baby swan?

What was the usual exclamation of the White Rabbit?

Napoleon, while imprisoned on an island, was supposed to have said in English a sentence of seven words which reads the same backward or forward. What was it?

The first man, when introducing himself to Eve, could also have used a brief sentence which would read the same whether read backward or forward. What is that sentence?

What is the most northerly city in the United States?

CATCH QUESTIONS

In old China, they used to measure the height of children to decide whether a child could travel for half fare or not. Now, how long *is* a Chinaman?

Which was the second largest island before New Guinea was discovered?

What was the highest mountain in the world before Mount Everest was discovered?

If a father gave one of his sons 15 cents and the other one 10 cents, what time would it be?

How can you change the length of your dog?

Why is a skunk in a cabin like a house on fire?

There were nine ears of corn in the nature cabin. Each night a rabbit carried away three ears; how many nights did it take him to carry away all of them?

A camper saw a duck in front of two ducks, a duck behind two ducks, and another one between them. How many ducks were there?

Does a red or white candle burn longer?

What is the best way to punctuate this sentence: "A dollar bill is blowing across the sidewalk."

When is a squirrel most likely to enter a cabin?

Would you rather have a *dog* chase you or a *cat?*

How did the farmer keep the mule from jumping through its collar?

When a clock strikes thirteen, what time is it?

Which would you rather have; an old, dirty five dollar bill or a brand-new one?

In Ceylon, people ride on the backs of elephants, climbing down a light ladder to reach the ground after a ride. Supposing you were on a big elephant's back but had no ladder; how would *you* get down from that elephant?

Why does a canvasback duck land on a lake?

What makes more noise than a black pig caught in a gate?

What is the least expensive way to use a speedboat?

If Mississippi took Missouri's New Jersey, what would Delaware?

If it takes exactly ten minutes to clean one big dirty window, how long will it take to clean a big dirty mirror which is exactly the same size as the window?

Tell, in a one rhymed line, how you think this ends:

> There was a young fisher named Fisher
> Who fished for a fish in a fissure;
> The fish, with a grin,
> Pulled the fisherman in—
> . . . .

Solve this one if you can:

> Round and round a rugged rock
> A ragged rascal ran.
> Tell me how many R's are in that,
> And I'll count you a clever man.

How far can a dog run into a wood? Why?

With what would you fill a barrel to make it lighter than when it is empty?

If twenty-one white socks and twenty-three black socks were put in a box and you were then blindfolded, how many socks would you have to take out, one at a time, before you would have a pair of the same color?

ANSWERS TO RIDDLES

The Pet. The little animal is a pup.

The Rabbit. O I C U!

The bootblack. So that the farmer can "make hay while the son shines."

The oceans. "We haven't a notion!"

Watchdogs. Skye terriers and airedales.

No cat. A kitten.

The parrot. Polysyllables.

Relationship. A step farther.

Double time. Today.

Flood-free France. Because the water there is always *l'eau.*

Star dog. Skye terrier.

Minus two. Sixty.

Talkative. The shortest day.

Three-footed. A yardstick.

Yardage. A carpet.

Etiquette. The tailor could be spoken of as "Mr. Sew-and-sew.

Garden scene. One minds his peas and the other his cues.

Hold on! The left elbow.

Language. Unquestionably.

Knightly. The pain was in the middle of the knight.

Help! Because he has to be a brother and assist her too.

Figuratively speaking. Because the difference is naught.

ANSWERS TO QUIZ QUESTIONS

Stripes on Old Glory. Red. There are no blue stripes, as campers will point out.

What Lincoln saw. Abraham Lincoln saw millions of passenger pigeons, which have since been completely exterminated by man.

Excalibur. King Arthur's magic sword.

Baby kangaroo. A Joey.

The peacock's tail. The only color on the brilliant discs is actually black. The illusion of color is caused by refracted light.

Aurora borealis. The Northern Lights.

Southernmost. Hilo.

Flag raising. Half-mast, because regulations require that the flag be raised to the top of the mast before lowering it to half-mast.

Star spangled. Five rows of six stars alternating with four rows of five stars.

The swan family. Father is called a cob, mother, a pen, and a baby is a cygnet.

The white rabbit. "I'm late, I'm late!"

Napoleon. "Able was I ere I saw Elba!"

Adam and Eve. "Madam I'm Adam."

Northernmost. Fairbanks.

ANSWERS TO CATCH QUESTIONS

Chinese measurement. How Long *is* a Chinaman!

New Guinea. New Guinea, of course!

Mount Everest. Mount Everest, of course!

Time is money. It would be a quarter to two.

Dog-gone! Let it out in the morning and take it in at night.

Skunk simile. The sooner it's put out the better!

Eerie! Nine. The other two ears were his own.

Duck! Three.

Candlelight. Neither. Both burn shorter.

Punctuation. Make a dash after it.

Open house. When the door is left open.

Cave canem! Safer to let the dog chase the cat.

Farmer and mule. He tied a knot in its tail.

Unlucky number! Time to have it repaired.

Filthy lucre. Cleanliness is commendable, but the old *five* is worth four dollars more than the new *one.*

Elephant ride. You can't. Down comes from a duck.

The canvasback. For divers reasons. (This duck really dives for its food and does not "tip up" in shallow water while feeding.)

The noisy pig. Two black pigs.

Economy. Make her fast.

Missouri's New Jersey. I suppose she'd Havana's but Alaska.

Reflect! Five minutes. A mirror has only *one* side.
Fishing. Now, they're fishing the fissure for Fisher.
How many R's? There are no R's in *that*.
Dog trot. A dog can run only halfway into a wood. When it reaches that point, it will be coming out.
The barrel. Although some science-minded camper may suggest helium, the correct answer is *holes*.
Socko! Three socks!

CAMPFIRE SINGING

The saying that "a singing camp is a happy one" is usually right. Much comradeship and spontaneity can be aroused in campers of all ages through singing, especially when a happy choice of suitable, stirring songs is made. Sometimes older campers, when they get the chance—perhaps with the fallacious idea that they are being sophisticated—introduce offbeat, off-color, discriminatory, controversial, and gruesome songs and parodies which neither contribute to a camp's gaiety nor make much sense. Such numbers should be diplomatically and, if necessary, firmly discouraged by the leader. Needlessly stupid songs and pointless parodies, and equally needless repetitious songs with endless verses, have little place on a campfire program. When otherwise acceptable songs have dozens of verses, they will not suffer by being trimmed, only four or five of the best verses being used. In its original form, "The Chisholm Trail" had over one thousand verses, but even the most ardent of the singing cowboys rarely sang more than a dozen or so!

Song leaders or others who lead the singing should use catchy songs with catchy tunes and a rather simple musical range which even unmusical campers find within their limited vocal scope. It is a thankless task to try to promote a song which campers dislike or are unable to sing easily and well. The best songs are usually the tuneful and gay ones which campers enjoy singing, and the more dreamy, nostalgic, and romantic numbers which are in order when the campfire begins to burn low.

SONG REPERTOIRE

Leaders, and especially song leaders, should have a handy, classified repertoire of suitable songs and music for all occasions. A repertoire is best arranged by suitable song groups: patriotic, marching songs, ballads, early American, sea chanteys, rounds, cowboy and western, international, old favorites, sentimental songs, and recent popular songs, to mention some of the convenient divisions. Supplemented with an alphabetical index, this serves better than even a very good memory. Many a music counselor has expressed regret that she or he did not include some particular song in an otherwise rousing campfire program. The regretted omissions invariably arose from the fact that the singing part of the program had either not been set down far enough in advance of the fire to allow for eliminations and second-thought additions, or the numbers had been chosen from memory either through lack of a written repertoire or failure to consult an existing list when the singing program was drawn up. A song leader who includes the name of the composer in the case of really worthwhile numbers and is able to say, "Here is one of _____'s popular pieces," gains prestige and has a far better chance of being able to put more semiclassical and classical numbers across than one who makes no mention of the composer of the piece about to be introduced.

Songs become dated, some much sooner than others, and should not be used with groups which find no real pleasure in singing such numbers. Some popular songs die suddenly and completely and do not regain favor until many years later, when they may be revived because of the scarcity of worthwhile current compositions. On the other hand, some really old favorites do not outlive their popularity despite the passing of camp seasons and years, and a music counselor can lose out by not knowing some of the "old-timers" which appear on the undernoted memory refresher lists. Camp directors have the opportunity to observe that the most popular songs, judged by the gusto and frequency with which they are requested and sung by the campers, are not always the ones which the music counselor likes best. Once the author asked a group of campers why they sang a certain song so often, his curiosity being aroused by the listless way in which they sang it. "You must like that song," he remarked. "No," was the rather terse answer, "*we* don't—*she* does!"

SPECIAL MUSIC

Before briefly touching on special singing appropriate for the more musical groups of campers, it may be well to mention suitable musical accompaniment for campfire singing. One of the most versatile instruments is a good accordion, closely followed by the less versatile guitar and banjo. One or more well-played harmonicas can also provide helpful accompaniment. Percussion instruments and good rhythm bands, humming, whistling, and clapping also provide a suitable background at times. Group singing can occasionally be enhanced by suitable rhythmic movements of hands, head, arms, and body, but this usually depends on the age and tastes of the group.

Part singing and dual song singing, in which a group is divided into two parts to sing in unison two different songs which harmonize and blend well, and recitative songs, serious or gay, with a good accompaniment, make fine additions to campfire programs. Suitable poetry recited, by a group divided into light and dark voices, to a musical background can be splendidly effective.

GENERAL MUSIC

Since practically all camps have either songbooks or songsheets which contain many of the old-time favorite airs and a number of the newer ones, there is little point in attempting to set down here words and music for the infinitely small number of appropriate songs which the space available permits. Ambitious music leaders will find alphabetical lists of titles and first lines for well over 12,000 varied songs in the public library, and dozens of worthwhile song collections are also available. They can be taken home or to camp, often for the entire summer.

The only original contribution which the author attempts to make to campfire singing is a humane version of "Alouette," which he has been goaded into writing after listening to too many counselors and song leaders who, with savage face and gesture, led the campers in plucking the luckless lark to pieces. The words fit the usual melody of this well-known song.

Canadian *voyageurs* have taken poor "Alouette" apart around the campfire for many years. The same helpless lark has taken an awful plucking in modern camps for too long a time. This version of "Alouette" is an attempt to come to the rescue of that much-abused songster.

"ALOUETTE"
Version for Bird-loving Campers
A-lou-et-te, tris-te a-lou-et-te,
A-lou-et-te, je te sauv-er-ai.
Pe-tit ois-eau de l'au-rore,
On n'te plume-ra pas en-core;
Pas en-core, pas en-core; Oh!
A-lou-et-te, jol-ie a-lou-et-te,
A-lou-et-te je te lâch-er-ai.

A-lou-et-te, gen-tille a-lou-et-te,
A-lou-et-te, on n'te plume-ra plus!
On ne plum-era pas ton cou,
Ni ton bec et ni ta queue,
Ni ton bec, ni ta queue, Oh!
A-lou-et-te, vole chère a-lou-et-te,
A-lou-et-te je te lâch-er-ai.

A-lou-et-te, joy-euse a-lou-et-te,
A-lou-et-te je te sauv-er-ai.
Je lâche-rai tes captives ailes,
Chante tes ber-ceuses dans le ciel,
Dans le ciel, dans le ciel; Oh!
A-lou-et-te, chant-ante a-lou-et-te,
A-lou-et-te je t'en-ten-dr-ai.

"THE LARK"
A Free Translation
Lark, sad lark,
Lark I shall save thee.
Little bird of the dawn
They shall not pluck you again; Oh!
Lark, pretty lark,
Lark I shall free thee.

Lark, gentle lark,
Lark they shan't pluck you again!
They shan't pluck your neck,
Nor your beak, nor your tail; Oh!
Lark, fly dear lark,
Lark I shall free thee.

Lark, joyful lark,
Lark I shall save thee.
I shall release your captive wings;
Sing your lullabies in the sky,
In the sky, in the sky; Oh!
Lark, singing lark,
Lark I shall hear thee.

campfire shows

CAN DO?—DID DO!—CAN YOU?

This is a Story-Riddle Play from Old Japan, which can be acted out in coeducational or girls' camps. There is one act with four scenes. The audience participation angle of the story gives all members of the audience a chance to show how bright they are in the question part of the last act.

Camp leaders, with the willing and clever co-operation of the campers, are usually so well able to stage and improvise a little play that no effort is made here to set down a regular script to be followed. Instead, the characters and what they do will be outlined, as will the scenes where the action of the story-riddle play takes place. The playwriting and casting are left to the play director and senior campers.

It should be noted that all suggestions are made to endeavor to simplify the production of this little play. With a little help from the theatrical department of the camp, an ambitious play director can add considerably to the effects in any way desired. Care should be taken, when staging this play outdoors, not to use backdrops or bulky scenery which will obscure the view of some sections of the audience.

Naturally, if this play were to be presented in a recreation hall, one could add greatly to the lines, costumes, props, and scenery. Costume changes could be made in the dressing room, and the curtain would hide the scene

and prop shifting. Any time required behind scenes could be filled in by Japanese juggling acts and other numbers in front of the curtain.

THE CHARACTERS:

CHERRY BLOSSOM
WILLOW } Three young Japanese girls
LOTUS FLOWER
MAMAKOKO: the girls' mother-in-law
NAGA, SAKI, and KOBE: the three brothers, who are also the girls' husbands and sons of Mamakoko
YUASKA: the wise woman

Note. The three husbands have such small parts that one or two things can be done about them. Their roles can be padded in Scene 1, so that they have more to do, or they can be dropped entirely from the cast. In this event, the three wives simply speak of the fact that their husbands had been to see their mother and brought back the message about the wives seeing Mamakoko the next morning.

THE SCENES

Scene 1: In a garden
Scene 2: In a courtyard
Scene 3: Outside a hut, in the country
Scene 4: In a courtyard (same as Scene 2)

SCENE 1

The three little Japanese maids are seated in a garden, chattering. From their conversation we learn that they await the return of their husbands, who have been sent by the girls to ask their honorable mother if the three wives may return to their native village for a month's holiday. It appears that the girls have been married to the brothers for a year and that they have worked hard for their mother-in-law and need a rest. None of the girls seems to expect much sympathy or understanding from Mamakoko. As one of the girls puts it, "Mamakóko will say 'nono'; then we can't go."

To the girls' surprise the three husbands, wearing long mustaches, shuffle onto the scene, with hands thrust into loose sleeves, and give good news. "The honorable Mamakoko no say 'nono'—she say 'gogo,' " Naga tells them.

The girls are so happy that they raise their little paper parasols, open their little paper fans, and sing and dance "Three Little Maids," from the *Mikado* (or a similar dance and song number). Not to be outdone, or perhaps to show pretended indifference, Saki sings "A Wandering Minstrel I" (or as much of that or a similar song as the play director thinks the audience can stand). The girls gush about how sweet Mamakoko is until Kobe hushes them with the remark that their honorable mother-in-law expects them in her honorable presence, in her courtyard at 6 A.M. sharp the next morning. The girls show fear and ask why? Kobe explains that the honorable one simply wishes them to bring a few little things back with them when they return from their holiday. The girls feel so relieved that they ask Kobe to sing. Kobe, somewhat of a clown, borrows a fan from one of the girls and, turning slowly in a circle on the same spot, fans himself and sings any little Oriental type tune, such as "Tit Willow" or a selection from the *Mikado* or other source.

The couples then pair off and go off stage.

Costume suggestions for Scene 1. The girls wear flowered dressing gowns or something similar, to represent kimonos, and bath sandals or slippers. Their hair is arranged in a more or less Japanese hair-do, with a flower stuck in it. They carry paper parasols and paper fans. The boys wear slacks or jeans, yellow or beige T shirts or loose shirts, if they do not wish to wear flowered dressing gowns; they have bare feet. Long mustaches made of heavy black wool can be pasted on.

Props suggested for Scene 1. Very little in the way of props is required. The scene can be acted out under and about a big beach parasol, decorated in Japanese style by pinning a few paper flowers on it. There can be three little chairs or stools for the three girls. A short length of trellis fence can be stuck into the ground, where it will least interfere with the audience's view. The trellis does not need to be more than a couple of feet high. A few paper flowers may be twined, vinelike, on the trellis.

SCENE 2

Mamakoko is seated on a chair before a little table. She raps it impatiently with her fingers and looks closely at an hourglass (egg timer) from time to time, turning it over briskly as she does so. The three little girls file in, bow very low before Mamakoko, then stand in line at attention before her. Mamakoko gives them the usual line about their happiness being her happiness and then gets down to business with a meaning smile.

"You may go for thirty days but not one day longer, or you may not return to Weechewow," she informs them. She makes them promise, which they all do together. She then tells them that she wishes each of them to bring her back a little present. "I will have to work much harder when you are gone," she explains, "and so I ask each of you to bring me back a little gift in return. The presents which I ask are all very simple things. You will, because you are all clever girls, find the little things which I ask right in your own village."

She gives each girl a tiny, gaily colored envelope. "There is a little message inside each telling you what I want. Do not open these envelopes until two days before you leave your village to return here. This I ask because I do not wish you to think about us here in Weechewow while you are in your village. There your thoughts should be only for your parents and families."

The girls, in an aside, comment on how thoughtful and kind Mamakoko is, and all agree to promise anything in order to be off on their holiday.

"Now," continues the mother-in-law, "I know how forgetful and thoughtless you often are and that you do not always keep your promises, but this time you *must* do so." (She bangs the hour glass on the table to emphasize the importance of the matter.) "Two promises you must make and keep. If you do not, each one of you, bring me the little gift asked for, none of you can come back here. Your husbands have agreed to this. Secondly, you must return exactly thirty days from now. Promise."

The girls promise, bow deeply, and walk off stage in single file, fanning themselves violently.

Costume suggestions for Scene 2. The mother-in-law wears rather an elaborate "kimono," a high-piled Japanese hair-do, and sandals of some sort. The girls can wear the same kimonos as before, but each should carry some sort of bright laundry bag, as a traveling case.

Props suggested for Scene 2. A small table and chair for Mamakoko. A glass for timing eggs, if there is one handy, or an improvised one. A few long-stalked paper flowers can be stuck in the ground around the ends of the table to create a courtyard garden effect.

SCENE 3

The three girls are seated in a circle on the ground, close to a little hut. Each girl takes her little, open, colored envelope and reads aloud the note inside. Lotus Flower says before reading her note, which is the first to be read, "Ten times today have I read this and I am still no wiser." She reads aloud. " 'Lotus Flower, bring me many cool breezes in a paper.' If only I knew how to bring Mamakoko even one warm breeze I would be happy," Lotus Flower sighs. "Please read me your puzzle, Willow."

Willow then reads: " 'Willow, bring me something which nobody has ever seen before.' That seems to be the hardest task of all!" Willow exclaims in tears.

"No, mine is," says Cherry Blossom. She reads aloud: " 'Cherry Blossom, you must bring me fire wrapped only in paper.' Oh! Oh dear, that is impossible, I fear," sighs Cherry Blossom.

"We must do something at once!" Lotus Flower exclaims. "You know that we must start back tomorrow, and you know what it says at the foot of each of our orders."

"Yes," answers Cherry Blossom, reading from her note. " 'If you cannot bring me this simple thing, *none of you must ever return to Weechewow.*' "

"Simple thing," continues Cherry Blossom heatedly, "why none of our friends, not even the wise men of our village know what she means. Mamakoko is a fox. She did not wish us to open our orders sooner because we would have had more time to try to find out the answers to her puzzles. Oh dear, oh dear, I do wish somebody could help us."

Suddenly a high-pitched woman's voice comes from inside the little hut.

"Perhaps I can help you in your trouble, children."

The three girls spring to their feet.

"Who is she?" asks Lotus Flower.

"You ask her," suggests Cherry Blossom.

"That's right, my dear. You know my name, I hear. I am Yuaska, called the Wise One." An old woman hobbles from the hut toward the startled girls. "Now, tell me what each of you requires."

Each girl reads her note aloud, once more.

"Your mother-in-law is a very clever woman," Yuaska says, "but she will be greatly surprised when each of you arrives with the thing which she demanded but hoped you would never find.

"Do you really know what the things are?" the astonished girls chorus.

"Of course," the Wise One replies. "I have all these things in my home. Wait here for just a moment, and I shall bring them out to you."

The girls stand just outside the hut and wait impatiently. In a few moments, Yuaska comes out carrying three parcels, prettily done up in fancy paper, each one tied with a bow of gaily colored ribbon. She hands Cherry Blossom a little flat package about 15 inches square. To Lotus Flower she gives a little oblong packet about a foot long and 3 inches in diameter. The girls gasp when she hands Willow a tiny parcel, not larger than a *small* matchbox.

"Now listen carefully, while I tell you how to present these gifts," says Yuaska. She whispers for a moment into each girl's ear. As she does so, each one laughs happily and exclaims, "You *are* clever!"

The Wise One waves to them as the girls scamper gaily off scene.

At this point, while the scene shifters are at work and there is nobody on stage, the play director asks the audience thoughtfully: "Can any junior campers guess what is in these packages? I wish I knew! Don't anyone tell me now if you have guessed, but think about it carefully, because I may get a chance later on to ask you to tell me the secret."

Costume suggestions for Scene 3. The girls can wear the same kimonos they wore in the former scenes. Yuaska wears a plain dressing gown, a white wig made of white fiber or cotton wool, etc., and bare feet or sandals. The three parcels are all ready in the hut when the Wise One goes into it to fetch them.

Prop suggestions for Scene 3. The hut is easily made by thrusting four poles, each about 8 feet long, into already prepared holes, one hole in each corner of a square about 6 feet in diameter, then hanging strips of sacking, canvas, or other cloth which is handy, onto the poles. Loops of string may be fastened to the top parts of the cloth so that it may be hung easily. The hut does not require a roof, but it should be impossible for the audience to see inside it. The cloth used for the hut can be stained or painted or decorated in any other way that the play director sees fit.

SCENE 4

Mamakoko is seated at the little table, smiling to herself. There is a sort of little arbor about two paces behind her. This is actually a sort of screen set up in the form of a triangle with a narrow opening, so that the audience cannot see inside it. Inside the arbor there is a tiny table, or upended box, with a nutcracker on it and a big box of matches.

Mamakoko talks aloud. "Well, I am quite sure that I have seen the last of those lazy girls. Never will they find out the answers to the riddles I set them. He, he, he! Little did they guess when I let them go that I set a trap to keep them far from my dear sons. It is well that I sent all of the boys off to the annual Kumanbuynow Fair yesterday. Their steamer will not be back for two days. I can tell them when they return that the girls got back but decided to go home again—What's this!?" she suddenly sees the three girls walking toward her, each carrying a package.

The three girls approach the table in single file and all bow together, most ceremoniously. "Happy shades of afternoon, Mamakoko," they chorus.

"So you're back," the mother-in-law greets them curtly.

"Why are our dear husbands not here to greet us?" asks Cherry Blossom.

"They had to leave for a day or two to go to the yearly

sale at the Kumanbuynow Fair," Mamakoko replies. "But what of my gifts? I hope that you have not dared to return without the presents which I ordered you to bring?"

"Oh no, dear Mamakoko," they say altogether. "You asked for such simple little things that we feel ashamed to have brought them back to you."

Mamakoko slumps suddenly forward and apparently bumps her head violently (sound effect) on top of the table. She straightens up and stretches out an imperious hand toward the three girls. "Show me," she commands. "You first, Lotus Flower. Have you brought me many cool breezes in a paper?"

"Yes, Mamakoko, I bring them to you." Lotus Flower walks inside the screen, opens her parcel and waits for a few moments, until she hears the play director say, "Now we shall see who is right!"

As Lotus Flower walks behind the screen, the play director turns to the audience. "I wonder what she has brought?" he asks the audience in a stage whisper.

Quite a few bright junior campers may call out what they think it is. Some will be right, others wrong. The play director should make a mental note of the campers or group having the correct answer.

"Now we shall see who is right," the play director says, as the cue for Lotus Flower to return.

Lotus Flower walks on stage carrying a folded fan. She approaches Mamakoko, opens the fan and fans her mother-in-law with it. "Now you can enjoy many cool breezes. They are, as you can feel, in this paper."

Mamakoko takes the fan, bows slightly, and lays it on the table. "And now, Willow, have you brought me something which nobody has ever seen before?"

"Of course, Mamakoko. It was your wish," says Willow, walking behind the screen. She hides the nutcracker in a pocket or kimono sleeve and waits for the play director's cue words: "What she has brought is a mystery to me."

Just as soon as Willow disappears inside the screen the play director addresses the audience, as before: "What on earth do you think Willow has brought her mother-in-law?" He waits for a few moments for the answers and guesses, then says: "What she has brought is a mystery to me."

Willow now comes from behind the screen. She goes slowly to the table, opens her tiny parcel, takes out a hazel nut, or any nut with a single kernel, from the little box, cracks it open, and holds out the kernel to Mamakoko. "I am sure that you have never seen this before, Mamakoko," she says with a smile.

"No indeed, not ever," admits Mamakoko, holding out a visibly trembling hand for the kernel, which she places on the table beside the fan.

"And now only little Cherry Blossom remains to surprise me with her cleverness," says the mother-in-law

in a sweet, sweet voice. "Cherry Blossom, have you brought me fire wrapped only in paper?"

"Indeed I have. That is what you asked me for, Mamakoko," replies Cherry Blossom cheerfully. She takes her parcel inside the screen, opens it, takes out the Japanese lantern, lights it and waits for the cue from the play director: "We will soon know!"

Again the play director addresses the audience, just as soon as Cherry Blossom goes behind the screen. "She is a clever girl if she has brought that," he comments. "What do you think she has in the parcel?" He listens for the answers, as before, then says "We will soon know!"

Cherry Blossom walks from inside the screen up to the table, holding high the lit lantern for her mother-in-law's inspection. "Here is your fire wrapped only in paper," she says. "It will look pretty hung in your bedroom."

Mamakoko takes the lantern, bows very low, blows out the lantern, and places it beside the other gifts on the table. "Thank you all so much, very much, too much," she stammers, smiling and bowing to the girls. "You are all good, smart girls, and I will tell your husbands how very clever you are as soon as they get back from the Fair. I am going to try to make you even more comfortable and happier than ever before, you'll see. Now, how about a nice bowl of Sukiyaki, daughters?" *(Curtain)*

Costume suggestions for Scene 4. Little or no costume change is required here. Any change made will depend on the costumes available and the time element in changing from one kimono into another.

Prop suggestions for Scene 4. The same table and chair used in the same scene layout as in Scene 2. The little arbor screen can easily be made from the cloth used for the Wise One's hut in Scene 3. The chief thing is to be able to set it up rapidly, so that it does not interfere with the view of the audience when in place, and in such a way that the campers cannot see inside it. The upended box, or small table, is handy for girls when they undo their packages. The big box of matches is for the use of Cherry Blossom when she lights her lantern. The nutcracker is not required, provided somebody in camp can produce a lichee nut, which can easily be opened with the fingernails.

FAKE FAKIR

This little skit can be made both effective and funny by the choice of a good Fakir. Dignity, poise, and calmness in the face of adversity are the chief requirements necessary in putting on this comedy of errors.

The campfire director magniloquently announces that the campers are honored by having The Great Singh in their midst. He will proceed to entertain them with incredible feats of mystic Eastern magic. The Fakir now walks pompously into the campfire circle, wearing a big turban and clad in the gorgeous flowing robes of the mysterious East—improvised from a bed sheet and

a pillowcase. He walks to a small table, about the size of a card table, and stands behind it. The table is covered with a tablecloth which hangs down about 6 inches all around. A big box, which holds the Fakir's paraphernalia, stands on a stool beside the table. (The table should either be a very old one, or better still, a small table built with a top of light wood slats, of which the center one can be made of *strong* cardboard. The reason for this will be seen a little further on.)

The Fakir raises his hand for silence and then speaks to the onlookers in slow, broken English, which should be quite understandable. First of all, he announces that he will do his famous "Big Balloon into Little Balloon Illusion." He takes a large, inflated balloon from the box, or even better, it is brought to him by someone who, the instant the balloon is in the Fakir's hands, rushes out of the campfire circle. The Fakir, holding the big balloon by the neck, *carefully* inserts a pin into the top of the large balloon, which should promptly explode, leaving a smaller balloon, of an entirely different color, in its place. This little balloon, which can be orange or yellow in color, has been blown up inside the big balloon—which should be dark blue, green, or red in color—by having the end of its neck protrude from the neck of the big balloon. This is easily done by folding the neck of the large balloon back, in a rolled-up position. When the little balloon is inflated, the neck is tied with a single knot close to the balloon and snipped off with scissors. The small balloon should be inflated fairly

fully but not too tightly. The big balloon is now blown up fairly tight, and the neck tied with a single knot. Knotting the balloons' necks is a far more efficient way of assuring that they remain inflated than tying the ends with wool, or even an elastic band. Sometimes the bursting of the big balloon causes the small one to burst too, though it will not if they are both properly blown up. Should the little balloon burst, the Fakir in a few flowery, flowing words can explain, perhaps, why things went wrong.

Unperturbed, serene, no matter how the balloon number turned out, the Fakir goes on to his next illusion. Fakirs always create illusions, never do "tricks."

"I will a magic flower for you grow," he announces, as he places a big, *tall* crepe-paper-covered can on one corner of the table. He pours water *carefully* into it, from a large watering can. The amazement of the onlookers grows with the growing of the flower, which rises inch by inch in full exotic bloom from the can. Unfortunately, the Fakir, flushed by success, pours too much water into the can, and the flower—attached to a little circle of wood—pops out and lies on the table. (The flower was a paper one on the end of a 4-inch-long piece of strong, straight wire wrapped in green oiled paper or cloth to give the illusion of a stem. The other end of the wire was stuck into a little buoyant raft of lightweight wood or a large, flat cork weighted on the bottom so that the flower remains topside up.)

Such a *contretemps* as the exposure of how his flower

illusion was carried out does not ruffle the Fakir. While someone removes the can and flower, he goes right on to his next number, which he announces as "The Disappearing Ping Pong Balls." He takes three ping pong or small red rubber balls from his box of tricks and calmly states that, one by one, he will make them vanish before the eyes of his "audience most distinguished." It prepares for a laugh, but sure enough, the Fakir covers a ball with a small yellow or red silk scarf or piece of cloth, pushes the ball around on the table, then suddenly shakes the empty scarf toward the audience. No doubt about it, *the ball has actually disappeared!* Two other balls vanish in the same mysterious manner, leaving no doubt in the minds of the puzzled onlookers as to the Fakir's ability when he really tries.

The campfire director can add a few "magic boners" to the Fakir's repertoire at this point, before the magician goes on to the grand finale.

For the last number, the man from the East performs a well-known stunt, that of swiftly snatching the tablecloth out from under a bowl—which should be fairly heavy and of little value—leaving the bowl sitting in its original position in the center of the table. This little trick requires only a little practice to accomplish successfully, the practising being done before campfire time, of course.

Should the Fakir succeed in snatching the cloth from under the bowl without mishap, which he should endeavor to do, he goes on to the final act. Should the bowl follow the jerked cloth and land on the ground, the Fakir simply explains that such an illusion was too simple for him—but wait! He now places some old strong earthenware cups, bowls, and saucers on the table, spacing them a few inches apart. (In case of breakage, which might leave a few earthenware splinters in the campfire circle, enamel ware can be used equally well.) The Fakir, after walking twice around the table to studiously ascertain the exact placing of the dishes, now selects the best side from which to accomplish the big yank-off. He grasps one side of the tablecloth and intentionally pulls the cloth toward him in such a way that all of the dishes fall on the ground, and on him, as he falls on his back onto the ground.

His fall, alas, knocks over the table, revealing how his illusion-masterpiece, "The Disappearing Ping Pong Balls," was performed. The round hole cut in the center of the table tells the tale and the campers correctly guess that there was a slit cut in the tablecloth, just above the hole, through which the balls were pressed at the will of the Fakir.

For the first time since the performance began the Fakir is flustered. He scrambles clumsily to his feet and rushes out of the campfire circle pursued by the campfire director, who returns triumphantly carrying the Fakir's turban in one hand.

The flat cardboard box into which the ping pong balls

dropped when they were pushed through the slit in the tablecloth and then the hole in the table top, should be securely fastened onto the underside of the table and directly beneath the hole, with strips of adhesive tape all around. This box must be knocked off by a flying foot or waving hand of the fallen Fakir, while he lies beside the upset table, in order that the hole in the table top will be revealed. If the campfire light is not strong enough at that moment to expose the hole, a leader can pretend to give a hand to the fallen Fakir while a flashlight which he holds shines through the telltale hole in the table top.

SWAMI AND FAKIR

Swami and Fakir is a good stunt or skit which can be carried out in a way that will keep the audience guessing throughout the first part of the act. It is usually the first number on the program, since it is easier to stage that way, for a reason to be seen later.

The leader grandly announces that they are honored by having with them the great Swami Dhram Shir Lall. The Swami then walks pompously into the circle. He is arrayed in the usual flowing robe and turban, easily improvised from a bed sheet and pillowcase. He sits down at a little table, like a card table, which is fittingly draped all around with some sort of dark print or cotton, or a dark blanket. In all cases, the drapes reach the ground. The Swami is ceremoniously blindfolded by

the leader, but his ears are left uncovered. Two or three of the audience may be asked to assist the leader, to make certain that there is no trickery. Half a dozen volunteers are then asked for, and they stand close to the audience but facing the Swami. The leader, who now stands at some distance from the Swami, asks them, two at a time, to make any motions they like, such as shaking hands, dancing together, changing hats, and similar movements. The audience is surprised to hear the high-pitched voice of the blindfolded Swami state what each couple is doing. Sometimes he may even describe the clothing worn by them. He leaves the circle amid considerable applause.

His place is taken by an American type of Fakir wearing a big false moustache. He makes fun of the Swami's performance and calls for his own medium in order that the spectators may see some real thought transference. The medium, a bright boy or girl who has had one or two rehearsals, comes in and sits down on a chair. The medium is then blindfolded, and the Fakir stands beside her.

He holds up four fingers and then taps the medium lightly on the head four times with a wand made of rolled paper. "How many fingers do I hold up?" he asks.

"Four," answers the medium without hesitation.

"Extraordinary!" cries the Fakir. The medium does as well when one and three fingers are held up, the number of fingers corresponding with the number of taps which the Fakir gives quite obviously.

A ripe banana is then held before the medium. "What color is this nice ripe banana?" asks the Fakir anxiously.

"Yellow," the medium replies instantly.

She is just as accurate when the Fakir asks, "What color is this orange?" and, "What color is this half-dollar?"

"Now to more difficult feats," says the Fakir. "On what am I writing your name?" he asks, as he writes the medium's name on a slate with a scratchy slate pencil.

"You are writing on a slate," the medium announces in a faraway voice.

"Unbelievable!" exclaims the Fakir. "Tell the audience what I have written," he commands.

"You have written 'Mary,' " answers the medium, if that happens to be her name. The Fakir and medium then hurriedly leave the scene, taking bows to right and left.

Two attendants now make a spectacular entry in order to call attention to what they are about to do. They lift the Swami's table high in the air and carry it out of the campfire circle. In the spot where the table was, squats a small boy who is apparently fast asleep. Everyone in the audience now realizes that he served as the Swami's eyes, from underneath the table. The leader awakens the boy, who scuttles hastily out of the circle. It was he who watched what was taking place through small peepholes cut in the cloth, and reported it in a low voice to the Swami.

CAMP COMEDY KITCHEN

This skit is bounded only by the imagination of the leader who stages it, as any number of additions can be made. Too many skits depict a day in camp without mention of the kitchen. This is a pity, for the kitchen, regarded in lighter vein, can prove the source of many laughs.

The scene opens and closes in a kitchen. There is an imposing "stove"—easily constructed from a few orange crates or boxes covered with black paper—a couple of tables, a low stool or chair, and a small cupboard, for the props. The stove gives off quite a lot of black smoke. The smoke comes from some smoldering rags in a tin can, hidden inside the stove. The cook, immaculately clad in white and wearing a chef's hat, has a well-padded stomach. He gets into the smoke from time to time and much theatrical coughing results. He has four assistants, each one more clumsy and apparently less bright than the other. The cook loudly beats a large pan with a ladle. On this "assembly" signal all his assistants rush to him, nearly carrying him off his feet, then go into a huddle.

The cook announces that they have come together to plan a "scrumptious" menu for the next day's meals. He asks his aides to put on their thinking caps and come up with some helpful ideas. They all make ludicrous suggestions, such as "bees' knees on toast, bubble and squeak, bobcat pajamas sauté, butterfly pie," and so forth. At the mention of butterfly pie, one of the assistants grabs a butterfly net from the cupboard—a fish net will do—and, encouraged by the shouts of his fellow assistants, chases an imaginary butterfly around the kitchen several times. He finally misses it and ends the chase with the net over the enraged cook's head.

One assistant polishes and blackens the stove—and his face, chiefly his face. Still another assistant sits down on a fluffy, imitation pie which the cook has just taken from the oven and placed on the chair. Several times, the assistant nearly sits on the pie, which he apparently does not notice, before actually doing so. This keeps the audience in suspense.

The fourth assistant dips a cup into a pot on the stove and tastes the contents. He loudly praises the wonderful soup. The cook angrily shouts that it is "coffee." To decide which is right, the three assistants taste the disputed contents of the pot. Three assistants are quite positive that the concoction is soup, but the indignant cook and another assistant stick to the coffee theory. The matter is decided by vote. Each writes on a slip of paper what he thinks the pot contains. They drop their slips into a bowl and then appeal to a leader, or guest in the audience, to count the ballots. The ballots are solemnly counted, and the vote is declared to be three to two in favor of soup. The democratic spirit prevails, so they unanimously decide to serve the contents of the pot as soup next day.

The cook beats the basin again, and the assistants fall on him in a body. When they get disentangled, he announces that he is going to make doughnuts for next morning's breakfast and asks for their co-operation. They show great interest as he pours some flour on the table. One assistant clamors to make the holes. Another assistant suggests that the doughnuts be made square for a change. One begs for a few to use as sinkers when he goes fishing. The cook calls for a yardstick so that he can measure each doughnut to make sure that it is exactly 3 inches in diameter. Other assistants get rulers and demand that the doughnuts be 6 inches in diameter. They all become so excited that, with the help of the rulers, flour flies in all directions. The flour causes violent theatrical sneezing, which ends the doughnut business.

The cook places a frankfurter on the table. It promptly jumps off and chases a terrified assistant around the kitchen, while the others climb frantically onto tables and chair, one leaping into the chef's arms, so that both fall on the floor. Finally the chef and his assistant pursue the mad hot dog, apparently being bitten at times as they get a momentary hold on it. To end the skit, the assistant who is being pursued by the hot dog rushes from the kitchen, and campfire circle, chased by the others in the act. (The frankfurter, for the sake of better visibility, can be replaced with any big wurst, reinforced with adhesive tape to withstand rough usage; or an artificial one can be made from a piece of wood, painted a reddish color. A thin piece of strong fishing line connects the assistant and the frankfurter.)

THE STARGAZERS

The leader gravely announces before the skit that they are favored in having with them a great astronomer, Professor Leo Nunki. The professor enters, clad in an improvised gown and a type of hat worn by professors at commencements. He takes a bow and stands beside a large telescope. It is made of cardboard, mounted on a wooden tripod, and tilted at an acute angle. The small end is on the level of the eye of a "star gazer" seated on the chair directly in front of the small end of the glass. The large end goes through a hole, cut to fit, in a large square of dark cloth, or two old blankets, which almost touches the ground. This screen is to hide from the star gazer's view the astronomer's assistant and his small table, on which are the necessary properties required for this act. The assistant has a strong stool or chair to stand on, so that he can easily reach the height of the large end of the telescope. A lit flashlight is tied on outside and close

to the large end of the telescope so that its beam illuminates the large end of the glass. The audience can see both ends of the telescope and the assistant at work, but the star gazer seated on the chair cannot see the assistant. He has to look through the telescope to see what is going on at the other end.

The leader calls in three star gazers who have been rehearsed in their parts. One sits on the chair, and the two others stand behind it awaiting their turns.

"Now, my little man," says the professor, "what planet would you like to see?"

"Venus," replies the star gazer, puting his eye to the telescope. The professor's assistant now picks up a small doll from the property table and, mounting the chair, holds the doll a few inches away from the large end of the telescope. "Wonderful," exclaims the star gazer. "She is beautiful."

"Perhaps you would like to see a constellation now," the professor suggests.

"Yes, please," says the star gazer. "May I see the Little Bear?"

"Ah, you mean Ursa Minor," says the professor as his assistant holds up a teddy bear in front of the end of the telescope. "Next," says the professor, and the second gazer sits on the chair.

"May I see the Little Dipper, please?" he asks.

"Certainly," replies the professor as his assistant holds a little dipper, from the kitchen, in front of the telescope. "What next?" asks the professor.

"The Snake, please," requests the gazer.

"No doubt you mean Serpens, the Serpent," remarks the professor. The assistant holds up a jointed wooden snake before the telescope.

"Remarkable," says the star gazer. "Just like a milk snake."

He now gives his chair to the third and last seeker after knowledge. He is dressed in old overalls and an old shirt. "Show me the Little Dog," says he.

"One usually says 'please,'" remarks the professor, "but you may see Canis Minor, just the same." The assistant holds up a little stuffed dog. "I don't believe that was a real star," the star gazer comments loudly.

"Well, my little man," remarks the professor patiently,

"why do you not ask for something really real, say a constellation such as the Milky Way? There can be no deception there."

"That's it," cries the rude star gazer. "Give me the Milky Way."

As soon as the professor mentions the Milky Way, the assistant picks up a quart bottle of "milk" from the property table and pantomimes with it gleefully, for the benefit of the audience. (The "milk" is cornstarch or flour thoroughly dissolved in water.) The assistant removes the cap from the bottle and holds the bottle close to the end of the telescope but just underneath it. As the star gazer places his *closed* eye near the end of the telescope, not right against it, the assistant empties the entire bottle of "milk" into the telescope. Of course, the rude star gazer is at the receiving end and soon becomes a major part of that galaxy which he demanded to see—the Milky Way.

CAMPFIRE SHADOWS

Either two large white sheets fastened securely together end to end, or a length of light, white cotton cloth 12 feet long by 7 feet high, is needed for this amusing guessing or deductive stunt. Two 9- or 10-foot-long straight, smooth poles should be forced down into deep, narrow holes which have been prepared in advance by driving a crowbar into the ground at the exact distance required between the two poles. This distance is decided by the length of the sheets or cloth used. These screens are tied or thumbtacked firmly onto the posts. The screen should be quite taut for the best results. Two leaders can hold the poles in place during the performance, but this is not necessary if the holes have been well made and the poles fit them tightly.

This shadowgraph screen is set up about 6 feet in front of the campfire on one side of it, and if the campfire director wishes the entire campfire audience to see the show at the same time, he can set up a second screen on the opposite side of the campfire. With a little crowding for this particular performance, all the campers are there for the preview. Of course, a cast of actors is needed for each screen.

Once the screen is in place—and it can be set up quite quickly—the show begins. When a guessing contest is in progress, only the section of the audience which cannot see around or behind the screen, takes part. The performers then move, one at a time when it is a solo act. walking strangely or disguising themselves by funny actions and motions so that the onlookers cannot easily guess who is behind the screen.

Leaders or senior campers who are good at animal mimicry can help to stage part of the show where various animals are represented in shadow, one or more performers forming the outlines of the animals with little or no props. A bear, for instance, is easily imitated without any gear, and quite a good make-believe monkey can also be thrown on the screen without artificial aid. Some big birds, such as ostriches and emus, require only a little advance work and a few pieces of heavy cardboard, held correctly in place by a performer, in order to appear lifelike in shadowgraph animal land.

Firelight shadow screen skits should be very short ones. Very suitable are parts of *Hansel and Gretel,* not overlooking the witch; Oliver Twist, asking for "more"; and many others requiring only a minute or two, two or three characters, and perhaps some striking prop which will help to identify the story when the characters are not too easily guessed. Literary characters, such as Huckleberry Finn, Robin Hood, Long John Silver, and others who are easy to recognize can be used. Characters with a distinctive silhouette can be made even more recognizable by the character carrying a fishing rod, a bow, or some other easily made and identified prop.

It is suggested at this point that the ancient and stereotyped shadowgraph stunt of portraying an operation, with yards of garden hose being removed from a "patient" as intestines, or a big alarm clock to illustrate why the patient's time was running out, be left out of the picture.

A campfire as a shadowgraph projector must take second place when compared to the more scientific shadowgraph projection methods such as powerful flashlights, reflector electric lamps, or other safe types of lamps or spotlights. Such artificial lights are best set up at one side of the campfire circle, and they can be counted on to assure crystal-clear shadows on any suitable screen. However, a campfire burning brightly and giving a sharp, clear light can be coaxed to contribute still another of its multifaceted entertainments when given a chance and fed with dry, clear-burning sticks at proper intervals. The sticks can have been dipped in melted paraffin wax to assure instant combustion when dropped into the fire.

Care must be taken to see that the performers keep very close to the screen in order to cast natural-size shadows, since the distance from the screen determines the size of the shadows projected. Actions should be broad and sweeping in order to register on the screen clearly. The shadows of performers or props must never overlap, unless intentionally, since merging shadows ruin the effects.

PICTURE GALLERY

This includes odd characters, old masters, and stars for a campfire exhibition, and is an easy exhibit to make and set up even for the first time. After that, it is almost as simple as setting up an easel, which is actually what the necessary props amount to, plus cloth curtains for front, backdrop, and sides. A leader, with very little help from the camp handyman and the donation of a few damaged sheets, will put the exhibition in business.

Almost as important as the equipment for putting on a show is a clever art director, who acts as master of ceremonies throughout the exhibition. One who is adept at ad lib, and a master of rhetoric and repartee is the ideal art director. The art director should keep the audience amused, even instructed, between the behind-the-scenes preparation for the presentation of each picture and the announcing and lecturing on each subject, in the most professional style, while it is on view. The art director may also have to cover up when the framework totters because of a clumsy stagehand, or when the camp director appears out of turn as "The Chief," when he is announced as "The Three Graces" before the curtain goes up. A really good art director can direct many campers into what to them is an almost unknown realm when, at the end of the camp season, they visit picture galleries and museums in order to see what real art is. Ring up the curtain!

A character study. If there is a real "character" of any age in camp who will pose as the subject of this picture, fine. If not, someone can be made up to represent an old man, an old woman, or an old master.

A good egg (a well-rounded subject). The subject of this living picture can be the camp director, a popular counselor, or a camper. When this Picture Gallery stunt is used a second time, at a future exhibition, and the audience feels that it knows just who the "good egg" will be, it is amusing to have a real hard-boiled egg appear in the frame.

A well-matched pair. This can be made an amusing picture by having two ill-assorted campers, counselors, or a camper and a counselor, standing side by side within the frame. For a second show, on another night, a real pear, with a number of large wooden matches stuck in it, will get a laugh from the audience.

The front page (a journalistic study). This "picture" can be the front sheet of a newspaper, or a pose may be taken up by two campers or counselors who enact what is, or may shortly be, front page news.

A chip off the old block (a study in heredity). A suitable picture may be that of a father and son posing side by side, or a camper alone. For a repeat performance of Picture Gallery, the subject may be a big chip from a real block of wood.

Tongue-tied (silence is golden). This picture of a very talkative camper, with his or her tongue tied with a bow of clean ribbon will get a laugh. On a second program, a shoe or sneaker, with its tongue tied with a big bow of ribbon, will be a good substitute. Any double subject of this sort makes an excellent encore, provided the art director has the second subject ready to make its appearance in the frame.

Two good souls (made for each other). Similar to the above picture, this one can depict a team of two counselors or campers standing arm in arm. As a stunt, a pair of big shoes can be shown, with the soles facing the audience.

The campers' friend. A good subject for this picture can be the camp owner, camp director, cook, head counselor, or another popular counselor. A second subject, which may get hisses instead of cheers, can be the camp bugle, or the bugler with his bugle at his lips.

The granny (an example to be avoided). Perhaps the best subject for this picture is a large "granny" knot tied on a thick piece of rope.

The light that failed (global darkness). A suitable portrayal is either an obviously burned-out electric light bulb, or one painted gray-black outside to imitate the real thing.

PARADE OF STARS

The field of astronomy may easily be invaded for subjects and ideas, as the few examples below illustrate.

The constellations are shown by means of cutting out the star formations from a large sheet of stiff cardboard, the cut-out holes being the "stars" which the audience sees while a photographic spotlight shining behind, but not through, the stars makes them stand out well. If one wishes to make certain stars shine with greater realism, the effect is easily achieved by pasting colored tissue paper, yellow, golden, red, etc., behind the cardboard over the star cutouts. To remind campers of the brilliance of some of the planets, a spotlight may be shone directly through the cutout of a planet, the beam directed slightly upward.

To make this effortless lesson in astronomy really worthwhile, most of the constellations shown should be those visible in the summer skies during camp season.

Cassiopeia. This is a fine constellation to show. The bright stars comprising it, the little double cluster of three stars arranged in pyramid form slightly to the north of this constellation in the summer sky, and the shape of Cassiopeia—a big W to some and an M to others—make it easy to distinguish in the heavens.

Ursa Minor. The outline of the Little Bear is a useful constellation for campers to be able to recognize. For variation, instead of the outline being pictured, a teddy bear may be shown.

Ursa Major. The Great Bear, also known as the Big Dipper, deserves an important place in the parade of stars. Its use as a pathfinder can be demonstrated by having an arrow cutout, backed with red tissue paper, cut through the pointer stars in the Dipper to call attention to Polaris, the Pole Star, which should also appear on this constellation cutout.

Canis Major. Can be the outline of the Great Dog, or

for a laugh a stuffed toy dog may be used.

Corona. This beautiful, wreathlike, constellation is so easily recognizable in the summer sky that it makes a good subject.

The Milky Way. This can be that wonderful star group, represented in vague outline or, for an encore, a camper drinking a glass or carton of milk.

Gemini. This is a prominent group. The two bright stars Castor and Pollux, which mark the Twins' heads, being roughly five degrees apart, form good measuring points. The bottom stars in the Big Dipper's bowl point to Castor, and the campers have already met the Big Dipper in the person of Ursa Major. Of course, if there are real Twins in camp, they are a natural to double for the constellation Gemini, the Twins.

Venus. This bright planet, with a spotlight flooding through the cutout to remind campers of its brightness, can be impersonated easily—by one of the camp belles.

With these few suggestions to work on, counselors may use the ingenuity which is their hallmark, to take over from here. "The sky's the limit!"

MASTERING THE OLD MASTERS

The masterpiece field too may be invaded for suitable subjects when older campers form the audience.

Dance of the Nymphs. Though it seems a pity to parody anything so lovely as this masterpiece of Corot, the title of the picture leaves it wide open for such treatment. The art director in charge of the exhibition can take over from here, and hope that none of the campers becomes curious enough to look up a copy of the original for comparison.

The Bohemian Girl. An older girl camper or counselor who scoffs at dieting can best do justice to Franz Hals' robust original.

Laughing Cavalier. A counselor from the boys' side of camp can, with some help from the dramatic or arts and crafts department, play this role without too much "dressing up." The costume of the subject of Franz Hals' dashing painting need not be followed too closely.

Laughing Boy. This picture requires very little "make-up," as the subject of the Indian artist is a young Navajo brave in simple dress.

An amusing piece of "business" can be worked into some of the "Laughing" picture stunts by the subject, or someone just behind the backdrop, laughing loudly for a moment just before the picture is shown. A similar signing-off laugh can be given just as the picture is covered, after its exhibition. The wrong sort of laugh often sets the audience laughing.

Girl's Head. Without seeking a likeness to represent this striking Goya girl, any photogenic counselor or camper from the girls' side of camp will make a good subject. A very striking effect may be achieved in this picture by stretching a piece of cloth, exactly the same color as the backdrop, across the lower inside part of the frame, so that only the head from the neck up is seen.

Mona Lisa. It should not be too difficult for the art director to select the right girl counselor for the impersonation of Da Vinci's masterpiece. The subject must be in the mood, of course, and this may be induced by the art director asking her, just before she goes on, what she intends to do on her day off, or how she liked dancing with "Bud" at the counselors' dance.

The Invisible Man. Departures into the field of fantasy can be made quite amusing when carried out in the following way. Only the top half of the long frame should be used for these subjects, the frontdrop being used to screen the lower half. The art director announces, just before the picture is uncovered, that the subject about to be shown is a most unusual one. In fact, the subject of the picture will be invisible, as the title of the picture suggests. The subject, the director goes on to explain, has been instructed to repeat the magic words, "Cadabra aba, you can't see me."

When the screen is pulled back and the picture uncovered, the subject, with a nonchalant smile on his face, is visible to the audience from about the waist up, as though he had not used the magic words. The catch is that he is supposed to believe that he *is* invisible.

The art director, apparently much embarrassed, cries, "You're NOT invisible!"

The counselor acting the part of the subject looks greatly astonished and exclaims, "Honest? I said the words you told me to!"

"What were they?" questions the art director.

"I said, Aba cadabra, you can't see me."

"Aha!" exclaims the art director, "you said the two mystic words backward. That's why you're not invisible."

The counselor looks upset and says pleadingly, "Can't I have another chance?"

When the art director asks the audience "Can he?" there is nearly always an answering shout of "Yes!"

"All right, you may have another chance," the art director tells him, "but this time be sure to get it straight."

The screen is closed for a moment, then pulled back. Sure enough, this time the subject is invisible to the audience, but it distinctly hears his anxious question to the art director: "I am invisible this time, am I not?" (The counselor is on his hands and knees behind the frontdrop with his mouth upward, just below the picture frame, as he asks the question. This makes the sound of his voice appear to come from inside the empty picture frame.)

"You are indeed," the art director exclaims cheerfully. "I wish you to see that there is no deception, no strings,

no wires," he tells the audience. He waves his pointer up, down, and across the inside of the empty picture frame. Then, with a motion hidden from the audience by his body, the art director pulls the bottom bar of the picture frame forward, so that it falls to the ground, along with the frontdrop.

The audience then sees the "invisible" counselor on his hands and knees, made visible by the dropping of the frontdrop. The counselor pretends to panic. He creeps a few feet to the right, then to the left, shouts "I've been framed!" and disappears behind the backdrop of the picture frame, followed by the art director.

HOW TO MAKE THE PICTURE FRAME. The frame which is easiest to build, and the most solid type, can be made from ordinary 2-inch by 4-inch pine lumber. If large screws or bolts are used in its construction, the entire framework may be taken apart and stored in a small space for next season's use. Two long uprights, each 7 feet 6 inches long, and three crosspieces 4 feet 6 inches long are required for the actual picture frame. The crosspieces are fastened with the 4-inch width outward, one at the top and one at the foot of the frame, on the front of the frame side. A 4-foot-6-inch plank 2 feet wide and about 1 inch thick is securely fastened onto the top of the two uprights of the picture frame. It can be made more secure and more easily removable by supporting it on two metal angles used for holding up shelves. One angle is attached to each upright. The third crosspiece is simply fastened to the uprights by two stout spike nails 4 inches long, which fit through a hole of the same diameter as the nails' thickness, 2 inches from each end of the crosspiece. A hole should be bored in the center of each upright 40 inches and 30 inches from the ground. These holes should not be less than ½ inch in diameter, and the spikes which fit through them should be of the same diameter. The spike is cut off if necesssary, so that it is 4 inches long. A spike passes through the crosspiece from the outside of the frame, one on each side, holding it in position at the height required when showing pictures requiring a half-length picture frame. It will be seen that holes to receive the crosspiece may be bored at any desired height in the uprights. The crosspiece is easily put in place and removed by the art director as required. A canvas or other piece of opaque cloth is tacked to the inside of the movable crosspiece to hide the lower half of the frame. This screen cloth is 4 feet 6 inches wide and 40 inches long, unless holes are bored to hold it 50 inches from the ground, in which case the cloth would be 50 inches in length. When this screen cloth is used at a 30-inch level, the foot of it simply lies flat on the ground outside the picture frame.

The entire outside of the frame should be covered with a strong, opaque piece of cloth mounted on a spring roller, like a window shade, fastened to the top of the frame and operated by a very short cord hanging down from it. The art director should be able to speedily raise and lower this shade when presenting and blacking out each art exhibit. Another, less effective, way to screen the pictures is by hanging a cloth curtain by means of metal rings onto a metal or thin, smooth wooden pole fastened to the top of the frame. This curtain is pulled aside and shut for the showing of each picture.

The completed frame is easily held in place by two straight 12-foot poles or pine two-by-fours. One end of a pole is fastened to the top of the picture frame on one side, and the other end is pegged securely to the ground behind the frame. A pole is fastened to each top outside edge of the frame, with a spread of about 5 feet or 5 feet 6 inches between the poles at ground level. The ground ends of the poles may be easily fastened by driving an 18-inch stake into the ground on each side of each pole and lashing the pole between them. The frame itself should be tilted *slightly* backward before the poles are tied to the pegs. A backdrop should be fastened to the outside of the shelf at the top of the frame. It should be of heavy cotton or canvas or any other opaque cloth. It must reach from the shelf to the ground. A medium-weight wooden pole attached to the foot of this backdrop will assure its remaining in place and at the same time allow the living pictures going into the frame to lift and lower the backdrop as they pass under it. The color of this backdrop is important, as it is actually the background for all pictures being presented. It should be of a neutral shade, such as beige, light gray, or some other shade which will not conflict with the colors worn by the pictures which appear in front of it.

A length of cloth hung on each long pole, stretching from the picture frame top to about 2 feet from the end which is pegged to the ground, will form a little dressing room for the living pictures, as will the space between the backdrop and the inside of the picture frame, when the curtain is lowered between pictures. One or two counselors from the dramatic staff should be on hand to see that the costumes are worn correctly and well and that there is only a brief interval between each picture shown.

The art director will require a pointer, a lightweight tapered stick about 3 feet long, with which to point out the exhibits and, when necessary, close and open the sliding curtain in front of the picture frame when a window shade spring roller arrangement is not installed.

The art director will also have the responsibility, with the aid of an assistant when desired, of putting in place and removing the crosspiece to meet the needs of each picture exhibited. Bust views of smaller campers will require that the crosspiece be pegged into the 30-inch-high holes. Larger campers may require the crosspiece in the the position 40 inches from the ground, while the full-length portraits will require the removal of the crosspiece altogether. These moves are very quickly and easily

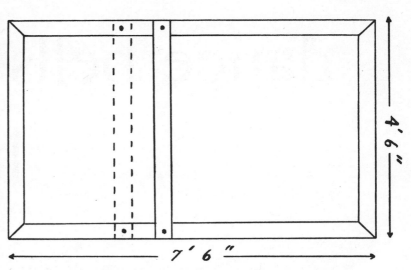

done, especially when a note is made on the art director's list of exhibits telling at which height the crosspiece is required for each picture and when the crosspiece should be removed for the showing of full-length pictures.

Additional height adjustments can be made for almost any objects exhibited by placing them on boxes or small tables, the tops of which reach just to the top of the crosspiece or slightly under it, the table or box being hidden by the cloth screen attached to the crosspiece.

Objects on exhibition may also be held up on thin sticks painted the same color as the backdrop, which gives the audience the impression that the objects are suspended in space. Actually, they are being held up by a counselor who is hidden behind the cloth screen on the crosspiece fastened at the 40-inch level.

The picture frame may also be set up in a makeshift form, with almost no construction work involved, by simply setting two 10-foot-6-inch poles 3 feet into the ground in post holes of the same diameter as the poles being set into them. Two 4-foot-6-inch poles are lashed between these two uprights, at top and bottom. A piece of heavy canvas 7 feet 6 inches high and 4 feet 6 inches wide, with the entire center cut out, leaving only a 4- or 6-inch border, is stretched tightly between these poles. The 4- or 6-inch strips at sides, top, and foot should be painted with dark paint to resemble a picture frame. Two long poles are fastened by the ends to the top of the two upright poles, and the other ends are pegged to the ground, as in the frame made from the two-by-fours. These two slanting poles will support the crosspiece, lashed about 3 feet from the two upright poles, to which will be tacked the canvas backdrop and substitute for the wooden shelf spoken of in the frame already described. Cloth curtains can also be hung from the slanting poles to form a dressing room. A crosspiece for the showing of half-length pictures may also be used. In a pinch, this simple frame will serve the same purpose as the more elaborate one.

dance bells

by firelight

DANCERS

NOBODY WHO HAS STUDIED INDIAN lore and has a knowledge of the Indian and his ways believes that his dances were haphazard affairs and that just any movements, especially jumping ones, will serve for Indian dance steps. There were many different dances to illustrate the life of the Indian—his success in the hunt and on the warpath; his personal hopes, triumphs, and defeats; and his joy and sorrow. The Indian dancers were clever mimics and pantomimists, and they were able to reveal through rhythmic expression and expressive movements of the hands, arms, legs, and body the thoughts which motivated the dance. Even if the Indian danced in deep shadow, so that his face was almost invisible, his body told the vivid story. Hesitation, fear, reassurance, triumph, gladness, and sadness were graphically illustrated as his body moved in rhythm with his thoughts. This is because the Indian danced first in his mind, then with his body, after projecting a strong mental picture.

DANCES OF THE AMERICAN INDIANS

There is little space here to go deeply into Indian dancing. The subject merits several volumes dealing only with the dance. It may prove helpful, however, to set down some of the basic steps and movements and to detail a few of the dances of the Indians, in order that they may be performed in the council fire circle in as Indianlike a manner as possible. Here are some typical dance positions, postures, movements, and steps.

Angles. They were apparent throughout the dances. The movements of hands, arms, legs, knees, or feet usually formed an angle when fully extended or in half-extended positions.

Body. In the quieter movements of the dance, the Indians used a relaxed, upright position, with the straight, easy carriage always apparent. In dances of challenge and in those depicting prowess in any field, the Indians used swagger steps, with the body swaying and the shoulders carrying out the same movement.

Hands. The hands were carried in a natural position in most dances, and nearly always in the quieter movements of the dance the hands of the Indian dancer were half closed. The best hand movement is achieved by letting the middle fingers almost touch the palms of the hands. Carrying a bow, fan, rattle, or lance in a dance helps to develop a natural hand style.

Feet. Many tribes used basic body movements and steps of great similarity. The toe-heel, heel-toe, flat-foot, trot step, fast and slow march steps, back scrape step, shuffling step, strutting step, and those used in animal mimicry were typical of the Indian style of dance.

BASIC DANCE STEPS

The same dance steps were used by a number of tribes, but each tribe had different names for them. In order to simplify nomenclature, no translations of the Indian names for the following steps are given, but a simple descriptive name has been given for each step or groups of steps. Nearly all the steps set down are easy ones to learn, and they can be done well after a little solo and group practice. The easiest steps and the ones which come most naturally to beginner dancers are given first, except in a very few cases, where steps are given to assure grouping of certain styles or patterns of steps.

Marching steps are simply a series of steps in march time, marching at various tempi and with either short or long steps to meet the requirement of the dance being done. These steps are done in a proud, upright position in the straight forward-march style, or they can be carried out in place, without advancing, until another advance step carries the dancer forward.

Trotting steps are a series of short running steps done in various tempi on the ball of the foot. Like the marching steps, they can be done advancing forward or diagonally, or in place, without movement in any direction.

Leaping steps. In a few of these steps, such as the elk or caribou leap steps, the dancer progresses by long, high, leaping steps, one foot at a time being stretched well ahead of the dancer. In solo dances, a dancer may leap almost straight up, one foot at a time, as though trying to reach an object just above his head. Leaping steps, always one foot at a time, may be taken sideways or in any other direction.

Jump steps are made on one or both feet at the same time and taken in any direction.

Hop steps are usually made on one foot at a time. It is a form of skip step, done on the ball of the foot with the knees raised high. Frequently this step is carried out with double hops on each foot. *Skip steps* are spring steps on one foot, keeping the foot close to the ground.

Flat-foot step is similar to the hop step but is even easier to execute, as the entire foot is lifted in a completely flat position from the ground and put down again in the same manner. The movements should be well defined, and the body from the waist up is held straight and without movement.

Southwestern step is inserted here, because it too was a flat-foot-stamp used by the Pueblo people. This step was used in general dancing to some extent, as well as being regarded as a ceremonial step. The feet are raised alternately, and horizontally, about 7 inches from the ground. As the right foot is lifted, either it is put down forcibly in place or a short forward step is taken with it. The left foot follows, but is kept close to the ground with knee and leg almost rigid. The same step is done when the left foot is the one raised from the ground and the right foot and leg are almost inactive followers. The body is held straight, with the arms bent in a horizontal position, with elbows close to the body. This step is usually done in three-four time, with a two-beat pause at times for variety.

Tap steps are made by lightly tapping the ground with toe or heel. These steps range from single taps, made with either foot, to five-beat taps. When there is more than one beat, the taps are made from the outside on whichever side the foot is used, tapping inward until the foot used is directly under the body, whereupon the other foot takes over the tempo tapping.

High-stepping steps are carried out, as in the Caribou Dance, by raising the legs one at a time horizontally, bringing knee to waist level, after which the foot is replaced on the ground with a firm stamp.

Toe steps are carried out on the toes and ball of the foot.

Toe and heel steps and their variations are common steps in the dance of the Indian. These are done in a double-beat time, the toe being raised and brought down to earth on the first (loud) beat of the tom-tom, after which the heel is sharply lowered on the second (soft) beat. While toe steps are spoken of in Indian dancing, the toes in nearly all cases can be interpreted as ball of the foot.

Heel and toe steps are the opposite from the steps described above. The heel comes down first, and the toe follows on the second beat of the drum.

Double toe and heel step is a far fancier but not difficult version of the toe and heel step, which looks impressive when done by good dancers. This is how it is done to double-beat drumming: Jump on both toes, with heels raised. Drop left heel, raising and advancing right foot. Jump on both toes, heels raised. Drop right heel; raise and advance left foot. These steps are either done in place or while advancing. Often done in fast time, they are most effective when done as a variation between simpler dance steps, and when danced in a zigzag pattern—two steps to the left, then two steps to the right.

Spring steps are short springy steps from foot to foot, danced either in place or while advancing or retreating.

Stamp-beat step is a four-beat step, the first beat being given flat-foot on the ground. Then three lighter beats, which follow immediately, are given with the toes of the foot in action. Usually in this step the foot starts in a position some little distance to one side of the upright body and taps its way to the center, directly under the body. The right foot generally leads these movements, and the left foot follows when the right one has completed the four movements.

Drag or scrape steps are used frequently in Indian dance movements. These steps are done by the dancer stepping forward on the toe of one foot and then scraping it back along the ground until it is in line with the foot which has not moved and which performs next. The same movement is done backward, when the dancer steps back instead of forward and drags the foot which stepped backward forward into place alongside the foot which remained in place. These steps can be executed while moving forward or backward instead of dancing in place. The heel should always be brought down with a snap when completing these steps.

Side steps are often taken in a drag-step style. With the feet together at the start, the left foot is carried clear of the ground and about 15 inches to the left, with the toe pointing downward and touching the ground. The heel is brought down firmly and quickly, while the right foot scrapes across the ground and takes its place beside the left one. This pattern is reversed in doing the steps to the right side.

Pony step, while used as a simple cross-step to the side in either direction when moving around a circle, can also be executed as a forward or backward movement. This step, when fancied a little, looks attractive and appears to be more difficult than it actually is. It is performed by swinging one leg around in front of the other until the swung foot rests on the ground, whereupon the leg in the rear swings forward and around the one which has just terminated the step. The foot which crosses can do the heel and toe step, once the dancer is sure of himself when carrying out the simplified step. The feet are crossed in a similar step, used backward or forward, in a step sometimes known as the *twine step.* The pony step can be made a swingy, swagger step and danced solo in a wavy pattern which is smooth, jaunty, and amusing.

Crouch dance steps are always difficult ones for dancers whose legs are not kept limbered up by practice.

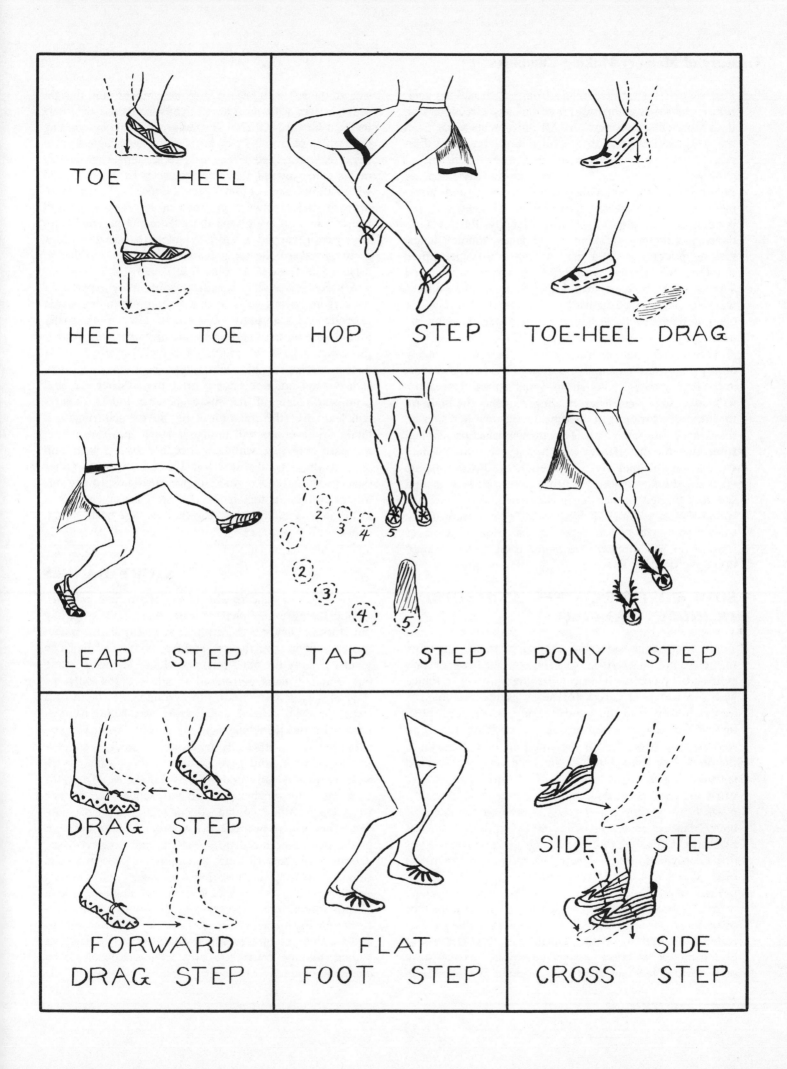

TOE   HEEL

HEEL   TOE

HOP   STEP

TOE-HEEL DRAG

LEAP   STEP

TAP   STEP

PONY   STEP

DRAG   STEP

FORWARD
DRAG STEP

FLAT
FOOT STEP

SIDE   STEP

CROSS   SIDE
STEP

Perhaps the easiest step made from the crouching position is the single jump step, made in any direction, with both feet held close together. All movements made from the deep-crouch position are, of course, far more difficult than those made from the half-crouch position.

Women's dance steps were used for solo style dancing rather rarely, but when they were, the steps and movements generally depicted typical work of some sort, depending on the habitat. Women cleverly illustrated, in dance pantomime, working in the fields, tanning hides, making pottery, or weaving. At times they performed dramatic solo dances descriptive of finding a wounded warrior or the body of a dead one. Many of these dances were executed in a ritualistic and ceremonial way which compared favorably with the action dance done by the men.

The women, in general, showed their best dancing ability in group dancing, the powwow style of dance, and circle dances. Though in some social dances the women's "steps" consisted of simply raising the body on the toes and lowering it in time to the two-beat music, they made out all right. The one satisfaction derived from this toe lift dance step by the versatile woman dancer was the fact that dance etiquette did not dictate what she should do with her arms and body, even though she was limited in her leg movements. The dances in which they sometimes danced with the men were of the social, go-as-you-please type consisting of a series of basic steps, as already described, used in any varied order the dancers liked.

SOME POSTURES, STEPS, AND ACTIONS IN INDIAN DANCING

There are a considerable number of these, but some of the more characteristic ones follow. The *I saw* or *look* actions may portray a brave looking into the distance with forearm held across forehead, as the real Indians always looked, and the hand hanging in a natural position. *Head* actions were made by nodding the head rhythmically in time with the tom-tom beat. Sometimes the nods were short, but for others the head was lowered considerably and then thrown back. *Crouch* actions were often used by good dancers.

Dramatic postures and steps were used for effect in many dances, especially solo ones. Their effectiveness was caused chiefly by abrupt changes in position or sudden changes of tempo where the striking comparisons made the changes more spectacular.

Fear steps are quite effective, and were used in many warrior dances. The dancers portrayed fear in a number of different ways, though all steps and movements illustrated hesitation while the dancer was discovering and establishing what being, animal, or object was the cause of his fear. One fear step was executed by taking one step to the left with left toe, followed by one step to right on right toe, with the knees slightly bent and the body inclined forward. Often a variation was made by crossing the right foot over left, or left over right, progressing in the direction desired. Frequently these steps were danced in fast time toward the rear, because the brave feared what he saw ahead of him. Often a dancer held one hand, or both, palm outward in front of his face while still keeping an alert eye on the thing feared. When the dancing warrior carried a knife or club, he usually made gestures toward the thing feared, as though striking at it from a distance or keeping it at bay.

My dance is ending is indicated by many expert solo dancers in various ways. It is a signing-off ending which generally stops abruptly eight counts after an unusually loud thump on the tom-tom by the drummer, who knows the exact instant when the dance will terminate. The dancer works out his steps, style, positions, and final stance—and holds this for a brief period after the final drumbeat. Some of the more modern Indian dancers will leap over the fire or out of the council ring as a finale, while others will plunge a torch into the fire on the sixth drumbeat, withdraw it on the seventh beat, and hold it dramatically aloft on the eighth beat. Other dancers at the end of their dance rush toward the onlookers waving a tomahawk and stop brusquely inches away, in a dramatic pose, for the last few beats of the dance.

STORY DANCES

Some Indian dancers who were superb pantomimists, without being exceptional dancers, were fond of acting out stories. They did this by means of expressive movements, actions, and the use of face, body, and limbs to vividly portray the mind pictures which they were acting out. Some dancers performed in silence, and only the thud of a swift foot striking the ground, the sound of a rattle, or the tinkle of dance bells was heard, accompanied by the throbbing beat of a softly beaten drum. Other dancers—especially in animal mimicry dances—sniffed, snorted, and gave suitable animal calls, which were frequently answered with striking effect from the darkness with which night had surrounded the council ring. Some of the solo dancers concentrated on one subject, while others introduced a number of different ones in the course of the dance. For example, dancers used actions to indicate sighting the enemy or game, tracking, stalking, freezing in a variety of poses, and shooting with bow and arrow. The dancer, in sign language, asked, "From where comes the wind?" He found out by pretending to throw a wisp of grass or dry leaf into the air and watching intently in which directioin it traveled. His actions told of retreating, advancing cautiously, then charging.

The Buck Dance was a story-action dance generally performed by one or more young braves. It told of hunting down the enemy and, after a fight, either conquering him or dying in the attempt to do so.

ANKLET

ROLE OF THE DANCE STORYTELLER. Sometimes storytellers or heralds were used to tell the story underlying the dance being performed, or about to be performed. An effective storyteller can often enhance the understanding and appreciation of a dance which requires interpreting by the spoken word as well as by the dance. This was especially true of some of the complicated story-dances of the Indians of the Northwest Coast.

The storyteller, when seen, should be dressed in ceremonial regalia, and he stands or sits motionless close to the chief's chair while he tells the story. His voice should be soft and loud by turns and sufficiently dramatic to point up the event which he relates and which the dancer is portraying. At no time should the storyteller's motions, posture, or change of position project themselves to the disadvantage of the dancer. The storyteller should be only a voice, the voice of the dance which is being performed.

Another good way to use a storyteller is to have him tell the story from some point outside the council circle where he will not be seen by the warriors-in-council.

SPECIALTY DANCES

The dances which follow are among those which the Indian dancers took special pains to do well and dramatically. The subjects, animals, or birds and other things depicted were ones held in reverence, or at least respected, by the Indian dancers of the various tribes performing the dances. At times the dances were solo, but

sometimes as many as six skilled dancers participated.

Eagle Dance was an impressive dance performed with eagle head-and-beak mask and elaborate "wings," danced both by tribes of the Plains and the Pueblo people of the Southwest—the latter using the Southwestern step, while the Plains dancers used steps more descriptive of the strange stride of an eagle on the ground and others illustrating the soaring glide of the eagle in the air. This dance was often done as a solo, but at times two or even three good dancers danced in unison. The great respect which the Indians had for this magnificent bird caused them to dance with all the skill at their command. Frequently the dance finished with the death of the eagle, ending with a dignity, grace, and pathos worthy of Pavlova's interpretation of the movements of the dying swan. Study and some research on the part of the dancers who wish to perform this dance is recommended.

Wolf Dance. In this dance too, only the best dancers dared imitate the movements of a wolf at a dance council fire. The wolf was regarded highly for his scouting ability, stealth, and daring, and only the dancers who had studied wolves well undertook to imitate them before warriors who had hunted the wolf and knew its wit, wile, habits, and movements.

Strong Heart Dance is a special dance, often-performed by a chosen brave whose valor equals his dancing ability, for the entertainment of visitors. Usually it was danced among the tribes of the Plains, like many other dances in this section.

War Dance. This impressive dance was performed by braves of a war party before setting out on a trail which might end in death for some of them.

Scalp Dance was a dance of braves, young and old, staged to celebrate a victory.

CHALLENGE DANCES

The solo dancers of numerous tribes sometimes started challenge dances of various sorts by challenging another dancer of the tribe, or sometimes a visiting dancer, to copy their difficult dance actions.

PIPE DANCE CHALLENGE. The Chippewa had an amusing dance in which all dancers had to be prepared to meet an additional challenge, that of the drummer who caused all the dancers as much difficulty as possible by sudden changes in tempo during the dance. Such changes were, of course, made at the most unexpected moments.

The first dancer leapt into the ring, carrying a pipe with a bent bowl. As he danced he tried by his posture to imitate the shape of the pipe bowl and at the same time kept a wary eye and intent ear on the beater of the tomtom. This was not an easy task, especially when he depicted the smoke rising in puffs and bent far forward, from the waist, in a low crouch to represent the pipe's curved bowl. When he had finished or was almost worn out by the violence of his interpretation and contortions, he chose a new dancer from among the onlookers, who had to try to surpass the imitative performance of the first dancer.

The first dancer indicated who was to be next by passing him the pipe immediately, stamping on his foot, or kicking him on the leg. This did not really hurt, as the dancers wore soft-soled moccasins. Sometimes four or five dancers would be called on, one by one, to try to better the Pipe Dance of the dancers before them, and the onlookers had a happy, exciting time. While there was always some horseplay in such dances, there was also much dance skill exhibited, and the best dancers would have felt disgraced had their dance bells tinkled after the tom-tom had unexpectedly ceased to throb.

CHALLENGE DANCE OF THE FLAME. This is a spectacular and exciting challenge dance, which can also be made into a story-dance. A young brave who is a good dancer enters the council ring and boastfully speaks of his prowess as a dancer. He then challenges any of the onlookers to outdo his interpretation of a flame. For the dance, he dons a special loose-fitting garment of flame and gold colors and a tall mask representing flickering flames. These can easily be made, and the dancer should be able to slip into them quickly and easily. Two good dancers enter the circle, one at a time, and contest spiritedly against the challenger. Two or three distinguished-looking judges talk together after each contest and announce that the challenger is the winner. This dance theme can end here, but there is a more striking ending.

An old man among the spectators, who appears to walk with some difficulty, enters the ring and speaks with the judges, who announce that the old man challenges the original flame dancer to a contest. The dancer appears to be unwilling, but the judges persuade him to grant the old man's request. The old man asks if he may borrow the costume of the flame dancer, who grants the request rather unwillingly. Having put on the flame garments, the old man raises his arms skyward in prayer for a few moments, then begins to dance. To everyone's surprise, he gives a remarkable performance, ending with a spectacular leap over the blazing fire. The judges state that the old man has easily defeated his young rival, whereupon the young dancer humbly declares that he will work hard in order to become a better dancer, and he leaves the ring with the old man, his arm around the old dancer's shoulders.

SOME AMERICAN INDIAN DANCES RECOMMENDED FOR DANCE COUNCIL FIRES

These dances are especially recommended, because they are group and fun dances in which most of the warriors-in-council will be able to take part without much practice. By learning some of the steps described in this chapter, and with a little improvisation, dancers will get along quite well in basic dance steps and in the free-and-easy powwow style of dancing. Some of the dances are the following.

Stop Dance. This amusing dance, favored by the Lakota and other Plains tribes, is one in which the dancing braves compete against the tom-tom player. The drummer tries to catch the dancers off guard throughout the dance, as they must stop *instantly* when the drum ceases to speak. Those who fail to do so retire from the dance until only a few fast, wily dancers whoop it up in the dance circle. Fearless braves who really wish to compete should wear ankle and below-knee bells, or at least ankle bells; for this dance. The dance can also be performed in a circle, dancers moving clockwise and facing the line of the direction of the dance, or it can be done in the free-for-all powwow style which assures more action and fun.

Owl Dance was a social dance of the Plains Indians. It was for men and women and was generally performed in a circle. Simple basic steps were used, and the partners could either dance together throughout the dance or change partners as often as they liked.

Feather Dance was used by the Cheyenne to test the agility of the young braves. It was danced in a circle. During the dance the dancers pulled feathers out of the ground with their teeth. The feathers were usually short ones, stuck in the earth in a circle in front of the dancers. Sometimes the attempts to pull the feathers out of the earth could be made whenever the dancers wished to do so, but at others the pulling had to be done on a specially marked beat of the tom-tom. For modern council fire Indians this dance will prove more difficult and provide more exercise than touching the toes with the knuckles.

Iroquoian False Face Dance, for which the Seneca were noted, was usually performed as a medicine dance by medicine men dancers in order to cure sick persons. The Dance of the False Face Society was another thing! This dance, given to hold the troublesome false face spirits in check, was carried out in a free-for-all manner, each dancer wearing a loose-fitting costume, easily made from sacks, and a big false face mask of one sort or another. They shook turtle-shell rattles, gave wild leaps, often ending a few inches away from the onlookers, danced clockwise twice around the dance circle using the hop step, then broke up into solo dances which consisted of creeping, wriggling flat on the ground, sneaking about with the masked face extended in a thrust-forward position while the legs moved in an unnatural position, and similar posturing.

Prairie Chicken Dance, an active dance of the Plains, was danced by braves who imitated the exhibition actions of the male prairie chicken as he wooed and won his mate.

WOODLAND
CARVED   MASK

As good Indian dancers performed, the dance was a wonder of bird mimicry which caused more admiration than smiles; but with modern council fire Indians in the roles of amorous prairie chickens, the warriors-in-council may be more inclined to laugh than utter loud "Hows" of approval. It is amusing to watch the dancers as they strut, "drum" rapidly with their feet, jump and peck at their rivals in the course of the dance, and make loud booming noises for the benefit of the female chickens. This dance is fun, though, and like the other bird and animal imitative dances which follow, it can be done without too much advance preparation. When a few dancers show special virtuosity in any of these dances, they can do them in pairs or in fours as special exhibitions during a council fire program.

Turkey Dance can be carried out instead of the Prairie Chicken Dance, because while it is not a mating dance, all the movements of the dance are descriptive of turkey movements as they feed, fight, "fly," strut, and finally roost.

Owl Dance is a different type of bird mimicry dance, which—with amusing cardboard masks and amusing noise effects—can bring smiles to the faces of the most sedate braves-in-council.

Frog Dance can either be done as an imitative animal-couple "wooing" dance or, for more movement and fun, by a group of dancers. The actions are those of a frog as it sits, hops, jumps, "sings," and catches insects. The hand, held close to the side of the mouth ready to shoot out suddenly, serves as the fly-catching tongue. Body paint and a realistic mask can greatly help the transformation from brave into frog.

Bear Dance is another dance which can be made amusing, as most Indian tribes regarded the black bear as a sort of clown which entertained by amusing antics. A number of dancers, from four to eight, can take part in

185

this dance; the addition of a small cub or two will add to the comic effect. The loose, shuffling bear walk should be well imitated, both when the bears are walking on all fours and when they are erect. Attention should also be paid to the manner in which the forepaws are carried. The forearms outstretched, with the hands hanging down loosely in front, will produce a bearlike effect. The bears walk on all fours, then erect, amble fast, amble leisurely, waddle, roll, crouch, pretend to climb a tree, find grubs, eat, and sleep—until another sleepy bear stumbles over the sleeper. The bear cub in the meantime falls over himself and the other bears, gets lost and into all sorts of mischief, gets spanked by its mother, and generally helps the fun along.

Buffalo Dance was danced well by the Lakota and other Plains tribes, in honor of and in thanks to the buffalo, to whom they owed so much. At times this dance was performed by six painted braves wearing realistic masks depicting the horned heads of bison. There was so much realistic movement and ritualistic significance in this dance that modern council fire dancers who wish to add it to their repertoire are advised to carry out some research and study before undertaking it.

DANCE PATTERNS. For most Indian dances, either solo or group, the dancers moved around the dance ring clockwise, in the pattern shown in Diagram A.

When the dances were of the animal mimicry type, the dancers moved or bounded across the ring in alarm or to meet, greet, challenge, or fight another dancer or dancers, as shown by diagonal arrows in Diagram B. Some-

In all such dances the dancers moved across the dance circle at any point, following the dance leader.

Powwow Dance. This is an exceptionally good dance to enliven a dance program, because every dancer is on his own, dancing without fixed steps or sequence, being carried away by the spirit and spontaneity of his dance. This dance was a favorite of the Plains tribes, who regarded it as a sort of war dance; but it was also danced by the Indians of some Woodland tribes. The principal steps used were the toe-heel, double toe-heel, and flat-foot steps. The drumming was generally in double time —*loud,* soft, *loud,* soft—and the dancers shouted loudly as they spread out all over the ring to perform. Their ringing yells of "Ho, ho!" "Hu ya!" or "Hey, hey!" and wild yelps and yipping filled the air as the dancing became more and more frenzied. Soon the dance may develop into a challenge powwow of the *Sti-yu type,* each dancer trying to outdo the other in dancing the double toe-heel step and dancing two or three steps to each drumbeat. All modern council fire braves can take part in this spirited dance. The novice dancers may open it, then leave the ring to the best dancers, who continue, with more space in which to exhibit their prowess. The dance can end with all dancers rushing from the ring together, or two or three of the best dancers may remain for a few moments to end the dance with some scintillating solo steps.

Strike the Pole Dance. A stout, painted pole about 9 feet long is driven into the center of the council ring about 8 feet away from the fire. The top of the pole may be decorated with a fringe of feathers or strips of bright-colored cloth. Six seasoned dancers, each carrying a strong hardwood club about 20 inches long, erupt into

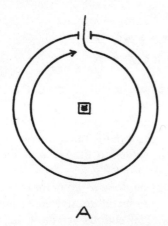

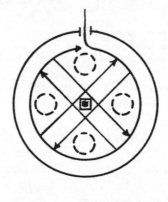

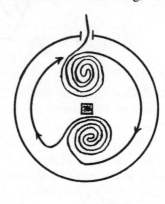

A   B   C

times the "animals" danced in little circles of their own in certain parts of the dance, as indicated by the small broken circles shown in Diagram B.

In the Snake Dance and follow-the-leader types of dances the dancers spiraled, with the leader at the head of the file, and wound and unwound from the two or three tight spirals done in the course of the dance, the first winding up being done counterclockwise and the second one clockwise, as shown in Diagram C.

the ring and dance to a fast tom-tom tempo, counterclockwise around the dance circle, with eyes fixed on the coup pole. Having circled the area once, the dancers take up positions close to the outside edge of the council fire area, with the same space between each two dancers. One dancer then races up to the pole and strikes it once, savagely, with his club. He then circles the pole in a striking solo dance and again strikes the pole, leaping swiftly away from it after the stroke and assuming a dramatic pose.

The drum is silent as the pole is struck. When it commences to drum again, after a moment's pause, the first dancer trots over and takes the place of another dancer, who thereupon rushes at the pole to strike it and then perform his solo dance. The dance continues until each dancer has performed. All six or eight dancers then begin a Powwow Dance, stopping simultaneously at a distinctive and prearranged drum beat or beats, then charging and striking the pole in unison. They keep their clubs on the pole, staring at them, waiting for the drumbeat—which stopped as the pole was struck—to recommence. As it throbs again, the dancers move toward the council ring exit, using the flat-foot trot. Just as the dancers reach the exit, they turn abruptly and together charge and strike the pole as before. After a moment's silence, as the drumming starts again, they trot swiftly out of the council ring.

Rattle Medicine Dance. The Indians often used rattles in their dancing, because the rattles inspired them to dance well and greatly accentuated their dance rhythm. To these dancers the rattle was good medicine. The most effective rattle dances were generally carried out as solos. At times the dancers co-ordinated their rattle time to tom-tom time, and at others they danced only to the rattle rhythm. Such dances are, perhaps, best performed in three parts. The first time, the dancer circles the council ring clockwise. He holds a rattle in each hand but keeps them so close to his body and swings them so easily that they make comparatively little sound, often being almost drowned out by the loud jingle of the dancer's sleigh-bell anklets. During the second circuit of the ring, he uses the rattles with much more vigor and effect, holding them far from his body as they whirr loudly, timing his brusque steps and body movements to the time kept by his rattles. Throughout this circuit he maintains an upright body position. The third circuit, which is often the finale, is a perfect frenzy of rattle rhythm. The dancer crouches, leaps, whirls, makes his rattles engage in a rhythmic duel with his belled anklets as, in the crouch position, he drums his heels savagely on the ground in an effort to make his bells' voice peal above the raucous rattles. He completes this circuit, using a number of half- and full-crouch steps until he reaches the exit. He then throws one or both arms high above his head, rattles silent, and leaps out into the blackness of the night.

Women's Dance. One form of the Give-Away, or Friendship Dance, is the Women's Dance. In these dances, gifts were exchanged during, before, or throughout a number of dances. It is described here for use as an amusing dance when some visiting maidens from a nearby maidens' council fire band have received the invitation sticks which entitle them to share a council fire program with the young men. The maidens, with shrill shrieks, take over the ring and perform in powwow style for a few moments, after which they turn their undivided attention to the braves-in-council. Each girl rushes up to the brave she has her eyes on and drags him, apparently against his will, forcibly, by the shirt or belt, into the dance circle as her partner. Each pair then dances in place, circling clockwise for a few moments, then all dancers move clockwise around the dance circle. After a few moments the maiden holds out her hand and says "Pay me!" whereupon the brave with whom she dances gives her a bead, a small string of beads, a colored feather, or a piece of decorated leather which he has prepared in advance.

The girls may demand payment several times in the course of the dance, and as a rule the brave feels bound to honor her request. After a few circuits of the ring in couples, the dancers form two circles, braves in the outside circle and maidens in the inner circle. The two lines face each other and move in a circle, the men moving clockwise and the women counterclockwise. The dancers use a springy skip step throughout the dance or, if they can do so easily and rhythmically, a cross step as they circle. After a few revolutions the dance becomes a partner one again, the women clutching their partners as they come opposite them and again pulling them into a duo dance. After a short while, all the couples dance clockwise to and out of the exit, where the dance ends, and the participants return to their seats. Instead of this ending, the dancers may return to their places directly from the postions which they occupy in the ring, just as soon as the drum tells them that the dance has ended.

DANCE COUNCIL FIRES

When modern Indian groups have developed sufficient interest in Indian dances and a varied and sufficiently large repertoire has been acquired, a special dance council fire can be held from time to time. In a council fire of this sort, dances dominate the event. As in all outstanding council fire programs, the success of the dance fire will depend on staging and pacing. Change of pace in the different dances presented, and having group dances follow solo dances, will add greatly to the effectiveness and spectator interest.

The council fire should burn brightly for most of the dance powwow, and a fire tender should be on duty throughout the performance to see that it does so. Brightly burning torches placed around the dance circle at regular intervals will add to the brightness of the scene.

It will be found good medicine to have groups and the solo dancers circle the dance circle clockwise at least twice in order to show off the regalia and trappings. The most amusing antics in animal mimicry dances and the most dramatic steps in the more serious dances should always be carried out where they will be best lighted and seen to the greatest advantage.

This is another council fire program where things can be made to happen in all parts of the council fire area at

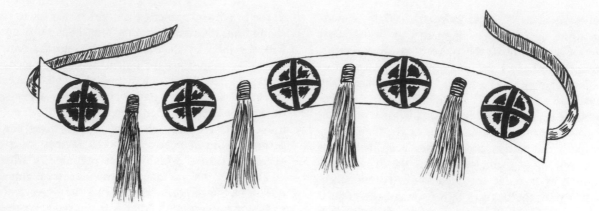

the same time, so that the dances do not degenerate into one special show being given in the vicinity of the chief's chair only.

COSTUMES, MASKS, BUSTLES, BELLS AND ROSETTES FOR DANCERS

Dancers should wear as few trappings as possible for the more strenuous sort of dances, but what is worn should be as attractive and striking as possible. A breech-clout, moccasins, the correct type of headdress, wrist-bands or cuffs, belled anklets, and a rattle when the dance being done requires them, can prove a suitable and effective costume for a dancer who is not impersonating a bird or animal nor costumed for a special dance requiring specific dress.

A light dance shirt, lightweight trousers, suitable head-dress, and whatever other paraphernalia is needed for the dance to be done is also good dance dress. Anklets and below-the-knee-bands adorned with tinkling bells, arm bracelets, and sometimes bustles and rosettes of different sorts, may also form part of the dance costume, depending on the dance being performed and the tribe of the dancer doing the dance.

Dance bustles and rosettes can add a colorful touch to a dance costume when their use is not overdone. When a dancer wears a big bustle, plus shoulder, arm, and wrist rosettes, he often seems so bedecked with them that he has the appearance of an earthbound dodo making futile efforts to become airborne. When required, dancers carry bow, arrow, lance, or club; for some of the South-western dances it is necessary to wear tabletas and carry cloud-making bowls, rainbows, and other symbols required for the dances of the Pueblo people.

Throughout this section the illustrations of costumes, headdresses, and regalia will help dancers to choose the correct costumes, motifs, and the other things necessary for a dancer. No attempt has been made to show, step by step, how the garments are made. There are a number of books which have space to give these details, and they can be referred to when necessary.

COSTUMING BIRD AND ANIMAL DANCERS
Animal and bird masks, such as those shown in this chapter, will help to transform dancers into animals and birds.

PUEBLO MASK

Additional disguise is added by wearing special dress, easily made from large sacks cut to the pattern desired and dyed in the colors best suited for the animal being represented. Buffalo and bearskins can be fashioned from burlap sacks. "Wings" of cloth and feathers, tails, and horns of different sorts can also be securely fastened to dancers with striking effect.

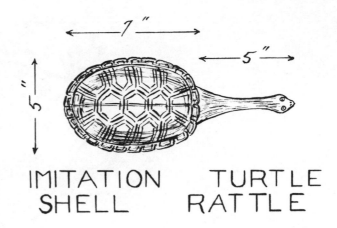

IMITATION TURTLE SHELL RATTLE

FEATHERS, FUR, SKINS, AND TURTLE SHELLS FOR DANCE REGALIA. Because of the realization of the tragedy being brought about throughout the world by man's failure to observe and obey the natural laws of conservation, it is important to discourage the use of fur, skin, and feathers which are the natural clothing of all animals and birds, styled and tailored by the Creator. The Creator did not give squirrels tails to be transferred to shields or used as decorations on headdresses, nor tail feathers to a magnificent eagle that it might be killed and these feathers worn as a bustle decoration for a human posterior. Even the humble turtle and tortoise have their missions in life, and were not intended to end prematurely as dance rattles.

Excellent substitutes and imitations for such things—which will help to stem the rapid depletion in the fast-shrinking bird and animal world—can easily be found today to take the place of the real thing. The feathers of domestic geese, turkeys, and chickens, killed for food, supply an abundance of suitable feathers which can be substituted for those of wild birds. Establishments supplying such feathers for use in making regalia for modern council fire Indians have even colored the feathers to look like eagle feathers. Artificial skin, fur, and hair can be bought for less than the natural covering stripped from dead wildthings. The Great Spirit intended wild animals to wear the skin, fur, or hair with which he adorned them for the term of their natural lives.

Turtle-shell rattles, when one of the many other colorful kinds will not serve, can be made quite satisfactorily from a small wooden box, such as a cigar box, covered on both sides with a cut-out scale drawing of a turtle, which can be colored to closely resemble a real turtle. The handle of the rattle should be securely fastened to the wooden box in the center, in which are the small pebbles or fairly large wooden beads which supply the rattling noise. With a little care and a few simple tools, so fine a rattle can be made in this way that at a few paces distant it is almost impossible to tell, even in daylight, the difference between the imitation rattle and one made from a turtle shell. Frequently the imitation rattle looks better and more colorful, in addition to providing a more satisfactory rattling sound, than a real turtle-shell rattle.

CEREMONIAL DANCES

Space does not permit an attempt to describe even a few of the lengthy and splendid religious, mystery, seasonal, harvest, and weather dances performed by dancers of the Plains, Woodland, Northwest Coast, and the Southwest. While the dance reasons for most of these dances were clear, the dance patterns and steps of such dances were frequently intricate and had to be followed in sequence and with precision in order to be acceptable to both the Indians and their gods. To add to the difficulty of performing these dances in an authentic manner, a number of them lasted throughout an entire day, a day and a night, or considerably longer!

Among some of the best known of these dances are: the Sun Dance, Medicine Pipe Ceremonial Dances, Medicine Bundle Ceremonial Dances, Ghost Dance, Elk and other Mystery Dances, Rain Dance, Wolf and other Secret Society Dances. The Southwestern tribes performed Growing Corn, Planting, Rain, and other harvest Dances. Similar prayer and celebration dances were also carried out, with different ceremonial procedure and steps, by tribes of the Plains and Woodlands. Books have been written about these dances and are available in the libraries.

People often ask, "Were these ritualistic, religious dances performed by the Indians really effective? Did they assure better crops? Did they bring rain?" A personally witnessed experience will answer one of these questions. At the Calgary Stampede a few years ago, many of the Indian tribes who were participating in the parade, and in some of the cowboy events in the arena later on, turned up at the fairgrounds in full regalia on the evening before opening day. They asked, for the last time, that the Stampede committee allow *all* of them and their families free entrance to all the events in the arena throughout the entire week of the Stampede. This mass admission demand nonplussed the officials, but the final decision, like the former ones, was that all Indians not actually participating in the arena activities and contests would have to pay the full admission price.

APACHE MASK

"Then," said a magnificently clad Blackfoot chief, "we will do the Rain Dance, now!"

The officials, certain of the good early July weather which practically always favored the Stampede, and made doubly confident by a hurried call to the weather bureau, said that they saw no reason why the Indians should not perform the Rain Dance then and there if they wanted to.

In a very short while, Blackfoot, Cree, Chippewa, Blood, and Stoney braves, wearing the magnificent costumes and trappings of their tribes, were dancing the Rain Dance, sweating as they moved in intricate patterns beneath the warm evening sun.

The Stampede officials and many interested spectators looked on. In half an hour a dark cloud crossed the sun. A sunny evening abruptly changed from a bright to a gray one. Then came the rain, in torrents. The amazed officials held a hasty conference, then asked the chiefs for terms.

They were simple: "No Indian pays at the Stampede." When the officials tried to set a limit to the number of free entries, the chiefs merely said, "No Indian pays, or we do Rain Dance again tomorrow morning."

As the terms were hastily agreed to and the gathering dispersed, the sun shone hazily through the dark clouds for a few minutes, then shone forth as brightly as before.

MUSIC FOR INDIAN DANCES

Without doubt, drums are the most helpful and effective instruments to accompany council fire dancers. This category includes the rhythmic tom-tom, the *tombe* of the Pueblo people, the dramatic Chippewa and Ojibway drum, and the water drum of the Iroquois and Navaho.

Rattles of various kinds take second place as suitable accompaniment for Indian dances. There are a number of rattles which can be made and used effectively with a little practice.

Perhaps the next best musical instrument is the voice. Rhythmic use of the voice proves attractive as a dance accompaniment. The Indians were far enough advanced

in musical knowledge not to worry about mere words. The all-important song-thought was amply expressed by the tone and tune. This is fortunate for the modern Indians of the council fire, whose knowledge of the Indian language may begin and end with "How!" The "words" of the song which accompany a dance can be merely "Hey-a-hey! Hey-a-hey! Hu-ya-hu!—Hu-ya-hu! Ho-ya-ho! Ho-ya-ho! Ho-ya-ho!—Eh-ya-ha! Eh-ya-ha!—Kah-nin-dah!

Kah-nin-dah!—Eh-ah-ye! Eh-ah-ye!" and the like, chanted in rhythm to the dance being done. It is doubtful that actual words, partially drowned by drum throbs and rattles, would be more intelligible and articulate than those heard today in grand opera sung in English.

As drummers give the correct dance time to the singers, drumming is important. Modern braves with "an ear for music" will not find it difficult to beat out the required rhythm on a tom-tom or drum, once they have learned how to handle the stick or sticks. The basic beat for many Indian dances is two-four time—*loud*-soft, *loud*-soft—and the rhythm is *one,* two, *one,* two. Some dances require three-four, four-four, and six-eight time, but a drummer will soon acquire this timing too. The tom-tom player who can improvise and keep good dance time while doing so will be the one in most demand to accompany solo dances, and he will also be able to improvise successfully as he beats time for impromptu group dancing in the council ring.

Whistles, giving one clear note or varied notes, can be used advantageously at times, chiefly to heighten the dramatic effect of the dances. Bells, in and outside of the council fire circle, produce pleasant rhythmic effects. Beating hardwood sticks together is more effective than modern camp-made wooden clappers, but the "beating

DANCE RATTLES

HORN

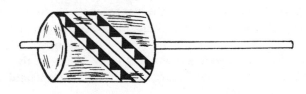

TIN CAN

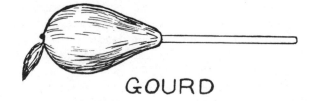

GOURD

board," so popular with the Indians of the Northwest Coast, is a fine addition to council fire dance music. These boards are simply made from 3-to-6-foot lengths of smooth, hardwood planks drummed on with solid, round-ended hardwood sticks, each about a foot long.

TOM-TOM TIME. Before a drummer plays for even the simplest form of Indian dancing, he should be able to beat all the basic times without difficulty and be able to change from one time to another smoothly. When a tom-tom player has achieved sufficient skill to be able to accompany solo dancers performing improvised dances by merely watching the dancer's leg movements, and follow all time changes accurately throughout the dance without hesitation, he is entitled to count coup—or even grand coup!

To make drumming easier, the basic times used in the usual Indian dances are set down in the following paragraphs. When a player knows that a certain dance is performed to two-four time, for instance, he has only to look at the illustration of drum beats and practice the time set down.

There are a number of special drumming effects which a drummer will acquire with practice, such as the quick pattering of bird or small animal feet which proves so effective in some of the animal dances.

KEEPING TOM-TOM TIME

o   .   '

LOUD tap   soft tap   Accented tap

TYPICAL TOM-TOM BEAT

'   '   '   '

o . . .   o . . .   o . . .   o . . .

The three closely spaced soft taps occupy the same space of time as the one loud tap. The first soft tap of each group is accented as shown.

OTHER TOM-TOM BEATS

two-four and two-eight (double time)

o .   o .   o .   o .

and

. o   . o   . o   . o

three-four and three-eight (triple time)

o .   o .   o . .

four-four and four-eight (quadruple time)

o . o   o . o   o . o .

and

o . . .   o . . .   o . . .

six-eight time

o . . o . .   o . . o . .

Authentic Indian dance music suitable for council fire use is published by several music companies, and there are some phonograph records of vocal and instrumental American Indian music on the market which provide Indian dance time and atmosphere. Authentic Indian songs and music will also be found in the *Bulletins and Annual Reports of the Bureau of American Ethnology,* Smithsonian Institute, Washington, D. C.

Most of the drums and rattles illustrated in this book can easily be made from materials found around the home or camp. Others can be bought inexpensively at one of the stores which specialize in supplying materials for the use of modern Indians. The humble tom-tom can be made from a big wooden salad or chopping bowl, artistically decorated, and the top skin-covered. It will prove a useful addition to the music of the council fire and an incentive to the dance.

INDIAN DANCES AND DANCERS OF THE NORTHWEST COAST

Dancing played an important role in the life of the Indians of the Northwest Pacific Coast. Many tribes

danced throughout the greater part of the year whenever they got the chance, but all tribes danced almost constantly for several months during the splendid winter ceremonies. Among the Bella Coola, social dances in which men and women joined took place every night of the year except during the salmon run. During these dances the owners of songs danced to them, and often a good deal of improvisation took place.

RATTLE

Dances of one sort or another kept the dancing Bella Coola in nearly constant motion. Their dances included supernatural, ceremonial, social, and those of secret societies. A youth of a prominent family of this tribe might decide to give an *a'alk* dance, which was attended by invitation. Long before the night set for this dance, professional composers of music, singers, and mask-makers went to work to compose a special song and make a striking, artistic mask for the donor of the coming dance feast. The work of these skilled artisans was carried out with the utmost secrecy, so that the nature of the dance-song and mask were known only to the donor of the potlatch, his immediate family, and the craftsmen until revealed at the dance.

Frequently, songs and dances were the personal property of a certain family, and no other family or person would dream of borrowing or copying them. These dances varied greatly, since many were personal dances which had come to the original owners in a dream, while others had become the property of a dancer through gift or purchase, making them the sole property of the person who had acquired them.

A patron of the dance and his dancers would prepare a dance of several days' duration. This dance was often built around an ancient legend. With a chief song-keeper

DANCE   APRON

and a chief baton-master in charge, the dancers unfolded the legend in dance, posture, and song. Those invited to the dance were given wooden batons for beating plank drums. The music which accompanied the dance-legend was made by singing, drumming, clapping, and rattling. Almost immediately after one dance-legend had been performed, another one began under a new sponsor.

The indomitable Nootka, Hunters of Whales, danced a great deal, often throughout the entire winter. They were one of the very few Northwest Coast groups to stage cultural dance myths. Nearly all other tribes performed general pantomime dances.

Secret society dances, parts of which could at times be given in public, were magnificent and at times hair-raising affairs. Such dances had supernatural significance and were generally astonishing and eerie performances. A great number of dancers participating in these dances made use of the animal masks and complete animal disguises spoken of in the following pages.

Special ceremonial and pantomime dances were not only used to celebrate the initiation of a young man into a secret society but were often staged for the reception of an important guest. Honors for such a guest generally included laying precious furs on the ground for him to walk on and scattering eagle down on him, the down being regarded as a symbol of peace, respect, and good will. Sometimes the honored guest, after full dance honors had been accorded him, danced solo as a token of his esteem for those who did him honor and also as a graphic way of saying, "Thank you!"

Other vivid dances of the Northwest Coast depicted the departure or return of a whaling crew or a raiding party, the ceremonies performed at the catching of the first salmon of the season, or the honors accorded a bear which had just been killed. Modern council fire chiefs can improvise striking dances along these lines. Less elaborate dances can also be staged in the everyday dance costumes described in the following paragraphs.

SIMPLE DANCE COSTUMES FOR NORTHWEST COAST DANCES. For ordinary dancing as part of a council fire program, the dancers wore dance aprons resembling breechclouts with a fringe, and at times colorful, short, fringed blankets for some of the introductory and slower steps. Some dancers wore decorated headbands to keep their hair out of their eyes, and others often donned high-crowned or other special dance hats. These dance aprons, hats, and blankets are shown in the illustrations. Some dancers wore a gaily colored dance shirt and breeches or leggings. Like their brothers of the Plains, many of these dancers wore deer-hoof rattles as anklets. As a rule, true to the tradition of the Northwest Coast, these dancers danced in their bare feet; but sometimes various types of simple or decorated moccasins were worn. Such moccasins can protect the feet of tenderfoot warriors who dance at modern council fires.

The Tsimshian men generally danced attired in splendid Chilkat dance blankets with light backgrounds and white fringes which reached to just above the dancers' knees. Under these blankets they wore dark, rather tight-fitting trousers. Large necklaces, often woven from cedar bark and fiber, adorned their necks, and their feet were shod in light-colored moccasins.

COUNCIL FIRE DANCING NORTHWEST COAST STYLE. Modern council fire chiefs will have no difficulty in staging suitable dances if the performances are done in pantomime to illustrate a story confined to animal mimicry, or if they stage special dances thought of—or dreamed—by a solo dancer.

Quite a number of the steps, such as the flat-footed, shuffle, march, skip, and hop steps described earlier in this chapter, were used by the dancers of the Northwest Coast. They were danced in practically the same manner, though many steps were repetitious to the point of being monotonous. One thing which many of the Northwest dances had in common was the great number of jump, spring, hop, and crouch steps used. This is accounted for by the fact that, like the Plains Indians in the Prairie Chicken Dance and other similar bird and animal dances, many of the movements made by birds, fish, and animals were carefully copied and used by the dancers.

ANIMAL MIMICRY DANCES. This type of dance was usually carried out with great realism both in regard to movements and disguises. Bird and animal dance masks, such as raven, eagle, hawk, wolf, bear, whale, frog, and others, were worn for these special dances. Quite frequently, the performers wore not only the masks but the skin, real or imitation, of the animal represented. Some of the masks and costumes worn are illustrated on these pages. Feather-covered skins were worn for dances in which the dancers became birds. When skins and feathers were not readily obtainable and the dances had to be staged in a hurry, blankets and cleverly made cloth cut-outs took their places quite effectively.

The Northwest Coast Indians found a number of animals especially suitable for imitation in their dances. The whale, as it surfaced, spouted, and sounded, was a favorite subject for mimicry. Dancers, especially chief harpooners of the Nootka, Makah, Haida, and Quillayute, built ceremonial dances around the movements of the whale. The leaping salmon, almost as important to many Northwest Coast tribes as the buffalo was to the Plains

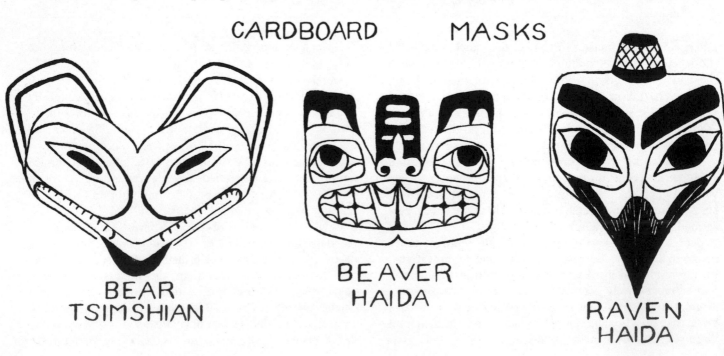

CARDBOARD MASKS

BEAR
TSIMSHIAN

BEAVER
HAIDA

RAVEN
HAIDA

tribes, also provided many motions which were used in the dances. Another unfailing source for dance steps and postures was the slower, shuffling movement of the grizzly and black bears, followed by swift, striking slaps and hooks with the forepaws, as the bears either played or struck at enemies from the upright position or scooped salmon from shallow pools, with quick sweeps of extended claws. In such bear dances, waddling steps and the movements of advance and retreat were usually carried out in an upright position. In the animal mimicry dances, especially when wolves were being imitated, the dancers frequently leapt among the onlookers, scaring them by pretending to strike or bite them. It is not surprising that the spectators jumped swiftly back to escape the long, slashing claws which the dancers often fastened to one or both hands for this dance. The more inspired and realistic among the dancers cast pretense aside, and sometimes spectators got severely mauled before they could break away.

NORTHWEST COAST DANCE MUSIC; INSTRUMENTS AND SINGING

Always the music was rhythmic, and often varied and weird, when the dance held sway at a Northwest Coast dance fire. The instruments most frequently and effectively used were skin-covered or wooden hand-drums, beaten with fingers or hardwood or softwood sticks. Some tribes—the Coast Salish, for instance—used wooden drums with a single head of hide, and plank drums.

DRUM

Occasionally, huge log drums were also used at the great winter dance festivals. Suitable music for the dance was also provided by: long wooden planks and wooden bowls,

beaten with sticks; hardwood sticks struck together in dance time; clappers of wood, shell, or metal; simple and

RATTLE

elaborate whistles ranging from the leaf whistles, generally used for luring animals, to elaborate shell and wood whistles with varied tones; beautifully carved and colored wooden rattles, also hoop rattles strung with shells and shaken sideways; and hand-clapping, in time to the dance being done. Voices singing, chanting, and making various other musical and weird noises, singly or in chorus, were often combined with the instrumental orchestra for added effect.

For general informal dancing the onlookers shouted and sang in time to the steps, and to encourage the dancers when they began to feel tired after five or six hours of dancing without a break. The chant for cadence in double, two-four, time was: "Hai! Hai!—Ho! Ho!—Hu! Hu!" Triple, three-four, time was: "Hai! Hai! Hai!—Ho! Ho! Ho!—Hu! Hu! Hu!" and for quadruple, four-four, time: "Hai! Hai! Ho! Ho!—Hai! Hai! Ho! Ho!" The beat of each chanted syllable was sung in exact time to the step being done, while the drums and other instruments played a rhythmic accompaniment.

OFF-STAGE DANCE ACCOMPANIMENTS AND EFFECTS. Striking off-stage noise effects, mechanical and human, were used to great advantage by most tribes. Usually they reproduced the noises of thunder, running water, and wind. The croaking of frogs was skillfully imitated by rubbing big rough horse-clam shells together. At exactly the right moments, "ghost" voices would make

the onlookers shiver, and occasionally bull-roarers which really roared were used for certain sound effects. The sound of waves breaking on the shore, followed by the sigh of the surf and sound of receding water, was cleverly produced by the use of large and small specially made rattles. These sounds came from somewhere outside the council fire area, from nearby or some distance away, as required by the dance. All such sounds were made at exactly the right moment. These instruments and sound effects were used to the greatest advantage during the magnificent winter ceremonies, on other ceremonial occasions, and at the ritualistic dance performances of various secret societies which carried out a part of their ritual in public.

POTLATCH DANCE FEASTS

Potlatches—give-away dance feasts—were for the wealthy, but the art of giving until nothing more was left to give was also practiced by the poorer people. The exceedingly few wealthy people who were stingy were often forced by the other people to be the unwilling donors of dance feasts. This is how it was done. A small group of dancers and singers called at the house of the involuntary host and began to perform. The village heralds, quick to realize what was going on, were soon heard throughout the village. Their loud, trained voices gravely informed the people that Tight Fist was giving

a dance feast at his house. The invitation was taken up with alacrity and glee, and soon Tight Fist, who would rather have been keel-hauled than publicly branded as an unwilling host, found himself passing out huge quantities of food and drink to his hungry "guests," whose numbers swelled with each passing moment.

THE POTLATCH OF TIGHT FIST (A DANCE PLAY)

This little dance-play is based on the dance feast of the unwilling donor, as described above. It requires no script, and council fire chiefs will find that with a little improvisation and rehearsal it will prove an attractive addition to a dance fire or any other council fire program. Council fire chiefs can stage it with dialogue, partial dialogue, or entirely in pantomime, as they think best. A little effort in producing *The Potlatch of Tight First* will prove worthwhile, as it can be made entertaining and amusing—and, with a few good dancers and careful casting, artistic.

The play opens with four or five dancers and singers, and a drummer or two, talking animatedly together at one end of the council fire area. At the other end, or to one side, is the housefront of Tight Fist's house. This can have a decorative front, such as those illustrated in this book, but it should have a regular cut-out doorway to provide an entrance and exit for the players. One or two colorful blankets can be hung on poles beside the housefront. The housefront pole, shown in the drawing, forms the entrance into the house. The entrance, as will be seen, is through the base of the pole. Let us return to the dance group. The dancers point to Tight Fist's house and then walk toward it, to the accompaniment of the drum or drums. Unless a narrator tells the story, they speak of Tight Fist's stinginess.

The group stops a few feet away from the entrance to the house and dances a few steps; then the voices of the village heralds can be heard announcing that Tight Fist is giving a potlatch. As other villagers, selected in advance by the council fire chief, begin to converge on Tight Fist's house, the dance group begins to dance in front of the house but not directly in front of the doorway. Soon, a head appears at the door of the house, slowly followed by a body, and Tight Fist comes out to meet the group. He is wearing a typical Northwest Coast costume, similar to one shown in the drawings, and has the appearance of a very old man. He appears to move with some difficulty but, after watching the dancers during a few lively dances, asks permission from his "guests" to try his hand, or rather feet, at dancing too. Amid much ill-concealed amusement, the old man asks for a drummer or two who can improvise and follow his steps. When they have taken up their positions —either sitting, kneeling, or standing—Tight Fist, to the apparent amazement of the onlookers, performs a splendid, serious dance, full of grace and rhythm, followed by a comic dance, a regular firecracker for fast movement and fun. (During the dances, the villagers sit or squat on the ground, so that the movements of the dancer are not hidden from the warriors-in-council. Tight Fist can either dance in the clothes which he is wearing when he steps out through the doorway of his house, or he can go back "inside" and make a quick change into a dance costume of some striking sort, or he can wear the costume under a blanket when he first comes on scene. Dance anklets can be used effectively in the second dance, as the bells will help to accentuate the rhythm.)

Loud "Hows!" and the beating of drums greet Tight Fist's performance. He then graciously invites the entire group into his house for the feast. A realistic finale can be accomplished by the group filing through the doorway into the house and, of course, dispersing quietly after stepping through the doorway.

In this dance-play, if the council fire chief decides to have it carried out entriely in pantomime, a seen or un-seen narrator can introduce and unfold the story as the dance progresses.

Through the voice of the narrator or the conversation of the dancers at the beginning of the play, or an introduction by the council fire chief, the reason for the impromptu potlatch dance being held should be made clear to the warriors-in-council before or immediately after the playlet begins. Advance knowledge of Tight Fist's miserliness and the fact that he is an unwilling, though apparently gracious, host adds to the humor of the situation.

Council fire chiefs have considerable scope in the choice of dances for this play. Should it be given as part of a dance fire, the performance can last for an hour or more, or occupy the entire dance program. Good dancers can perform solo numbers in addition to general dancing by a group or groups. An effective touch can be added by having a few extra dancers in the original group, and these extras can be disguised as animals and perform animal dances. Again, instead of Tight Fist doing a regular type of solo dance, he can perform a challenge dance, challenging anyone in the group of dancers to outdo him. He may chose to imitate a whale, bear, or salmon for this number, and his steps, postures, and antics throughout his dance make him a hard man to equal.

EAGLE HAT

The Indians of the Northwest Pacific Coast were masters in the art of dance circle surprises, and neither time nor trouble was ever spared in planning, rehearsing, and introducing unexpected effects which would please, startle, astonish, or puzzle the onlookers.

chapter 18

A WORD TO COUNCIL FIRE CHIEFS about staging the following plays may prove helpful. Each play can easily be adapted so that the scene can be laid and the story told and acted out in the council fire area of a Plains, Woodland, or any other Indian group.

ADAPTING PLAYS

In the first play, *The Bewitched Moccasins,* the story is about a young Kootenay brave, whose tribe, though neighbor to the Indians of the Northwest Coast, were akin to the Plains Indians in their mode of life. This brave can be made to belong to any tribe of Plains Indians. The first change suggested is that all the braves-in-council remove their shoes or moccasins, so that the feel of their bare feet will transform them into North-

west Coast Indians. Youthful imagination and the magic medicine of the fire will make this transformation easy. A second suggested change is that the brave chosen to play the role of the Nootka boy wear the simply made costume of the Northwest Coast, as illustrated in this book, and be able to kick a football accurately with his bare foot. A little practice will soon take him out of the tenderfoot class, especially as the ball is only an inflated bladder and not a football. As will be noted while reading the play, practically all the dialogue is carried out in sign language. The only other change which will add realism to the little play is for the two chiefs, or older braves, who take the parts of shamans to play their role in simple costumes without Plains head-dresses, while the council fire chief and the storyteller can also discard their coup-feather-bedecked war bonnets for this occasion. A Woodland habitat group can stage the play in the manner described above.

For the second play, *Raven Outwitted,* no change in costume or props is required. Raven—the trickster, the maker of magic—was known to practically all the Indian tribes of the Untied States. If any modern Indian groups know more of Manabozo, another trickster and maker of magic, he can take the leading role instead of Raven. The play can then go forward as set down, with one simple exception: The fish cooked by the boys need not be herring; they can be nameless, or they can be any other fish caught in the habitat of the Indians holding the council fire.

In the third story-play, *The Eagle Guide,* no change of any sort is required. Actually, the story is woven around an old Pueblo legend, but there is nothing in the tale to reveal the name of the tribe in difficulty. The only suggestion of the tale's origin exists in the name of the character called Sky Sign. However, the names of the young braves, who dare much in order that their people may be saved, can be changed at the will of the council fire chief staging the play.

council fire
indian plays

THE BEWITCHED MOCCASINS

A tale told by the tribal storyteller and acted out by shamans, a Kootenay brave and Nootka warriors. The action takes place in a council fire area, during council. The storyteller, standing beside the chair of the tribal chief, tells the tale while it is carried out in pantomime in the council fire area.

STORYTELLER

ACTION *(in pantomime)*

Hear, O warriors, the story of a young man of the Kootenay who lived far from the ocean. He thought that he was better than our young men because he had hunted the buffalo on the plains and wore better robes and moccasins, while our young men wore but dance aprons and went barefoot. One night he came to our council fire, as he had right, because he had married one of our young women who had wandered far from our tribe. Though we did not like to hear his boastful words, he was greeted as a brother by all of us.

Our chief asked the Kootenay to show our young men how he lived on the great plains, how he rode on a horse, and how he hunted the buffalo.

The Kootenay enters the council fire area, touches his buckskin shirt and leggings, arranges the feather in his hair, and pulls at his colorful moccasins. He then advances to the fire and raises his right hand high in salute to the tribal chief, who beckons him to come closer.

The Kootenay brave walks proudly around the council fire; then, as the Nootka do not understand his language, he imitates riding on horseback and hunting the buffalo; by signs, he shows that he lives in a tepee and wears moccasins.

As the Kootenay pointed to his moccasins, an old shaman entered the council fire area. In the sign language, he told the Kootenay boy that he would like to see if he could run fast and if he were quick and strong like the Nootka young men. Soon the shaman beckoned to a Nootka who went toward him, raised his hand in salute, then stood beside him.

As the Kootenay proudly points to his moccasins, an old Shaman enters the council fire area. He asks the boy by signs if he can run fast, wrestle and kick. Then he asks if the Kootenay will race a Nootka. The Kootney nods his head vigorously and the Shaman beckons a Nootka into the area.

We saw our Wise One look at the Kootenay moccasins and then at the barefoot Nootka. When we saw the Kootenay take off his moccasins and hand them to our shaman, we wondered why. We knew that the earth of the place of the council fire would feel soft to the feet of the Nootka. Always were his feet bare. He felt not the bite of hard, sharp rocks. We wondered, yes, but our shaman knew best.

While the shaman explains by signs and lines them up for the race, he suddenly appears to notice the gay moccasins of the Kootenay. He shakes his head and points to the bare feet of the Nootka. He signs to the Kootenay that he should take off the moccasins so that he will not have an advantage. The Kootenay hesitates for a moment or two, then takes off his moccasins and hands them to the shaman.

Treasury of Memory-Making Campfires

We saw two Shamans enter the place of the council fire. They were given the moccasins, and took them to another part of the place of the council fire. All our warriors were looking at the shamans, because they shook their rattles and danced. We could see that they were making medicine. The Kootenay could not see, because he was trying to understand our shaman, who in sign language told him about the race he was to run. Had our visitor but spoken the Chinook jargon, much sign talk would have not been needed.

At last the Kootenay understood. He took his place beside the Nootka, and our shaman told them to go. The race began, but we still watched the two shamans, because we saw that they made much magic over the moccasins. We thought that the moccasins would have to obey such powerful magic—and soon they did! They did strange things which we could not understand. Then both moccasins walked by themselves, following a shaman. Strange things were seen and done at our council fire that night. We saw bewitched moccasins that walked where they would. What would the Kootenay, who ran with much pain around the council fire, do when he found that magic now lived in in his bright moccasins?

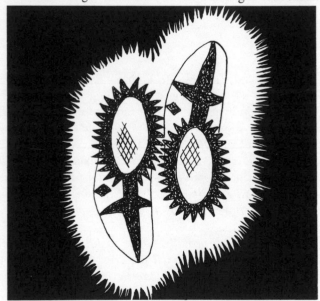

The race was now almost over.

Our boy was winning, perhaps because the Kootenay could not run well in his bare feet.

Yes, our boy was the winner!

Two other shamans now come into the area and the old shaman hands the moccasins to one of them. They take them toward the other end of the area and lay them on the ground. They call attention to themselves by shaking their rattles, and they begin to dance and make medicine around the moccasins. The Kootenay does not see what is taking place, as he is too busy trying to understand the signs of the old shaman, who at last makes the boy understand that the race will be three times around the council fire area. The Kootenay lifts his feet uneasily. He feels them. He appears to step on something that hurts one of them. He jumps and holds the foot in his hand.

The Kootney now understands. He is ready. The shaman calls "Go!" Though the boys race, the warriors-in-council watch the two shamans too, because they dance and perform antics around the moccasins. One slips them onto his hands and stoops and puts them on the ground as though he were walking in them. He pretends to try to follow the other shaman across the area, but the moccasins appear to go in any direction except the one which the shaman wearing them on his hands desires. Then he takes them off, and the two shamans shake with silent laughter while they again make strange passes and do strange things with the Kootenay moccasins. At last, the moccasins follow one shaman who walks backward across the area, while the other shaman begs them by signs to come back and follow him instead. Now the warriors-in-council know that the moccasins are bewitched. They wonder what will happen next. One shaman replaces the moccasins while the race is being run. They appear to wriggle in his hand as he carries them. When he lays them down he signals dramatically to them to lie still.

The two runners race rather slowly around the council fire area. The Kootenay stumbles and limps a little at times and makes poor time until near the end when he tries hard to catch up to the Nootka. The Nootka wins by a fair lead.
(A little practice, or timing, or both is required to give the shamans time to perform their magic during the start of the race and before it finishes. Some stalling in getting the race under way will help, and the old shaman can keep the Kootenay occupied at the end of the race, if necessary, while the moccasins are being returned.)

The Kootenay went to pick up his moccasins, but our shaman stopped him. A Nootka came into the council place. He carried a blown-up bladder which we use to kick in some of our games. I wondered why.

Then I knew! The shaman wanted to see whether the Kootenay or a Nootka could kick it further. Our boys kick the bladder well. I wondered if the Kootenay had learned how to kick. Our Nootka kicked first and kicked well. Then the Kootenay was going to kick, but first he wanted to put on his moccasins. I feared that they would prove of little help to him. The shaman signed "Wait," so the Kootenay kicked barefooted. The ball flew far, but not so far as our Nootka sent it.

The Kootenay was going to try with his moccasins on. Poor youth! First the Nootka kicked, and the ball traveled far. It was thrown back, and the Kootenay tried. He ran at the bladder, kicked—and missed it!

He tried again and again but could not hit the bladder. He looked as though he were bewitched. Perhaps some things were!

He tried again, but he seemed to have no power over his legs. They did what they wanted him to do—not what he wanted them to do. But my words are as twisted as the Kootenay legs! He fell to the ground. He looked puzzled and angry.

The shaman threw the bladder out of the place of the council fire. Our tribal chief beckoned to the Kootenay. He tried to walk to him, but his feet seemed to want to follow another trail.

He tried again, but the poor brave and his moccasins could not follow the same trail!

The Kootenay stood still, then tried to reach our chief by walking backward—but now his moccasins carried him forward!

He took off his fine moccasins. He threw them away! He smiled! He laughed—at himself! Someday he will be a great chief! He pointed to his naked feet, then walked straight to our chief, who greeted him as though he were a victorious young chief returned from battle.

The Kootenay reaches for his moccasins, but the shaman signs for him to wait. The shaman beckons to a Nootka seated in the front row of the warriors-in-council. He goes into the council fire area, carrying a blown-up volleyball or other bladder, which looks somewhat like the inflated intestine of a sea mammal. Some dried corn kernels or small pebbles will give it weight.

The shaman explains, by signs, that he wishes to see whether the Kootenay or Nootka can kick the bladder farther. The Nootka kicks it first, and it flies out of the council area. The Kootenay holds a sore foot and indicates that he wishes to put on his moccasins. The shaman tells the Kootenay by signs that he should try once with his bare foot. He tries, and the bladder nearly goes out of the council fire area.

The Kootenay indicates that he can do much better with his moccasins on. The shaman hands them to him, and he pulls them on. The Nootka boy kicks again; the bladder flies out of the area. It is thrown back, and the Kootenay prepares to kick. He takes a short run and kicks with all his might. Much to his surprise, he misses the bladder entirely and nearly falls down. He tries again, with the same result. He apparently loses patience and tries to kick the bladder several times. Each time, he fails to connect with it. His legs seem to get tied in a knot after each kick. Finally, he misses again and sits down hard. He scratches his head and feels his moccasins.

The shaman picks up the bladder and throws it out of the council fire area. The Kootenay shakes his head in great puzzlement. The tribal chief stands up and beckons to him. The Kootenay appears to try to walk toward the chief, but to everyone's amazement and amusement, his moccasins seem to carry him in the opposite direction. He tries again, and again his bewitched moccasins carry him off in the wrong direction.

The Kootenay stands still for a moment or two then tries to walk backward toward the chief's chair. This time his moccasins carry him forward, to the very edge of the council fire area. He stoops, pulls off his moccasins and throws them out of the council fire area. He smiles broadly, laughs loudly and heartily, points to his bare feet, then walks straight over to the tribal chief, who greets him with a broad smile and a very friendly salute. He signs to him to sit beside him.

*   *   *

SOLUTION FOR THE BEWITCHED MOCCASINS. The effect of the moccasins following the shaman across the council fire area is easily produced by the shaman who is followed by them. One way is to push a sharpened fishhook, from which the barb has been snipped, through the toe of each moccasin. A strong black thread or length

of thin black fishline, about 40 inches long, is fastened to each fishhook. The other end of each fishline is attached to a small black metal ring fastened to each legging or trouser leg of the shaman, about halfway between the knee and ankle. At this height the moccasins will "follow" him easily, with the soles on the ground, as he backs away from them slowly across the council fire area.

With a little practice the shaman will even be able to turn around and walk away from the other shaman and then turn and return to the other shaman with the moccasins following smoothly, right side up, behind him. The walking backward suggestion in the script is to permit an amateur shaman to assure himself that the moccasins are performing satisfactorily. It is an easy thing for the shaman to withdraw the fishhooks when he picks up the moccasins, and tuck the lengths of thread through his belt or elsewhere, so that they will not hang down and get in his way.

The clowning between the two shamans in this scene can be very funny, and they should not be too far away from the light of the council fire, in order to make the "magic" most effective. The moccasins can be made to appear to wriggle and jump out of the shamans' hands without much effort on the part of the medicine men.

It cannot be too strongly stressed that much of the effectiveness of the magic of modern shamans is lost because of *too little*, rather than too much, illumination. This applies strongly to such a scene as *The Bewitched Moccasins*. The black thread, even fishline, is invisible a foot or two away from the council fire, so keeping some distance away from the fire is not needed in order to cover up how the magic is worked.

Once the bewitched moccasins are on the Kootenay's feet, it is up to him to pantomime the fact that they are very much bewitched.

RAVEN OUTWITTED

A tribal storyteller relates this folk play as it is lived again—this time in the council fire area—by a group of six or eight Indian boys of various sizes and Raven, the transformer, magician, and trickster played by a chief. The simple props required for this play, and how they are used, are described at the end of the play. As the storyteller, standing beside the chair of the tribal chief, unfolds the tale, it is acted out in pantomime.

The council fire area is empty, and the fire burns rather dimly when the tribal chief rises to speak. He tells the warriors-in-council that their storyteller is coming to tell them a tale of Raven—"Raven, the Maker of Magic! Raven, the Wise One! Raven, the Foolish One! Raven, the trickster! Listen well, O warriors, as the tale is told," concludes the tribal chief, as the storyteller enters the council fire area, to the accompaniment of a slowly beaten, hidden drum. He circles the council fire and then approaches and stands beside the chair of the tribal chief.

STORYTELLER	ACTION *(in pantomime)*
Hear, O warriors, a tale of Raven, Maker of Magic, who has helped and tricked his children since the world was young. Raven was full of tricks, and clever, but at times men were more clever than he. Yes, sometimes Raven was too clever for his own good. It was at these times that even children counted coup, as you shall see.	
One day, a band of Indian boys came into a clearing in the forest. They started to light a fire. Some of them gathered wood and built the fire; then older boys struck fire from stones, so that the fire could be lit. Soon their little fire burned bright, and they held herring, which they had brought from the fish traps, close to the fire on pieces of bark. The herring did not cook well in that way.	*As the storyteller speaks, six or eight boys, wearing Indian costumes, file into the council fire area, lay down baskets which they carry and a bright blanket or two. They proceed to light a little fire, after gathering some wood for it, toward one end of the council fire area. The method of lighting the fire is told at the end of the play. When the fire has been lit, supposedly by friction, the boys take four or five herring out of the baskets and hold them out awkwardly, on flat pieces of wood or bark, close to the fire, as though trying to cook the fish.*
The feast would have been a poor one had not Raven, who looked like an Indian, walked through the forest at that time. He saw the boys. Raven smelt the half-cooked herring. He rubbed his stomach and smacked his lips at the thought of a feast. Raven was always hungry, always ready to eat.	*Just then, Raven enters the council fire from the end opposite where the boys are squatting around the fire. He carries a rolled-up bundle under his arm. He stops, sniffs the air, looks toward the fire, rubs his stomach, and smacks his lips hungrily.*

Raven moved very quietly over to the fire and stood beside the boys before they heard him. One of the boys noticed Raven and jumped up in fright. So did the other boys. Raven raised his hand in a sign of friendship and told them not to be afraid. He said that he had come to help them. He took a few of the boys and went to look for sticks. They found some, and Raven, with his sharp stone knife, quickly pointed the sticks at both ends. He showed them how to push one end of the stick into the fish and the other end into the ground, so that the fish were just out of the fire and cooked well without burning.

The boys thanked Raven and asked him to eat with them. Raven said, "No." He had become so very hungry that he had decided to eat *all* the herring—not share them. Yes, he had made up his mind to trick the boys. He walked away from the fire until he came to some bushes. Then he disappeared. He had gone behind some bushes where the boys could not see him. Then he unrolled his bundle. It was not a blanket that Raven carried. No, it was a bearskin which a brown bear had worn only one sleep ago! He quickly pulled the skin over his shoulders, wrapped it around his body, and used his magic power so that his face looked like a bear. Then he left his hiding place and shuffled like a bear on its hind legs toward the campfire, growling savagely! As he got close to the fire, the boys saw and heard him and ran fast into the forest to hide, leaving the fish behind them. Raven took all the fish and ate them—yes, every one of them. He then shuffled off to his hiding place and waited.

After a while, two or three of the bigger boys returned to the fire. They called to the others, still hidden in the forest, that the bear had gone. All the boys were starting to gather up the baskets and things which they had left behind, so that they might run back to their village, when Raven, dressed as an Indian, came walking toward them. When Raven reached the fire, the boys told him of their adventure with the big brown bear and said that they were going back to their village in case the beast returned.

Raven laughed and told them, "It is too bright a day to go back to your village. Stay and I will show you what to do if the bear returns. Let two of the big boys go back to the village for more herring—and maybe some salmon. . . ." Here the mouth of Raven watered so much that he had to stop speaking for a while. "When the boys come back with the fish, you will have a great feast. My, what a feast you will have! With a glad heart would I stay to enjoy the feast with you, but I must be off, far into the forest. If the bear does return, have some sticks and

Raven moves very cautiously and quietly around the council fire area, until he stands just behind the boys, who sit in a half-circle formation with their backs turned toward him. Suddenly, one of the bigger boys sees Raven. He jumps quickly to his feet; the other boys do the same. Raven raises a hand above his head and smiles broadly. He speaks in pantomime to the boys, looks at their attempts to cook the herring, and solemnly shakes his head. He signs to some of the boys to follow him. He leads them to where the sharpened sticks have been cached and helps to carry them back to the fire. There, he appears to point all of the sticks and shows the boys how to push one end of the stick into the herring and the other end into the ground in front of the fire, so that the fish appears to cook just out of reach of the flames.

The boys act pleased with the way their fish are cooking and, by signs, invite Raven to feast with them. Raven shakes his head and points into the forest. He walks away from the fire and disappears into the shelter. Here he unrolls his bundle, which is the blanket-bearskin, and ties it on securely over his shoulders. When the blanket is arranged, he takes up the bear-head mask and puts it on, bending over to hide it as much as possible, so that it will not be noticed by the warriors-in-council until it is placed in position.

He now shuffles rapidly toward the boys around the fire. (As this play is in pantomime, Raven disguised as a bear should not growl, but it is very effective if he does so, loudly and fiercely, at this point.) When he reaches the fire, all the boys have fled into the forest, so he pretends to eat all the fish, with much smacking of lips and rubbing of the stomach. He then waddles off to his hiding place and takes off his mask and blanket.

Raven looks cautiously around the side of his shelter until he sees the bigger boys go back to the fire, then sign to the other boys to return.

Then Raven walks toward them and, by signs, asks them why they are leaving. The boys gather round Raven and, by graphic signs, tell of their adventure with the bear. Raven appears to reassure them and they gradually lay down the baskets and blankets.

By signs, Raven advises the boys to stay at the fire and send two of the bigger boys back to the village for more fish. He shows them what they should do if the bear comes back, by pretending to beat a bear with a stick. He points to the forest, where the boys can find clubs and sticks.

clubs ready. Be not afraid of him. Black and brown bears are not fierce and brave like grizzly bears. Take clubs and drive him away."

Then Raven taught the boys to sing a song that would make them brave when they met bears. The words of the song were, "Who's afraid of the big brown bear, not we Indian boys." They walked in a circle as they sang the song, and felt very brave. "We fear no longer," they told Raven; "if the bear comes back, we shall chase him away."

Raven smiled and walked back to his hiding place while two of the boys went off to the village. Those left at the campfire went to look for thick sticks to use as clubs and soon came back with some. They waved them over their heads and pretended to attack a bear. "Now we are ready for the big brown bear," they sang bravely. Then they sat around the fire to wait for the return of the boys who went for the fish.

Soon the two boys returned with more fish in a basket, and once more fish—yes, even salmon—cooked in front of the bright fire. THEN THE BEAR CAME BACK! As soon as it shuffled on its hind legs close to the fire, the boys attacked it fiercely with sticks and clubs. The bear tried hard to escape, but the boys made a circle around it and beat it again and again. The bear dropped on its four legs and tried to push its way between the boys in the circle, but it could not get through.

Then something strange happened! It looked like magic, but it was not. The bear stood up, threw off its skin, and there stood Raven. He tried to rub his head and body all over at the same time, while he told the boys that he had only pretended to be a bear to see how brave they were. That, he had seen! Now he would go away quietly and leave the brave boys to enjoy their feast.

"No, no!" the boys shouted. "You have taught us how to be brave, and so you must stay and feast with us. We have salmon, and you shall be our guest of honor. Stay! Stay!"

And so Raven sat down to another feast—after all, he *was* very fond of children!

Raven lines the boys up in Indian file and teaches them a bear-scaring song as they march around in a circle. (Once again the usage of pantomime may be broken effectively, at this point, by having the boys sing "Who's afraid of the big brown bear, not we Indian boys.")

Raven stalks off into the forest, disappearing into his hiding place. Two boys carrying a basket leave for the village, while the remaining boys look about until they find the clubs and sticks which have been hidden around the edge of the council fire area. They return with the sticks and clubs, pretend to attack a bear. "Now we are ready for the big brown bear," they sing before squatting around the fire to await the two boys who went for more fish.

Very soon the two boys return, fish are once again roasting on the pointed sticks in front of the fire, which is kept burning brightly all the time. The boys sit happily around the fire—then they see the bear shuffling upright toward them. They spring to their feet, and when the bear is close enough, they beat him soundly with their sticks and clubs. The bear, still shuffling upright, tries to escape; but the boys circle it and continue to beat it. The bear drops onto all fours and tries to force its way out of the ring of attackers. It cannot do so, and the boys continue to beat it.

Suddenly the bear jumps upright and throws off the mask and blanket. The boys leap back in astonishment. Then Raven tries to explain, in pantomime, that his trick was performed in the spirit of fun, though the way he rubs his head, shoulders, and body shows that it did not turn out quite as funnily as he had hoped it would. He signs that he must go far into the forest and leave them to enjoy their feast.

The boys shake their heads and show Raven, in sign language, that they are grateful that he taught them to sing the bear song which had taught them to be brave. They pull him toward the fire and he joins their feast.

❊ ❊ ❊

PROPS REQUIRED
Some bushes or a small shelter
A bear-head mask and "bearskin"
Eight thin straight branches, pointed at each end
Ten or twelve "fish"
Two baskets
Two bright blankets
A few pieces of thin wood, about 14 inches by 6 inches
Some rough, very dry grass and thin tinder sticks

Small, dry branches
Two large smooth stones
Some matches, large, friction sort, *not* safety matches
Six or eight heavy-looking clubs and sticks

HOW TO MAKE AND USE PROPS
Bushes are stood up at one end of the council fire area. Raven hides behind them, out of sight of the other

players, when he changes into his bear mask and skin. When a shelter is used instead of bushes, it can be made of heavy green cloth or rough sacking. The bear-head mask is hidden in the bushes or shelter.

Bear-head mask can be made from cardboard, *papier maché,* or a big brown paper bag. Except for the fact that it does not give a chance to the arts and crafts people, a bear mask of the Halloween sort, which can be bought for around fifty cents, is the easiest solution.

"Bearskin" is made by using either a large piece of brown cloth or a brown double blanket. A few short lengths of string or tape should be sewn on, so that it may be tied on securely. This bearskin is rolled and carried under Raven's arm on his first entrance.

Thin straight branches, pointed at each end are hidden somewhere at edge of the council fire area where they can easily be found when needed.

"Fish." Five or six of the fish are made to represent herring, about 8 inches long, and the other five or six fish are salmon, about 15 inches long. They can be cut from thick cardboard and painted a silvery color. A small hole is punched through the middle of each fish, through which the point of the sharpened branch may be pushed.

Baskets. The fish are carried on scene in these.

Bright blankets are suggested for their decorative value.

Rough, dry grass and thin tinder sticks should be very dry, so that they will flare up at once.

Small, dry branches should be about 1 inch thick and 12 inches long. The boys can arrange them in a log cabin type of fire.

Stones. The boys appear to light the fire by striking the two stones together.

Matches. These are the large friction kind. Actually, a match is struck on one of the stones in such a way that the onlookers cannot see it. A bunch of dry grass is lit by the match, and the fire set alight.

Thin wood. These are flat strips about 14 inches by 6 inches. The boys pretend to cook the herring on these pieces of wood. About 6 strips are required.

Clubs and sticks are made from dark-colored, heavy paper, rolled up to look like real clubs and sticks, or they can be made of rolled cardboard. These "weapons" should be strong but not too heavy, so that Raven will not be hurt. They are hidden away at the edge of the council fire area, where they can be found easily and quickly.

THE EAGLE GUIDE

As this tale of magic from a time long past is told by the storyteller of the tribe, it is acted out by two young Salish warriors of long ago. The storyteller, standing beside the chair of the tribal chief, tells the tale until it unfolds in pantomime.

STORYTELLER.   The sun has gone, O warriors, and the black blanket of night covers the forest. I can now tell you a story of great magic of long ago. It is a tale of mystery and powerful medicine, of an eagle guide and two young warriors who sought a new land, where their tribe could dwell safely in peace and escape the dangers and hunger of their old village. When night made the land dark, a young warrior called Sky Sign had a powerful medicine dream. He dreamed that in the dark he heard the shrill cry of an eagle. He knew that eagles did not scream in the night. Magic was near!

In his dream, a great eagle appeared in the sky above him. It told him that it knew of the sorrows of his tribe. The bird told the young man that if he would follow its slow flight, it would lead him to a new land where his tribe would be safe from its enemies and live with glad hearts in peace. Then Sky Sign—for that was the name of the young warrior who dreamed—awoke. He was troubled and glad. Troubled, because he feared that it was maybe only a dream, and glad that if it were not a dream he had been chosen to help his tribe. He left his blankets and ran to tell his friend Little Bear of his dream. Little Bear slept, but Sky Sign shook him until he was awake and told him of his dream. Little Bear sprang to his feet. "Let us follow your eagle guide," he cried. Together they got weapons, food, and new moccasins. Together they stood staring up into the starlit sky. No eagle could they see. (*It should be noted at this point that though the eagle of this tale leads the young Indians northward, the direction may have to be changed when the story is being enacted at a modern council fire.*)

"Maybe it was only a dream," Sky Sign said sadly. Their hearts were heavy, and their eyes no longer looked up into the sky.

Then they heard the shrill *Kre-e-e-e-e* of an eagle. Above them appeared the dark form of a great bird. It was motionless. They could clearly see its white head and tail by the dim light of the stars. As they watched, its great wings beat slowly, and it flew toward the star-that-does-not-move. The two young men ran toward the north, in the direction taken by the eagle. The big bird seemed to fly so that it was not lost to their eyes. Always their keen eyes could see the white of the tail above them. When the sky began to turn the color of roses, the eagle disappeared.

The two tired warriors fell to the ground and slept until the sun rode high in the sky. When they awoke, their eyes searched the sky for their eagle guide, but the bird was not there. The young men snared two rabbits, ate, and hid in the forest for fear of war parties from other tribes, until the sun was gone.

Darkness came, and then they heard the cry of an eagle. Their eagle guide was above them. Again it flew toward the north. It traveled far and fast, but they followed, though their legs were tired and their breath cried in their throats. When the first light came, the eagle rose high in the sky until they could see it no more.

The two young warriors were sore of foot and tired. They fell to the ground and slept. They did not move until the sun had gone to make place for the new moon.

Their eyes searched the sky for their guide, but they saw it not. Long they watched and waited, but the great bird did not come. "Maybe our eagle guide has gone to the spirit world and will come no more," said Little Bear.

"All is lost, and we cannot help our people if the eagle comes not," Sky Sign answered.

"Let us go on toward the star that lights the sky in the north," said Sky Sign. "The eagle points always toward that star. It may be there, behind those mountains, that the new land awaits our people."

"I cannot go on," said Little Bear. "My feet and body are tired and will not do what I say."

"You must go forward," cried Sky Sign, "or our people will soon take the long trail to the shadow land, and we too shall walk without shadows. "Come!" commanded Sky Sign.

"No! You are stronger and older. Go on to the north alone while I lie here and await my call to the land of shadows."

After much talk, Sky Sign got his young friend onto his feet, and once again they went slowly northward with dragging steps. Their hearts were on the ground, because with no eagle guide they had no hope. Then—!

STORYTELLER

(Dramatically, the storyteller stops and gazes southward into the distance. He springs backward in feigned astonishment.)

Maybe my eyes have been given strange magic tonight, or the keen sight of the eagle guide has been granted me for but a little time, that I may better tell the story of the great magic that helped the young warriors as they tried to save their tribe. I seem to see those who followed the eagle guide. Yes! they are coming toward our council fire! Watch well, O warriors-in-council, for those who come toward us seem neither to see our fire nor hear my voice. Magic is in the air. So shall I speak no more, for they can show, far better than I can tell, the strange things that came to pass on that last night of their wanderings. This only will I tell—their mysterious guide did not fail them!

(SOUNDS FROM THE FOREST, AND ACTION IN PANTOMIME)

In the forest, from the direction of the south, the noises of breaking sticks and dragging feet are heard.

These noises are heard first in the distance, then closer and closer toward the council fire area. The sound stops for a moment or two and then begins again. Nobody is visible in the direction from which the noises come.

Slowly, two young Indians approach the council fire area. They come from the south. One is taller and appears less tired than his companion. They both walk on weary feet and stop and speak to each other by signs at the entrance to the council fire area. Then the shorter warrior drops heavily to the ground, just inside the council fire area. His companion tries to pull him to his feet, but the smaller warrior struggles a little, half rises, and then falls to the ground again.

The taller warrior who is standing searches the sky. Apparently he sees nothing. He holds up his arms in a gesture of prayer, then throws himself on the ground a few feet away from his companion. Both lie still for a short time. Sky Sign rises slowly to his feet. His eyes search the sky in all directions. Suddenly, he gazes fixedly into the sky. He stretches up his arms in an atttiude of prayer and with a shout points dramatically upward. As he watches, an egale feather falls downward, then stops,

and floats and sways in the air. It is high overhead, and its quill end points northward. It sways and moves quite plainly as Sky Sign watches, then moves slowly and steadily for a distance of about two short paces, toward the north. Sky Sign falls on his knees beside Little Bear and shakes him violently. He then drags him to his feet, pointing to the feather with one hand while he pulls with the other. Little Bear sways on his legs shakily for a moment, looking in the opposite direction from where the feather hovers, then drops to the ground again with a gesture of despair. Again, Sky Sign pulls him to his feet and turns him so that he can see the eagle feather. Little Bear almost falls backward in his amazement, then he stretches out his arms in prayer.

Together, he and Sky Sign slowly follow beneath the eagle feather as it glides at turtle's pace across the council fire area and disappears in the distance, followed by the two Indians who are soon swallowed-up by the darkness.

The forest is silent again.

(The storyteller gazes into the forest in the direction in which the two young Indians have disappeared.)

Now my story has been told nearly to its end. The mysterious eagle feather guide, which led when the eagle came no more, guided them to the land of promise. Before the light of the new moon shone over the forest, Sky Sign and Little Bear led their people to their new village.

I have spoken!

     ✻   ✻   ✻

Solution for the Eagle Guide. Despite the spectacular appearance of the eagle feather, as described in the story-play, and the almost thoughtful leadership it displays as it waits for and suits its pace to the two tired Indian boys who follow it, it is surprisingly simple to carry out the illusion.

A long white feather measuring about 14 inches from the tip to the end of the quill and with a width of about 3½ inches at its widest part, is the first requirement. The extreme tip of the feather should be colored black and a number of small lead pellets put inside a slit made in the end of the quill. An easier way of weighting the end of the quill is to wrap two or three strips of lead, such as is used for sinkers while fishing, around the quill point. The point is then wound around with a piece of white adhesive tape, so that the lead is held securely in place and all of the feather is white at the quill end. Cut a length of strong black thread 20 inches long and make a simple knot 9½ inches from one end. Tie this end securely onto the quill part of the feather, 2 inches from the very point. A clove hitch covered by a reef knot makes a good fastening. Now tie the other end of the thread around the backbone of the feather 1½ inches from the very tip. It is important that *both* of these knots finish *on top* of the backbone of the feather, the top side being the one that is uppermost when the feather is suspended by the knot on the thread.

Tie a black metal ring about ½ inch in over-all diameter to one end of a 12-inch length of strong black thread. The other end should be tightly fastened to and directly beside the knot on the thread which is tied to the feather.

A sheath has to be made for the feather. It is easily made from a piece of strong, stiff black paper or brown paper colored black. The over-all measurements of this envelope-like sheath should be 16 inches by 5 inches, with a 1-inch flap left all the way along one side for attaching the sheath to the overhead line. The side with the flap is the top of the sheath.

Both ends of the sheath are left open, and a small hole is punched through the top at one end, ½ inch from the top and the end. This hole also goes through the flap. A short length of strong black thread or fishline is passed through this hole in the sheath-envelope.

All that is now required to complete the gear is an overhead line made of a length of black nylon fishline about 100 feet long. It will be seen that no arbitrary length for the overhead or operator's line can be set, since the distance will vary for each council fire area. Since there is little strain on the overhead line, except the initial strain of stringing it in position *without sagging* between two suitable trees, a spool of strong black button thread can sometimes be used, provided it does not have to be strung too great a distance. One end of the overhead line is tied high and securely to a tree or branch somewhere

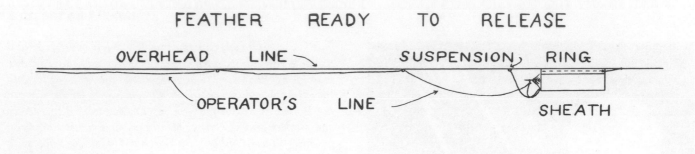

FEATHER READY TO RELEASE

OVERHEAD LINE — SUSPENSION RING

OPERATOR'S LINE

SHEATH

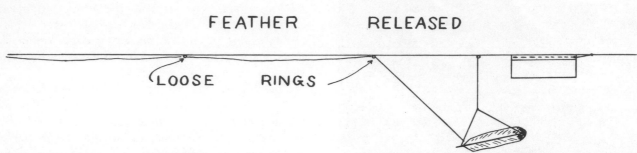

FEATHER RELEASED

LOOSE RINGS

outside the entrance to the council fire area at the end from which the Indian boys enter and the feather "magically" appears. The line should be tied as high as possible —at least 20 feet or, if possible, 25 feet. Its height will have to be decided by the maximum height a chief can safely reach from the top of a stout, high stepladder. Stepladder-reach is advisable, because adjustments may have to be made from the same perch. *Before* the first end, at the entrance to the council fire area, is made fast, it is *first* threaded through six to ten black, metal rings ½ or ⅜ inch in diameter, then through the ring attached to the line from which the feather is suspended. The line is then unwound gradually from the spool and carried directly across the council fire area, passing 6 feet or so on either side of the council fire to the point where the Indian boys will follow the feather out of the council fire area and out of the range of vision of the warriors-in-council.

Though the eagle feather trail of the young warrors in the story led *north*, the direction taken by the modern council fire Indians will have to be decided by the compass point in which the entrance to the council fire area lies, and the easiest exit in the most direct line from there into actual cover or the cover of darkness. At that point, the other end of the overhead line is made fast to a tree at a point 3 or 4 feet higher than at the other end. An end ring is tied securely onto the overhead line about 2 feet from where the line is fastened to the tree. A very good way to make the line quite taut, with the least wear and tear, is to screw a fairly large, strong screw eye into the tree at the required height. Now pass the end of the overhead line down through the screw eye and pull on the line until it is taut. The end of the line may then be wound several times tightly around a nail driven 3 feet below the screw eye into the tree, and tied securely. Now the envelope-sheath is attached to the overhead line just inside the council fire area at the point where the feather

is to appear. It must be remembered that the place chosen should be in full view of all the warriors-in-council, though about one-fourth of them will have to turn their heads to see the entry of the Indian boys. Another important factor in choosing the place for the appearance of the feather is to try to select a point where the feather will have the *maximum* distance to travel from its appearance to its disappearance. The sheath for the feather may be pinned, sewn, or stapled to the overhead line, the fastenings passing through both the flap, which is placed over the line, and the other side of the sheath. The piece of fishline on the sheath is now securely fastened to the overhead line to hold the sheath in place when the feather is jerked out by the operator.

The operator's line, a black nylon fishline or one of heavy black linen or strong cotton buttonhole or carpet thread, should be 20 feet longer than the overhead line. The end of the operator's line is now passed through the six to ten loose rings on the overhead line and *then* tied to the thread 1 inch above the quill point of the feather. The sketches show how simple it is to set up and use the entire, easily made equipment required to carry out this spectacular illusion. All that now remains to be done is to carefully push the feather, *tip first,* into the sheath so that just the extreme point of the quill end and the connecting threads stick out of the end of the sheath which is nearer the council fire. The operator's spool of line is now slowly unrolled to the other side of and beyond the council fire, the loose rings on the overhead line through which the operator's line passes being spread out 6 or 8 feet apart in order to hold the operator's line well above the council fire area. These loose rings are distributed along the overhead line at the desired distance apart after the sheath has been fastened in place and the feather is pushed carefully inside it, ready for the pull on the operator's line. In the case where an unusually long stretch of overhead line is required, a number of additional loose rings may be added. These rings are designated as loose rings because they are not fastened in any way to the overhead line; when the operator, from his place of concealment, pulls the feather from its sheath, the rings on the overhead line are collected—after they have served their purpose—by the master ring from which the feather is suspended.

The operator should carefully note that only a gentle pull or slight jerk on the end of his line is required to make the feather slip from the sheath and fall into the position in which it will travel as he pulls it very slowly toward him, pausing from time to time to get the maximum effect from the illusion of the guiding feather. Too hard a jerk on his line will cause the feather to leap out of the sheath and travel immediately several feet further than is desired along the line. The feather's travel should begin from just a short distance below the sheath.

It is most important that the operator see what is taking place in the council fire area from his place of concealment, if at all possible. He can operate best standing upright behind a tree. However, if unable to see the feather and players from the time of their entry into the council fire area, he should be warned by a prearranged whoop or other signal of the exact moment when he must pull the feather from its sheath. From then on he should require no guidance, since he has only to pull in his line very slowly, stopping from time to time for effect. Slight, short tugs on the line are very effective from time to time. They make the feather quiver and seem alive, but some advance practice in this is advised prior to the actual exhibition. Such practices can be carried out in daylight when there is nobody around. The operator must bear in mind that the most effective part of the entire illusion takes place as the feather drops mysteriously from the sky and the two Indian boys follow it slowly across the council fire area, in full view of the warriors-in-council.

The fall of the feather is a striking part of the performance, and the older Indian boy must not fail to draw the attention of the warriors-in-council to it. He does so by giving a surprised shout and pointing dramatically up into the sky just above where the feather will make its dramatic appearance. After he has pointed and gazed for a moment or so, in order that the warriors-in-council will be looking at the right spot, the feather suddenly and mysteriously appears.

THE GODS FORGIVE
A HOPI KACHINA PLAY-PAGEANT

By having leaders rehearse a few children for the leading roles and the others for the remaining parts, one can stage this play so successfully that there is little need for a script. The impromptu play has always worked out well, and the scope given the leaders and players has been very cleverly used by them.

In this one-act play, such properties as colorful blankets, pottery, and baskets, when available, can be used to good advantage. They lend atmosphere and add beauty. The play can be performed in forty-five minutes, or it can run for an hour and a half. This is decided by the time at the group's disposal and their imagination and ability to the leaders who stage it.

The play opens in the council ring, with all the players on the scene. Some are weaving, some are making pottery, some are busy with basket-making, while others are tanning skins. Some boys are playing and wrestling; other little groups just talk. All gradually leave the council ring except the heroine, little Blue Sky, and her friend White Cloud.

The players wear the simple Hopi costume of a sort of kilt and tight-fitting short-sleeved shirt. It may be dec-

orated with crayon or pieces of colored cloth, feathers, and a colorful belt. The popular Pueblo colors for costumes and masks are red, yellow, black, white, orange, and green. Sneakers colored with crayon, or moccasins, decorated with colored cloth, may be worn. The drawings show improvised Hopi costumes made for this play. The players do not wear masks, since only the Kachina gods wore masks at the time of our story. The masks for the three Kachinas are easily made from cylinders made of rather heavy cardboard, the ends being fastened together at the back so that each mask fits easily over the head of the wearer. Holes are cut for the mouth, eyes, and nose. Ears, noses, and decorations are stapled or glued to the cylinders. The drawings show two masks of this type.

Any number of boys and girls from twenty to fifty, may take part in the play. The play is evolved from the old Hopi legends. Though the role of little Blue Sky may have no Hopi foundation, it could easily have one. What better way is there of accounting for the fact that since the time of this play only Hopi men are permitted by tribal law to make replicas of the colorful Kachinas?

SCENE 1

The place is the usual council ring with the fire in the center, when the play is staged in camp. In a hall or playground, a circle about 24 feet in diameter is formed by placing chairs or benches in a circle. An imitation council fire, for the night scene, can easily be made in the center of the circle by using a large electric lamp and flameproof fire-colored paper.

It is late afternoon when the scene opens, and little Blue Sky the Hopi girl is talking to her little girl friend White Cloud. They discuss with awe the fact that Sun Path, their chief, has announced that three of their Kachina gods will attend the council fire ceremony that night. The players relate that several of the Kachinas come from the West each year to give counsel to their people and instruct them in agriculture, building, hunting, pottery-making, and other arts. This is the first time that the little Hopi girls have had permission to attend such a ceremony. The two girls leave to prepare for the big event.

SCENE 2

It is now night, and the Hopi file in solemnly and sit down around the council fire. They leave a circle 20 feet in diameter free between the front row and the fire. Sun Path, their chief, sits a little apart from the others, with two or three lesser chiefs beside him. Sun Path tells the eager people that their gods will soon be with them and asks that they be received with all honor. He warns the younger people that although the Kachinas who will soon appear may look strange and act awkwardly, they are very

wise and most powerful. Just as Sun Path finishes his speech, a loud roll like thunder is heard off stage.

Now three strange figures stalk into the council ring. They are clad in the full regalia of Hopi Kachina gods. Their costumes are similar to those of the other players, only more colorful and more elaborately decorated. All three gods wear grotesque masks. (The four types of Hopi Kachina masks shown on these pages may serve as models. Actually, there are more than 240 different masks.) One or all of the Kachinas make short speeches, telling the people to be very attentive during the few days of their stay and learn well the lessons which the Kachinas have come so far to teach them. The speeches ended, the Kachinas stalk awkwardly about the council ring. One walks in a knock-kneed fashion, one walks bowlegged, while the third falls down occasionally. They then stalk off-stage out of sight, followed by the Chiefs.

The Kachinas are hardly out of sight when half a dozen of the young men run into the ring and give exaggerated imitations of the clumsy movements of the gods. The younger people are laughing at these really funny antics, when suddenly there is a terrific roll of thunder off stage, and the infuriated gods bounce back into the ring. The young men who imitated them flee in terror. The Kachinas shout in their anger that they are leaving the mocking, thankless people at once and forever. They prophesy bad crops, bad hunting, and general misery until the people are all truly repentant. (This is related in Hopi legends.) The Kachinas then stalk out and disappear. Chief Sun Path enters and advances to the middle of the council ring. He sternly reproves the people for their lack of courtesy and warns them that their future is black because of it. All then slowly leave the council ring.

SCENE 3

(Two years later.) Again the council ring is the scene of action. It is daylight. Little Blue Sky, White Cloud, and some of their friends are in the council ring. They speak of the terrible times they have been through since their gods left them. They relate that many of their people have died of starvation. The corn will not grow, and the Hopi are always hungry. Soon all leave the council ring. Blue Sky returns alone, carrying a bundle wrapped in a brightly colored blanket. She opens the bundle, spreads the blanket on the ground, and very carefully places three small model Kachina dolls on it. These little figures, about two feet high, should be replicas of the three gods who were insulted by her tribe. Blue Sky holds them up, one by one, and talks to them while she arranges their costumes. She tells the little figures how sorry all her people are for having been so very rude. She says that she has just finished making the Kachina models so that they may be set in the place of honor in the village. She asks the gods to forgive her people and come to them once more.

Just as she finishes her lines, a loud triple roll of thunder comes from off stage. Blue Sky falls forward on the ground with her face buried in her hands. The three Kachinas rush into the council ring and look at Blue Sky, then at the replicas of themselves. Using her name, one of the gods softly commands Blue Sky to look up. She does so in a frightened manner and then hides her face in her hands again. One of the Kachinas raises her gently to her feet. He tells her that her thoughts and her prayers have softened their hearts and that they have decided to give her people another chance. Now Chief Sun Path comes hesitantly into the council ring, followed by the other chiefs and the repentant people. They walk wearily and keep their heads bowed until one of the gods addresses them and commands them to look up. They then gaze on the strange scene before them: Blue Sky standing close to the gods, and beside them, the Kachina dolls. The gods tell the Hopi that because of Blue Sky they have returned to give the people another chance—the last. The gods make the condition that the people must sometimes wear masks like the Kachinas, masks which the Hopi once mocked. Each year the masks must be worn at the sacred ceremony when the people pray for fertile fields. The people murmur their thanks.

The Kachinas promise a bountiful harvest, good hunting, and happiness in the coming months. Then one god commands forcibly that from then on no girl or woman should be allowed ever again to make a Kachina doll. (Hopi legend tells us that this command was strictly obeyed, and so it is to this very day.)

PART 5

OUR INDIAN HERITAGE

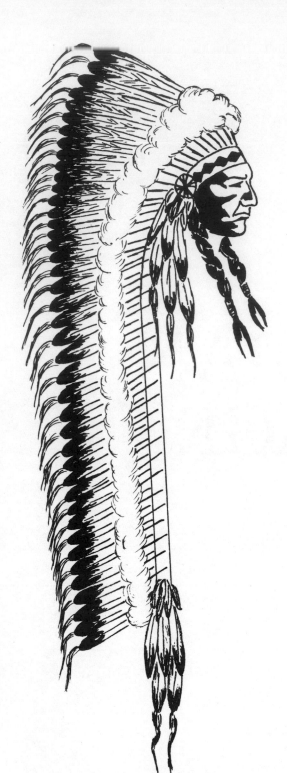

chapter 19

indian designs and regalia

MOTIFS AND DESIGNS FOR DECORATING INDIAN DRESS

The pages of design given in this chapter will help council fire chiefs to select suitable ones for the costumes of their bands. The Woodland designs have a distinctive beauty all their own, and were usually worked in vari-colored beads on a dark background. It should be noted that the floral designs Numbers 1, 2, 3, 7, 8, and 9 were often made with a variety of different flowers and leaves on the same stem or branch. The designs 4, 5, and 6 are geometrical patterns.

The Plains designs were largely geometric, consisting of triangles, squares, and other figures with straight sides, which represented natural phenomena, tracks, and other things mentioned below. There were no fixed meanings attached to many designs, since peoples and tribes frequently had different meanings for the same symbol. The general subjects of motifs were often everyday objects known to the Indians. Some illustrated the power of nature—showing the sun, wind, moon, and stars—or depicted beasts, birds, and insects. Another favorite sign topic was the natural features of their surroundings, such as mountains, hills, rivers, trails, and trees. Frequently, circles figured in the Plains symbols, as a circle was good medicine. The page of Plains tribes designs illustrates a few of the motifs of that habitat group. Design Numbers 1, 2, 4, 5, and 7 are Sioux; 3 and 9 Arapaho; 6 and 8 are Dakota.

The favorite colors of paints and beads used in Indian painting and design were red, yellow, black, blue, green, and white—which was often used as a background. White depicted snow, winter time, the time for Plains warriors to tie up their ponies' tails and take to the war trail which would lead to glory or death. The colors used had symbolic values which differed in meaning according to habitat.

THIS BRANCH OF INDIANCRAFT was as specialized as their headdress-making and feathercraft. Every symbol and design, like almost every feather, had a specific meaning and represented some actual object. Some special owner designs on clothing were believed to protect the wearer from danger. Often these designs and their significance were never spoken of by the brave wearing them, and what they meant and were supposed to do was unknown even to close friends. The belief was that some magic and power would be lost in speaking of the symbols.

AUTHENTIC INDIAN DRESS

Research is required on the part of council fire chiefs who are not satisfied with their braves wearing a motley collection of Indian trappings copied from many tribes. Such chiefs wish their warriors' dress and regalia to look as much like the original dress of the Indian tribes which they represent as possible. This also applies to the designs used, as different Indian groups used different designs, many of which had great significance. A council fire chief does not wish one of his Woodland group braves to lay aside his feathered *gustoweh* and appear at the council fire wearing the tailed war bonnet of a Plains chief. Many of the drawings in this book serve to illustrate correct dress and headdress of various habitat groups, but several volumes would be required to go into costuming for the American Indians in detail. A visit to one of the museums which display American Indian dress, weapons, and handicraft is recommended for council fire chiefs in search of authenticity. If they can use a camera or take along an artistically inclined brave from their groups who can make sketches of the various costumes, regalia, and trappings of particualr interest to their groups, so much the better.

BOYS' INDIAN PONCHOS

The robe poncho illustrated is a handy Indian garment when one has to be turned out in a hurry. It is easily made and has the advantage that it can be worn without breechclout or leggings, as a pair of blue jeans can take their place. These ponchos can be made from an old blanket, heavy cotton cloth, or even sacks, cut to the size shown in the drawing, which fits the average council fire brave—but each brave should be measured for his poncho to assure a good fit. Since a great number of tribes wore various forms of poncho, in addition to some of the Plains and Southwest tribes, the only thing required to make the poncho suitable for wear at various council fires is that the correct design of the tribe represented by the wearer be used. The head goes through the across-and-down slits shown just above the top decoration pattern in the Navaho poncho in the drawing. The cross-slit is 6 inches, and the downward slit about 3 inches. These slits are cut out a little to make the poncho more comfortable. The two tapes shown at the top of the illustration go down behind the back section of the poncho and are tied around the waist, in front, under the poncho.

BOYS' INDIAN DRESS OF THE SOUTHWEST

Costumes of the Southwest, such as those worn by the Navaho, Zuni, and Hopi, can be quickly improvised by simply wearing a breechclout or blue, black, or tan jeans, with a dark-colored shirt closed in front and laced at the back, a colorful belt and headband, a necklace, a big bracelet, and black or dark leather short boots with a big silver buckle on the outside of each boot. If a breechclout is worn, short leggings tied with a colorful strip of cloth just below the knee, and plain moccasins mostly hidden by colorful angora type anklets, can be worn. The dress of these peoples was varied and ranged from beautiful ceremonial garments to a pair of jeans and a store blanket. Headbands, worn chiefly to keep their hair out of their eyes, were a usual feature of their dress. The chief thing to be observed when decorating any of these costumes, belts, and headbands is to be certain that the designs used belong to the tribe which the warrior wearing them wishes to represent. The dresses of the Southwest were so varied and colorful that great choice and scope of costumes are available for council fire warriors who represent any of the tribes in that territory.

The typical Zuni dress shown in the drawing is not difficult to imitate, as white, light blue, or light khaki slacks, with a 6-inch slit cut in the foot of each trouser leg along the outside seam, takes care of the lower part of the costume. A long-sleeved black or navy-blue shirt is worn outside the trousers. A white cloth belt colorfully decorated, a bright headband, a string of beads, a big "silver" bracelet decorated with a large blue stone, and the boots mentioned above complete the costume.

Today the dress of the Navaho does not differ greatly from that of the everyday garments of the Zuni and Hopi. Jeans, bright-colored store blankets, and dark wide-brimmed felt hats can be seen on all sides in the

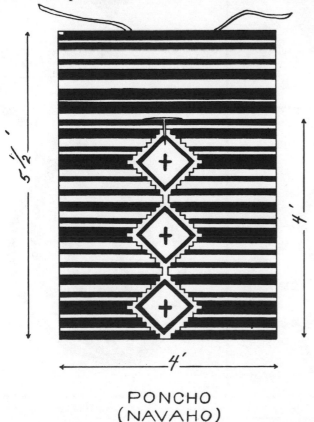

PONCHO
(NAVAHO)

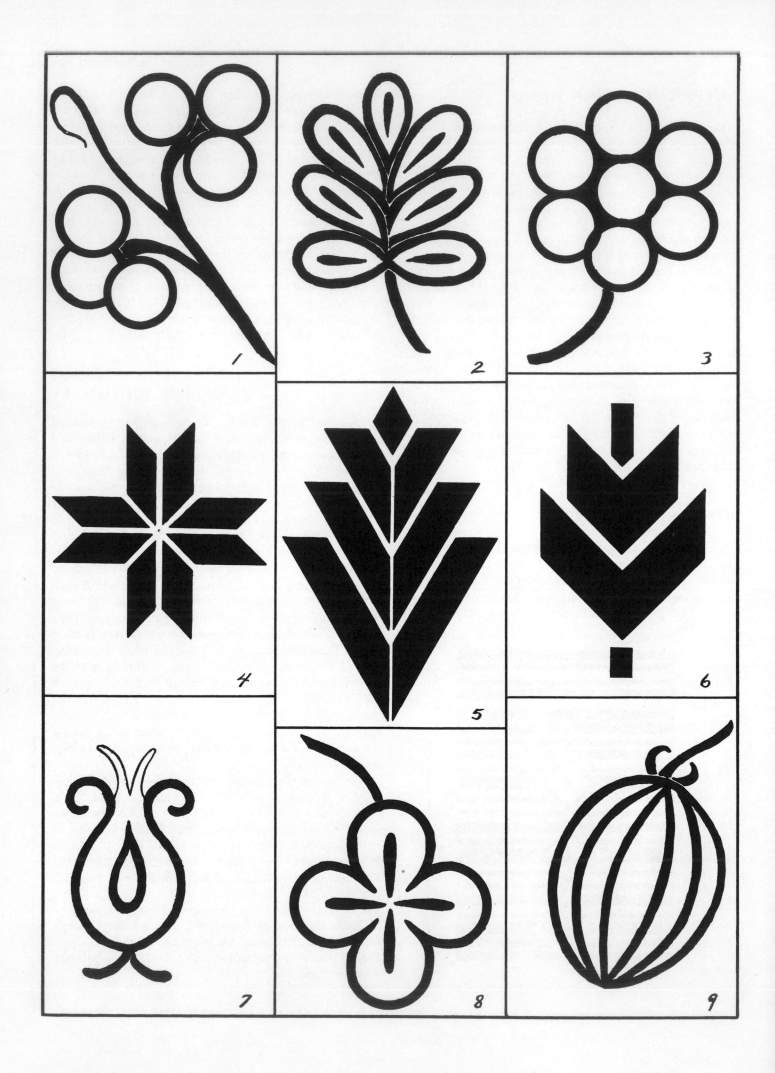

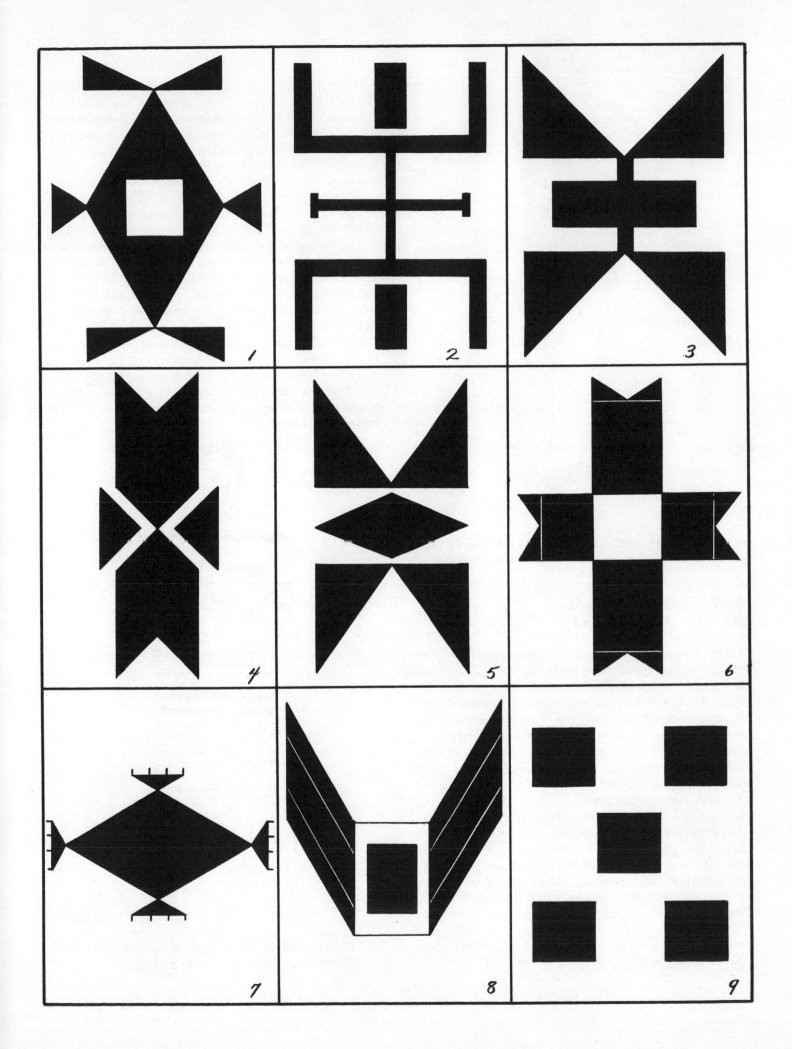

ZUNI

Pueblo and surrounding country. Breechclouts replace jeans and the blankets are cast aside in warm weather.

BOYS' INDIAN DRESS OF THE SOUTHEAST

The dress of the Seminole is chosen for description and illustration because it is by far the most colorful and distinctive costume of the entire southeastern area. Tribes to the north of that habitat wore Eastern Woodland types of dress—the Tuscarora, for instance—while other groups, such as the Shawnee, affected dress which resembled that of some of the Plains tribes, though the Shawnee wore turkey-feather headdresses with the feathers standing upright from a leather headband and a sort of turkey-feather trailer hanging down the back, which distinguished them from other tribes of the Southeast.

The drawing of the Seminole illustrates how much their dress differs from that of nearly all other American Indian tribes of the United States. The costume shown is a cotton or calico robe with a light background, often in white or a buttercup yellow, with stripes of gay colors. These stripes are usually red, green, blue, black, and orange, though other colors are also used. The dress consists of a waist-length tunic with long puffed sleeves. The knee-length kilt is gathered at the waist.

A very different garment is a one-piece, loose-fitting smock type of garment which comes to just below the knees as a rule. It is of dark-blue or black calico, with a V-shaped fringed collar hanging down in front to upper chest level. It has long, slightly puffed sleeves, and gaily colored designs decorate it from just above the waist to halfway to the knees. These stripes are in light colors, as is the fringe on the V-shaped collar. There is generally a light-colored design running around the collar just above the fringe.

The Seminole wore high-topped soft-soled moccasins which were puckered to form a single seam along the instep. Some were decorated with a little colored tassel attached to the toe. On ceremonial occasions the Seminole wore a strange headdress which looked like an Oriental turban, made of cloth or leather and decorated with feathers, often egret plumes, which rose high in the air above the turban.

Today, in addition to the calico robes described above, the Seminole men wear dark or light-colored jeans, bright-colored shirts, and either a wide-brimmed felt hat or bare heads.

PLAINS AND WOODLAND DRESS

VESTS. Copied by Plains and Woodland tribes from vests worn by the white men, like trousers, they are an addition to Indian attire of comparatively recent date. An Indian vest can easily be cut out of suede, buckskin, other lightweight leather, or cloth, using an ordinary vest as a pattern. Most Indian vests opened down the front and were held together by being laced with thongs in two or three places, as shown in the drawing.

These vests can be painted or beaded in bright-colored simple Plains or Woodland designs. A 3- or 4-inch fringe of cloth or leather, each fringe about ¼ inch wide, all around the foot of the vest adds to its Indianlike appearance. They look best when worn instead of a shirt rather than over a shirt.

INDIAN STYLE TROUSERS. Though trousers were not worn by Plains and Woodland Indians until long after the white men came, they can be a very useful part of a council fire group Indian costume. The trousers can be a pair of old dark jeans or khaki slacks. The Indian touch is given by sewing on a 2-inch strip of bright cloth all the way down the outside seam of each trouser leg. A 3- or 4-inch-wide fringe of cloth or buckskin, each fringe about ¼ inch wide, can take the place of the cloth strip.

Woodland groups can also use strips of cloth and add further decoration by beading them in Woodland designs. Strips and patches of beads can be bought in various trading posts which sell Indian supplies to modern Indians. Such patches can be sewn on easily and save much time and effort otherwise spent on camp-made beadwork.

Trousers like the ones described can be made more quickly and easily than the long leggings, or short leggings and breechclout, required when trousers are not worn. With moccasins and colorful Indian type shirt left hanging down outside the trousers, such trousers can easily be mistaken for long leggings.

SHIRTS AND WAR SHIRTS

The section and illustrations on motifs and designs for Indian dress opened this chapter because they are suit-able types of decorations for use on council fire dress and regalia. The shirts worn by the American Indians varied according to habitat, and there was an easily recognizable difference in both styles and decorations worn by Plains, Woodland, Southwestern, and Northwest Coast Indians. The two Woodland shirts, often worn with beaded belts, shown in the drawings illustrate the cloth and buckskin types. Another sketch illustrates a Plains shirt, cut in the Woodland style but covered with a V-shaped flap at the neck. The Indians made shirts from almost any material found in their villages, tepees, longhouses, hogans, and pueblos. These materials ranged from sacks to splendid elk and buckskin. Some of the earlier shirts were of the poncho type; they pulled over the head and were open at the sides. These shirts were known as war shirts and were sometimes laced or tied at the sides to hold them in place. The Apache left their shirts open at the sides but used leather thongs to lace the sleeves together. Even shirts made from the most ordinary materials were made splendid by painted designs, beads and beaded work, fringes of cloth of bright colors or buckskin, and appliqué work, as was the custom in the various tribal areas.

Modern council fire braves can make a war shirt easily and speedily by cutting the cuffs and collar from any old colored shirt, or a white one may be used and suitable designs painted on it. Many things can be done with such shirts to turn them into good-looking Indian type shirts. For instance, the buttons in front of the shirt can be cut off and the shirt laced together up the front with a gaily colored strip of cloth or tape. Fringed collars can be attached to these shirts, and the sleeves can have fringes sewn onto the back seams of each sleeve. Such old shirts, provided they are strong enough to last through at least an entire season of council fires, can also be painted or crayoned in various correct designs, and strips of beads and colored cloth can be sewn on them to add further to their appearance. These shirts, worn outside a pair of dark-colored jeans, do away with the need for both breechclout and leggings. It does not take long for a brave who can use a needle and thread to make an effective Indian shirt from a few flour or sugar sacks.

BREECHCLOUTS

This cool, comfortable, informal garb varied less throughout the various habitats than did most of the Indian apparel. Though the decoration and designs were different, the actual loin cloths were much alike. They can be made from heavy unbleached cotton or cotton flannel; the favorite colors were red or blue. The breechclout served not only as underwear but also as a decorative part of the costume. As a rule the breechclout should be about as long as the wearer is tall, and its width is one-third of his waist measurement. It was decorated with painted, and sometimes beaded, designs at both ends and worn as a sort of back-and-front apron. The decorative front and back hung down over the belt which held the breechclout in place. The drawings show how the breechclout is worn.

APRONS

The aprons worn by some Woodland, Southwest, and Northwest Coast Indians were a sort of kilt without pleats, as will be seen from the illustrations in this chapter and in Chapter 17. The dance aprons of the peoples of the Pueblos and the Northwest Coast were the most ornamental of all, because they were worn for sacred dances and for great ceremonial occasions.

PUEBLO KILT

These aprons can be made most easily from lightweight canvas, but buckskin or any suitable cloth can also be used. The illustrations show that the Woodland apron was made from two decorated squares of cloth which were worn one in front and one behind, held in place by colored tapes around the waist. To allow one to feel a little more securely clad, the two squares can be held together with a short lace fastened about halfway down the apron on each side. Woodland aprons are, of course, only decorated with Woodland designs.

The Pueblo aprons were of the wrap-around sort, and

their chief adornment was a splendid sash which held the apron in place and hung down on the right-hand side of the front of the apron. This sash was entirely decorated, though some of the aprons were less adorned, having the designs mainly around the foot of the unfringed apron or on either side of it. The aprons for adults were about 30 inches long and 18 inches wide, with a sash 6 feet long and 10 inches wide.

The Northwest Coast aprons were splendidly decorated, with the main decoration painted directly on the front of the apron, which was deeply fringed all around and tied behind or at one side by supporting tapes. The Indian name for this apron means "dancing blanket," or "the fringe around the body." The decorative work of the Northwest Coast was seldom geometrical. Most of the designs and motifs depicted supernatural beings, animals, and family crests. The basic colors of the Northwest Coast tribes were a bright yellowish-red, black, pale yellow, and a shade of copper-green.

LEGGINGS

There were a great variety of leggings worn by the Indians of the United States. As a rule the Northwest Coast tribes wore short leggings reaching from ankle to knee and tied just below the knee, the whole legging generally being fringed and painted in a decorative manner. Some of the Woodland tribes, the Iroquois, for instance, also wore short leggings as well as long ones. These leggings were usually decorated on the lower third, beginning just above the ankle. Leggings were beaded, painted with various designs, and decorated in a number of other ways, including quill work and appliqué. Beaded garters were often worn over the leggings just below the knee. Most of the other habitat groups, especially the Indians of the Plains, wore long leggings fastened to the belt thongs by loops. Leggings may be worn with breechclouts, aprons, shirts, or coats, such as the Cree wore.

There are a number of good materials from which leggings may be made. One of the cheapest methods of making serviceable leggings is to cut them from bleached, heavy cotton sacks. Such leggings are easily painted with suitable designs, and they may also be embellished with fringes cut from red or blue flannel or flannelette of various bright colors, and lightweight leather when it is available. Laces or thongs should be attached at the top of the leggings on each side toward the back, to tie around the belt to hold them in place. A fringe sewn on the outside of the leggings will add to their appearance. The Blackfoot, like their Woodland brothers, usually decorated their leggings toward the foot, in the lower third. Suitable designs for Plains and Woodland groups' leggings will be found among the two full pages of design illustrations in this chapter.

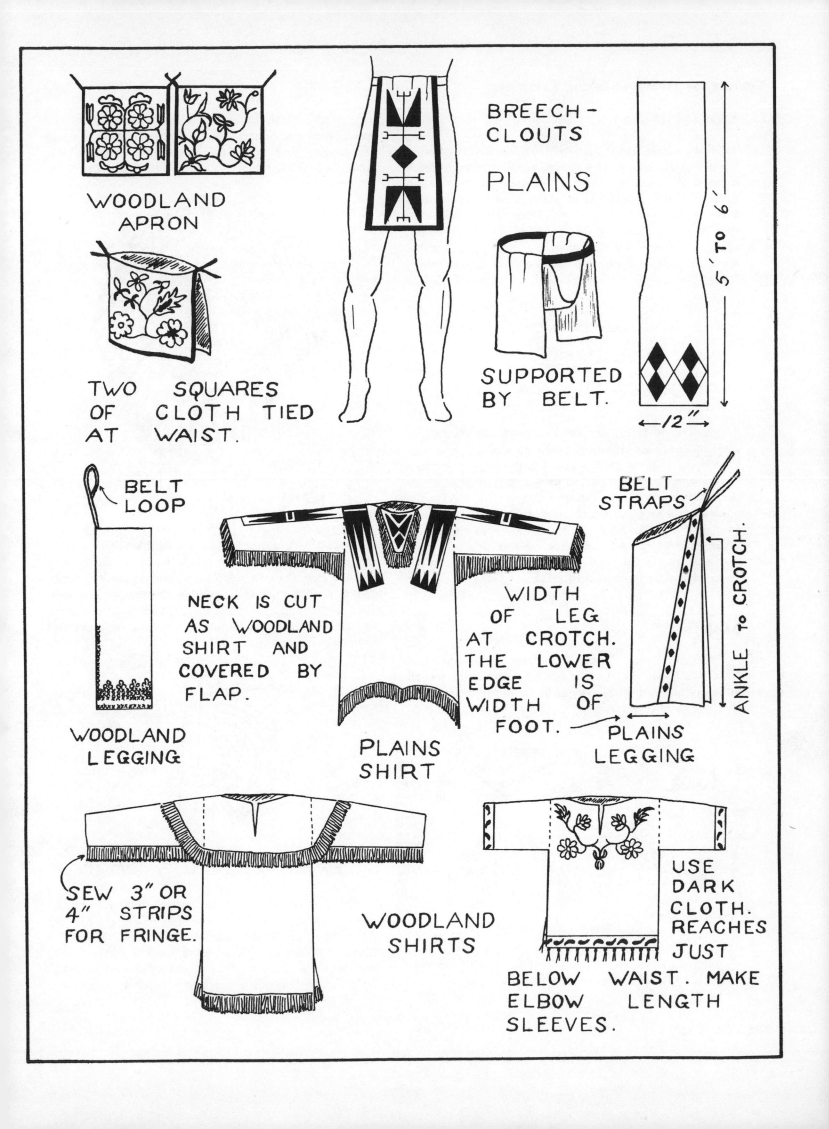

WOODLAND APRON

TWO SQUARES OF CLOTH TIED AT WAIST.

BREECH-CLOUTS

PLAINS

SUPPORTED BY BELT.

5' TO 6'

12"

BELT LOOP

NECK IS CUT AS WOODLAND SHIRT AND COVERED BY FLAP.

WOODLAND LEGGING

PLAINS SHIRT

WIDTH OF LEG AT CROTCH. THE LOWER EDGE IS WIDTH OF FOOT.

BELT STRAPS

ANKLE TO CROTCH.

PLAINS LEGGING

SEW 3" OR 4" STRIPS FOR FRINGE.

WOODLAND SHIRTS

USE DARK CLOTH. REACHES JUST BELOW WAIST. MAKE ELBOW LENGTH SLEEVES.

MOCCASINS

Most modern council fire Indians own a pair of regular moccasins which, with a little decoration added, can be used quite well for the footwear part of their Indian dress. The decoration can be a fringe of leather or imitation leather fastened to a strip of brightly colored cloth, tied around the ankle so that the fringe falls over the top of the moccasin. Good improvised moccasins, like the mock-moccasins shown in the drawing, can be made from a pair of old sneakers painted with a suitable Indian

MOCK - MOCCASINS

design. To add to the illusion, the sneakers can either be dyed in a solution of strong tea or painted a buff or yellowish color as a background for the design. Further camouflage can be introduced by wearing a pair of imitation Angora anklets, pictured in Chapter 17, around the ankles just above the sneakers, so that they come down over their tops. An even simpler method is to wear a pair of brightly colored socks and roll the tops down to touch the sneakers. As a temporary measure, the designs on the sneakers can be marked with crayons.

MASKS

Throughout the Plains, Woodland, Southwest, and Northwest Coast habitats, masks of many kinds played an important part in the way of life of the Indians.

There were clown masks for play, articulated and two-face masks, chiefs' masks for ceremonial wear, animal masks for dancers and secret societies, false-face masks for healing, and masks for magic. These masks were made from many things. The heads and skins of animals,

WOODLAND
CORN HUSK MASK

heads and feathers of birds, corn husks, leaves, leather, cloth, and bark were among some of the materials used. The mask decorations were made from substances even more varied than those used for mask-making. Paint, shells, small animal skins, sea lion bristles, ermine tails, hair and hair tufts, feathers and feather tufts, and strips of varicolored cloth were among some of the decorative material employed.

PAPER BAG MASK

The modern council fire Indian is fortunate in having much suitable mask material within reach. He can use paper bags, cardboard, and cloth for quick results, as many really artistic and effective masks of many kinds may be made from cardboard and cardboard cylinders by gluing on attachments such as ears, noses, horns, and varied decorations.

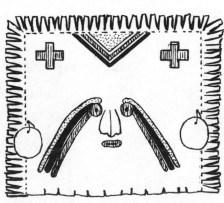

ZUNI
CLOWN

ASSINIBOINE
MASKS

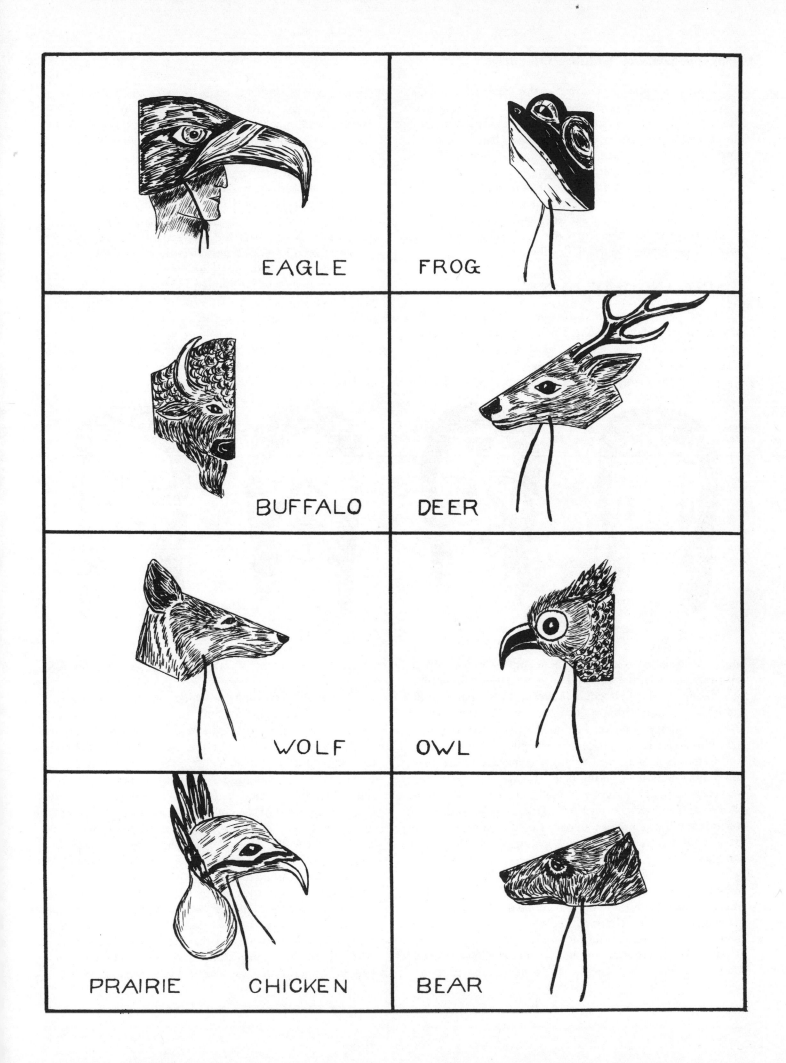

EAGLE

FROG

BUFFALO

DEER

WOLF

OWL

PRAIRIE CHICKEN

BEAR

Among the masks pictured in this chapter, the eagle, frog, owl, and prairie chicken ones are made from cardboard cylinders worn in a vertical position. The buffalo-head mask is worn with the wearer's head completely inside, and his eyes look out, with some difficulty, through the buffalo's eyes cut in the mask.

The deer, wolf, and bear-head masks are made from cylinders which are worn tilted at an angle so that the top of the mask rests on the forehead.

All these masks are worn tied on with tape attached to each side and fastened under the chin.

PAINT AND WAR PAINT

Facial painting may also be considered part of Indian dress, since paint was worn for adornment, ceremonies, mourning, and other reasons, as well as for a preparation for war dances and warpaths.

Two or three days in the sun, taken in easy doses at

This is not to be recommended for council fire braves! They will attain better results, painlessly, by doing as the Nootka and other warlike tribes did, using paints for facial decoration. First these warriors coated their faces liberally with deer tallow, melted fat. On top of this foundation coat they applied dry ochre colors, and charcoal for black, usually using a flat, smooth stick of the desired width with which to apply the colors.

Face painting was regarded as a fine art by nearly all Indians. Both chiefs and braves gave it much thought and pondered long over the selection of design and color when applying an original design to their faces. Many of the most effectively painted chiefs wiped the designs disgustedly from their faces many times before they achieved the desired results. Council fire braves will find that certain colors and markings look better than others when applied to their faces, and it is good medicine in such cases to adopt such coloration as their own for special occasions.

FACE PAINTING

the Indian village—that is, the camp—should provide the average paleface with a fair coat of tan. This proves a blessing on the first council fire night, as painting the entire face, and perhaps the upper part of the body, is rather a messy job for beginners; also, the regalia is likely to suffer in the process of painting. With a natural-tan foundation, it is easy to apply some decorative paint lines, even a pattern, to the face. Bright-hued color sticks or grease paints may be bought at theatrical supply stores and in some drugstores. Grease paint will come off quickly if one applies a coat of cold cream to the skin as a base before applying the paint. Water colors are excellent for face painting, since they wash off easily when the last fitful flicker of the council flame is but a memory. Cold cream or cocoa butter, applied with a piece of cheesecloth, are fine for removing face paint. The drawings show four simple patterns of face markings which are effective and easy to apply.

Some of the Indians of the Northwest Coast tattooed themselves instead of using paint for decorative purposes.

SCALP LOCKS

This warlike decoration, which can be worn on the headdress to council fires and on ceremonial occasions, can serve a useful purpose in modern council fire group work. First of all, it should either be earned by the brave carrying out a grand coup or be awarded when the brave earns and claims his third coup feather. It adds distinction when the coveted scalp lock award is given only with the approval of the council fire chief and his council of advisers, after its recommendation by the brave's immediate chief. The council fire chief can warn a scalp-winning brave that he will lose his scalp for unworthy conduct. The forfeited lock will not be returned until it has been won back by a worthy deed. Should a brave be foolhardy enough to pledge his scalp lock in a council ring dual challenge and then lose the contest, the brave who defeats him may keep the scalp lock permanently. After seven suns have come and gone, another scalp lock may be awarded the scalp-lockless warrior, with the solemn warning that should this one be lost, many moons may pass before another one will be granted.

The scalp lock may be made from a 4-inch length of braided black horsehair sewn onto a 1-inch strip of scarlet cloth 3 inches long, or a more elaborate and lengthy lock up to 8 inches long may be worn. These longer locks can be sewn onto the same sort of strip as the shorter ones or onto a 2-inch circle of scarlet flannel. Since horsehair is not always readily available, the locks can be made from coarse cord or a piece of combed hemp rope. The cord or rope should be soaked in warm water for an hour or two to soften and, when dry, dyed black with any good household dye.

NATURE'S DYES

The Indians used a great number of the roots of flowers, plants, and bushes in making some of their dyes; but because some of these plants are nearing extinction today, no mention will be made of them here. Unrecorded too, in the interest of conservation, will remain the many sorts of bark and branches used in the manufacture of dyes by the Red Men. It is a depressing sight to see bark and branches stripped ruthlessly from living trees for use in the experimental making of dyes, especially since so many attempts to secure satisfactory colors end in failure and eventually commercial dyes have to be employed to get the desired results.

Before listing a few of nature's dyes which should give good results without having to destroy wildwood growth, it should be pointed out that today inexpensive, easy-to-use household dyes can be bought which will do the required dyeing work quickly, easily, cheaply, and well. In an emergency shades of buckskin, tan, or khaki can be achieved by boiling or soaking white cotton cloth in a strong solution of tea. Tea will assure the color remaining reasonably fast, and leaves the cloth odorless after dyeing.

Natural dyes which can be made without destroying the roots of living plants and flowers are listed in the order of their usual demand.

Several things of importance must be remembered before experimenting with dyes. Soft water only should be used for boiling the various solutions of leaves, berries, or nut hulls. Cotton, calico cloth, or linen will dye more easily than wool, rayon, or silks. All materials should be steeped for a few moments in soft water and then rung out before being steeped in the dye solution. Old metal pots without lids make good dyeing vessels. All cloth being dyed should be stirred and lifted frequently with a long flat stick and exposed to the air several times before being taken from the dye pot, wrung out lightly, and hung up to dry. Some Indian tribes washed out the loose dye in soft water before hanging the dyed cloth on trees or bushes to dry. Some of the dyes listed will not run; but if others are not rinsed from the dyed material, they will run and drip if the wearer is caught wearing the dyed clothing in the rain.

Some sort of fixative, known as a mordant, will generally aid in setting the colors and making them fast. Simple mordants may be things such as salt, vinegar, or alum, and it is generally best to use alkali fixatives with acid dyes and acid fixatives with alkali dyes. Tribes of the Southwest often used wood ashes as a mordant. Sometimes the cloth to be dyed is best steeped in the fixative solution and then wrung out, prior to placing it in the dye, while at other times the fixative solution is stirred into and mixed with the dyeing solution. Dyeing with nature's color is a visual process to a large extent, in order to assure the desired color. The length of time that the material is boiled or steeped and the amount of material which produces the dye will determine the final color.

Dyeing with natural colors is an experimental business, and the results achieved will often be decided by trial and error. At times the result is startling, at others, surprisingly beautiful.

TAN AND BROWN SHADES. The *fresh* hulls of ripe wild black walnuts boiled for an hour or so in an old open pot will give shades ranging from light tan to dark brown, according to the strength of the brew. The hulls, of course, are removed before the cloth is soaked in the dye and kept there until the shade desired results. Sometimes the leaves of the tree are used in addition to the hulls.

A very strong solution of boiled sumac leaves and stems gives a good shade of tan, but unfortunately the color is liable to fade fairly quickly unless the brew is very strong and the cloth is kept in it for several hours.

REDDISH SHADES. A strong brew of chokecherries, sumac berries, or elderberries produces varied shades of red.

YELLOW SHADES. As a rule, the Indians used various roots to make yellow dyes. The Navaho made a rich shade of lemon by boiling the flowering tops and stems of goldenrod for at least four hours. A fixative, such as alum—one ounce of powdered alum to three-quarters of a gallon of soft water, plus a quarter of an ounce of washing soda—should be added to the dyeing solution and boiled with it to assure fast color.

A strong solution of "sneeze weed," a sort of wild aster, when boiled for several hours, makes a good yellow which usually retains its color.

A heavy brew of fresh green peach leaves boiled for two or three hours and pounded with a wooden beater until the leaves are in shreds, makes a yellow dye, as will a similar solution of sunflower blossoms.

BLUISH SHADES. The Indians of the Southwest got blue dye by boiling strong solutions of the larkspur flowers. The purple iris also yields a purplish-blue dye when the flowers are boiled in soft water for several hours. The solution must be strong to give good results, though wood may be dyed purple by merely rubbing purple iris blossoms onto it. A strong solution of pokeweed flowers and stems also provides a purplish dye. Varying shades of blue can also be secured by boiling strong solutions of the fruits of privet, sloe, elder, and whortleberry.

GREEN. Equal quantities of nettle and elder leaves and stems boiled together for an hour or so produce a shade of green which varies with the strength of the dye mixture used. The berries and leaves of privet when boiled together also produce green.

BLACK. Wild fresh black-walnut hulls mixed with an equal quantity of sumac berries with their stems on, when boiled together for a few hours, produce a good black.

COUP FEATHERS AND HEADDRESSES

Often, too little attention is given to correct headdress, the use of feathers, and especially the wearing of coup feathers and grand coup feathers.

Not all modern braves know that the term coup derives its meaning from the French word *coup* (pronounced *coo*), which means an effective stroke, or achievement. A *grand coup* means a still greater exploit or achievement. The word *coup* appears daily in French newspapers—*coup de grâce* or *coup d'état,* for instance. Many chapters could be written on the subject of coup feathers.

These exploit feathers were first earned and then worn with pride by Indians of the Plains tribes. One, two, or three eagle feathers worn in a warrior's hair told, by the manner in which they were decorated and worn, exactly what the wearer had done to earn them. The Omaha and other tribes of the Plains considered the coup feather more as a war honor, gained on the warpath or in battle, than as an award for other feats of bravery. An eagle feather worn *upright* in the scalp lock was a war honor *first class,* used to denote that the wearer had struck an unwounded enemy with the hand, bow, or coup stick. An eagle feather worn *horizontally* was a *second-class* war honor, awarded for touching a wounded enemy, while a *third-class* award, represented by a feather hanging *straight down* from the scalp lock, was given to the first two men to strike a dead enemy. Naturally, there were as a rule other enemy braves waiting to avenge a dead warrior, so that there was nearly always a certain risk in this feat.

In other Plains tribes, coup feathers were decorated with tufts of horsehair, often dyed red. Red bars painted on the white part of a feather represented various coups, according to the markings. They replaced the feather worn at an angle by the Omaha. Some exploit feathers were painted with a red spot, others were notched at various points, and a feather split from the top down could denote a brave who had been wounded a number of times. A warrior who had been wounded in battle could wear a feather which had been dyed red. Many other coup feathers were marked in other ways and had special significance. It can be truthfully said that coup feather spoke a language of their own. It is not too hard a task for a modern council fire chief to find out, through books in his nearest library, just what significance the various feathers worn by the warriors of a certain tribe had. Should there be too many rules to be observed, a council fire chief can adopt some simplified rules governing the wearing of feathers by the members of his band. The point that they must be *earned,* like most worthwhile things in life, is worth stressing. There is no good reason why chiefs and subchiefs should not set an example in the wearing of coup feathers.

Some tribes of the Eastern Woodland and Plains habitats wore headdresses made from deers' tails. They were called roaches and are illustrated, along with a number of other headdresses, in these pages. The roaches were dyed red in certain tribes, when the warrior wearing the

ROACH

HEADBAND

headgear of these peoples. Mandan chiefs wore splendid horned headdresses with trailers, and Sioux medicine men also wore horned bonnets at times. High-ranking chiefs of the Six Nations were also entitled to wear horned head-

red roach had earned one of the first three war honors. Feathers used for further decoration of roaches had also to be earned. Indians were trained from youth to know that honors did not come easily.

The Blackfoot and some other tribes of the Northern Plains wore winter caps made of fur. Some of these caps, which looked like simple turbans, were decorated with quillwork and painted strips of rawhide. The feathers often worn in this winter headdress were also won, not just fastened to the cap because they looked striking.

Eastern Woodland groups wore headdresses of buckskin, deerskin, other animal skins, and feathers. The latter is a sort of skull cap made from large and small feathers, and perhaps some downies, with a long feather

dresses, but powerful women counselors of these nations had the power to have that distinctive headdress removed when the chiefs so dishonored proved unworthy to hold their high office.

This brief run-down of Indian headdresses has left the striking war bonnet of the Plains Indians to the last. These magnificent bonnets, carried in special *parfleche* cases and tended with great care by their owners, were often donned by chiefs just before they went into battle, often when they sensed that the battle in which they were eager to engage would be their last. These magnificent war bonnets also had their coup and grand coup feathers, tufted feathers, and others with special meaning. It is not to be wondered at that, in modern times, tribes other than those of the Plains have cast envious eyes on the Plains war bonnet and have been delighted when some

GUSTOWEH

MANDAN HORNED BONNET

standing up from the center of the cap and worn in a socket, so that the feather twirls as the owner walks. This headdress is the *gustoweh,* or "real hat," so called by the Iroquois.

The Apache, people of the Pueblos, and other tribes of that habitat wore completely different headdresses, especially for ceremonial dress. A headband was the usual

227

BLACKFOOT WAR BONNET

ill-informed cinema director has insisted that they wear that striking regalia for an "Indian" film which did not feature, nor even deal with, Plains Indians. Many of these war-bonneted "extras" became so enamoured with their headgear that they have been wearing it ever since, to the delight of tourists, most of whom would not recognize a man as an Indian unless he were wearing a Plains war bonnet.

When considering the many and varied headdresses of the American Indians, one can see that Indian headgear was not the sort of thing that can be picked up, like a white man's hat, at a moment's notice at the nearest hat shop. Most of the headdresses mentioned are illustrated on these pages, and a number of books are available to council fire chiefs at the library, telling just how each headdress can be made. Many can be made quite simply, often using the crown of a man's felt hat as a base, and all the warriors who sit around the modern council

APACHE HEADBAND

fire should be encouraged to make their own headgear. It is true that a Plains warrior will have much more trouble making his than an Apache will in devising his headband.

NECKLACES

Chiefs and braves often wore necklaces of many sorts, as is illustrated by chiefs bearing the names of Big Necklace and Little Necklace. A brave who killed a bear was entitled to wear a bear-claw necklace. Sometimes the strangely colored elk teeth were made into striking necklace. The advantage of wooden beads is that they can were strung onto a buckskin thong, in sequence, and worn as necklaces. After the arrival of white men and traders, the beads were usually made of wood or glass.

Today fine necklaces can be made by stringing wooden beads of the size desired on a strong cord or leather lace. The advantage of wooden beads is that they can be colored to suit individual taste. The predominating colors, recommended to give an Indian touch to the decoration, are red, black, and yellow. Glass and plastic beads also make good necklaces. Imitation bear claws can be cut from soft wood or bought in stores which sell material for Indian arts and crafts. A good arrangement for necklaces is to string a colored bead between each two bear claws.

BREASTPLATES

The more showy breastplate decorations are harder to make and less comfortable to wear. They are best, perhaps, reserved for strictly ceremonial occasions. They are certainly not the thing to wear when challenges are in order. The breastplates, worn by many Plains tribes look as though they were made from pipe stems. Traders supplied them under the name hair pipes. Modern council fire Indians can make breastplates in a number of ways. They can be made the hard way, from uniform-size bones of certain kinds, such as the bones from chickens' legs.

PLAINS ARMBAND

They can also be made, with less trouble, from reed pipe stems or the stems of corncob pipes. Considerably smaller "bones" can be made by cutting off the quill ends of large feathers, such as goose or turkey feathers. The lengths cut for breastplates should all be the same. All bones are strung on cords, preferably brown to imitate buckskin, and a colored bead may be strung between each two bones. The strings of bone can range from 4 to 7 inches in length, according to the breadth of chest they are to adorn, and they can be painted with white or cream-colored enamel paint. A small loop is left at each end of the thong on which the bones are strung. The rows of bones are suspended across the chest so that they touch, or almost touch, each other. A colored cord is tied onto the loop of the top row, on each side, and then passed down through and fastened to each row in succession until the bottom row is also attached, and the ends of the cords are passed around the waist and tied behind the back. Another way to string the bones is to thread

quills, or tufts of colored hair hanging from them. The wristbands were about 1 inch wide, while the arm bands had a width of about 2 or 3 inches. They were both made in the same fashion, beadwork sewn onto a soft band of leather or cloth, just long enough to encircle the wrist, or the arm just above the elbow. Usually the two ends were laced together with a thin, soft thong. Short, narrow strips of cloth of varied colors can hang down from either the wrist or arm bands as further decor. Arm bands made of 3-inch-wide strips of tin were often worn just above the elbow.

CUFFS

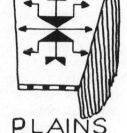

WOODLAND   PLAINS

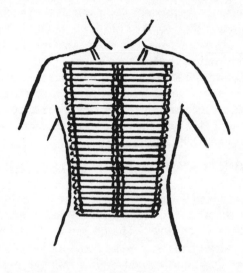

one long cord through all of them, making rows by bending the cord at the end of a row and starting the next row directly beneath. This style is fastened to the wearer as described above, or one can dispense with the little loops at each end of each row and simply fasten the colored retaining cord around the end of each bend, at each end of every row of bones. Colored cord, narrow rickrack, or a colored cloth strip can be woven down between the bones in the center of the breastplate. This not only serves as decoration but helps to hold the rows in place.

WRISTBANDS, ARM BANDS AND CUFFS

Other decorations used among the Indians, especially those of the Plains tribes, were wristbands and arm bands, often beaded and sometimes adorned with small feathers,

Wide, beaded cuffs were sometimes worn instead of wristbands.

Gloves and gauntlet gloves were introduced by white men, as were Glengarry bonnets, and are not recommended as part of Indian regalia.

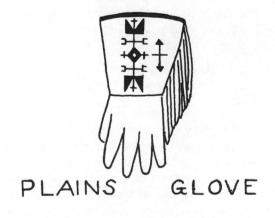

PLAINS GLOVE

229

DEWCLAW DANCE ANKLET

ANKLETS

Anklets of various kinds were not only worn by dancers while performing but were also worn by Indian dandies—yes, they had their dandies too! Anklets can easily be made by using strips of bright-colored cloth about 2 or 3 inches wide, just long enough to go around the ankle and lace with short, soft thongs at the back. These bands are worn just above the anklebones, which help to keep them in place. They can also be made of soft, colored leather and may be decorated with short tufts of white or colored hair sewn onto the band at about 1½-inch intervals. They may also be beaded or decorated with tufts of imitation Angora wool, or the entire anklet can be made of this wool, sewn to and hanging down from the band just above the ankle so as to reach the top of the moccasin. This type of anklet is known as a fetlock, named after the long hairs on the back of horses' legs just above their hooves. The wool can be worn in its natural color and looks well undyed, or it can be dyed red or some other color.

Dancers, of course, usually wear belled anklets to accentuate the rhythm of the dance.

There was an almost endless variety in anklets, not only of material and design but also of noise-making devices. In earlier days, when metal bells were unknown to Indians, dancers wore anklets of dewclaws, like those illustrated. Dewclaws are small, purposeless claws found above the actual deer hooves. These claws rattled together as the brave danced. Many other sorts of rattles and jangles were devised by Indian dancers and attached to their dance anklet bands.

GARTERS

Wrap-around garters, often made of brightly colored yarns, were frequently worn by Indians of the United States. Plains tribes used thirty to fifty strands of thick varicolored yarns, each strand measuring from 24 to 40 inches. These strands, in bundles of equal length, were tied together in three or four places, leaving about

6 inches of the garter hanging loose at each end to hang down in front of or on the outside of the leg, according to how the garter was tied. Some of the Woodlands tribes used a beaded strip of buckskin or cloth about 3 inches wide, with tassels of brightly colored yarn at each end. These garters were worn just below the knee, either on the bare leg—when only breechclouts were worn—or tied around leggings. Bells were never attached to such wrap-around garters, but some tribes used small, 3-inch long feathers suspended from the bands so that the feathers dangled in front of the legs.

The men of the Pueblos, especially dancers, also wore garters of various sorts, frequentlly strips of woven cloth or buckskin which were tied just below the knees so that the ends hung down on the outsides of the legs.

BUSTLES (CROWS) AND ROSETTES

The Indians of some Plains tribes who had earned high battle honors were allowed to wear the decoration known among them as a "crow." The chosen dog soldiers wore crows as official badges of office on important ceremonial occasions. They had earned their crows the hard way; and it was from the ranks of those who had the right to wear them that the tribal police, often known as "dog soldiers," were chosen.

Though these warriors wore their bustles at some ceremonial dances, to think of a crow as a "dance bustle"

ARM BUSTLE

DANCE BUSTLE

WRIST ROSETTE

cheapens that splendid decoration for prowess. The highly ornamental bustle, which used to be made from an entire eagle and crow skins, lavishly decorated with feathers from "birds of the battlefield," has become flashy and entirely devoid of symbolism. An overly bebustled brave, even a dancer, looks more comic than warlike, loaded down with his bustles and rosettes.

There are a number of books which describe the making of bustles in great detail, so it is sufficient to state here that bustles may be either oblong or round in shape, and usually have two trailers, called "trails," one on each side of the centerpiece. They are suspended just below the small of the back by a colored cloth sash. All three bustles shown in the drawings, including the little wrist rosette, are made from feathers. A miniature mirror, or circle of highly polished tin, usually winks from the centerpiece of the "dance" bustle, shown in the center sketch. The smaller rosette, also worn at times on the front and sides of some war bonnets, is often made from beads worked on cloth or leather. It is not too difficult to make any of the three bustles shown in the drawings by using a circle, or tube for the oblong ones, of strong cardboard for a foundation and sewing or tying the feathers onto it. The big bustle for the back can measure anywhere from 24 to 36 inches in diameter. The arm bustle, usually worn above the elbow, measures from around 8 to 15 inches in diameter. The rosette type has a diameter from about 2½ to 6 inches, according to whether it is worn on the back of the wrist or on a headdress. Judging by the size of bustles worn by some council fire dancers these days, one is tempted to write, after mentioning maximum size —and up.

So many magnificent decorations of various kinds can be made and worn with Indian regalia that the best advice on the subject of bustles is not to unduly stress that much-abused ornament and to leave the wearing of it to dancers, unless a council fire group really wishes to study

and emulate the bustle-wearers of the Omaha and their prized crows, which only the bravest of the brave could wear.

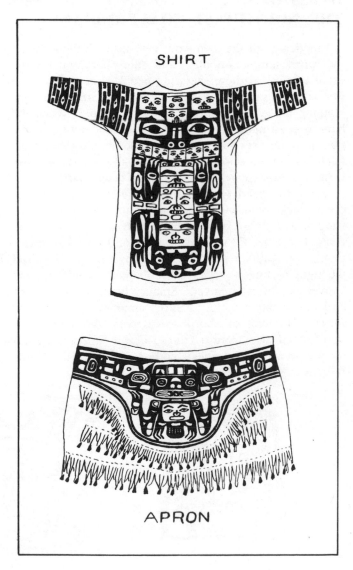

SHIRT

APRON

HAT

EAGLE   MASK

DRESS OF
THE NORTHWEST COAST INDIANS

Practically all the men wore very little clothing during the warm summer months, and going barefoot was the usual custom of these seafaring peoples. Because of the rain and dampness of the climate during part of the year, clothing made from cedar bark was favored. When the bark was stripped from the tree and well pounded, the fiber became very soft and made fine clothing and blankets. During the rainy season nearly all the coastal tribes wore a simple poncho woven from cedar bark, with a hole for the head to pass through. Elaborate blankets, often black, blue, yellow, or green, decorated with long fringes, were worn by the chiefs, nobles, and some warriors. These beautiful blankets were of Tsimshian origin, though the Chilkat group of the Tlingit people acquired the right to finger-weave these blankets, which became known as Chilkat blankets. Smaller blankets were worn as dance blankets. Colorful shirts, sometimes called dance shirts, with long or short sleeves were worn by some tribes. Men also wore a fringed apron fastened around the waist, which resembled the breechclout of the Plains Indians to some extent.

Headdresses and masks with movable parts, which covered the entire head and face, were frequently worn by chiefs, shamans, and performers at ceremonies. These masks were often made to resemble animals or birds, and the eyes rolled or the beaks opened when a string was pulled by the wearer. Headdresses were often made from a wood plaque, carved and colored, and worn in front of the brow, with sea lion bristles and a few flicker feathers sticking up in front. Weasel skins hung down to the wearer's shoulders from the sides and back of the plaque. When attending potlaches and other important ceremonies, wealthy men wore such headdresses with the family crest carved on the plaque. Feathers were little used as head decorations. The Bella Coola and a few other tribes sometimes stuck from two to six feathers in their hair, but the feathers were not worn in the form of a regular headdress. The boys of many tribes stuck feathers in their hair. While the men of some tribes wore their hair long, others cut it a little shorter than shoulder length and either wore it in a knob on the top of the head or held it clear of their eyes with a colored headband.

LEGGINGS

Leggings were worn by a number of tribes. They fitted below the knee and reached to the ankle. They were usually colorful and contrasted strangely with the bare feet which often showed below them. Moccasins were occasionally worn with leggings by some of the northern tribes. Some tribes wore collars, bracelets, and anklets made from or decorated with abalone shells, soft copper, and sea lion bristles.

War or ceremonial paint may be worn on the face and body, if desired. The Indians of the Northwest Coast were real artists when it came to painting themselves, and elaborate and startling effects were obtained by the use of simple colors. Water colors are suggested for modern warriors, as they wash off easily, though grease paints may also be used effectively.

HAT

Big hats made from spruce roots, as shown in the drawings, were generally worn throughout the rainy season and also when fishing, whaling, or attending ceremonies. Loose cloaks of red or yellow cedar bark were worn during the winter months. These cloaks were generally tied on around the shoulders, leaving the arms free for action. The chiefs and the richer people decorated the cloaks with borders of sea otter or other valuable skins. Most tribes wore colorful belts which held their clothing in place. A number of tribes painted their faces very cleverly on special occasions; others, like the Haida, had faces, hands, and bodies elaborately tattooed.

The clothing described is varied enough to leave considerable scope for the dress worn by modern warriors-in-council. The easiest form of regalia can be the fringed dance apron of leather or cloth painted and decorated with colors such as red, yellow, black, green, white, or blue. A gay blanket, leggings and simple moccasins, or moccasins, only, and a colorful headband with a few feathers tucked into it if the owner wishes, complete the costume.

ROBE

Colorful robes, made and designed like the ones shown, can be made either from imitation buckskin or red or blue cloth.

CHILKAT   BLANKET

ROBE

Masks, with or without moving parts, can be worn at times by chiefs, shamans, dancers, and other performers at the council fire. Eagle, hawk, or animal masks made so that the birds open and close their beaks and the animals their mouths are very effective.

GIRLS' INDIAN COSTUMES

Because so many groups of council fire maidens have chosen the Plains or Woodlands as their habitat, the costumes for these two groups are given in more detail than those from other tribal habitats, though the costumes for practically all other groups throughout the United States and Canada are also illustrated.

The drawings of the Plains dress give a clear idea of what the well-dressed Plains girl can wear at council fires. Girls have a much easier time than boys when it comes to making colorful Indian dress. Most girls can sew and do some rough pattern cutting, which helps a great deal when assembling a complete Indian outfit.

PLAINS DRESS. The costumes shown in the drawings are decorative and easily made. The dresses can be made from closely woven cotton cloth, calico, for instance. Before cutting the material, a pattern should be made from newspaper and fitted for size. An old sport dress

can be placed on the newspaper as a guide, since the Indian garments were not tight-fitting. The front and back of the dresses are cut exactly alike, but the back does not have to be decorated. The designs should be sketched on the material after the garments are made, and then colored with paints or crayons. When wax crayons are used, the material should be ironed with a fairly hot iron on the reverse side in order to fix the crayon color in the cloth. There are a number of excellent textile paints on the market when one wishes to make a fine dress which will serve for several council fire seasons.

The poncho-style dress can be made from the same weight material as that used for the regular dress. Again, a pattern should be cut from newspaper, and an old skirt can be used as a guide for the skirt part of the costume. To make the poncho, measure from the shoulder to just below the waist and then double the material, so that there is the same amount both in back and front. Now exactly in the center of the fold cut a crosswise slit about 6 inches long, with another, downward slit about 3 inches long running from the center of the cross slit. This is for the head to go through, and the slits should be cut out a little to fit the neck comfortably. Care must be taken that the decorations and motifs used copy those used by Plains women. The skirt is wrapped around the waist, and the belt tied at the side, the fringe turned down over the belt.

Girls with long hair can dress it in two braids, tied at the ends with brightly colored ribbons. The headband can

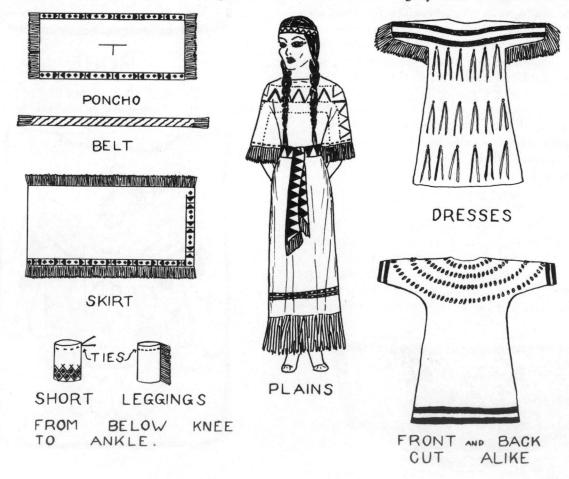

PONCHO

BELT

SKIRT

SHORT LEGGINGS
FROM BELOW KNEE
TO ANKLE.

TIES

PLAINS

DRESSES

FRONT AND BACK
CUT ALIKE

FRONT

HEADBAND

BACK   WOODLAND

DRESSES

BOTH   SIDES   ALIKE

be of plain, colored cloth with a design painted on it, or it may be beaded. The short leggings, reaching from just below the knee to the ankle, can be made of heavy cotton cloth decorated and fringed on the outside, or they can be made without fringes. The moccasins can be made as described under boys' Indian dress. Colorful necklaces can be worn if they add to the appearance of the costume chosen. Many girls' camps have council fires once a week, and some of the girls have made beautiful and elaborate costumes for these occasions, using real buckskin or suede.

WOODLAND DRESS. The Woodland costumes can be cut out in the way described for the women's dress of the tribes of the Plains. They too can be made of heavy cotton cloth, and the back and front of the dresses are cut alike. Though many of the Woodland women decorated their dresses with elaborate beadwork, usually using dark beads on a light background, a considerable number of their costumes had painted designs instead. Paint, bead, and porcupine-quill designs were sometimes combined on the elaborate ceremonial costumes.

The headband, as shown in the drawing, is more elaborate than that of the Plains. The women of the Woodland sometimes wore a number of silver, glass, wood, or other beads. The moccasins, which were painted or beaded,

ZUNI   NAVAJO

and a brightly decorated belt. Favorite colors among them are green, yellow, and red. They are fond of large ornaments made of silver—and their interesting necklaces in silver represent the pomegranate, and not the squash blossom, as is generally believed by Pueblo visitors. The Zuni girls have worn their hand-woven dark dresses since long before Columbus arrived, and they are just as popular now as then. The women still wear their shoulder-length hair straight. Head scarves and blankets have reached them through the traders, and those who are not tradition-minded have adopted them for everyday wear. Blankets, when worn, are draped over the head and shoulders like a shawl. The easiest way to imitate the white footwear and leg covering of the Zuni girls is to wear white sneakers and then wrap them over with strips of strong 3-inch-wide white cloth, continuing to just below the knee, where they may be held in place by a garter.

The Hopi girls dress very much the same as do their Zuni neighbors.

The Navaho costume can also be made of cotton cloth, in light shades of red, blue, yellow, or green. The blouse has long puffed sleeves. The skirt is a dirndl type, ankle-length, trimmed with a band of bright ribbon near the hem. A considerable amount of silver and turquoise jewelry is worn. The boots, reaching to above the ankles, can be made of heavy brown cotton cloth buttoned at the outer seam with "silver" buttons. Store blankets in gay colors and with long fringes have become popular with Navaho girls.

were similar to those worn by the men, and short leggings were often worn. These were beaded, and tied just below the knee.

GIRLS' INDIAN DRESS OF THE SOUTHWEST.
The Zuni costume can be made of black cotton cloth decorated with a band or two of bright ribbons near the hem

GIRLS' INDIAN DRESS OF THE SOUTHEAST.
The Seminole costume is pictured to give a clear idea of the sort of dress favored by these people. The costume is made from a light-colored cloth such as cotton, and the gay-colored stripes can be painted onto the cloth or they can be appliquéd. The dress background can be of cream color or pale yellow, and the stripes in varied colors of red, blue, green, and black. The woman's dress, as will be seen from the drawing, is very long; but it can be made shorter to allow more leg freedom for the council fire activities, when a high-topped moccasin laced on one side with a thong can be worn.

GIRLS' INDIAN DRESS OF THE NORTHWEST COAST.
Though the dress of the princesses of these clans was elaborate and resembled, to some extent, the clothing worn by the men, the dress of the other women and girls of these peoples was comparatively simple and easy to make. Bright colors can be used in making these costumes, and almost any rough cloth or blanket material can be made into serviceable dresses. The costumes illustrated are of the sort which were usually worn by the women of the Northwest Coast.

PRINCESS   MAIDEN

236

council fire ceremonies and programs

THERE ARE MANY SIDES to a council fire ceremonial program, from the solemn ceremonious preparation for the fire-lighting ceremony to the impressive closing ceremony which terminates the council fire. Apart from these two ceremonial acts, the other ceremonies can be both grave and gay, combining spectacular feats, challenges, song and dance, colorful pageantry, medicine men's magic, and the merrymaker's laugh-provoking "magic."

This cairn, forty miles west of Calgary, was erected as a tribute to the Red Man.

back. The drawstring is brought around and tied in front of the bag, holding the two halves in place. A belt can be passed through the fold, so the bag can be worn at the warrior's side.

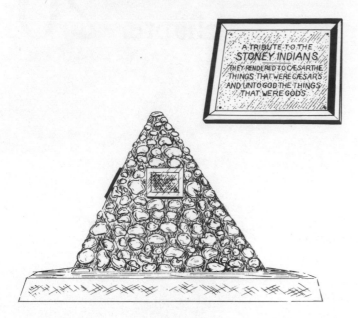

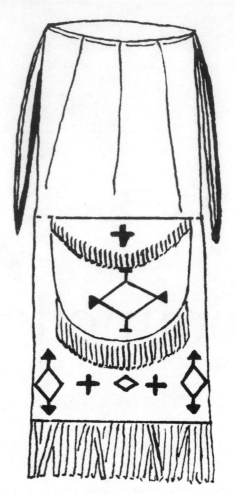

PARFLECHE TINDER BAG AND PEACE PIPE POUCH

Many tribes of various habitats used decorative tinder bags in which to carry their precious fire-lighting equipment of different sorts and tinder. When the council fire Indian of today uses flint and steel with which to ignite the tinder, the bag can be small, measuring about 6 or 8 inches long and 6 inches high. When a bow drill is used for fire lighting, the bag has to be considerably longer to accommodate the bow, fire board, drill, and socket. This fire-lighting gear will require a bag 24 inches long, plus a 6-inch fringe flap to fold over the top of the pouch. The width of this pouch can range from 8 to 12 inches.

These pouches can be made of rawhide, regular leather, suede, or heavy cloth decorated with painted designs or beaded, in addition to being fringed. It is equally handy for Plains, Woodland, Northwest Coast, or other tribes of council fire Indians. Care has to be taken that the habitat designs be correct, unless a warrior wishes to decorate his bag with an original design to identify it as his property.

The bag shown in the drawing is of Plains design. It is 24 inches long and 10 inches wide, fitted with a drawstring at the opening. A pocket with a fringed flap is sewn onto it about halfway down. It can be used as a long or short bag to suit the type of fire-lighting equipment carried. When used as a long bag to carry the bow drill or the pipe for the peace pipe fire-lighting ceremony, it is carried by the drawstring. For carrying smaller articles, the bag is folded in half with the top half doubled over toward the

PEACE PIPE COUNCIL FIRE OPENING CEREMONY

There are a number of council fire opening ceremonies based on the use of the peace pipe. A handsomely decorated calumet, such as one of those illustrated, is used in the ceremony. The pipe may be ceremoniously carried, in an artistic pipe bag or naked, held out at arm's length in both hands with the arms directly in front of the body. The pipe or pipe bag rests on the palms of both hands of the council fire chief or medicine man who carries it to the fire. The pipe may also be brought to the council fire by the keeper of the peace pipe on the call of the chief. The pipe used for the ceremony may actually function or may be an ornamental one, in which case the smoke-blowing is carried out in pantomime or the stem of the pipe may be pointed in the directions mentioned.

The simplest form of peace pipe ceremony, which is usually performed at the opening of the council fire, may be carried out in this way. The chief either points the stem of the pipe or blows a puff of smoke toward the sky, Lodge of the Great Spirit, then a puff toward the earth, Mother and Giver of Food, after which the four (sacred number) puffs are wafted toward the Spirits of the Winds at the four cardinal points, usually in the following sequence: East, South, West, and North. Some tribes change this honor sequence, depending on the tribal habitat. This is a matter for the council fire chief to decide—because the Pawnee, for instance, and some other Plains tribes carry out the puff-blowing in this order: West, North, East, and South.

The chief, smoker of the ceremonial pipe, says: "Sky, to you I smoke as an offering for many good things which you have sent us. Earth, to you I smoke for your many good gifts. East, to you this offering is made that the sun may return to us when darkness is gone to make place for light. South, our offering is made that your warm breath may comfort us after the cold of the night. West, to you I smoke as the sleeping place of the sun and for your sky colors. North, to you this smoke offering goes up that your keen wind-knives harm us not when you make the painted leaves dance and when the snow-blanket covers the earth. I have spoken."

FIRE-FROM-THE-SUN CEREMONY

The Fire-from-the-Sun ritual may be made longer and more elaborate when desired, but it is not advisable to let it take up more than five minutes. This advice applies to all such ceremonies, for the braves are eager to see the fire burst into flame and the more active program begin.

When the braves have taken their seats in council, the chief and medicine man stand by the unlit fire, facing west. A runner and the fire tender stand close beside them.

THE CHIEF (raising both arms skyward with the palms up). O Sun, dweller high above the Thunderbird, hear our prayer. Before the flap of your teepee closes and leaves us in darkness, give us of your fire, that its smoke may rise with that of our fire to Wakonda the Great Spirit. (*The Chief then hands the runner a torch about*

2 feet long. The torch is made of dark wood, so that a 3-inch strip of dark absorbent cloth, saturated in melted paraffin wax and wrapped around one end of the torch, is almost invisible.)

THE CHIEF. Runner, speed swiftly to the West and bring us fire.

RUNNER. As a deer from a wolf will I run, O Chief. (*He speeds toward the West. When he is just out of sight of the council ring, he lights the torch, waits until it is well alight, then runs speedily back to the chief—holding the torch far ahead of him as though he fears its fire. As the chief sees the runner approach, he signals to all braves-in-council to stand. The chief then takes the torch, kneels, and thrusts its blazing end between the logs into the heart of the fire, where it ignites the tinder. He leaves the torch in the fire, and as the fire flames and smoke rises, he raises his arms skyward, as does the medicine man.*)

THE CHIEF. O Great Spirit, as the flames of our council fire leap upward toward thee and its smoke carries the fire mystery to the greater mystery which is thine, be with us now. Protect us from the fury of the winds, the darkness of the forest and the wiles of our enemies. Let thy wisdom be with us tonight as we sit in council—this is our prayer.

GULL WING
COUNCIL-FIRE-LIGHTING CEREMONY

This brief ceremony, which is carried out just before the council fire is lit, is one which can be used by any council fire group organized along Woodland lines. It is especially suited for any group of the Six Nations. This is how the ceremony is performed.

After the braves have filed into the council ring, they stand at the places where they will sit during the council fire and remain there while the council fire chief, other chiefs, and the medicine man stand in front of the unlit fire. Since the Iroquoian tribes carried out the ceremony prior to building the new council fire, the following adaptation is only symbolic, as the fire is ready to light.

The council fire chief solemnly declares: "With this sea-gull wing I do as Hiawatha did, dust the place of the old fire. See, I scatter the ash and embers of our last council fire, that this new fire may burn bright and shine in our hearts. I have spoken."

After he has said these words, the fire is immediately lit by the method decided upon for that evening. It might be good medicine to have it lit upon this occasion by an Onondaga, the tribe which was traditionally keeper of the fire.

In this ceremony, as in many others, the council fire chief can use his initiative so that even if his group is one composed of Plains tribes, he can arrange for a Woodland chief—correctly dressed—to light the fire.

COUNCIL FIRE INVOCATIONS

These little Fire Prayers may suggest the rhythm and pattern of the Pueblo people, although actually they are not Pueblo. They have been set down for use as the fire is being lighted by any habitat group, Plains or Woodland.

Thy flames will be bright; may they burn bright in
  our hearts,
In our hearts may the flames of friendship burn bright.

May this fire burn in beauty; in beauty may it burn.
In our hearts may this fire shine in beauty;
In beauty may this fire shine in our hearts.

May good medicine thoughts come with this fire;
When the Dawn Star looks over the edge of the world,
When the ashes of this council fire are cold,
May the friendship in our hearts still be warm.

EAGLE FEATHER FIRE OFFERING

For use by Plains council fire groups with some form of "magic" fire-lighting ceremony.

O Great Spirit above, send us fire.
Fire for life, fire for light,
Fire for peace and friendship.

Then, after the fire comes:

We give thanks for this precious flame
And as our fire smoke rises to thy tepee
May it serve as a trail between us.
See! to the flames I sacrifice this eagle feather;
It is offered humbly as a sign of our thanks.

COUP POLE CEREMONY

A simple but effective way of having Plains council fire braves count coup can be carried out in this way. When the time arrives for counting coup and feather claiming, the council fire chief gives a prearranged signal, and a chief and two older braves carry a coup pole into the ring. This pole is 7 feet long and tapers from about 6 inches at the top to 3 inches at its pointed end. It is painted bright red, and 2-inch-wide yellow rings can be painted around it at 8-inch intervals from the top to halfway down the pole. It is driven firmly into the ground a few feet to one side of the chief's chair.

The chief, two subchiefs, and a medicine man take up positions on either side of the pole. The chief carries a coup stick 4 feet long with a 2-foot length of scarlet flannel 2 inches wide tied onto it, so that it hangs down, as shown in the feathered coup stick in the drawing. The chief's coup stick has no feathers attached. The medicine man carries a number of long white goose feathers with the tops dyed a brownish black to resemble eagle feathers. The braves who intend to claim coup feathers for some exploits performed since the last council fire are formed into a line on the opposite side of the council fire, facing the coup pole. On a signal from a chief standing just in front of the braves claiming coup feathers, a warrior from the right of the line runs swiftly around the fire and stops a few feet in front of the coup pole. The council fire chief hands him the coup stick, saying as he does so, "It is said that you come to count coup. Take this coup stick, strike the pole with it, and tell the chiefs and braves-in-council what you have done to make claim of a coup feather. Let your coup-counting words be short and your voice loud, that all may hear."

The brave who is making the claim steps forward and strikes the pole sharply with the coup stick, then turns and briefly proclaims the exploit for which he hopes to earn a coup feather. His chief joins the council fire chief and medicine man, and the three confer and make the decision as to whether the feat declared deserves an honor feather. Since the brave's chief knows in advance what the claim will be and has told the council fire chief of it prior to the council fire, it takes only a few moments to make the decision which follows the claim. The decision is nearly always favorable, because the chiefs have

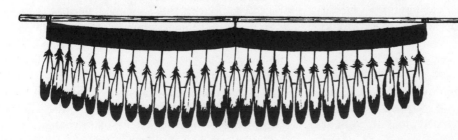

asked the braves whom they considered had insufficient reason to claim a feather to wait until the next council fire burns.

It is perhaps wise to withhold one feather in about every four claimed, because the brave has shown nervousness in making the claim, has not made his reason for claiming the exploit feather quite clear, or has not been sufficiently emphatic in stating his claim. The chief's refusal to grant every feather claimed stresses the fact that coup feathers are not easily come by. This makes a strong impression on the braves-in-council who will make claims for coup feathers at future fires. When the council fire chief withholds an exploit feather, he points out just why it had been denied but tells the claimant that he may make a similar claim the next time the council fire burns.

The feathers earned may either be presented after the feather claiming, or the presentation can be made at the next council fire, as decided by the chief.

WOOD-LAND ROACH

COUP AWARDS OF THE NORTHWEST COAST

Although there were no actual "counting coup" ceremonies or coup feather awards among the tribes of the Northwest Coast, warriors were given the opportunity to declare their successes in war or peace at a council fire, as were the Plains Indians. Warriors who had been selected beforehand by their clan chiefs were called by the tribal chief to come to his chair. Each warrior then declared the act or acts which he had performed that he thought were worthy of notice by the chiefs and warriors-in-council.

A warrior might begin his declaration by saying: "I, Little Wolf, when the sun was high two suns ago, did find deep in the forest a big cave in which many warriors can camp. Because it has not before been found by the warriors of our tribes, I claim the right to be known as the one who found the cave which was unknown to others."

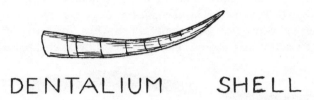

DENTALIUM SHELL

Should the tribal chief, after inquiries in council, find that Little Wolf was actually the first to discover the cave, he praises the warrior, comments on how every warrior should keep his eyes wide open when in the forest and elsewhere, and decides that Little Wolf will be awarded a dentalium shell to fasten to his copper as a record and reward for his discovery. Imitation dentalium shells, which were prized by the tribes of the Northwest Pacific Coast, look like miniature elephant tusks, as the drawing shows. They are about 1 to 1½ inches long, and replicas of them can easily be made from wood by the arts and crafts people. These shells can replace the coup feathers of the Plains tribes. They can be awarded by tribal chiefs to individuals or clans for special feats of courage, strength, endurance, ability, storytelling, or achievement in sports. The shells may be colored, and a red shell can be awarded for a major coup, blue for a lesser coup, and yellow for a minor coup. These awards can either be mounted on the warrior's personal copper or added to the coup shells on his clan's copper.

A really important event in which an entire clan participated can be pictured on the clan's totem pole, when considered of sufficient importance to merit that honor.

GIFT OF DANCE AND SONG CEREMONY

The council fire chief or the medicine man tells the warriors-in-council that two chiefs, or a group of warriors, from the powerful Haida of the Northwest Coast will attend the council fire in order to present their brothers of the Plains, or Woodland, with a dance and/or song. He explains that such a gift has great value throughout the vast Northwest Coast Territory and that once it has been bestowed it can never be taken back, nor can that same gift be given to another tribe. He says that the tribe, or tribes, in council have little of equal value to offer their brothers from the Coast. They can give beaver pelts, which have far less value than those of the sea otter of the Coast, or blankets, which have little value when compared with the magnificent Chilkat blankets of their Coastal brothers. The gifts of a dance and song which the visitors bring are living things; a part of their creators have gone magically into them. What, he asks the warriors-in-council, can they offer in return?

A chief or warrior, who has been given suitable suggestions in advance by the council fire chief, rises and says that this thing or that thing might be a worthy gift to make in return. The council fire chief and his counselors may decide on a really worthwhile present within their scope and means. The warriors show their approval

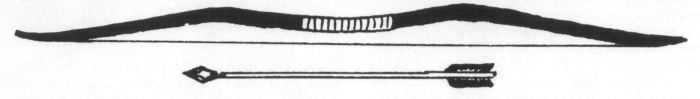

of one or more of the suggestions made by "he who stands in council" by giving the usual "How! How!" or "Ho! Ho!" of assent. Soon after a suitable gift, or gifts, has been decided on and placed beside the chief's chair, the visitors arrive.

The leader of the Coastal visitors greets the assembled chiefs and braves and tells them that though their visit will be "brief as the fall of a leaf," they will leave something with their brothers that may be passed down through "moons too many to count." After the visitors have been welcomed by the council fire chief, and perhaps another chief or medicine man, the Haida, either in a group or as a solo number, present their dance and their song by slowly and carefully dancing the steps of the dance. A dancer from the tribe which is being visited, on an order from the council fire chief, follows the visiting dancer through the steps, when the dance is being performed for the second time, in a painstaking manner. Every step, the onlookers feel, must be exactly right. After this, he performs the dance alone, to the loud "Hows!" of approval from the visitors. (A little practice prior to the council fire will make a good dancer

step-perfect.) Following the gift dance, a singer, or singers, from the group of visitors sings the two- or three-verse song. Some thought and work on the part of the council fire chief and his counselors will provide a striking song, which can be sung in English if necessary, but with Indian phrasing. A singer or singers from the tribe receiving the visit will first follow the song along with the visitors, when it has been sung for the second or third time, and then sing it alone.

After the dance and song have been performed and accepted, the council fire chief presents the visiting Haida with the gift the council has decided on.

When the visitors leave, either following the presentation or at the close of the council fire, they are given a brief farewell address by the council fire chief and leave amid the vociferous "Hows!" of the warriors-in-council.

MEET THE OTHER INDIANS

Just as "one half of the world does not know how the other half lives," so it is with many tribes of modern council fire Indians today. Observation reveals that too many tribes do not even know how "the other" three-fourths lived. This is not unreasonable when one considers that the organization to which they belong has been built on a one-tribe or one-nation basis. Pride of tribe, and at times a not-too-certain source of even finding authentic information about the tribe to which they belong, have proved barriers to expanding their general knowledge of the Indians of the Americas and their many and interesting ways of life. This is unfortunate, because an over-all picture of the Indians of the United States and Canada is of value to modern council fire Indians.

Here is a way to impart such knowledge which is easy to carry out. Usually, a council fire chief will find that some of his subordinate chiefs have considerable authentic information concerning other tribes of other habitats, but because these chiefs work as part of a Plains or Woodland tribe council fire group, they have little or no opportunity to put such knowledge into practice. These chiefs will prove of great help in introducing an extended Indian program. By having them interpret a dance, story, or custom of another tribe of a distant habitat at the council fire from time to time, a big step in the right direction will have been made. Such interludes must be interesting, entertaining, and comparatively brief. Of course, little detailed instruction along the line of arts and crafts of other tribes can be given during a five- or ten-minute period, but there are many ideas that can be adopted to advantage. They will change the pace and add interest to the regular council fire program. Some suggestions follow.

TRIBE IDENTIFICATION.   A chief can wear an authentic, though camp-made, costume of some distant tribe and be introduced by the council fire chief at some point in the council fire program. The "visitor" briefly explains various points concerning his clothing and weapons and tells why they are suitable for the habitat in which he lives and hunts. He can also point out similarities in clothes and weapons to show that there are common bonds among all tribes.

CHALLENGE.   A chief may bring a challenge which is new to the warriors-in-council, from another tribe. He may wear the costume of the tribe from which the challenge comes, or he may demonstrate the challenge while wearing his usual council fire dress. There are many distinctive Indian challenges, forty different ones being given in this book.

DANCE.   A chief brings a new dance of another tribe to his council fire. He demonstrates the steps—there should not be more than three—slowly and carefully, shows them to a good dancer chosen by the council fire chief from among the warriors-in-council, and then performs the steps once again while the chosen warrior dances them at the same time. A little private practice sometime before council fire will be helpful.

SONG.   A "visiting" chief sings a new song, one of only two or three verses, and then "teaches" it to one of the singers in the council fire group. Of course, the singer chosen to learn the song has had the chance to practice it secretly in advance, though he follows the words and tune of the gift song, after it has been sung twice by the donor, as though hearing it for the first time.

SAND PAINTING.   This demonstration is most effective when the chief performing the ceremony is clad in the simple costume of the Navaho, who were renowned for their splendid sand paintings. The Navaho can wear blue jeans, a dark shirt, bright headband, and gay belt. The visiting Navaho tells the warriors: "Night has come, but when the sun was above me I made a sand picture.

That picture I made disappear before the sun left to make way for the moon, for so it is commanded. So must such painting be made. Now, for the short time that it takes to sing our 'Walking Song,' I have asked the Rainbow People to let me make a little sand picture." Here he kneels down before a large square or circle of dark-colored cloth, between 3 and 4 feet in diameter, which has been stapled or pegged to the ground close to and on one side of the fire. This cloth blends with the ground and is invisible to the warriors-in-council. The Navaho takes colored "sand" from a bag with two or three pockets sewn inside it and makes a large, simple design on the cloth. He does this by letting colored powder trickle from between his forefinger and palm onto a design which has been clearly, but from a distance not noticeably, drawn on the cloth before it was stapled in place.

If real sand of distinct colors is available, that is by far the best means of making the painting, but should none be available there are good substitutes. A white sand substitute may be made from white sawdust, which will trickle better than salt or flour and is not wasteful. Yellow sawdust can replace yellow sand, and perhaps charcoal which is not too finely pulverized is the best substitute for black sand. Black and white are the two most effective colors from the standpoint of visibility when the painting is done in only two colors. For more ambitious sand paintings, when time is available, additional colors can be made by tinting not-too-fine sawdust with inexpensive tints or dyes, which can be bought at five and ten cent stores. The sawdust must be thoroughly dried before being used. Colored rocks which are soft enough to grind into powder, under the strokes of a hammer, are found around some camps. A few trial strokes should be given such rocks, which are first covered with a piece of stout canvas in order to be certain that the rock will not splinter and cause damage to the eyes. Such rock powder is effective and easy to use.

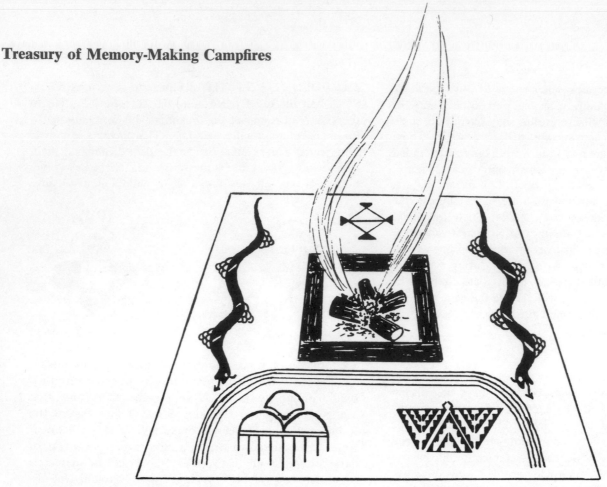

The two simple designs shown here can be made in two colors, black and white, and can be done quite quickly. The first design illustrates the morning star, the second a turtle. There are many other suitable and simple designs to choose from.

When the visiting Navaho has completed the sand painting and all the warriors have had a chance to see it well, the sand painter obliterates the design entirely, by stroking the sand with gentle sweeps of his hands into or toward the fire.

"In beauty was it begun; in beauty does it end," he chants as he removes all traces of his work.

One big drawback of a real sand painting or sand paintings used as decoration in the council ring on special occasions is the fact that they take up room which may be required for other activities. The second disadvantage is that it is a great pity to walk or run on a sand painting, which is really a medicine picture, so that even a portion of it is obliterated. About the only way to avoid this is to use four strips of heavy white canvas or very heavy cotton ranging from 3 to 4 feet wide, according to the width in which the material is sold. If the canvas is 4 feet wide, two of the strips must be 12 feet long, and the remaining two need be only 5 feet long. Should the material be only 3 feet wide, then two of the strips should be 10 feet long and the remaining two strips 5 feet long. The two longer strips are laid opposite each other, one on each of two sides of the fire frame. The two shorter strips are laid at the other two sides of the frame, and there will be a 6-inch overlap at each end

of these short strips where they touch the longer strips. The ends are tucked under the two long strips and securely sewn in place.

When finished, the effect is as shown in the drawing, after the desired design has been painted in colorful shades on the canvas. Black, dark reds, blues, and greens show up well on the white background. A fireproof solution can be bought and sprayed on the canvas so that chance sparks will not set it smouldering, but with a good fire tender there is little chance that the canvas will be burned, since it is on ground level and protected by the fire frame. Should the fire burn on the raised square of ground, as suggested in Chapter 1, there is even less chance of the "sand painting" being scorched. Such a painting looks very well in the firelight and resembles a real sand painting closely. Much of it can be seen from all sides of the council fire area.

Four warriors should put the painting in place before the fire is lit, stapling it securely to the ground at the points shown in the drawing, with the camp-made staples described in Chapter 6. These four braves can also, when desired, *swiftly* remove the painting from its position around the fire frame, even while the fire is burning brightly, by first removing all the staples and then rolling and quickly lifting and removing the canvas to one side of the fire, where the rolling is completed and the canvas taken from the council ring. It will be noted that only one side need be lifted above the fire while the canvas is being removed.

These various ways of meeting "visiting" braves from

some of the other tribes are mere suggestions, which can be amplified by council fire chiefs in their search for more varied and authentic Indian programs.

THE INDIAN MERRYMAKER

Though the council ring was always respected and as a rule used only for council fires of a serious nature, an exception was made and a gay note struck from time to time. At such times women of the tribes and visitors received the invitation sticks, and fun reigned around the council fire.

The chief cause and promoter of the fun was the tribal merrymaker. Too little is known of this clever and cheerful fellow, who in days gone by was recognized, respected, and appreciated as a sort of official jester.

THE MERRYMAKER'S AUCTION

One of the merrymaker's many amusing feats was to trade in the council ring, on the night when he held sway, some comparatively worthless object for one of considerable value. He might, for instance, trade a reed flute which he had made with little trouble for a valuable blanket or a buffalo robe. He performed his astonishing feats entirely by his witty words, amusing antics, and profound psychology. He would assure the assembled people that when his flute was played with unusual skill, the wildest creatures could be literally lured from the forest depths to dance rapturously to the tunes tootled by the owner of the flute. Bears and wolves would become as harmless as mice when they heard the strains of the flute. The merrymaker would at this point give realistic imitations of bear, wolves, deer, and even skunks dancing happily to the magic music. Without the flute—here he would give a grotesque and very funny pantomime of a weary and clumsy hunter engaged in a fruitless chase— the hunter would get his fingers caught in his moccasin, headband, and bowstring and end up sitting on the business end of one of his hunting arrows. As the audience roared and rolled in the aisles of the forest at his ludicrous antics, he would suddenly bring them to their feet with the offer of his wonderful flute in trade for something else, of great value. Almost immediately he would be offered a fine bow and arrows, a buckskin robe, or beautifully beaded moccasins, all of which he would spurn. Then some chief or brave, under the subtle spell of the merrymaker's almost hypnotic suggestion, would eagerly offer a buffalo robe, a canoe, or even a horse, in exchange for the fabulous flute. Reluctantly the merrymaker would make the trade for the object of greatest value which pleased his fancy, and everyone was satisfied.

Strangely enough there were no complaints in the days or moons following such auctions, and on the very next occasion there would be just as many eager bidders ready to fall under the merrymaker's spell.

THE MERRYMAKER'S LOCO STICK

On a social council fire night, when women of the tribe are present, the chief invites three or four women and the same number of braves into the council ring and keeps them engaged in conversation for a minute or so. As they stand around in little groups, the merrymaker enters the ring. He is grotesquely attired and carries a gaily decorated ceremonial staff. He saunters nonchalantly around the ring and walks among the groups. The braves, and especially the women, in the groups apparently suddenly realize that the merrymaker is being closely followed by a huge, ferocious-looking rattlesnake. Red fangs hang from its open jaws, and it appears to lunge at some of the people in the ring as the merrymaker, swinging his ceremonial staff, comes close. Both braves and women jump away and then run out of the council ring. The merrymaker looks as though he is astonished by their actions and looks all around to see what is alarming them. He apparently sees nothing and strolls around the council ring, which gives everyone a better chance to see the big rattler which appears to be following him without his knowledge.

As the braves and women call out a warning, or point behind him, he looks back but only appears to be puzzled. He walks out of the council ring and returns, after a moment's absence, without staff or snake. He carries, held high above his head, his "loco stick," a short stick decorated at one end by a gaily colored magic tassel. He audibly tells the chief that some of the people appear to be seeing things and asks permission to give a few of them his loco stick test, to see if they are well balanced. The merrymaker then leads two of three of the subjects to a spot perfectly free from obstructions of any sort and as far as possible from the fire. He then asks the first victim to hold the loco stick by its end, raise it high above his head, fix his eyes on the magic tassel on the other end, and wait for the word "Spin!" On this signal he is told to whirl around eight times as rapidly as possible, in the same direction, while keeping his eyes fixed steadily on the tassel. He must then lay the loco stick on the ground in front of him and jump over it with his feet together.

The merrymaker, after his explanation, gives a partial demonstration of how the loco stick must be used; handing the stick back to the first subject, he says, "Spin!" The unfortunates who take this "test" are usually so giddy after the eighth speedy turn that they lay themselves on the ground as well as the stick. Having made his tests, the merrymaker gives each of the subjects who fails to pass the test a few wrapped candies to cure them of "seeing things," and they return to their places.

HOW TO MAKE THE RATTLESNAKE AND LOCO STICK. The rattlesnake can be made from a 6-foot length of heavy rope about 2 or 3 inches in diameter. It is covered with a greenish-brown tough cloth to represent the skin, and the cloth is securely fastened around the rope. A head with red fangs protruding from the mouth is attached to one end, and a tapering tail is made at the other end. The snake can be made as realistic as time allows and craftsmanship permits. Sometimes realism is carried to the point where a small round metal box with a few pieces of buckshot inside is fastened inside the snake's tail to produce a rattle.

The snake is attached by a 3-foot length of strong, thin black fishing line to the foot of the ceremonial staff. The merrymaker, by careful manipulation, can bring the snake very close to those in the council ring. He must be careful not to get the almost invisible fishing line entangled in their legs. With a little practice, he can make the snake perform tricks, such as coiling and striking.

The loco stick is easily made from a 7½-inch length of ½-inch-thick dowel stick, rounded at each end, with a tassel of bright cloth or strands of wool 1½-inches long securely fastened onto one end. The cloth is cut into narrow strips to give a tassel effect. The completed loco stick is pictured here.

THE MERRYMAKER'S MEDICINE

The merrymaker is in an even merrier mood than usual. The chief has consented that he try his skill as an amateur medicine man. The chief has warned him that he must limit his efforts to braves or women who require "cures" and leave such things as war, weather, and good hunting medicine strictly to the real medicine man. The merrymaker willingly agrees, and one by one women of the tribes and braves who require "treatment" advance into the council ring. The would-be medicine man opens his gay medicine bundle and prepares to perform.

He rubs some salve on the back of a brave who apparently has to walk in a doubled-over manner. In less than a minute, after a few preliminary efforts to straighten up, he is marching around the council ring as straight as a dog soldier. One woman is carried before the "medicine man" on a rough litter, which is laid on the ground. One of the four braves who have brought her for treatment explains that he is her husband and that she has been sick for one moon. She can, he says, neither stand up nor talk. He hints that he does not much care whether she can talk again or not, but he does want her to be able to walk, even if it is only slowly, and work. The medicine man gives her some liquid from a cup. Nothing happens for a moment or two; then with a loud yell she leaps from her litter, knocks over three of the braves who carried her in, hurls a few uncomplimentary remarks at top speed at her husband, rushes once around the council ring shouting, and rushes—still yelling—from the council ring. A brave from a distant tribe is led in by a companion. The patient has a very sad expression, and his friend explains that he has not been able to laugh, or even smile, for many, many moons. The medicine man does a few grotesque dance steps in front of the patient, who only looks sadder than ever. Then the medicine man reaches into his medicine bundle and pulls out what appears to be a rabbit's foot. He makes passes with it around the patient's head but without result. He then holds the charm under the sad one's chin. Instantly the solemn one lets out a roar of laughter which nearly sweeps the medicine man off his feet. The patient continues to shake with loud and lusty mirth until the chief commands that he be taken from the council ring. This is done, and his laughter is heard until it dies away in the distance.

Now an enormously fat woman, draped in a large blanket, is led into the council ring by a little thin man. He tells the medicine man that he is the fat woman's husband and that she eats him out of lodge and tepee. He fancifully describes her tremendous appetite and begs that she be "reduced"—fast—so that he will not have to hunt night and day for her and she will be able to get in and out of the tepee without knocking it down every time. The medicine man speaks to the fat woman, but she only chuckles deeply and says plaintively, "Heap hungry—when will buffalo herds come?" The medicine-man-for-a-night dives for his medicine bundle and takes out what looks like a big pink pill. He exhibits it to the braves-in-council and then pushes it into the woman's open mouth before she can get her hands out from under her blanket. With a loud gulp she apparently swallows the pill; then an amazing thing happens. Her enormous stomach appears to melt away before the eyes of the astonished braves-in-council and her delighted husband. He throws himself gratefully at the feet of the medicine man, then leads his now skinny wife from the council fire.

The chief then proclaims that the merrymaker medicine man has done well, and the merrymaker stalks from the council ring amid the "Hows" of the braves-in-council.

SOLUTION FOR THE MERRYMAKER'S MEDI-CINE. As will have been deduced, all the "cures" have been previously arranged by the chief, "medicine man," and "patients." Good actors should be chosen for the various roles of patients. The reducing process is assured with the aid of an old sawed-off umbrella. Most of the umbrella handle is cut off, leaving just enough for the patient to grasp firmly as the umbrella is closed and opened. The point is also sawed off close to the ribs, outside. The fat patient appears in the council ring with the umbrella opened under the blanket, the point facing out, and the short handle held horizontally against the stomach. The large, losely worn blanket—which should be securely fastened at the back of the neck and behind the back—completely hides the umbrella. The patient's hands are underneath the blanket, holding the umbrella. As it is closed, the point (what is left of it) is gradually tilted toward the chest. Thus when completely closed, the umbrella can be held vertically, close to the body, without a bulge being seen by the onlookers. A little practice on the part of the patient will create an almost perfect illusion. The large round pink and white pills are balls of candy.

COUNCIL FIRE CEREMONIAL PROGRAMS

The various ceremonies given in this chapter can be built into suitable programs, which will differ somewhat according to the Indian groups represented by the council fire group staging the program. The suggestions which follow are outlines of complete council fire programs, each of about one hour and thirty minutes duration. A council fire chief will see at a glance why the word "about" is used in connection with these programs. There will be activities and challenges which the braves-in-council will wish repeated, perhaps several times; so programs have to be flexible enough to allow the addition or deletion of several numbers without affecting the overall interest and enjoyment of a program.

Though the complete program outlines which follow are ones of general interest for the average council fire band of Indians, programs composed almost entirely of dance and song will prove popular, as a Dance-Song Fire, with groups which specialize in these arts. For the more athletically inclined and younger groups, stirring Challenge Fires can be organized. The interspersing of the three distinct types of challenge given in this book will provide the necessary change of pace to make a Challenge Fire worthwhile. There is no reason why a splendid Pageant and Story-Play Fire, a Story and Story-Play Fire, or a Medicine Men's Magic Fire should not meet with equal approval and success.

COUNCIL FIRE PROGRAM NUMBER ONE

1. The heralds, or chiefs, give the Call to Council Fire signal by voice and tom-tom.
2. The council fire is ceremoniously lit. (This may be done by flint and steel or bow drill, or by one of the more spectacular methods described in Chapter 4.)
3. Brief introduction of guests by council fire chief.
4. A fast-moving group dance, followed by a solo dance.
5. Counting coup and feather-claiming ceremony and awards.
6. Medicine men's magic. A demonstration such as the Medicine Feather Dance, The Mystery Snake, or The Coming of the Ducks, etc.
7. Challenges: varied clan challenges and challenge games. (See Chapters 9 and 10.)
8. Indian and perhaps other suitable council fire songs.
9. An Indian story told by a chief or medicine man.
10. Ceremonial closing of council fire. The finale can be the singing of the splendid Omaha Tribal Prayer.

COUNCIL FIRE PROGRAM NUMBER TWO

1. Call to Council Fire by drum or tom-tom.
2. Lighting the council fire by one of many methods, chosen by the council fire chief.
3. Brief introduction of visiting chiefs and other guests.
4. A fast-moving snake or similar dance around the council ring by all warriors.
5. Coup-counting ceremony, with awards to be decided on and made at next council fire.
6. Man-to-man challenges: three or four fast and competitive challenges contested by chiefs and warriors. (See Chapter 11.)
7. Coup stories and coup questions. One or two of the stories taken from Chapter 14 can be used in this contest, and the coup questions can be taken from Chapter 22. Braves from different bands should compete, and if they fail to reach correct solutions, chiefs may be called on to solve the unsolved problems.
8. Indian songs, group and solo.
9. A challenge pageant of one sort or another, contested by at least two of the groups at the council fire. Some suggestions for this contest will be found in Chapter 23.
10. Ceremonial closing of council fire by chief, or suitable song or prayer.

COUNCIL FIRE PROGRAM NUMBER THREE

1. Call to Council Fire, in any way decided by council fire chief.

2. The council fire is spectacularly lit by one of the methods described in Chapter 4.
3. Visitors are briefly introduced by the council fire chief.
4. Indian play. Suitable ones are given in Chapter 18.
5. Group and solo dance; a fast-moving group dance with many participants, followed by a solo one.
6. Coup story contest and coup questions. Material for this will be found in Chapters 14 and 22.
7. Medicine men's magic. A medicine man performs one or more feats of "magic," such as those detailed in Chapter 21.
8. Challenges. Varied, fast-moving ones such as KICK STICK (Woodland version), KIWA TRAIL, TWIN FROG RACE, BEAR CAVE CHIEF, etc., to be found in Chapters 9, 10, and 11.
9. Coup-counting ceremony and coup awards, presented by council fire chief.
10. Council fire is closed by ceremony or song.

Interesting numbers such as one selected from Meet the Other Indians, in this chapter, can be added to any one of the above programs.

PAGEANT AND CHALLENGE PAGEANT COUNCIL FIRES. Such fires can also be held, but as a rule they are best given to entertain visiting groups, since practically all the warriors-in-council are participants in such programs. However, several of the Northwest Coast challenge pageants, such as a combined Totem Pole Challenge Pageant and Talking-Stick Tale Challenge Pageant, and the Ceremonial Potlatch Pageant, can be staged as a complete council fire program, the participants

living the lives of the rugged people who held such colorful events. These programs are also interesting and eye-filling for any spectators who may be invited to look on. The challenge pageants and potlatch pageant mentioned are described in detail, along with others, in Chapter 23.

NORTHWEST COAST COUNCIL FIRE CEREMONIAL PROGRAMS

A number of striking activities for these programs will be found in Chapters 4, 9, 10, 11, 14, 17, 18, 21, 22, and 23. An effective Northwest Coast ceremonial council fire program can be carried out in this sequence.

1. Fire-lighting ceremony, after the entry of chiefs and warriors into the council fire area. The fire can be lit by a magic fire method or in the usual way.
2. Honored guest or guests introduced by the tribal chief in a few well-chosen words. A small quantity of white down can be scattered on the guests' clothing as a sign of high honor. Eagle's down meant good will, respect, and peace.
3. Individual or group dances may be given, or a special dance such as the Dance of the Lightning Snake, described in Chapter 21, can be performed.
4. Coup declarations by the warriors, and awards.
5. Dual and clan challenges.
6. A coup story may be told, or coup questions asked. See Chapters 14 and 22.
7. A feat of medicine men's magic can be performed by a shaman or chief. See Chapter 21.
8. The tribal chief may tell an Indian story or give a brief talk along Indian lines.
9. Ceremonial closing of council fire.

The suggested program can be different at each council fire. Different feats of medicine men's magic can be performed; different methods of fire lighting can be used; a short Indian play such as *The Bewitched Moccasins,* given in Chapter 18, can be performed. A greater part of the program can be devoted to Indian stories, coup stories, and coup questions, or a longer challenge period can be used.

chapter 21

medicine men's magic

Now That Night Has Wrapped the Great Blue Wigwam in a black blanket and the faint mystery music of shadows quivers in the air of the council ring, the far-off gods make medicine. Their medicine men, workers of lesser magic for the Great Ones, stand ready. In the golden glow of the council fire, they will make powerful medicine for the braves-in-council before the stars pale and the darkness leaves to let morning come.

Even some of the more experienced camp people seem to believe that there was little magic, real or otherwise, at Indian gatherings and council fires. Early American and Canadian history proves this contrary. It is on record that there was much magic of almost every sort performed by Indian medicine men, not only of the Northwest Coast but also of the Plains and Woodland tribes, the Corn Planters, and other tribes of the Southwest. It is known that included in this magic were some medicine bags with false bottoms from which appearing and disappearing snakes and otters came and went. There were also knives and arrows with concealed vents from which "blood" poured forth onto the "victim" on the pressure of a finger, or on contact. However, there were also really astonishing feats performed in bright firelight, even in daylight, which could not be explained by white men. Top-ranking officers of the armies which invaded the Indian territories, medical men, and scientists have left records of their bewilderment as to how many of these medicine magic feats were performed. The things which puzzled them, for which they could find no explanation, are detailed in official writings which are still a matter of record.

A considerable amount of the ceremonial magic of the Pacific Northwest Coast Indians which appears in this book is founded on what the author was privileged to see, and hear firsthand accounts of, from old chiefs, medicine men, and shamans. In order to describe the visual effect of such magic on the onlookers, this is set down as though seen through the eyes of those present, without any attempt to theorize on how the effects were produced. The attempts at explanation in this chapter merely try to tell how the effects achieved by the Northwest Coast Indians can be more or less duplicated by the use of some imagination and "improvised" magic on the part of modern tribal and clan chiefs, for the amusement and astonishment of the young white warriors solemnly seated around the council fires of today.

THUNDERBIRD FEATHER

This is strong magic for a breezeless night, which any shaman worthy of the name can perform, to the wonder of the warriors, while the council fire burns bright. It is also magic which can be carried out safely indoors.

The warriors see a shaman enter the council fire area. He carries a strip of folded bark in his hand. He raises his hands high above his head and says in a loud voice: "O Thunderbird, when the sky was lit with your light, one of your feathers of fire dropped into my hands. Thinking I would be burned, I tried to drop it to the earth, but your feather burned me not. That feather of flame became a red feather, which I now carry, and I ask power to send it back to you. Maybe, my heart tells me, it is not good for a humble shaman who has so little power within himself to have such strong magic; and so I wish to return it to the sky above. If it is your will that I may have the flame-feather, let it return to me. Thus will I know your will."

When the shaman has finished speaking, he carefully takes a long red "feather" from between the folded strip of bark and holds it up toward the sky. The feather does not move. "You came to me in flame; maybe it is your wish that you go from me in flame," the shaman tells the feather. "Bring me fire, O Fire Tender," he calls.

The Fire Tender lights a twig at the council fire and takes it to the shaman. Holding the feather out in front of him at arm's length in his left hand, the shaman sets the end of the feather furthest away from him alight. The feather burns slowly, but the ash remains on the burning feather. When the flame has almost reached the fingers of the shaman, he gently releases the still flaming ash. The ash floats downward for a moment then rises quickly up into the air. Higher and higher it floats while the shaman and warriors-in-council watch. Then the ash floats slowly downward. The shaman gently catches it in his two hands. As he does so he gives a loud shout, for he holds outstretched between his hands the red feather which flew skyward but a heartbeat before. The shaman holds the feather high, gently places it in its sheath of bark, and silently leaves the council fire area.

SOLUTION FOR THUNDERBIRD FEATHER

This illusion is very simple to create indoors and, provided the weather co-operates, outdoors. It should be performed on a dry, *breezeless* night. Before appearing at the council fire, the shaman has cut two strips from a sheet of 30-by-20-inch *flammable* red tissue paper. Since the tissue paper sold in most ten cent stores these days is non-flammable, it is best to look for the paper required in any big stationary store. As the sheets are 20 inches wide, it is easy to run down a 4-inch strip and cut it smoothly from the sheet. The paper is thus cut, as it must be, with the grain. Both strips of paper are rounded at one end to represent the top of a feather. One strip is carefully doubled in two, so that it now measures 4 inches wide and 10 inches long. The end that has not been cut in the shape of a feather is now trimmed, using the other end as a pattern. The doubled paper is pressed firmly with the fingers at the place where it is doubled. This piece of tissue paper is placed, still folded, between a sheet of completely dry, heavy cardboard painted on the outside to resemble birch or any other sort of bark.

The second strip of tissue is now pleated from one end to the other, like an accordian, in 1-inch pleats, then folded in half, making a small packet roughly 2 inches by 1 inch. The end pleats of the strip are now one at each

end, outside of the other pleats. While it is quite easy with a little practice to manipulate this strip without difficulty, the following additions may help a novice in even the simplest feats of sleight of hand to handle this key strip quickly at the right moment. To be able to grip one end easily with the fingers and thumb of the right hand, a 2-inch length of a flat toothpick may be stuck into the quill end of the strip by coating a very narrow strip of the "feather" at the extreme end with mucilage and folding it over the piece of wooden toothpick. At the other end of the strip—the one which is rounded to resemble the top end of a feather—a thin, narrow, wrap-around type of lead sinker used in fishing is bent tightly into several thicknesses to form a 1-inch-long strip of lead which is

TOOTHPICK　　　　　LEAD SINKER

stuck inside the very end of the tip, both sinker and piece of toothpick being fastened to the same side of the folded strip, one at each end.

The shaman holds the folded, pleated strip closed by slipping a large paper fastener over it. With a small safety pin, he fastens one end of the paper fastener somewhere on his person, out of sight but where he can reach it with the greatest ease and without drawing needless attention to his movement. It may be fastened just inside the neck of the shirt, at the front and to the right or left of the throat. Another convenient place to conceal the strip is just inside the loose cuff of the left shirt sleeve, the arm band of the shirt being used if the shirt has short sleeves, or in an outside breast pocket if the shaman's shirt has one. The shaman performing the magic can think up any other place where the strip can be reached and produced with ease at a second's notice when the time comes.

The shaman will be ready to perform in public after he has practised the trick a number of times in the open air in private. The number of trial performances is decided by the amount of practice necessary to make him proficient and certain of being able to carry out the illusion confidently and successfuly in public.

First of all, on a very calm day and when there is nobody around, he takes an exact duplicate of the 20-inch-long strip of tissue paper which he will use later at the council fire and folds it in two, so that is 10 inches long and 4 inches wide. He then holds it out straight in front of him at shoulder height and at arm's length, after having lit the foot of both ends of the strip, which he holds firmly by the lower corner of the folded part. He must be very careful to keep the strip quite steady and *horizontal* as it burns, so that it will burn slowly. The grip on the doubled end must be as close to the very end as possible, because the burning strip must be held until the flame is within an inch—less if possible—of the end which is being held. The strip must be held steadily to the last second and released very gently when the flame has almost reached the end, without the shaman making any attempt to propel it either upward or outward, since as much of the entire ash as possible must remain unbroken until it takes off. The amateur maker-of-magic may be surprised to find that the ash, when released with the tiny flame still burning on the end, may drop a little, then rise straight up into the air. The ash is quite visible by the light of a brightly burning council fire, as it is silver-gray in color and big enough to be seen by the braves-in-council.

As the ash floats slowly upward, providing the perfect natural *misdirection* which is so highly apreciated by professional magicians, the eyes of the onlookers are fixed on the rising ash. It is at this second that the shaman takes the hidden, pleated strip of tissue in his right hand, without a glance in the direction of where it is hidden. He holds it against the palm of his right hand while his fingers grasp the end on which the toothpick is rolled. He brings his hands together, and the fingers of the left hand firmly hold the sinker end of the strip. Naturally, these movements are carried out as quickly as possible while the paper strip is hidden by his hands. As he now places both hands, held together with cupped palms, under the falling ash he holds the strip into readiness for the second the ash drops into his hands or until it is close enough for him to snatch at it successfully. At that instant he swiftly opens his hands. He holds the red feather, apparently unharmed by its flight in flames, stretched out between them. Should the shaman, by malchance lose his grip on the sinker-weighted end of the strip, he has only to hold onto the toothpick end and flick the other end downward. The weight of the sinker will carry the strip, open, downward to its full length, giving the shaman time to grasp the strip somewhere along its length with his free hand and keep it open at full length directly under where the ash fell. The ash disintegrates instantly when touched, but even if it is entirely missed by a small margin the effect of having apparently taken the feather from the ash is almost as effective.

Various unexpected happenings can make the performance of this feat even more exciting for the shaman than the warriors-in-council. For instance, the slightest sudden breeze which springs up when the ash is safely afloat may cause it to glide out of reach instead of dropping almost straight downward, and the shaman must try to get under it in order to "catch" it immediately when it comes within reach. A fugitive ash may hover over the chief's headdress, in which case the ash must be caught before it settles into the war bonnet, or several coup feathers

may be produced along with the restored Thunderbird's feather.

Should the ash be seized on its upward flight in the grip of an uprising thermal, it will be carried so high above the council fire area that it will be lost to view and beyond recovery. In such circumstance it is best for the shaman to thank the Thunderbird for having taken the feather back. This is more effective than giving a shout and producing the "restored" feather after the ash has gone out of sight. The shaman must be sure to stand at least 8 feet away from the brightly burning council fire to avoid having the ash carried upward out of sight by the heat thermal of the fire. It should constantly be remembered that the least breath of breeze which strikes the tissue as it is burning into ash will break it up before it is released, and of course spoil the entire effect of the illusion.

Thunderbird Feather can be carried out effectively indoors, when there are no drafts and the place in which it is performed has a fairly high ceiling. There is no danger of setting the place on fire. A few sparks may scintillate on the ash just as it rises, but they will not ignite the most flammable object, and they die out almost instantly.

DANCE OF THE LIGHTNING SNAKE

A good dancer leaps into the council area. He is wearing one of the dance shirts or dance aprons illustrated in Chapters 17 and 19. The dancer holds a magic Lightning Snake high above his head and improvises dance steps while he holds the writhing snake now on one side of his body, now on the other, in front of him, and above his head. At times he holds it with only one hand, but when its apparent efforts to escape become too great, he holds it with both hands. After a short while, the snake wriggles free, while the dancer is on one side of the council area, and floats over the center of the council area, flying back and forth about 10 feet above the council fire. The dancer makes every effort to catch the Lightning Snake, jumping high into the air when the snake glides overhead, but the snake rises and falls and glides forward out of reach when the dancer tries to seize it. He nearly catches it several times, but always it manages to escape. He follows beneath it as it glides here and there, rising and falling as it circles the fire. Once the dancer grasps

the snake by the tail, but it squirms out of his grip and again glides about the center of the council area. At last, the dancer catches the Lightning Snake, holds it high above his head in triumph, dances once around the council area and then out into the forest.

SOLUTION FOR
DANCE OF THE LIGHTNING SNAKE

The Lightning Snake is operated by using the suspended thin, black nylon fishing line, or in this case even a strong black thread, stretched above and across the council fire area from the trees above. As the snake is light in weight, it may be suspended from only one thread fastened to light branches above any suitable part of the council fire area.

It is a good policy not to use more than one feat of "magic" which requires the overhead line at the council fire on the same night. There is the risk of twisted lines spoiling spectacular effects, unless two different sections of the area are chosen in which to work two different feats which will not interfere with each other.

The Lightning Snake may be made from a 2-foot length of fairly supple rope 1 or 1½ inches in diameter, wound around with a strip of pale-green cloth, about 3 inches of which is left at one end to form a tail which wriggles easily. The other end of the rope is wrapped to form the somewhat larger head of the snake. Close to the middle of the snake, directly at the point of balance, a very small metal ring is fastened. A length of strong fishing line or black thread is tied securely to this ring. The thread or line must be long enough to go through the overhead ring and then reach outside the council fire area to the point from which the unseen operator guides the actions of the snake. He should have about 35 feet of thread left by the time it reaches him from through the ring on the overhead line, in order to have plenty of slack with which to make the snake perform. This spare thread is best wound smoothly onto a spool. The spool may best be placed on a headless nail, driven into the trunk of a tree about 4 feet above the ground, with a small white disc fastened directly beside the nail in order to help the operator to locate it easily in a dim light. The tree chosen on which to fasten the spool should be the one behind which the operator can work unseen, though he should be in a position which enables him to watch every movement of the snake.

The choice of position offers considerable scope, as the operator may work from any side of the council fire area, provided the cover is good. The operator must be at his post several minutes before the dance begins, so that he does not draw attention to himself by taking up the position hurriedly at the last minute.

The thread can easily be unwound from the spool without fear of its becoming tangled if it is allowed to run out between the fingers of one hand while the spool is held in the other. This will assure a smooth performance of the snake as the thread is wound out and in to follow the movements and position of the dancer. A clever operating job adds greatly to the spectacular nature of the dance. The chief who operates the thread and the dancer should have several workouts before the performance, one of them in the comparative darkness of the council fire area in which only a small fire burns, so that both performers know what to expect. There must be complete co-ordination between the dancer and the thread operator, so that any emergencies—such as a tangled or too slowly paid out line, or the dropping of the spool—can be dealt with without the onlookers guessing that things are not going smoothly behind the scenes. For instance, when the dancer feels that the thread is being fed to him with difficulty, he can stop and dance in place for a moment or two without any one being the wiser; then when he feels the thread coming through easily again, he can continue his dance around the fire.

The dancer, too, requires some skill and practice in order to put on a good show. He can let the snake "escape" from his hands in such a realistic manner that nobody realizes that he has tapped it smartly on the head or tail in order to make it glide away from him, while pretending to catch it. Pretended grabs to capture the floating snake are really smart taps with the palm of the hand or fingers which drive the snake away from the dancer. Of course, the work of the thread operator at such times is of immense value in enhancing the illusion in helping the snake float at the right heights. The operator also raises and lowers the snake, jerking the thread slightly to make it squirm and keep it above the dancer's head, out of reach, when so required. A dancer and operator working in unison can give a wonderful performance and take care of all unexpected happenings without letting them interfere with the dance.

At the end of the dance, the operator may break the thread, close to the tree, so that the dancer can pull the thread out of the area by simply carrying off the snake, while the operator winds in the remaining thread. This is not necessary if the dancer, after dancing out through the entrance, takes his snake some distance away and lays it behind some bushes far enough away from the fire to make sure the thread will be high above the heads of the warriors-in-council. The dancer winds the operator's part of the thread several times around the snake as he lays it down. The operator simply winds any slack thread around his spool and loops the thread securely around the nail before leaving his position. The threads above the council fire area will be invisible to the keenest eyes, and they will also be high above and out of the way of further activities around the council fire.

MEDICINE STAR VANISHES

This story of powerful medicine and great magic can be told by the council fire chief to his braves-in-council—before they see the impossible happen before their eyes.

"Listen well, O braves of the Six Nations (or Seven

Nations, or other Plains group), and you will hear of strange magic, of the powerful medicine made by Medicine Star, a medicine man of the Six Nations. Many, many moons ago he came to where our council fire now burns, thinking that here he would be safe from his enemies while he took a sweat bath before he worked powerful magic for his tribe. Not often was Medicine Star wrong, but that time even his medicine power failed to tell him how cunning his enemies were; nor did he know that Black Sun, their medicine man, had had a spirit dream in which he saw many things that Medicine Star would not have had him know. So now Medicine Star came to where this council ring now stands, yes, to the very spot to which I now point. There he set up his sweat bath lodge, which looked like a strange tepee with but three sides. Soon the smoke from his fire rose like spirit fingers groping for the sky. His voice could be heard as he begged the Great Spirit to grant him the medicine power he needed.

"Even while he prayed, his enemies, led by their medicine man Black Sun, came to where we now sit. They surrounded the council ring, so that there were warriors on all sides to capture Medicine Star when he came out of his bath lodge. They heard his voice but saw him not. Soon his voice was no longer heard. They waited—and waited.

"Then Black Sun would wait no longer. He signaled the warriors in his party to attack the sweat lodge and take Medicine Star alive, but at first they were afraid of his medicine. They crept toward the sweat lodge and then ran backward, till their leader swore to use his magic against them. Only then did his warriors form a circle around the lodge and rushed upon their enemy with loud war cries. They reached the lodge, threw it to the ground, then with wild cries of terror ran into the forest. The magic of Medicine Star had been too great for them! He was no longer in the sweat lodge—he had vanished. Only Black Sun remained for a few moments after his band had fled. He approached the sweat lodge, stretched out eager hands to take it, then drew them quickly away and jumped backward. Twice more did he feint before lifting the medicine lodge, as did medicine men always before touching sacred objects.

" 'This will I take that it may help me to make greater magic,' he shouted as swiftly he followed his warriors into the forest.

"Today, in hushed voices, before darkness covers their lodges, the Six Nations ask themselves in voices as low as the rustle of aspen leaves, 'Where did Medicine Star go? Did he rise to the sky like spirit-mist in the smoke of his fire? Was he now a spirit-star?'

"There were no answers to their questions. There are some mysteries too great for man to find the answer—maybe they are hidden in the sky. Maybe if we sit still and wish, Medicine Star will come again to our council ring and make the same magic for us that he did to save himself from his enemies. My warriors, let us be still and silent, and wish."

Soon a slight sound is heard off in the forest. Medicine Star, and later his enemies, come. Once again the mystery and magic of many moons long past are enacted in the council ring.

Once again Medicine Star sets up his sweat lodge. His enemies come. He vanishes. Those who would capture him fly shrieking into the forest.

When tomorrow's sun is high in the sky, will not each warrior who sat in council on that night of mystery ask himself—"Last night in council did I see, or did I only dream?"

SOLUTION FOR MEDICINE STAR VANISHES

In order to learn the exact way to cause Medicine Star's disappearance in a most realistic manner, council fire chiefs should refer to The Vanishing Roman, in Chapter 15. It will been seen immediately that a great deal of the acceptance of that disappearance as a real mystery, even by adults, lies in the *marked difference* between the costume worn by The Roman and those worn by his would-be captors—which makes it impossible to recognize him when he suddenly *merges with them* dressed like them. His quick-change artistry behind the screen also contributes to the mystification of the onlookers, who imagine that it is impossible to effect so complete a transformation in so short a time. They cannot guess how little transforming is really done. So must the disappearance of Medicine Star appear to the warriors-in-council.

A few brightly colored Indian designs can be sewn to the outside of the three panels to give a medicine-magic touch when the sweat lodge is carried around the council fire area and later set up.

The chief or older warrior who plays the role of Medicine Star must be of very nearly the same height and build as the majority of the seven or eight attackers. This number should be sufficient to carry out the illusion, but additional attackers—certainly not more than two or three—can be added if the council fire chief staging the disappearance thinks best.

Medicine Star's dress and appearance must be as greatly different from the attackers, when he first appears, as it is exactly like theirs on his second appearance. This transformation is not too easy, because he must make a rather quick and complete change, in restricted quarters, prior to his sweat lodge being rushed by Black Sun and his warriors. This rush can be postponed if absolutely necessary, until a sudden silence after continuous audible muttering on the part of Medicine Star tells Black Sun that the concealed medicine man is completely prepared and awaiting the rush. Some other distinctive signal for the attack can be prearranged between the two medicine men. It must not be too obvious a signal, such as a whoop from Medicine Star, as it must not be possible to detect any collusion whatsoever between the two medicine men. It is also advisable not to have the attacking warriors stand in full view, where they can be counted easily, waiting for a signal. They should take cover behind trees and stick their heads out from around bushes, as real Indians would do, until Black Sun gives them the order to rush forward into the council ring. The two braves between whom Medicine Star will be standing at the instant the sweat lodge is thrown over must be posted so that they will rush the section of the panels which open, so that the hidden medicine man may merge perfectly with the attackers. As the exact position of the opening can be arranged in advance, even though it will be visible to the attackers, there should be no difficulty in the instant disappearance of Medicine Star.

Medicine Star can be spoken of, in the council fire chief's introductory story, as belonging to a different tribe from that of his attackers. He can wear a different headdress and costume from theirs when he first appears, but the very best and simplest way to avoid all such costuming difficulties is the following. Medicine Star wears a soft, painted mask which completely covers his face. This mask is held securely in place by an elastic band around the back of the head, so that it can be removed in a second. His face, under the mask, should be painted with exactly the same markings as those of some of his attackers, provided their faces are adorned with war paint. No headdress need be worn with such a mask. Medicine Star wears a blanket which reaches to just above his knees. This "blanket" is best made from cotton or some similar material, which is lightweight but *not* transparent, since it should have little bulk. It may be painted with a few fantastic medicine designs in bright colors. Great care must be taken by the medicine man that this blanket does not lift more than an inch or so above the knees at any time, as he carries his folded sweat lodge around the council ring, once or twice, before setting it up about 10 feet away from the council fire, on the side of the ring selected by the council fire chief. The reason for the blanket being maintained at knee level is that Medicine Star is wearing a pair of dark jeans, the same as those worn by the attackers. The legs of his jeans should be wide enough to allow them to be rolled up to a point well above the knees, and they *must remain in that position,* which is best assured if they are held in place by a strong elastic band around each roll, until the medicine man has disappeared into his sweat lodge. The front of the blanket, which can hang loosely, especially at the foot, can be held shut by large, effective snaps, so that

it is impossible for the onlookers to see that Medicine Star is wearing trousers. It will be seen that if the blanket suddenly flies open in front or lifts a little too much, or if one trouser leg slips down below blanket level, a solution to the disappearance may suggest itself to some alert chief or brave. Unless one of the slips mentioned occurs, the onlookers believe that Medicine Star is either wearing a breechclout under his blanket or that, in readiness for his sweat lodge bath of purification, he is already naked. This belief can be heightened by Medicine Star having bare feet, which is quite in order for one about to take a sweat bath, to be followed by magic-making. (His soft-soled moccasins, which should be similar to those worn by some of his attackers, are hung securely in position inside the folded sweat lodge, held firmly in place by the tapes described and depicted in Chapter 15.

This almost completes Medicine Star's disguise and gear, except for a shirt, worn beneath his blanket, which should resemble in color and design those worn by at least four of his would-be captors. Certainly, his shirt must not be distinctive in any way, either in color or decoration. Should body paint be worn instead of shirts, the markings on the medicine man's body must resemble closely those on the majority of his attackers. The only important thing remaining is a simple, *uniform* headdress for *all* participants in the illusion. This headgear can be a red headband with one medium-length feather sticking up from the band at the back of the head. The same headdress, to be worn by Medicine Star when he merges with his attackers as they push over the sweat lodge, is attached to one of the tapes tacked to one of the cross bars inside the sweat lodge. The drawing in chapter 15 shows these bars and tapes. The single feather in Medicine Star's headband must be sewn securely in place, or it may drop out when carried inside the folded sweat lodge. A wide band of elastic sewn inside and all around the headband will allow it to be put on in a moment and will also hold it securely in place. *Great care* must be taken by Medicine Star so that his feather does not show even for an instant as he puts his headdress on inside the sweat lodge ready to merge with the would-be captors. To avoid this risk and make the working of the illusion still easier, *none* of the participants in the illusion need wear feathers. Usually the Indians of Woodland and Plains discarded their headdresses when in heavily wooded country, and many of them simply wore a headband to hold their hair in place at such times.

Three more props, and Medicine Star is ready. These are a medium-sized tin lid, or a small square of metal, some quick-smoldering smoke-producing material, to be lit on the lid or metal square, and a small box of matches. A piece of thick cotton cloth 4 inches long and 2 inches wide, thoroughly impregnated in a soupy solution of saltpeter and completely dried before use, gives off a satisfactory, whitish smoke. The saltpeter solution, which is the same as that used for lighting delayed-action and magic fires, is made by pouring about three tablespoons of boiling water onto about three teaspoonfuls of powdered saltpeter and mixing them until the saltpeter is dissolved. This little cotton strip is rolled into a small, open roll before it is lit. A very good smoke can also be made from a similar roll, or a little larger one, of thick dark-brown paper; but one must experiment in order to find just the right sort of paper. It must smolder continuously for a few moments without going out. The smoke arising from this smoldering material represents the smoke from the sweat lodge fire. It also signals that all is working out on schedule within the lodge and that Medicine Star will be ready for the attack in a few moments. As soon as he lights the material it will begin to smolder instantly, throwing off a thick smoke. He must then stoop down slightly, holding the lid in which the smudge rests slightly above head level, so that the smoke rises above the top of the sweat lodge and does not get into his eyes. He must be certain that neither the lid nor his hand shows even for a second over the top of the lodge, as the fire would be burning on the ground in a real sweat lodge. When the smoke has risen for a little while—even a minute or two is not too long, as it increases the suspense—he places the smudge container on the ground and extinguishes the smudge with the toe of his moccasin. (Council fire chiefs can dispense with the realism of the smudge if they so wish. There is no good reason why a medicine man of Medicine Star's ability cannot take a sweat bath without a visible fire.)

Medicine Star now dons his headdress or headband, still stooping slightly, if he is wearing the single-feather headdress, so that the feather does not show above the top of the lodge. Then he waits for the war whoop which tells him that the attackers will rush him in a split second. He himself, as has been suggested, can trigger the instant of attack by suddenly ceasing to mutter audibly within the lodge, or in some other way. His silence indicates that he is all ready for the attack and waiting to merge with the attacking warriors when they overthrow the lodge.

Three points may require stressing here for those who carry out the illusion for the first time. First, Medicine Star should make his presence in the sweat lodge known right up to the last second. This prevents alert braves from deducting that he has already left the lodge, by a concealed trench, for instance, before the attack takes place. The second point is that the council fire may be blazing brightly at the moment of Medicine Star's disappearance. It reveals nothing when the illusion is well carried out, and it greatly heightens the mystification of the onlookers. A third point of major importance is that the screen should be pushed over so that the outer panels fold over the center panel, to hide the apparel tied to it by the tapes. (Medicine Star *must* unhook the latch before the screen is pushed over.)

The mystifying feat of The Magic Turtle can easily be performed by the medicine man or a chief, with the help of an assistant, or by a chief and the medicine man.

At a sign from the chief, the medicine man enters the council ring and tells the braves that he will make good hunting and good weather medicine that night. He explains that this powerful medicine will be made with the aid of a magic turtle which he has just found through a dream. From his medicine bundel he takes the turtle. (It is cut from a piece of soft leather gaily decorated in light colors, and is about 8 inches long and 4½ inches wide.) He holds it up in the firelight for the braves to look at and speaks glowingly of the magic powers of this spirit-turtle. He tells the warriors that no one can take it from him and keep it, for his turtle medicine wand always tells him where the turtle is. The wonderful wand, he says, leads the way to the Magic Turtle and flutters at it points out exactly where the turtle is hidden. The medicine man exhibits the thin wand. (It is about 2 feet 6 inches long, with a dozen narrow strips of white or yellow cloth attached to one end.) He says he feels that someone present doubts the power of the wand. Now they will see it put to the test. The braves will see that it will not work for anyone else. He gives the chief the Magic Turtle and wand and begs that a test be made. He offers to go out of earshot, some distance outside the council ring, under the escort of two chiefs or trusted braves, while a test is being prepared. The chief asks the braves if they wish such a test of magic and on hearing the approving "How, How" of consent, he agrees.

While the medicine man is being conducted out of the council ring, the chief—who has been told the secret of the wand by the medicine man—takes over. He suggests that the test be made a very difficult one. He calls softly for any six braves from different tribes, or two or three from each tribe should there be only two or three tribes in council, to enter the council ring. He arranges them quickly in two lines with three braves in each, the braves in the rear row standing directly behind those in the front row. As an apparent afterthought, the chief says that it will make the test still more difficult if more braves are added, so he calls for three more. When they come forward, he places them directly in front of the three braves in the front row or directly behind the three braves in the back row. The nine braves are now standing in a fairly exact square and should hold these positions. The chief then tells the braves-in-council that he is going to hide the Magic Turtle on one of the nine braves. Better still, he suggests that any three braves come into the ring and, by pointing, indicate the brave on whom the turtle should be hidden. This seems to be proof that the chief and the medicine man cannot be working together.

The chief then drops the Magic Turtle down inside the

back of the war shirt of the brave indicated. The chief suggests that they make the search for the turtle even harder for the medicine man by having a volunteer brave, the tenth, stand in front of the others and pretend that he is the guilty one. When this brave comes forward, the chief places him just in front of the others and facing in the same direction—that is, they all face the chief.

Another chief now gives a call or signal to indicate that the medicine man should be brought back. When he returns with his escort, the chief, without saying a word, touches the brave who stands in front of the others with the magic wand. The medicine man merely grunts and holds out his hand for the wand. The chief hands it to him and then stands near the edge of council ring. The medicine man then points the wand at the brave whom the chief indicated. The wand does not move, and the medicine man signals to the brave to return to his place in the council. The medicine man then goes slowly from brave to brave, pointing his wand at them, one by one. As the braves-in-council watch with great interest, the medicine man signals brave after brave to return to his place. Now only two braves remain. As the medicine man points his wand at one of them, it begins to quiver visibly, and does so even more violently as the medicine man moves closer to the brave. The wand flutters strongly as it indicates the brave's back. The medicine man puts his hand inside the shirt and, taking out the Magic Turtle, holds it up in triumph. Even should the braves beg for another test, and another, the result is always the same. No matter on whom the Magic Turtle is hidden, its presence is always betrayed by the magic wand, which proves to be infallible.

SOLUTION FOR THE MAGIC TURTLE

The diagram is almost sufficient explanation of this mystifying feat. As will be seen, the brave in front of the

nine braves is merely used as an "indicator." The nine points shown on his head and body correspond with the positions of the nine braves in the square behind him. The numbers are given only to show the relation of the various points on the brave "indicator" to the braves in the square. As the chief places the wand lightly on one of the points on the brave "indicator," he specifies quite clearly to the medicine man which brave has the turtle. The fact that the chief does not say one word, as the braves in the square can vouch for, adds to the mystification of the onlookers.

The medicine man knows which brave has the turtle as soon as the chief points to the "indicator," but in order to build up the suspense the medicine man does not let the wand "discover" the brave with the turtle until most of the nine braves have been sent back to their places. In the event of two repeat performances, at the request of the braves-in-council, the turtle may be discovered on the third try in the second test and on the first try in the third test. This will show the increasing power of the wand and make it even more difficult for braves with Sherlock Holmes tendencies to figure out how the feat is accomplished. In the case of a second test, the chief may not even use the "indicator" in front, but may use one of the braves (who has not got the turtle) in the front row as the "indicator." This will puzzle the braves who may believe that there is some connection between the tenth brave used as the "indicator" and the location of the turtle.

THE COMING OF THE DUCKS

The warriors-in-council are very still. Only the soft, sighing sound of the waves can be heard. The await a sign from their shaman which will tell them whether many ducks will come to add to their food supply for the winter.

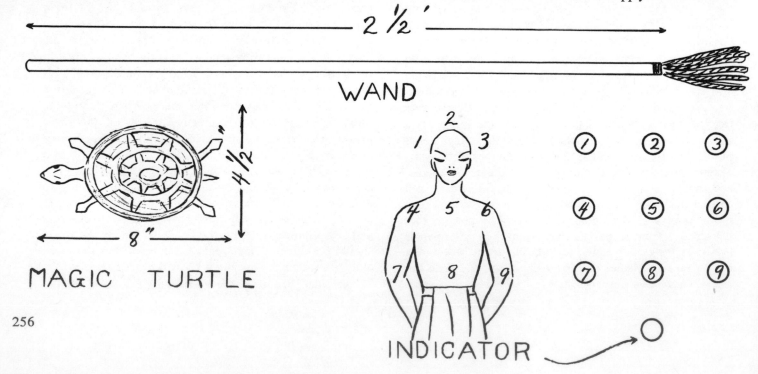

2½'

WAND

MAGIC TURTLE

4½"

8"

INDICATOR

Two clan chiefs slowly enter the council fire area. They carry a big water basket between them. It is heavy, and some water spills over its brim as they place it on a low stump close to the council fire. As the two chiefs leave the area, the warriors who have seen the duck-bringing magic before keep their eyes fixed on the surface of the water, which can just be seen a little under the rim of the water basket.

Slowly a shaman dances into the council fire area. He wears full regalia, under a bright Chilkat blanket, and a headdress of bear claws on his head. He carries a short staff in his hands. It is carved and painted and decorated with flicker feathers. The shaman puts his blanket on the tribal chief's chair and increases his dance tempo. The firelight reflects on his painted leather apron. Its fringes swirl as he whirls around the council fire. Gradually his dance steps slacken. He stops and makes an impatient sign, and two clan chiefs who carried in the big water basket again enter the area. They carry a water basket. At a sign from the shaman, they pour water from it into the great basket on the stump. Water now flows over the brim of the big basket onto the ground. The two clan chiefs leave the area. The shaman dances twice, slowly, around the fire. He stops and, with his arm held above his eyes as though to shield them from too great magic, gazes up into the sky. The warriors-in-council stare up into the dark night sky too. Some of them murmur that they can see ducks flying high. Others whisper that they can hear ducks calling. It is clear that the shaman does not do so, for he dances again, raising his hands high toward the sky and uttering ducklike calls and sounds as he circles the fire. Suddenly he stops, looks quickly upward, then cups his hand to his ear. He gives a number of low, ducklike calls.

The warriors-in-council are excited; "Kweh-kweh!" they call softly, using the Chinook word for duck. The shaman stares northward and listens. Yes, the warriors too have heard the unmistakable calls of ducks in flight! The calls come ever closer, sounding from high overhead at first, then gradually coming nearer to the treetops. The shaman dances again, his frenzied gyrations taking him closer and closer to the great water basket, as the cries of flying ducks sound close overhead. Those who know what may happen next have fear in their hearts in case the shaman is not quick enough. They should not have doubted his spirit power. He raises his feathered staff high in air as he softly approaches the water basket. Suddenly, three big mallard ducks appear on the surface of the water, and their loud, alrmed quacks mingle with the surprised and joyful cries of the warriors. The ducks bob on the surface of the water as though about to take off. The warriors hold their breath. The shaman again raises is staff. The ducks have come!

Two clan chiefs quickly and quietly run toward the water basket. They carry a large square of woven bark-cloth. Approaching, one on either side of the basket, they throw the cloth over it completely, covering ducks and basket. Loud, frightened quacks come from the imprisoned ducks. The two chiefs carefully tilt the water basket and let much of the water run onto the ground. Then, with the muffled quacking of ducks still coming from the basket, they carry it out of the council fire area.

The shaman, who has stood quietly with his arms lifted skyward while the chiefs attended to the ducks and basket, now slowly walks from the council fire area.

SOLUTION FOR THE COMING OF THE DUCKS

Shamans of some of the Northwest Coast Indian tribes used to make several ducks appear mysteriously on the surface of a big water-filled basket. Sometimes the ducks were small, sometimes life-size. All the ducks used were carved from lightweight wood and beautifully colored. The author devised a way to duplicate this feat of "magic" and believes that his method is similar to that used by one of the tribes, though probably his use of the overhead line, in this version is an innovation.

Because of the advance preparation required for this feat and the brief time of its duration, only a general description of how it can be performed is given. A little experimentation and practice on the part of chiefs and medicine men who wish to carry out this illusion at their council fires will soon supply the necessary skill.

A big deep wooden, metal, or canvas tub is needed. It can be wrapped in burlap to give it a woodsy appearance. The tub is placed on a box disguised as a tree stump, high enough to keep the top of the tub 3 feet above ground level. A small metal ring about ½ inch in diameter is fastened inside the tub, or outside if necessary, ½ inch below the rim.

The size and number of ducks used will depend on the size of the tub and the skill of the operator in anchoring and releasing them. Two standard size decoy ducks—inflatable, cork, or wooden—can be used, and they prove more spectacular than smaller models. The ducks are fastened to the bottom of the tub, inside, as follows. A small metal or bone ring about ½ inch in diameter is required for each duck, and two strips of waterproof adhesive tape 3 inches long and about 1 inch wide are required for each duck or pair of ducks used. The ring is securely fastened to the center of the belly of each duck with a strip of waterproof adhesive tape. A length of heavy smooth cord 12 inches long is needed for one duck, or a 22-inch length for two ducks.

Assuming that the overhead line described earlier is already in position, a ring should be tied to it 8 feet away from the council fire, on the side nearest the spot used by the concealed operator. The tub is placed on the "tree stump" below this ring. One end of a 50-foot length of black nylon fishline, which is the operator's line, is passed down through the ring on the overhead line, then through the ring on the rim of the tub. A guard ring, the same size as the one on the tub rim, is tied onto the operator's line 9 inches from the end, and then the end is tied securely to the middle of the 12- or 22-inch length of cord. One end of this cord is threaded through the ring on one of

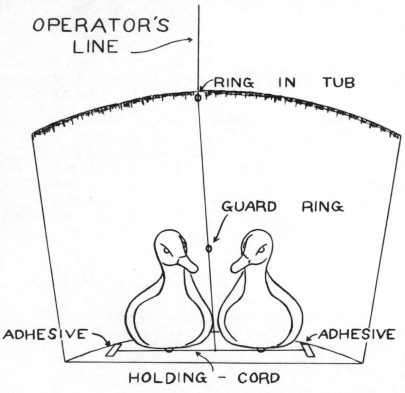

the ducks and then fastened securely to the foot of the empty tub with one of the strips of adhesive tape. String the free end of the length of cord through the ring on the other duck, then fasten it to the bottom of the tub with the other strip of adhesive tape. The cord is stretched in a straight line between these two lengths of tape, so that they hold it taut.

The tub is now slowly half filled with water, which can be discolored by stirring some wood ash or other substance into it, so that the ducks are hidden from view. The tub is now gradually filled with water, and the upward pull of the ducks should not be sufficient to pull free either end of the adhesive tape which holds the cord that keeps the ducks on the bottom of the tub. Only experimentation will test the ability of the adhesive tape used to resist the upward pull of the ducks, since the pull varies with the type of duck used and some waterproof adhesive tape is better than others.

When The Coming of the Ducks is to be the first event on the program after the lighting of the council fire, the tub full of water is placed in position before the warriors arrive. Another way to carry out the illusion, which permits it to be staged at any time during the council fire without the gear taking up space in the council ring, is to have four chiefs carry in the tub, about half or three-quarters filled with water. Weight will decide the amount of water to be carried in the tub, and additional water to fill the tub completely can be carried in wooden or camouflaged pails. The tub and stump should be ready just outside the council ring at a point where clear and easy passage is assured for the bearers. Some practice is advisable if this method is used, so the operator will be sure to pay out enough line to prevent the ducks being prematurely jerked free and shot to the surface while the tub is being carried in. The senior of the chiefs who help to carry the tub should be entrusted with the very important job of wrapping around one hand about a foot of the operator's line, just outside the tub, before helping to pick up the tub outside the council area. This allows the operator to let enough line roll off his spool without worrying about the untimely release of the ducks. When the tub is in place and the chief has unwound the line from his hand, without drawing attention to it, he gives a shrill whoop to signal the operator that his trigger line is clear and ready for use when the medicine man or tribal chief gives the prearranged signal.

A sharp jerk on the line by the hidden operator will instantly release the ducks when the time comes, and they will blob up and float on the surface in plain view of the warriors-in-council. The ducks will float right side up, of course, since decoys do so automatically. Ducks with a tendency to turn over in the water can usually be made to float right side up by fastening a lead sinker onto their bellies with a strip of adhesive tape. The Indians always weighted the bellies of the ducks which they carved so cleverly from wood, to assure the birds floating right side up.

After the ducks have bobbed to the surface and floated there for a while for all to see, two of the chiefs who carried in the tub should throw a sheet of cloth or canvas over it, presumably to imprison the ducks, before the tub is carried from the council ring. A few muffled quacks, made by one of the chiefs carrying the tub out, will add to the effect.

The Indian chiefs and medicine men spared neither time nor effort in preparing even a minor illusion for use in their council fire programs of magic and fantasy. Many rehearsals were held in secret; and when the illusions were carried out at the ceremonial council fires, there was never the slightest hitch or imperfection visible in any part of them. Perfection was sought and achieved.

MAGIC FEATHER DANCE

Shortly before the closing ceremony, when the chief brings the night's council fire to an end, he makes a solemn announcement. Their medicine man has been instructed in a dream to perform the Magic Feather Dance, the braves-in-council are informed. They are told to watch well, for they may never see such a sight again.

The medicine man, in full regalia, now enters the council ring and salutes the chief and braves. He then walks slowly toward the chief's chair, near which lies a brightly colored blanket folded once lengthwise and once crosswise. Slowly he picks the blanket up, hands it to the chief, and reveals another blanket underneath. On it lies a large eagle plume, its quill wrapped in scarlet cloth. The medicine man holds up the feather for all to see. He then takes a few steps toward the fire, holding the plume above his head. He now steps back, lays the plume ceremoniously on the blanket, and stands one long pace behind it. He faces the fire and raises his arms toward the sky. He stares at the feather which lies before him on the blanket. He then does a few slow dance steps and once more stands a pace behind the feather, with arms uplifted. Very slowly, the feather stands on end, then falls back on the blanket.

The medicine man now takes a short step toward the feather and holds his hands at shoulder level above it. The plume now stands on end and makes a series of little leaps, never higher than one foot above the blanket. Now the medicine man steps back two short paces with his arms held high above his head. The feather now really comes to life. It jumps two or three feet straight up into the air and swings from side to side before landing end up on the blanket. Now the feather dances and capers in time to the movements of the medicine man. (A tom-tom can be effectively used throughout this dance, the brave who beats the tom-tom keeping time as well as he can to the more rhythmic movements of the dancing plume.)

At last the medicine man ceases his movements, and the plume, after resting on end for a few moments, falls back on the blanket. The medicine man then raises the blanket on his hands and advances with the dancing feather on it close to the council fire. He lays the blanket with the plume on it gently on the ground. He then gets

the blanket which covered the plume before the dance and folds it carefully over the feather. After ceremoniously raising his arms above the blankets, he picks them up and returns them to their original position, close to the chief's chair. The chief then leads the solemn closing ceremony, and the council ends.

SOLUTION FOR MAGIC FEATHER DANCE

The movements of the dancing feather are caused by an almost invisible black thread, which is completely unseen by the braves-in-council. The thread is manipulated by the medicine man's assistant, who is concealed behind a tree or bush completely out of sight of the braves-in-council. The feather is weighted at the quill end by wrapping a few lead strips, such as those used as sinkers on fishing lines, around it. There should be just enough weight, evenly distributed, for the assistant to feel the pull of the feather even if he has to operate from a distance of 30 feet. (As will be seen, the feather will operate very smoothly, and there should not be sufficient weight on its end to give an appearance of heaviness as it "dances.") The lead strip is completely covered with a strip of bright scarlet cloth which covers the quill, conceals the lead, and decorates the plume. A 2-foot length of strong silk or cotton thread is securely fastened by one end to the rib of the plume about ½ inch from its tip, allowing the tip to keep its symmetrical shape. Nylon thread usually proves unsatisfactory, since it tangles too easily and is difficult to knot and handle with certainty.

The loose end of the 2-foot length of thread is fastened to the end of the strong black linen or cotton thread on a spool. This thread is used to manipulate the plume. This is done after the loose end of the cotton thread on the spool has been threaded through a small black metal screw eye or a small dark-colored bone or metal ring not more than ½ inch in diameter. The screw eye is screwed into the underside of a branch about 10 to 16 feet from the ground. This branch should overhang the council ring near the chief's chair. The overhead line used in staging the magic fire-lighting feats is another excellent means of making the feather perform. The small ring is tied onto this line directly above the most suitable spot for the "dance" to be performed. The best place to keep the feather when not in use is at one side of the chief's chair, a few feet away, so the blankets and feather need not be disturbed during the earlier part of the council ring activities. Since the thread runs freely, the blankets with the feather in place between them can be set at the very edge of the council ring by slackening the thread which operates the feather. The dance itself is performed several paces away from the chief's chair, nearer the fire.

A very important factor in the success of the entire performance is the chief or brave who manipulates the thread which makes the feather dance. He should be concealed from 10 to 30 feet from the chief's chair, with one end of the thread held securely in his hand, several minutes before the medicine man lifts the blankets. The operator must be completely hidden from the braves-in-council. He may operate in an upright or sitting or crouching position, in a place from which he can see the feather clearly *at all times* throughout the "dance." This allows him to pay out thread as needed by the medicine man at the start and end of the performance and to control the plume's movements all through the "dance." It is, of course, easier for the medicine man to time his dance and other movements with the motions of the plume than for his assistant to make the plume keep time with the medicine man. As mentioned before, a tom-tom can be used to advantage throughout this performance. To assure a perfect act and the mystification of the onlookers, the medicine man and his assistant should practice several times in secret before performing the feat at the council fire. They must determine in advance the best possible spot for the blanket on which the plume will dance, and this is often decided by where the assistant can best conceal himself. Another very important point is that the assistant be able to locate his spool of thread by the firelight at least five minutes before the start of the "dance." This is best done by placing the spool on a headless nail driven into a tree at the exact point from which he will operate. This nail may be marked by a small disc of white paper to assure its easy location in the dim light.

With some showmanship and forethought, the Magic Feather Dance can be made spectacular and mystifying. It can be performed a number of times without any of the braves being able to figure out just how it is done, although they well know that there is more trickery than magic involved, as in the actual Navajo Feather Dance. Having an able assistant who does not rush from a prominent position to manipulate the feather a few moments before the performance begins and then crash around in the underbrush looking for the spool of thread helps to create the illusion. All threads are, of course, carefully removed after the braves have left the council ring.

MEDICINE FEATHER DANCE

The Nootka warriors-in-council are very silent. They have come to see medicine man magic. They will watch closely and perhaps learn, if it be the will of the Great Chief on High, some of the mysteries of shamanism.

In the dark, somewhere outside of the council fire area, the music of rattles, drums, and wooden and shell clappers can be heard. Sometimes sounds likes those of the ocean—low, long, hissing sounds of little waves breaking on the sand and rocks—rise above the rest of the sounds, while voices rise and fall in time to the rhythm.

Suddenly there is only the slow beat of drums as a dancer moves slowly into the council fire area and dances around the brightly blazing fire. He holds a short white feather, about the length of a long hand, above his head as he dances. After he dances for a while in slow time, the drums increase their tempo and the steps of the dancer quicken as he approaches the fire. He stops for a moment, holds the feather high in one hand above the flames, and then drops it, quill end down. It spirals into the fire and burns with a colored light. Almost before it has finished flaming, the dancer gives a shrill shout, jumps into the air, and grasps something. Now he dances with a white feather at least twice as long as the one which he gave to the flames.

He continues to dance, turning and twisting with the feather held high. He dances close to the fire, holds the gleaming white feather above it as though about to drop it into the leaping flames, then dances away again. Again he goes close to the fire. It is not burning so brightly now—perhaps to make it easier for him to work his magic, some Nootka think. No! They think wrongly. A fire tender runs to the fire and pours some eulachon oil onto it. The candlefish oil falls from the richly decorated ceremonial ladle, and the flames greedily lap up the oil and blaze anew. As the dancer holds his feather just above the fire, the fire seizes it in flaming fingers. The dancer springs away from the fire, waving the blazing feather above his head as though to shake off the flames. He cannot do so. He leaps to the fire and drops what is left of the flaming feather into its heart.

The dancer circles the fire slowly, then more and more quickly, making high jumps into the air, grasping for something which he cannot seize. He crouches, hands held high above his head, gazing straight up into the sky. Suddenly he gives a shrill shout of triumph and springs high into the air. A great white feather, as long as his forearm, is drifting slowly down toward the fire. He seizes it as it floats downward, dances three times triumphantly around the council area holding the medicine feather high that all may see, and then leaps into the darkness outside the council fire area.

SOLUTION FOR
MEDICINE FEATHER DANCE

The dance as performed by the Indian shaman counted on the distraction of the onlookers' attention at critical moments and also on perfect timing at the moment of the changing of the feathers. Here are a few suggestions as to how the dance can be done.

The second feather may be concealed quill end down in the sleeve or quill end up in the neck of the shirt. It can be held in place by a stitch, just sufficient to hold it in place during the dance, yet light enough so that it may be snatched instantly from its place of concealment at the moment when the warriors-in-council are watching the first feather burn in a burst of colored flame. The color flame may be caused by putting grains of powder, sold commercially for producing colored flame, into the quill end of the feather. The onlookers, turning suddenly at the shout of the medicine man, see only that he had apparently snatched a longer feather out of thin air.

The release of the final and longest feather may best be done by the use of the overhead line. The drawings show clearly how the longest feather is made and fastened to the overhead line.

The 18- or 20-inch feather is easily made by cutting and joining lengths cut from two or three goose or other long white feathers. When the connections are made carefully, the one long feather looks perfectly natural. The more feather saved from each cut feather, the

longer will be the final feather resulting from splicing them together. The joining together of the two sections of the feathers is most easily done by inserting and gluing 1½ inches of a large match, smoothed to the correct size, ¾ of an inch into each section of the two feathers being joined, as shown in the diagram.

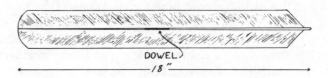

MATCH-STICK DOWEL

DOWEL

—18"—

This third and last feather is fastened to the overhead line and is released to float down to the dancer in this way. A small black metal ring, or a split ring, ¼ inch in diameter is tied securely onto the overhead line about 3 feet away from the council fire. Another ring of the same size is tied onto the overhead line 2 feet away from the ring, toward the direction in which the operator will be hidden. The free end of the operator's line, a length of about 90 feet of strong black thread or lightweight black nylon fishline, is threaded through the overhead line ring nearer to the operator's post by a chief—or better still, the operator—standing on a high stepladder. The line is now tied about 1 inch from the end to the bend in the top of a rippled, springy, metal hairpin snipped off 1¼ inches from the bend on top. A third ring,

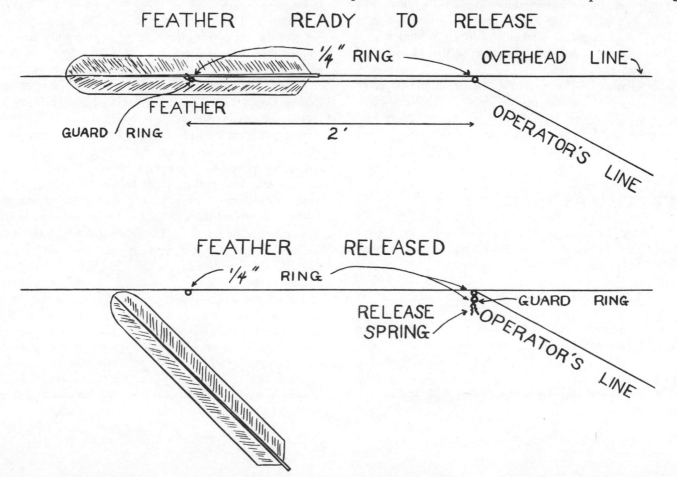

FEATHER READY TO RELEASE

¼" RING — OVERHEAD LINE

FEATHER

GUARD RING — 2' — OPERATOR'S LINE

FEATHER RELEASED

¼" RING

GUARD RING

RELEASE SPRING — OPERATOR'S LINE

the guard ring, the same size as the other two, is fastened onto the operator's line, as close to the bend in the hairpin as possible, by the remaining free 1 inch of line.

The feather is held tightly in place against the ring nearer the council fire by the simple method of putting one prong of the cut-off hairpin on either side of the quill, about in the middle of the feather, putting both prongs through the ring, and spreading the ends *slightly* to hold the feather securely in place. The bend at the top of the hairpin should hold the backbone of the feather close to the ring. It will remain in place for an hour or two when placed in position before council fire time, unless there is a wind blowing and the council fire area is in an exposed situation. Either the top of the feather or the quill end or both can be braced by its own tension on the overhead line, so that the feather lies in a horizontal position. Actually, it does not matter greatly in which way the feather is braced, since it will work equally well from any position when released. The only advantage of the horizontal position is that it tends to make the feather less noticeable. However, when horizontal, the feather must lie along and *underneath* the overhead wire, so that it cannot possibly be caught and held aloft in any way once the release cord has been jerked slightly by the operator from his place of concealment. Even if the big feather turns into a perpendicular position and is noticed by the onlookers in bright council fire light, it appears suspended in mid-air so that the "magic" of its fall at exactly the right moment is accented rather than diminished.

Trials will show that the feather is instantly released by a slight tug on the end of the operator's line, which is fastened to a spool or stick and hidden behind a convenient bush or tree, as in the case of the Thunderbird and Flying Torch fires.

Several practice drops of the feather should be made prior to the performance on the night of the council fire, and it will be found that despite the simplicity of preparing for and staging this illusion, the result is startling and apparently inexplicable when it is well done.

THE MYSTERY SNAKE

Only the sad, baying *hoo hoo hoo whoo* of a great horned owl, followed by its savage, hair-raising hunting scream broke the silence as the Nisqually warriors sat silently in the glow of the council fire. Their tribal chief had told them that tonight the shaman would call on the spirits to send them the Mystery Snake which would warn the medicine man of danger from their enemies and help him in his medicine cures. The snake was said to have much medicine power, and the warriors hoped that it would come at the call of their shaman.

There was the sound of a medicine rattle in the dis-

tance. Gradually the sound came nearer. Soon it was heard faintly just behind the tribal chief's chair. All eyes turned in that direction. Perhaps that is why only a few warriors, if any, saw the shaman glide silently into the council fire area through the main entry. The whirring of his powerful rattle turned the startled glances of the warriors in council in his direction. His rattle whirred the tempo that had just sounded and died behind the chief's chair. The shaman wore a brightly colored dance shirt, long leggings, moccasins, and the mask of a snake covering his face and head. He danced slowly around the council fire area, crouching from time to time as though listening. At times he made his rattle whirr gently, then stopped and listened for a reply. The warriors strained their ears too.

Yes, suddenly a low answering whirr could be heard coming from the end of the council fire area opposite the entrance. The shaman moved in a crouching position toward the sound—which stopped and was no more. The sigh of the warriors was like the night wind in the cedars. Then from the direction of the entrance to the council fire area a faint, distant whirr could be heard by those with the best hunters' ears. Softly the shaman glided toward the entrance, swinging his rattle in a series of broken whirring sounds. He crouched close to the entrance and raised his arms skyward. The whirr from just outside the council fire area ceased suddenly. The shaman rose, still facing the entrance, then backed slowly away from it with his outstretched hands motioning toward his body, as though bidding the snake to come.

With a loud whirrr the snake came. The warriors could see it quite clearly by the light of the brightly burning council fire. It was a great rattlesnake, almost as long as a man is high. Slowly it wriggled into the council fire area, coming ever closer to the fire. The shaman retreated slowly before it, never taking his eyes from the reptile nor ceasing the whirr of his rattle.

When the rattler had passed the council fire a short distance, the shaman advanced slowly toward it in a crouching position. The snake stopped. The shaman stooped still lower, then knelt facing the snake, which was a long pace away. His rattle called for an instant, low and insistent; then he laid it on the ground beside him and stretched both his hands toward the rattlesnake. He held them flat, palms upward and close together, so that the sides of the hands touched. The rattler glided toward them. The warriors-in-council could see the gray and black markings on the great snake. When the rattler came closer still, the shaman lowered his hands so that the fingers touched the ground and the arms sloped upward toward the shoulders. Slowly the snake slithered onto the hands, its head moving slightly from side to side, its eyes looking into the eyes of the shaman. Gradually the snake wriggled up the arms of the shaman and stopped with its head close to his face. A sharp whirr broke the silence. The shaman bent slightly forward and hissed close to the snake's head. The rattlesnake raised its head and rested it against the cheek of the shaman. The squeak of a field mouse would have sounded loud to the warriors at that instant.

Gradually the snake wriggled up the motionless right arm of the shaman and over his shoulder, then slid down his back onto the ground. It slithered between his legs for a moment and wriggled slowly out of the council fire area. The shaman who had risen when the snake slid to the ground, watched it wriggle away. He picked up his rattle, and with it whirring intermittently he glided slowly from the council fire area and disappeared noiselessly into the forest.

A long, low sigh seemed to hover above the council fire as the warriors breathed again. The Mystery Snake had come. It had spoken with their shaman, and he had spoken to it. Now all would be well.

SOLUTION FOR THE MYSTERY SNAKE

Having seen the snake come, in the course of a most realistic and convincing performance at a Northwest Coast Indian council fire, it is embarrassing for the author to have to resort to a camp-made snake and a black fishline in order to give the best and easiest explanation of how the illusion can be duplicated at a modern council fire.

The snake can be made, with a little help from arts and crafts, with a 5-foot length of rope 2 inches in diameter. The rope is padded at the end which is to form the head, in order to make it thicker and more natural-looking. A very small loop of strong, flexible black wire is tightly fastened to the snake's nose. Both ends of this wire may run for a distance of 4 inches down the snake's body and be tied there to assure the wire's remaining in place. This wire is covered as the entire body of the snake is tightly wrapped in strips of white cloth, which are then colored with the gray and black markings of a rattlesnake. An added realistic effect can be produced at the tail end by attaching a thinner, flexible piece of cloth-wrapped rope, so that the tail has motion which accentuates the wriggling movement as the snake slowly glides forward.

One end of a strong black fishline is securely fastened to the wire loop on the nose of the snake. The fishline stretches from outside the council fire area along the entire length of one side of the council fire area and

out the other end, to the point where it is operated by the chief who works the illusion. This end of the line is fastened to a spool or short round stick which is temporarily fastened to a tree at a height of about 4 feet from the ground. The exact situation of the spool on the tree should be marked with a small white circular patch, so that the operator, who already knows its approximate position, can find it easily in the semidarkness in which he will operate. The snake, which is placed outside the council fire area on the opposite side from the operator, lies in the grass ready to crawl into the council fire area as the operator winds in the line. Great care should be taken that there are no twigs or roots in front of the snake at any point from start to finish, so that its wriggling will not be interrupted.

The snake should be used soon after the council fire opening ceremony, in order that the chiefs and shamans using the council fire area will not get snagged on the practically invisible fishline. The chiefs who use the council fire area prior to the coming of the snake should be informed of the fishline and warned to step high, but not noticeably so, when crossing the danger zone on one side of the council fire.

The clever use of rattles outside of the council fire area, combined with a realistic performance by both shaman and snake operator can make The Mystery Snake appear a real mystery, hard to solve and spectacular to watch. Once the snake has approached close enough for the shaman to touch and guide its head with his finger, the movements made by the snake's head are easily controlled and can be made most lifelike by a little clever manipulation. Naturally, the shaman guides the movements of the snake up his arms and over his right or left shoulder by inclining his hands and bare arms, or arms covered with tight-fitting dance-shirt sleeves, so that there is no resistance to the snake's upward progress, as the operator pulls on the fishline. The medicine man must be sure at all times that he is not standing on the line; and when the snake wriggles down his back, he should be sure that the snake's head has cleared his legs by about a foot or so, before rising to his feet. He can best tell the snake's position at this point by glancing over his shoulder.

The props used for this and other illusions merit care in their preparation. A little time and artistic effort are well spent, as the props look better and more natural, can be used any number of times, and may be stored away for use during another season.

chapter 22

I count coup!

THE TRIBAL OR CLAN CHIEF who asks the coup questions given on the following pages calls a warrior to come to his chair. He uses the name which the brave is known by in council, and the name of the brave's tribe or clan is not changed, although the coup questions which follow are asked of warriors with Northwest Coast tribe names. The chief may ask braves from several tribes to sit in front of his chair and listen to the questions being asked. The first warrior who believes that he knows the correct answer stands up. The chief then asks them, in the order in which they stood, to tell him very softly what they believe the answer to be. The first one to give the correct answer counts coup. The chief should tell these contestants not to stand nor indicate in any way that they think they know the answer until the end of the question. When the warrior or warriors at the chief's chair cannot answer the coup question, other warriors are called on until the correct answer has been given and the coup awarded. The award may be a feather or an imitation bear claw for a Plains or Woodland brave, or a small crest painted on an oval of leather, an imitation dentalium shell or a miniature copper for a warrior of a Northwest Coast clan. Such awards can easily be made in the craft shop.

Of course, the coup questions should be asked in the Indian manner of speech. No questions or stories should be read from a book or paper at a council fire. No matter how interesting the story may be, it is very hard to retain

the listeners' interest. There is, perhaps, no point in trying to commit the questions in their entirety to memory, but great care must be taken to include *all* pertinent information in the questions asked, in order that the braves questioned—as well as the warriors-in-council—will have a fair chance to follow along and try to figure out the correct answer.

The chief in charge of this part of the council fire program—the questioning—will be saved considerable advance preparation if he uses the unseen narrator, whose role is described in Chapter 14, to read the questions. This will assure that they are read *precisely,* while the chief can concentrate on those braves answering the questions. Should he prefer to use a visible narrator—one in regalia—the narrator stands beside the chief and by torchlight reads the typewritten or very clearly written questions pasted on the back of a ceremonial fan, to preserve atmosphere. The council fire chief can call the braves to his chair before the narrator begins to read the coup question and send the braves back to their places after each coup question has been answered.

INDIAN COUP QUESTIONS

The answers to the following coup questions are to be found at the end of the chapter.

THE TRIBAL CHIEF. A messenger has come to me, O warrior of the Tsimshian, to tell us that hunters in the forest behind the Mountain-that-Rises-from-the-Great Salt-Water have found deer without horns and fur. That even the bucks have neither horns nor fur must be true, for the word has been sent by a great hunter. He has also told me why it is so. Men of your tribe are good hunters and wise in the ways of the forest trails, O Tsimshian, so maybe you can tell us why these deer of which I speak have no horns and no fur.

THE TRIBAL CHIEF. Listen well, O Salish who live far from the salt water, while I speak of a fish that you know well. The Old One has placed the arch of color which we sometimes see in the sky on the sides of this brave fish. Just after the sun had come I was on the bank of a swift stream of clear water. As I looked down into the waters I saw a great fish of the tribe of which I speak, swimming with a big pebble in its mouth. Where was it going, O Salish, and why think you it carried the round stone in its mouth?

THE TRIBAL CHIEF. Our hunters tell us, O warrior of the clan of Sea Otters, that they see both father and mother birds who are good to their young and protect them from all enemies while they lie helpless in their nest. One of the cruel enemies of the very young birds

265

is our friend the sun. Tell us how some fathers and mothers of the wings-of-the-air protect their young from its burning rays. Name the birds of which I think and tell us of the wise thing they do, that you may count coup.

THE TRIBAL CHIEF. You have hunted in our forests, O Chinook, and followed the hunting trails with hunters from many clans. Much have you spoken of our furred and feathered friends, and many things have you learned of their ways. You know that the first snow finds many sleepy animals in our mountains and forests. So sleepy are they that you will see them little or never until the green grass comes again. Both hands and all of my fingers do I need on which to count and name these sleepy ones, both big and small. Name five, O Chinook, to prove to the warriors-in-council that you know the ways of the animals of which I speak. Name eight and count coup as a hunter who is wise on the trail.

THE TRIBAL CHIEF. Many times have you eaten the mushrooms that grow in our damp shady woods, O warrior of the Bear People, but have you really seen, with the keen eyes of one who would learn the nature mysteries of the Sky Chief, how they grow? If you have seen them grow on straight and crooked stalks and looked well at them, you will know the answer to my question. I ask that all may learn. How would you bend greatly the stalk of a mushroom, when the stem stands straight as an arrow, without touching it with fingers or sticks. You may cut the stalk of the mushroom close to the ground first, if you believe that it will help in the bending. Tell us what you would do, and why you would do it, to make the straight stalk bent. If your words are wise, you may count coup.

THE TRIBAL CHIEF. Our people like the wind. It brings to us the smells of the sea and the forest. We like its soft breath and respect the power of its mighty strength and voice. Many of our furred and feathered friends like the wind too. Some of the wings-of-the-air ride and play on it. Can you tell me, O warrior of the Haida, which animal likes to have the wind rock it gently in the treetops, often until it sleeps? Name it, Haida, that you may count coup in council.

THE TRIBAL CHIEF. You have watched the sea otters play and swim with the speed of arrows, O Bella Coola. You have seen a mother of that tribe sleep far out on the ocean with her baby asleep on her stomach. Much do you know of these fast friends, who play much both in water that is salt and in the clear streams that you drink. The otters of streams are great hunters and often take the fish which they eat by surprise. You who have watched the wildthings in fast-flowing streams, tell us how these otters catch the fish that

is their food? Do they hide as though in ambush, or do they catch them in some other manner? Speak, that we may learn, O Bella Coola.

THE TRIBAL CHIEF. As a hunter of the Lummi you know that some furred and feathered things lie as though life had gone from them, when you cause them to fear greatly. Even some of the crawling, legless things will *hiss* at you, then when you frighten them they will turn over upon their backs and appear to die. Only some harmless snakes do this, so no danger awaits you when you go to them. Tell us, warrior of the Lummi, the surest and quickest way to find out if your eyes may believe what they seem to see. Is the snake alive or dead? How would you know?

THE TRIBAL CHIEF. Listen well, O warrior of the Yakima, while I speak of the worm-which-measures. We may learn something from that humble creeping thing. Who has not smiled as he watched the worm-which-measures measure a leaf or flower as it slowly crosses them. Does this greenish-brown worm say, when he reaches the far side of that which he measures, "Yes, it is six times longer than I"; or does he say, "The Sky Chief was watching so that, little and helpless as I am, I crossed that plain without being seen by one of my many enemies"? Yesterday, as the sun came, I watched a worm-which-measures begin to cross the petals of a white flower. It looked almost black against the white. Now, I thought, is the time for a wasp or a bird enemy to catch and eat that little worm. Why has not the Sky Chief given him colors to hide him or false frightening eyes, as he has given many of the little creeping things, to protect him? I watched, and my eyes could not believe that which they saw. Could the Sky Chief have given a wisdom as great as that which our warriors who are best at ambush warfare have, to that little worm-which-measures? Tell us what you think I saw, O Yakima, that the warriors-in-council may share my surprise.

THE TRIBAL CHIEF. You have hunted bear as well as whales, warrior of the Nootka. Not only black bear but grizzly bear too have felt the bite of your arrows. Your tribe is said to know much of the ways of the bears, which you honor by scattering eagle down on them after they have been killed by you. Tell us, that we may know, O Nootka, if you had only your war club in hand and were passing close to pine trees which you could climb fast, would you rather run to tree safety followed by a savage black bear or a grizzly bear? Choose now, and tell us why you so choose.

THE TRIBAL CHIEF. Summer, a time of change in the way of life of both man and beast, has taken over our land, O hunter of the Chehalis. Some of our furred friends of

the forest have built summer houses, just as some of our tribes build summer villages. The summer houses of the animals are far different from those in which they dwell in winter. Name one of these animals and tell us of its summer house, or name two of the same tribe, and count coup.

THE TRIBAL CHIEF. You have surely seen, O warrior of the Squamish, the peaceful beast with tree-cutting teeth and paddlelike tail which helps to guide it in the water and gives the loud alarm. Let us speak of this leatherlike tail, which they say is covered with scales. If this be so, these scales must be bigger by far than the scales on the sides of the biggest fish which live in our streams. Tell me, O Squamish, how many scales can be found on a tail of a beaver. Twenty, think you, or forty, or more? Speak, that we may learn.

THE TRIBAL CHIEF. You know the ways of our furred and feathered wildthings, O Nisqually. The Great Spirit marked some of the birds and beasts with markings which are as easily seen as bright stars in the sky. Some of these markings of which I think are black; others are white. We know that the Great Spirit wishes to protect the wildthings and so gave them colors which are often hard for even a hunter to see. Some may wonder if the black or white markings of which I have spoken do not make the beasts and birds more easily seen by their enemies. Do these marks not betray them to, rather than hide them from, the hunters? Name three beasts, or two beasts and one bird, O warrior of the Nisqually, which have either the white or black markings of which I speak. Tell us why they have these surprise markings, and count coup.

THE TRIBAL CHIEF. As you follow the forest trails, O warrior of the Klickitat, you may strike with a hard stick on the outside of hollow trees so that you may see the little furred and feathered wildthings look out of the holes in the trunks and branches to see who disturbs their sleep. In my mind's eye I can see nine furred and feathered wildthings which live in one of these treehole villages. Name but six for us, and count coup, that your tribe may think well of you.

THE TRIBAL CHIEF. You know, O Quinault, that old painted turtles are wise. The warrior who would pick one up before it slides into the lake must be keen-eyed, silent, and fast. Young painted turtles are not so wise, but the One Above has well protected them. They look like where they stand. Only one thing might have been seen quickly by their enemies—their eyes. So the One Above made their eyes hard to see until the turtles grew older and wiser than their enemies. What was done so that their eyes might remain hidden? Tell us, warrior of the Quinault, and count coup.

THE TRIBAL CHIEF. Let us talk of a big cat, O hunter of the Squamish, a beast that moves quick as light and as softly as wind-blown smoke from our council fire. The question I ask you is: How does this great cat teach her young to be quick to spring and sure to catch while she lies still upon a flat rock or the grass? She plays this game while lying purring there. Her hunting game tells her which of her young is best fitted for the first real lesson in hunting. How is this game played, O Squamish? Speak, and count coup.

THE TRIBAL CHIEF. Turn your thoughts from the ocean, O warrior of the Killer Whale clan, that you may tell us of a beast much smaller than the great gray whale. Our hunters tell us, because they have seen much in the forest, of birds that carry their young between their legs when they fly from danger and great cats which carry their young by the skin of the backs of the necks. Tell us this, that all may know: How does the mother black bear often carry her baby? Speak, and count coup.

THE TRIBAL CHIEF. Tonight, O hunter of the Squamish, I would speak of a strange bird, that is colored like an old buckskin dance apron and is one and a half times the length of your hand. A Woodland Indian storyteller has told us that the Great Spirit made this bird out of pieces that were left over after he had made all other wings-of-the-air. Because of this, the eyes of this bird are just in front of its ears. Because of this, it can see better when its enemies are behind it than when they are in front of it. Though this bird has the keen eyes of a hunter, it never sees what it eats as it feeds in the alder swamps. This strange feathered thing has a very short neck and almost no tail. It must have a singing place beside its feeding and resting place. Because the Great Spirit had to make this feathered friend in so strange a form, he felt sad for it. He thought, then gave it two wonderful things. As it flies, its wing feathers give a golden whistle which is a mystery of beauty. The love song which it sings as it seeks a mate is so sad and sweet that it will live always in the hearts of those who hear it. What is the name of this strangest of birds? Tell us and count coup, O Squamish.

THE TRIBAL CHIEF. Let us now talk of those who lived under water as fierce warriors for many, many moons and who can now fly but cannot walk. Perhaps my words are still mysteries to you, O brave, but soon I will pull aside the door of the tepee of your mind, and the sun of understanding will light it with its rays. I speak of the bright-winged hunters of the reeds, of those of the endless appetite—the dragonflies. Yesterday, I heard a merrymaker tell one of our women that now that our summer lodges are on the edge of a lake, she must be careful. Dragonflies—"darning needles," he called them—would come

from the reeds and sew up her lips as she slept. "Is that so, O Chief?" she asked me. "Are they of the bright darting wings our friends or our foes?" I answered her questions, O brave. What do you think I told her?

THE TRIBAL CHIEF. It is late in the Thunder Moon as you walk along the bank of our stream. Twenty paces distant from some brilliant red flowers, which now grow on the bank, you see a winged jewel dart from them and flit away above the reeds. If you know the flower, you will know its winged visitor. Tell us its name, O brave of the Mohawks.

THE TRIBAL CHIEF. Tell us, O brave of the Cheyennes, why the savage wolf, while hunting, will leave the newborn fawn lying safely in its covert and chase the mother as she breaks from cover? Were the wolves wise, surely they would eat the tender fawn, which has little or no speed, instead of chasing the swift mother as she bounds from her fawn's side. A cunning wolf must know that it may lose her scent, and a meal.

THE TRIBAL CHIEF. Come closer to your chief, O brave of the Six Nations, and let us talk of sweet sounds and bird notes. Our wise men tell us that to some men there are even sweeter sounds than the murmur of the stream in the willows, or the night noises on the shores of our lake. It is the sound of their own names! Some of our feathered friends seem to think as these vain men. Tell us, O child of the Oneidas, of at least six birds which tell us their names. By so doing, you may count coup. Name all six, and you may count three coups. Imitate them well, and you may count one coup for the voice or note of each bird you bring us.

THE TRIBAL CHIEF. Little Owl has told us that he was able to place his arrows in the heart of the wolverine. He did well, for we know the trouble and damage that beast of evil has caused. But did Little Owl do well when, in his anger at seeing his broken traps, he took his firesticks and burned our enemy on a blazing fire? Did not the Great Wakonda give his children some good even from an animal so bad? Tell us, O warrior of the Sioux would you have brought the body of the wolverine to our tepees, or would you too have destroyed all of him?

THE TRIBAL CHIEF. Your skill in felling trees, O brave of the Cayugas, brings to my thoughts the work of our little friends the beavers. The Great Spirit put little tomahawks in their mouths, and the trees fall before them. You, through the goodness of the Great Spirit, can think and therefore make a tree fall where you will. Our wise men tell us that the beavers, wonderful as is their work, cannot think. How then, O brave, can the beavers make the trees which they cut fall where they will?

ANSWERS AND SOLUTIONS TO COUP QUESTIONS

The hornless, furless deer. No deer has horns, only antlers; and deer have hair, not fur.

The fish and the pebble. The rainbow trout was on its way to build a nest on the bed of the stream. The pebble which he carried was to use in building the pebble nest, in which the female would lay her eggs.

The feathered sunshade. Eagles, hawks, and herons shade their young from sun glare by standing in the nest and spreading their wings as a canopy over the baby birds. Both mother and father birds take turns at providing shelter, which undoubtedly saves their young from death.

The sleepy wildthings. Among the animals which actually hibernate and those which spend most of the winter in their dens and lairs are: bears, marmots, raccoons, ground squirrels, woodchucks, jumping mice, bats, chipmunks, and prairie dogs.

Bending a mushroom stalk. All mushrooms, no matter how curved their stalks, grow with the bottom of their caps parallel with the ground. This is to assure the spores falling directly on the ground, so that a new mushroom crop is seeded. When a mushroom with a straight stem is cut off at ground level and the mushroom placed on its side on the ground, it will gradually turn so that the cap is directly upward and the stem greatly bent to assure nature's natural position of the mushroom top.

The treetop cradle. When the wind blows, porcupines are fond of climbing young flexible trees, the branches of which they may not eat, and swaying back and forth in the wind-blown treetop. Often a porcupine may be found asleep in the top of a favorite tree, on days when the wind sings lullabies in the treetops.

The fishing otter. The fast-swimming otter approaches the fish from the rear, because it knows that feeding and idling fish do so with their heads pointing upstream.

The "dead" snake. The hog-nosed snake will put on a great act when you come upon it suddenly. It *hisses* and threatens in a way that would make a venomous snake envious. When it finds that it cannot scare you off, it turns on its back and appears to die. You may touch it, even poke it gently with a stick, but it remains motionless in order to keep up the pretence of being dead. Turn it over on its belly and you will see how nature's instinctive defense slipped up. The snake will immediately turn over onto its back again— perhaps to convince you that it is really dead this time!

Measuring worm camouflage. When a measuring worm, sometimes called an inchworm, decides to spend some time feasting on a white- or yellow-petaled flower, it promptly tears off tiny pieces of the flower petals and sticks them all over its body, where they adhere, until

it is practically impossible to tell, even at close quarters, which is flower petal and which is measuring worm.

Treed by a bear. The Nootka, having a firsthand knowledge of bears and their ways, would certainly have chosen a grizzly bear, and for a very good reason—grizzly bears cannot climb trees, but a black bear does so easily.

Animal summer houses. The gray and fox squirrels build circular houses of sticks and branches, high in the treetops, for summer use.

Scaled paddle tail. While the blackish, leatherlike tail of a beaver has scalelike markings, they are actually surface markings, as there are *no* scales on a beaver's tail.

The give-away markings. The savage weasel—ermine, or vermin—according to the season and whether the fur is worn by its original owner or a human being, has a jet-black tip on its white tail, the only black marking on its entirely white body and tail, during the winter months. The antelope, the white-tail deer, and the cottontail rabbit are three of the mammals with tails with the undersides white. The flicker, of the woodpecker family, is one of the birds with white rumps. Strangely enough, these very noticeable markings have a surprise element which distracts attention from the animal or bird itself. When the distinguishing patch is hidden, which the animal can do at will, the beast or bird is extremely difficult to locate. Even dogs are often so fascinated with the white tails of deer that when this marking suddenly disappears, the dog not only loses sight of the animal but, for a while, its scent, and some time is lost before the trail can be picked up again. The black-tipped tail of an ermine makes it very difficult to locate the rest of the animal, and when the tail is coiled out of sight, the entire animal seems to vanish in the snow.

The tree-hole village. Some of the animals which may occupy homes in such trees are: raccoon, marten, skunk, rabbit, groundhog, and squirrel, depending on the neighborhood and the identity of the first-come tenants. Birds are especially fond of tree-hole homes, and likely ones to be found in these retreats—though, of course, not rooming together—are: wood duck, woodpecker, owl, sparrow hawk, blue bird, house wren, chicadee, crested flycatcher, nuthatch, according to locality and the position of the trees.

The camouflaged eyes. The eyes of a young painted turtle benefit by one of nature's most amazing camouflage tricks. Their eyes are marked by a dark, almost black band which completely crosses the iris, blending into the dark pupil on both sides. This marking makes the eyes, which would otherwise appear conspicuous,

almost invisible even at short range.

The hunting game. The mountain lion—catamount, cougar, or puma, as it is called among other things—uses the tip of her heavy tail to teach her babies to pounce accurately on their prey. As the mother mountain lion lies on the ground, she swings and twitches her long tail while her cubs try to spring on the almost tufted tip and seize it with teeth or claws. Since she is adept at keeping the tip of her tail out of the youngsters' reach, the one which connects most often with the tip is the one which is ready for advanced training in the pursuit of game.

The "headless" black bear cub. It is sometimes a startling sight, in the woods, to come suddenly upon a black bear mother carrying her tiny cub. The reason is that she often carries her little one with its entire head inside her mouth. The cub's instant activity, when she places it on the ground, shows that it is not affected by this strange method of transport.

The "remnant" bird. This remarkable, wise, and ungainly bird is the woodcock.

The dragonfly. Sometimes called a "darning needle," the dragonfly is one of our best insect friends. It is not only absolutely harmless to human beings, but it also devours our insect enemies. Were it not for the thousands of flies, mosquitoes, and other stinging insects which the always-ravenous dragonfly eats greedily, we would be far less comfortable on the lakeshore and in the woods surrounding it.

Red flowers and winged jewel. The flowers would be the flaming cardinal, and the bird would be the ruby-throated hummingbird. The cardinal flower is one of the favorite food sources of that species of hummingbird.

The newborn fawn. The wolf would pursue the mother, because wise nature takes care that the newborn fawn is practically scentless. At this time the doe has also a much stronger scent than usual, to lure wild animals away from her fawn while it is young and helpless.

Bird names. Among the birds which tell us their names are the bobwhite (American quail), cuckoo, whippoorwill, chickadee, phoebe, killdeer, and jay.

The wolverine. A wise hunter would skin the beast and treasure its pelt. It is the only known fur which will not frost when breathed on in freezing weather. This makes the fur valuable for edging parkas and making high fur collars for winter garments.

Beaver woodsmen. It is sad but true that the beaver, despite his brilliant engineering ability, has no idea in which direction the tree which he is felling will fall. The number of dead beavers found under trees which they have gnawed down is one proof of this fact.

potlatches and pageantry of the northwest coast

D ANCE BELLS TINKLE MUSICALLY in the shadow-paths of the silent forest as braves move quietly in Indian file toward the council ring. They are wearing ceremonial regalia, for tonight the fire will shine on the brilliant pageantry which is a colorful part of the way of life of the Indians.

Challenge pageants will put the skill, speed, and strength of the braves to the test. Dance, story, and song will unite to form mind pictures and medicine shadows in the flickering firelight. Let us share with the braves the magic of the council fire and its pageantry.

SALMON RUN
A CHALLENGE PAGEANT

The salmon run, when the Pacific salmon teemed in the rivers of the Northwest Coast on their way upstream to spawn and die, was one of the most important events in the lives of the Northwest Coast Indians. Great feasts, pageants, and celebrations were held in honor of the event. That is why this exciting challenge should be started off with a colorful pageant before the actual challenge is contested.

Before describing the pageant and challenge, let us line up the simple camp-made equipment required to stage this contest, including the salmon spears. The diagram shows exactly what is required for the challenge, and will prove helpful in making the necessary gear. Six salmon spears, two stout wooden stakes, two strong screw eyes, two black metal rings ½ inch or ¾ inch in diameter, one set of two "salmon" fastened to cords and dowel sticks as shown in the diagram, and about 30

chapter 23

feet of strong black fishline are required for one complete Salmon Run Challenge Pageant set, for six spearers.

Three torches are used for effect in the pageant entry into the council fire area and for illumination during the salmon run. Torches can be cut from a straight green sapling about 1½ inches in diameter. It is cut into 2-foot lengths, and a 4-foot length of gauze bandage which has been thoroughly dipped into liquid paraffin wax is wrapped around about 6 inches of one end. The other end of the torch is wired securely onto any straight pole 6 feet long and about 1½ inches in diameter. One end of the pole is pointed, so that it may be forced easily about 12 inches into the ground when the torch bearers leave them stuck in the earth to illuminate the salmon run. (Of course, long torches made from 7-foot saplings can be used instead of the green sections of saplings tied to ordinary poles, if sufficient thin saplings are available without spoiling a stand of young trees.)

Each of the six salmon spears is made from a 7-foot length of straight young wild cherry or a thin straight maple sapling about 1½ inches in diameter at the thick end and tapering to about ¾ inch in diameter at the thin end. Regular prepared poles 1½ inches in diameter, such as are sold in lumber yards, can also be tapered and used as spears. While the experience in working with natural woods is lost by this method, it is recommended when young trees are scarce in the camp area and there are no stands of young saplings which would benefit by thinning out. The finished spear should feel well balanced when poised in one hand, ready to strike. The heavy end is the point or striking end.

Each stake is 14 inches long and 2 inches in diameter, pointed at one end. On the top end of the stake a strong metal screw eye about ¾ inch in diameter is screwed into the wood up to the eye. Each stake should be driven into the ground for a depth of about 12 inches.

The salmon are best made from a thin strong plywood ½ inch in thickness, cut into ovals 12 inches long by 3 inches wide, and painted white on both sides. The dowel sticks are 15 inches long and ½ inch in diameter, and should be painted or stained black. One length of black fishline 1 foot long is attached through the ¼-inch hole in one end of each salmon, and another 2-foot length of line is attached through the hole at the other end of the fish, with the other ends attached to the dowels, as shown in the diagram. The ½- or ¾-inch metal ring is fastened tightly to the center of a 2-foot-6-inch length of black fishline, the ends of which are fastened to the ends of the dowel stick, as shown in the drawing. A notch made about ½ inch from each end of the dowel will secure the fishline so that it cannot slip, especially if the length of line is secured by a clove hitch. Fifteen feet of strong black fishing line is tied securely to the ring at each end of the salmon set. These are the lines which operate the salmon run, after one end is passed through

the screw eye on the stake at one end of the council fire area, and the other end is passed through the screw eye of the stake which is set up directly in line with it at the opposite end of the area. The diagram shows more clearly than words just how the entire salmon run equipment is set up. All is now ready for the challenge, and this is how the contest is carried out.

Two clan chiefs who act as salmon runners stand one behind each stake, holding the end of the fishing line, to which the two salmon are attached. The salmon can start the run from either end of the area. The job of the salmon runners is to make the salmon run the gauntlet of the six salmon spearers as the line is quickly pulled, hand over hand, making the fish travel swiftly from one end of the council fire area to the other. The six salmon spearers are ready, at the points shown in the drawing. The torches have been thrust into the ground, in the positions shown, so that light is thrown on the moving salmon as they approach the spearing points. While positions are marked showing where the tallykeepers stand at the start of the contest, they will soon be on the move up and down the line, in order to keep score and credit the salmon spearers with all salmon speared. The tribal chief keeps an alert eye on all activities; when he sees that all is in readiness, he gives the command to start the salmon run by shouting the word "Spear!"

On the chief's command, the salmon runner who has to bring the salmon to his end pulls sharply on the line, remaining behind the stake at all times as he does so. It is the job of each salmon runner to try to make it as hard as possible for the spearers to strike a salmon as it passes. To accomplish this he may change the speed at which the fish travel, stop them for a moment between spearers, and use other ruses to protect the salmon from the spears, without slowing up the speed of the contest. The salmon spearers require keen eyes and the ability to time speeds and move fast when the right time comes to strike. The spear must be held so that the hand holding it is above the spearer's shoulder prior to each strike. It must be brought up into the same position before a second strike can be made. Mere poking at a salmon with the spear, even when the fish is hit, does not count in the scoring. A good salmon runner will not give a spearer the chance to strike at either fish more than once while they are within reach of his spear. To make rivalry even keener, the salmon runners should, when possible, be from different clans from those of the contesting salmon spearers. The salmon runners stop pulling on the line immediately when they feel a salmon actually pinned down by a spear—glancing blows on the fish do not count. The tallykeepers will check each strike made and credit the spearer with it. When a tallykeeper has recorded the coup, he shouts, "Run!" and the salmon runner begins the run again.

The tribal chief may let the salmon spearers have

SALMON RUN

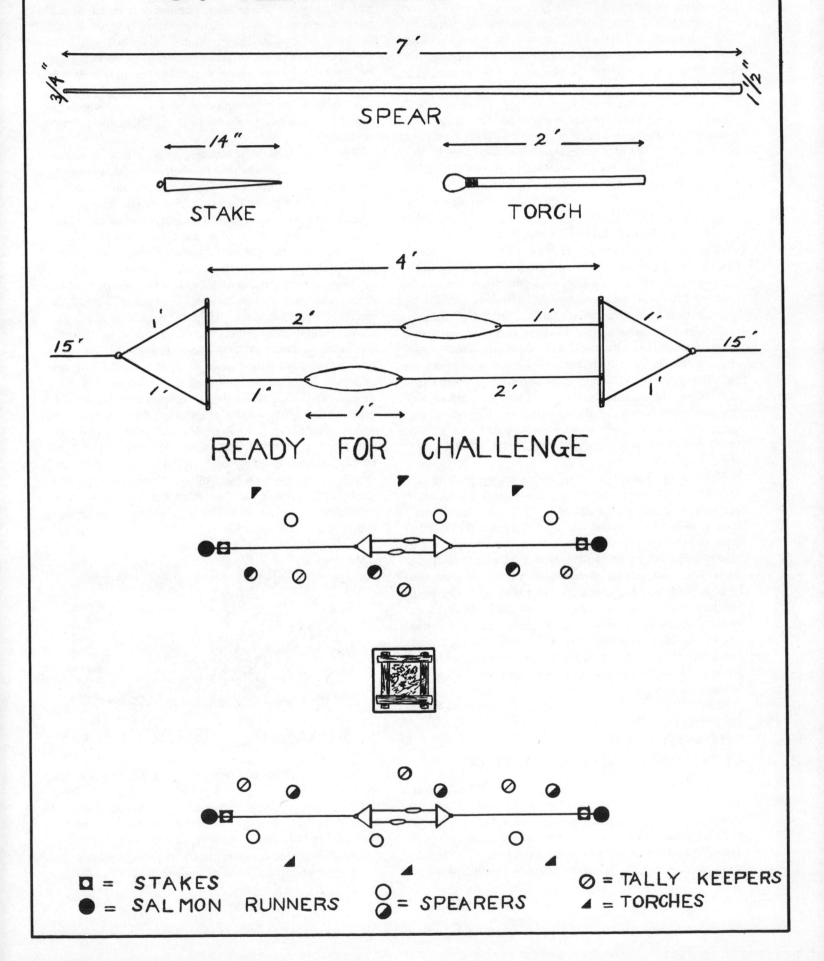

7′

3/4″   1 1/2″

SPEAR

14″

STAKE

2′

TORCH

4′

1′   2′   1′   1′

15′   1′   1″   2′   1′   15′

1′

READY FOR CHALLENGE

☐ = STAKES

● = SALMON RUNNERS

◐ = SPEARERS

⊘ = TALLY KEEPERS

◢ = TORCHES

either two or three runs before calling new spearers into the council fire area.

By using two complete sets of equipment, a Salmon Run can be contested on each of two sides of the council fire, allowing twelve salmon spearers to contest at the same time, six on each of the two sides of the council fire. This arrangement gives all of the warriors-in-council a close-up of the exciting event.

When two sets are in operation at the same time, each group of salmon runners and spearers contests entirely independently of the other. Separate scores are kept by the two sets of tallykeepers for each spearing group. An interesting event is to have the champions from each group contest for the championship at some future council fire.

The pageant entry into the council fire area may be effectively carried out in the following way. A tribal chief leads the march, followed by a torch bearer with flaming torch. Then come three salmon spearers, each carrying his spear, followed by two salmon runners, then a torch bearer and the three tallykeepers. One or two clan chiefs, followed by the third torch bearer, complete the parade. Should there be two groups of salmon run challengers, the second party follows the first group in the same order of march. Either one or two groups parade three times around the council fire area, taking up the positions shown on the diagram at the end of the march. Each group, when there are two of them, should know on which side of the fire its Salmon Run takes place.

The Salmon Runs should be set up in complete readiness for the challenge before the contestants parade into the area. There is plenty of room for the Indian-file procession to march around the area between the salmon runs and the warriors-in-council. It is a wise precaution to staple the fishing line to the ground at each end of the area. This will permit the marchers to pass over the lines without picking them up with their feet. The lines are best stapled down with two or three heavy wire staples, made by bending 5-inch lengths of heavy wire into staple form. The two ends of these staples are forced down into the earth so that the top is flush with the ground. These staples are, of course, removed before the Salmon Run begins.

THE POTLATCH— CEREMONIAL GIVE-AWAY FEAST

These colorful affairs are staged by the Indians of the Northwest Pacific Coast. The word *potlatch* comes from the Chinook Jargon, the trade language of the vast Northwest Territories, and means "to give" and "giving." Giving was stressed to the point where rich chiefs became poor, poor chiefs became rich, and tribes went to war or raided other tribes to provide gifts for distribution at a big potlatch. Some huge potlatches were announced three years or more in advance. When they were held, princes, princesses, chiefs, nobles, shamans, and other guests came from hundreds of miles around to honor and be honored at the magnificent ceremonial feast and give-away. Setting up a totem pole to honor a person, clan, or tribe, or to commemorate some great and striking event, was usually an important part of the potlatch ceremony.

The gifts given at potlatches were valuable, artistic, extraordinary, and endless in their astonishing variety. Splendid canoes, from the 75-foot ceremonial canoe to one-man hunting canoes, superbly carved and painted house screens, and beautifully constructed cedar chests were among some of the more important gifts. Wonderful weapons—spears, daggers, knives, clubs, rawhide and wooden-slat armor, battle helmets, bows and arrows, lances, and harpoons, in addition to other weapons of the chase and war—were lavishly distributed among the guests. Chilkat blankets, originally woven by the Tsimshian; magnificent clothing made of the most valuable furs, such as sea otter, and woven red and yellow cedar bark; ceremonial hats; marvelous masks,—which opened and closed and became animated by a slight pull on a thong—were expertly made for the potlatch and lavishly given. The variety of the presents was astounding! Let a very brief list of items that changed hands at one huge potlatch bear out this statement: A bowl of preserved berries, a crew of thirty or forty canoemen for a ceremonial canoe, a dead whale still very fresh, ten dentalium shells, fifty sea-otter pelts, an intricately carved bracelet, a priceless copper, a dance apron, six songs, four dances, fish nets and fishing tackle.

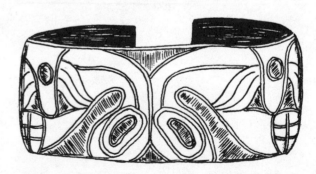

SILVER   BRACELET

The prince, chief, or noble who gave the potlatch distributed the gifts and made a grandiloquent speech about the illustrious person who was about to receive a gift, or many gifts. The one who received the gifts praised the giver and gifts in fitting, flowery, and dramatic terms.

Unbelievable care was taken to seat every guest in his or her proper place. Those of highest rank and achievement were given the seats of honor. As the guests were sensitive and constantly on the lookout to be certain that the honors accorded them were in keeping with their rank and that no person of lesser standing was offered similar courtesies, there were few intentional breaches of etiquette. The slightest breach could mean family or clan feuds, or even tribal war.

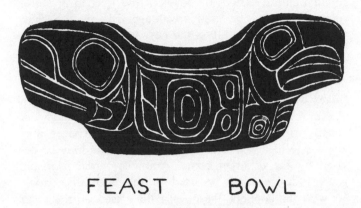

FEAST BOWL

Feasting, magic, dancing, dramatic performances, storytelling, music, hair-raising dances and acts by masked dancers, juggling, marionettes, sports, and challenges of all kinds found a place on the potlatch program. Modern council fire chiefs will be quick to appreciate the scope and variety of the entertainment offered at a potlatch and draw on it for their own council fires.

What did these fortunate Indians feast on? Whale steaks; seals; porpoise; fish—fresh and smoked—such as salmon, cod, halibut, and herring; many shellfish, including clams and mussels; crabs; edible seaweed; bear, elk, and mountain goat steaks; water birds, including geese and ducks; and birds' eggs. There were also huge quantities of fruits such as crab apples, gooseberries, salmon berries, and huckleberries, in addition to many vegetables and other delicacies. Usually the host made fun of those who had not eaten a terrific quantity of food, and his quips and jibes never caused offense.

Records of great potlatches given throughout the eighteenth century still exist, and it is interesting to know that quite recently a huge potlatch was given by the Indians of the Northwest Coast in Victoria, British Columbia.

A chief or noble giving a potlatch was known as "one who called the people in" and was greatly honored by his people and those of neighboring tribes. The term used to describe a giver of feasts arose from the "calling of names" ceremony, when callers in full ceremonial regalia publicly called the names of those invited to the feast. Potlatch invitation drums boomed; invitation sticks were sent out by canoe and runner, so that nobody entitled to an invitation was left out.

CEREMONIAL POTLATCH PAGEANT

Having read the background notes on how potlatches were carried out among the tribes of the Northwest Coast, the tribal chief of the modern council fire will be able to plan some spectacular potlatch ceremonies to be celebrated from time to time during the camp season. There is such a wealth of material to draw on that the only difficulty may lie in having too much rather than too little material from which to choose. A suggestion for a council fire ceremonial potlatch follows.

The "calling of names" should take place a day or two before the ceremony. The names called are those of the people who will receive "gifts," and perhaps those of other guests who do not appear on the gift list. Two or three tribal warriors in full regalia should call out the names at times when the campers are gathered together, in the dining hall or at flag raising, for example. If the calling is done over a period of two days, it keeps those whose names have not been called in suspense, since the list can be called in three or four parts, naming different guests each time.

A day or two before the potlatch, the warriors who will actually take part in carrying the gifts around the council fire area and arranging them for distribution should be chosen and given some chance to practice for the ceremony, to assure things going smoothly.

On the night of the potlatch, the council fire should be burning brightly, and the council area should be specially lighted by several paraffin wax torches on 7-foot poles, stuck into the ground at the end of the council fire area where the potlatch is held. Ceremonial pageantry starts the event. Chiefs, warriors, servants, and slaves parade around the council fire area bearing the "gifts." One torch bearer should march with each group of four or six warriors. Those in the procession carry bundles of brightly colored blankets, painted boxes, harpoons, spears, strings of shells, painted paddles, bows and arrows, "furs," and other gifts. Coppers, some carried in front of the chiefs, are beaten by servants and displayed to the onlookers as the bearers circle the council fire area. The gifts may be paraded two or three times around the area before the head of the procession halts close to the chief's chair. The gifts are then arranged near the chair, so that they are displayed to the best advantage. Those who took part in the parade now sit in the council fire area, and the tribal chief is ready to start the give-away. The potlatch can begin with music and singing, followed by a suitable Northwest Coast story or legend. This can be followed by a period of gift-giving. A colorful speech is made before each gift is given, and another speech is made in reply by the one who receives the gift, or gifts. The Indians of the Northwest Coast were not lacking in sense of humor, and while the ceremony never lost its dignity, many humorous remarks passed with the exchange of presents.

Challenges, magic and dances can be staged before the final give-away takes place. The ceremony may end with a tribal hymn, prayer, or song.

Gifts can easily be improvised for a potlatch. A single bright-colored blanket can be wrapped around a light box-like cardboard frame to give the impression that the bearer carries a bundle of blankets. Empty cardboard cartons of various shapes and sizes can be covered with plain or colored paper on which Northwest Coast designs have been painted with paint or crayons. Coppers can easily be cut from pieces of stiff cardboard or light plywood, using the shape and designs illustrated in this book when painting and designing them. Ordinary canoe paddles, on which paper bearing Northwest Coast designs has been pasted, can find a place in the gift parade. Most of the other presents suggested can be improvised with equal facility and will present a colorful and realistic appearance when on display.

POTLATCH GIFT-BOX CHALLENGE PAGEANT

This is another challenge pageant which can prove very popular, in addition to displaying some beautiful boxes. The actual boxes which the Indians gave away as valuable gifts at ceremonial potlaches were magnificent,

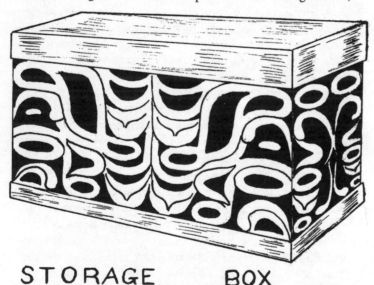

STORAGE BOX

being splendidly carved and painted. These boxes were usually made of thin boards of red cedar, often sewn together. The boxes were grooved where the fiber threads came through on the outside of the boards, so that the threads lay flush with the boards and were almost invisible when the boxes were painted and oiled. There were various sizes of boxes, from the great chests for blankets to the smaller food and trinket boxes.

For the purpose of a clan pageant, it is perhaps best to restrict the sizes of the boxes to a more or less standard

one. This makes judging easier and gives no clan unfair advantage from a viewpoint of size. The boxes may be made from strong cardboard or several sheets of cardboard glued together, or they may be made of light wood of some sort. They should be square or oblong. The square ones should be from 14 to 18 inches in width and height, and the oblong ones from 14 to 18 inches in width and from 24 to 30 inches in length. If there are suitable empty cartons or boxes in the kitchen or storeroom, they may be used advantageously by the clans which wish to make a box the easy way. All boxes must have lids.

It will be the decorating which counts, and that may be done on stiff paper pasted over the ready-made boxes. Boxes which are not ready-made can be glued together. The arts and crafts people may give advice, though not actual help. The boxes illustrated in these pages may give some idea of actual designs, but others may be devised by the different clans. Animals, birds, fish, and general designs may be used in the decorative work. As with the coppers, the usual colors used on the older boxes were red, yellow, buff, and black. The modern box-makers may use more modern colors, as long as their designs are graceful, striking, and colorful. The Indians made magnificent bent-wood boxes, which had to be steamed and worked before they took shape. Not only did they carve and paint these boxes but they also used sea shells as decorations. The pageantry and judging of this contest may be carried out in the same way as the Totem Pole and Copper Challenge Pageants.

NORTHWEST COAST CANOES IN COUNCIL FIRE CEREMONY

When a council fire area is situated at the edge of a lake, on a slope overlooking a lake, or on a point of land jutting out into a lake, Northwest Coast canoes can be used effectively as a part of the council fire pageantry. A canoe landing close beside the council fire area can be the point of disembarkment for chiefs, shamans, and other notables arriving for a ceremony. One or more canoes passing in front of the council fire area on the lake can be built into stories concerning Coastal clans, the timing being carried out by prearrangement between the chief or storyteller and the chief in charge of the canoe or canoes.

A killer whale hunt can be carried out on the lake close to the council fire area. The part of the lake on which the hunt takes place should be well illuminated by floating torches for the occasion. This hunt can be carried out as a challenge, with a big killer whale floating on the lake within easy sight of the warriors-in-council. Two canoes, manned by rival clans, paddle from equal distances on the signal to attack the whale, and each

WOLF MASK

STORAGE BOX

TOTEM POLE

COPPER

harpooner tries to make a rope fast to the dorsal fin of the whale and tow it away. The first crew to do so wins. The two canoes can be lit by torches held fore and aft. The whale can be made from several light planks or cut from a pine log, with a big dorsal fin attached. The fin should be shaped so that the noose, when once thrown over it, will remain fast and not slip up over the top. A battle with a killer whale can also be staged, in which the whale is attacked by the crew of two canoes and realistically pushed around with blunt lances. It is finally towed away in triumph.

The main drawback to this additional attraction to council fire pageantry lies in the fact that few if any camps have anything resembling an ocean-going Northwest Coast canoe. Fortunately, this state of affairs is easily remedied by building one or two. As the possibility of building the real thing is slight, let us be content with a safe, realistic, and usable replica. The building is gone into in some detail, because some camps may be glad of the chance to build such craft for an Indian Day or as a part of a Lake Pageant.

To construct a mock-up of a Northwest Coast canoe, first lash two regular canoes gunwale to gunwale with about a 2-inch clearance between the beams of the two canoes. A strong light pole about 3 inches in diameter is lashed securely across the bow thwarts of both canoes so that it projects not more than 1 inch over the gunwale of each craft. A similar pole is lashed across the stern thwarts, in exactly the same manner as the forward pole. (The 2-inch space left between the two canoes is to prevent the gunwales from chafing against each other.) The two canoes, when properly lashed, form the bow of a

Haida canoe. A second pair of canoes, lashed together in exactly the same way, form the stern. The drawing shows just how the two short poles are lashed, and also shows an additional pole lashed for extra support, if thought necessary, between the sterns of the forward canoes and the bows of the aft canoes to the long-side poles which are now described.

The two side poles should be about 40 feet long. They should be light but stout poles of seasoned wood, 2 or 3 inches in diameter, or they may be made of light saplings if a stand of young trees on the camp property requires thinning. These two poles are lashed, one on either side, along the outer sides of the two canoes which ride one behind the other, being fastened tightly to the shorter cross-poles which have been tied across the fore and aft thwarts of the side-by-side canoes. A distance of 1, 2, or 3 feet may be left between the bows of the aft canoes and the sterns of the forward canoes, based on the length of the canoes and side poles used. The average canoe used in camp is about 17 feet long, with a 2-foot beam. The drawing is based on these measurements. The forward ends of the two long poles are lashed together to form the bow of the big canoe. The stern for the big canoe is most easily formed by bending a flexible sapling, about 12 feet long, and lashing the two ends of it firmly onto the two long poles at the stern end of the two rear canoes. A similar arrangement can be used to form the bow of the canoe, should it prove difficult to bend and lash the two long poles at the bow. Two saplings, each about 15 feet long, are required to assure a pointed bow for the Haida craft. The ends of these two saplings are lashed to the two long poles, leaving sufficient length forward to be tied together

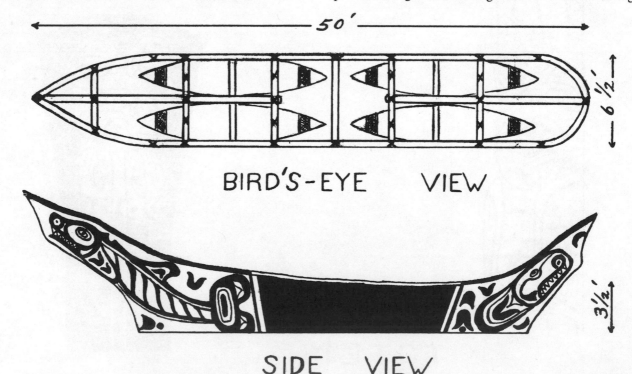

BIRD'S-EYE VIEW

SIDE VIEW

to form the bow of the big craft. The method used should be based on the resistance, strength, and flexibility of the saplings or poles available.

Additional suggestions for the reinforcement of the poles and lashings which hold the canoes in place are given here, though they may not be needed. A crosspiece about 4 or 5 feet long and about 2 inches in diameter can be lashed to the two poles forming the bow framework of the canoe. This reinforcement strut must not project beyond the poles to which it is tied. Its position is shown in the drawing. Additional reinforcement, when required, can be provided by the addition of a pole fore and aft, each from 20 to 25 feet long. The positions of these center braces are shown in the drawing. They work better when lashed over one cross-pole and under another, especially when they are more flexible than they should be. They should always be attached in the way that will give most support, strength, and rigidity to the particular framework under construction. It is impossible to set down any hard and fast instructions, or even measurements, for putting the most suitable framework together for any one canoe, since a great deal depends on three factors, which may differ greatly: (1) the length and beam of the canoes used; (2) the position of their thwarts; and (3) not only the length of saplings or poles at hand but also their weight and rigidity. When canoes are not available, quite a good mock-up can be made by using *two* rowboats pole-lashed one behind the other and propelled by real or improvised paddles. The wider beam and extra stability of a rowboat allows two boats instead of four canoes to be used in the construction of a mock-up of a war canoe.

The finished framework will be found rigid enough to fasten a light framework, representing the sides of a Haida canoe, to each of the long poles lashed on top of the gunwales of the outer sides of the four canoes. This framework can be made of light rods of bamboo or other wood, covered with a tough canvas painted to represent the sides of a Haida craft. The lower length of each framework should come a little below the water line on the outer sides of the lashed canoes when they have their crews aboard. When a little less elaborate job will do, a considerable part of the outer decorated canvas can be tacked directly onto the frame which holds the canoes together. With a little advance measuring and planning, plus some work, very good replicas of the sides of a big Northwest Coast Indian canoe can be made, and attached and detached when required. With a little care in the making, the entire mock-up will be found sturdy enough to use in the water carnivals which form part of the summer programs of a number of camps. A side view of a Haida war canoe is shown in the drawing.

One great advantage of paddling these mock-ups of Northwest Coast canoes is that the paddlers are in no danger of being tipped overboard, as it is quite impos-

sible to capsize the lashed canoes when the job is done in a shipshape manner. In paddling the completed craft, a paddler sits fore and aft in each of the four canoes, and another paddler may sit amidship in each craft. Sometimes the effect is better when those at the paddles kneel. Some advance practice is required on the part of the crew to assure that the craft handles and navigates well, even in a moderate wind, and that it can be brought alongside a dock or run carefully up on a beach without damage to either the canoes or framework.

WHY TOTEM POLES ARE CALLED TALKING STICKS AND STORY POLES

It may be well to take a quick look at the origin and purposes of "totem poles" before launching into the Totem Pole Challenge Pageant and the Talking-Stick Tale Challenge Pageant in this chapter.

Totem poles were cut, carved, and painted *only* by the Indians of the Northwest Pacific Coast and Southern Alaska areas. They were not connected with religion or religious beliefs, though they were reverenced because a great number of the beings, animals, and crests shown on the poles represented family, clan, or tribal totems and guardian spirits. The finest poles were carved from great red cedar trunks, huge trees towering to heights of 200 feet and more, with a diameter which often exceeded 8 feet. Controlled fire was one of the chief tools used in felling these forest giants. Once the spirelike shaft was cut to the desired length, the hewing and carving were done with long-handled adzes; elbow, hand, and D-shaped adzes; and chisels with stone, bone, and sometimes jade blades set in wooden handles. Handling and raising totem poles was always a very difficult task. This is not surprising when one considers that the average 45-foot pole with a 3-foot-6-inch base weighed around 4,600 pounds, even though the back might be hollowed out.

The great totem poles of leading chiefs and families bore heraldic designs, coats of arms illustrating mythological origin, family traditions, and important events—real and imaginary—many of which were family myths. The chief heraldic subjects of totems were: Thunderbird, Raven, eagle, hawk, cormorant, eagle's nest, wolf, grizzly bear, mountain goat, whale, beaver, killer whale, salmon, shark, sea-otter, blackfish, halibut, sculpin, frog, toad, fireweed, and others, which were carved and painted on many important totem poles. Stories of these birds, beasts, and fishes were woven into many versions of the legends, myths, and folktales and can still be seen carved on the original poles. Because of these tales, totem poles are often called "talking sticks" and "story poles." Totem poles were used by the nobility of the Northwest Coast as a means of recording their crests, family trees, history, and traditions by suitable representative symbols. It will be seen that the totem pole was to a large extent the social register of these proud peoples.

The earlier poles were carved and then colored in red, black, white, and sometimes yellow. These colors were made by the natives from clays, shells, wood ashes, and other coloring matters. Later, when European paints were available to the natives, other colors were added to those formerly used in the decoration of totem poles. Totem pole carvers were splendid artisans who selected, cut, carved, and painted the poles. They were paid from three hundred to three thousand blankets for each pole. The Haida and Tsimshian tribes were noted for the magnificence of their totem poles. They ranged in height from 50 to 70 feet, with a base approximately 4 or 5 feet in diameter and tapering gradually to the towering top. The warlike Nootka were the last to take up the art.

The question "Can totem poles be read?" is often asked. The answer is, yes—and no. People with a good knowledge of such things can identify most birds, animals, and fish, as they know how the carvers stylized these creatures. As the animals in the myths and legends pictured on the totem poles often appeared in human form, they had to be distinguished from real human beings by some feature or features added to the nearly human face. Erect ears on the top of a head, for instance, denote an animal. Large front teeth and a flat, scaly, cross-hatched tail easily identify a beaver, even without a stick—which a carver has sometimes added—held in the paws or mouth. Birds may be recognized by their beaks. A bill which curves back to the mouth indicates a hawk. Both the Thunderbird and eagle have beaks which curve at the tip, but the Thunderbird usually has two horns on top of its head to distinguish it from other birds. A straight beak tells that the figure on a pole is Raven, or a raven. The high dorsal fin of the killer whale is unmistakable; also the bulky body and shape of other whales.

One difficulty in recognizing some creatures in the totem pole story arises from the fact that most carvers took anatomical liberties with the birds and beasts which they depicted. They would visualize a bear cut along the back and open it out to assure a pleasing symmetrical appearance. Killer whales would be neatly split so that both sides, and sometimes the intestines, would figure on the talking sticks. Such treatment of subjects does not simplify totem pole "reading." Most of the carvers disliked blank spaces in their work and filled them in with eye, feather, and other designs.

The identification of figures other than those of animals presents far greater difficulty. Often the stories told by the carvers are so intimately connected with a family or clan history and doings—actual, lengendary, mythological, and sometimes imaginary—that even the most expert reader of totem poles would require intimate knowledge of the happenings illustrated to be able to even guess at what was meant by certain carvings on a pole. A general clue which often helps in reading a pole is the fact that, as a rule, the best carvers worked from the top to bottom of a pole in relating its owner's story. The top of the pole was usually decorated with the main crest, and usually the sequence of family events and myths told on the pole read from top to bottom.

The very fact that there are no hard and fast rules governing the making of a totem pole—as even the best work was not infrequently influenced by the whims, artistry, and the temperament of a master carver—makes it easier for modern clan chiefs to make a totem pole for council fire display without fear of breaking tribal taboos.

Raising a totem pole was always an occasion of great rejoicing, feasting, and gift-giving at a great potlatch ceremony which followed the setting up of the pole. The talking stick was dragged into place and raised with great ceremony and much effort. Sometimes a hundred or more people tugged and pulled on the fiber ropes of twisted nettles and cedar bark, which were fastened to various sections of the pole. As the people tugged and pulled, they sang haul-away songs, while the older onlookers also sang, beat skin drums, and shook rattles to encourage the pole-raisers. The butt of the pole was slid into and along a sloping trench which ended in a deep vertical hole into which the base of the pole was directed. When earth fell into this hole, a chief stepped down into the trench and removed the fallen earth with his hands. Considerable risk of being maimed or killed attended this work, and the chief who did it was well rewarded at the great potlatch which followed.

TOTEM POLE CHALLENGE PAGEANT

About one week before a council fire, the tribal chief proclaims a Totem Pole Coup Night. During the rest of that week, each clan makes a totem pole in its spare time. The pole may be made from cardboard or similar material, reinforced so that it will stand upright. The strong cylindrical packing tubes of various dimensions used for shipping rolls of linoleum make splendid totem pole material. Lengths of lightweight stovepipes fitted together to form the length required make an excellent interior for totem poles. The lower length of pipe can be securely fitted onto a round stake of correct diameter, driven into the ground where the talking stick is to be set up. The material of which the pole is made must be strong enough to allow animal heads, figures, or masks, also of cardboard or paper, to be fastened onto it. As much of the totem pole may be painted as each clan decides. The size of the pole should be limited to 12 feet in height, maximum, while the minimum height should not be less than 8 feet. The taller totem pole should measure about 18 inches at the base, tapering to about 6 or 8 inches at the top. While the taller pole may be judged less decorative than the shorter one, which counts coup, the additional length provides more space for decoration on the longer poles. Each pole should be painted and decorated with painted figures and totem animals based on real totem poles and the imagination of the totem pole builders. The usual colors used prior to the invasion of the Pacific Northwest Coast by white men were red, yellow, black, white, and various brick shades made by adding clay to the red and yellow colors. After the coming of the white man, native art declined considerably, though they had presumably better tools and a far greater range of colors to use in their work. Some of the magnificent poles, bearing animals and a wealth of heraldic design, towered as high as 70 feet in air. Naturally, the tribes which lived on or very close to the beaches along the coast used marine animals and fish a good deal on their poles, though a number also used land animals and birds. The inland tribes used marine animals less, though many used the salmon, which teemed in their rivers. Some totem poles, as well as various types of bird and animal masks, are shown in this chapter and may be drawn on for ideas.

Torches should be set up near the tribal chief's seat in the council fire area, where the judging will take place. When the warriors-in-council are seated, the clans competing enter the council area. They march in slowly, six or eight warriors from each clan, the totem pole being carried on the shoulders of some of the warriors and a torch bearer marching on either side of the pole. Each clan marches twice around the council area, then halts close to the chief's chair. They set up the totem poles directly behind the torches stuck into the ground, so that the poles may be more easily seen and admired. While one or two warriors may hold the pole in place, it is more effective when they are set up so that they stand straight and unsupported. A tapered, stump-like piece of heavy wood about 2 feet in length can be fastened inside the base of the pole when it is made, so that the totem pole remains upright on level ground. Another way to hold the pole in place is for clan warriors to quickly drive in four sharp stakes about 3 feet long, in a square formation, so that the pole will stand in the center with the stakes touching it. A couple of coils of strong cord, especially if the clove hitch is used, wound around the base of the pole and stakes will hold it securely in position.

When all poles are set up, the tribal chief and at least two other judges should carefully inspect the work of the totem pole makers, making comments which may be heard by the warriors-in-council as to the interest and merits of each pole. The judges decide which pole is best, and may also select second and third best if they wish. The winning pole can be set up in front of the tribal chief's house during a period of several dry days, to honor the pole and its makers. Special awards, such as miniature coppers or dentalium shells to be fastened onto

the clan's copper, may also be made as decided by the tribal chief.

While these totem poles require some time to make, and really artistic work can be produced with a little help from the arts and crafts counselors, the time spent on the original pole is not lost. The framework may be stripped of the initial decorations and redecorated for another challenge pageant, or the original poles may be used to decorate the council area on special occasions. The poles may also be used to decorate a part of the path leading to the entrance to the council area.

READING A STORY POLE

The speaker's staff struck the floor, and the chiefs, nobles, and warriors were silent as Chief Bear Hunter, wearing his magnificent ceremonial dress, began to tell the story of the great talking stick which had just been set up on the beach before his house.

"Long, long ago, when the world was young, my people set out over storm-tossed waters on the long water trail to the islands. For many sleeps my people fought the angry waves to keep their great canoe afloat, instead of going down to join the Ocean People and live with them in green darkness forever.

"When at last the sun lit calm waters, the hearts of my people were glad. They sang a 'Thanks Song'—and then the killer whales came! Two great killers of the ocean sought the blood of my people in the great canoe which lay still on sunlit waters.

"One big killer whale leapt high from the water, that it might fall on the canoe and crush it with its great weight. Then the great noise of thunder filled the sky. When the crash shook the heavens, my people closed their eyes. When they opened them again, a great shadow darkened the water. They heard the beat of mighty wings. Then a great bird, mightier by far than any eagle, swooped faster than an arrow flies and sank its fierce talons deep into the leaping killer whale. High above the canoe the Thunderbird rose, with the great whale held tight in its claws. Then as the Thunderbird climbed higher, the second great killer whale sped straight for the canoe. There was a great flash of light, bright even in the sunlight, as a Lightning Snake which rested on the legs of the Thunderbird flashed down and struck the killer whale on its head. Even before the Lightning Snake had turned to glide to the Thunderbird, the great fierce whale rolled over on its back and died.

"And so this day have I honored my people and my house by the story pole, which will tell those who look upon it the story which I have just told you. I have spoken."

TALKING-STICK TALE CHALLENGE PAGEANT

Clan chiefs, with the help of their clans, can carry out a striking totem pole challenge. Planning the coup will require some thinking, some knowledge of the crests and totems of the Northwest Coast Indians, and a considerable amount of imagination, in which all clan warriors may share.

FROG MASK

In council, the tribal chief tells the warriors that in two council fires' time there will be a Talking-Stick Tale Coup in which each clan can contest. The plan, he explains, is for each clan to invent an interesting tale of crests and myths, battles and adventures, and depict them on a totem pole. Then on the night of the council fire, a chief or warrior will interpret the pole, telling the significance and story of each crest and mysterious figure "carved" on the talking stick. The clan which counts coup and leads all others may not have the tallest or finest pole. It is the interest of the tales woven around the pole and the dramatic way in which they are told which will guide the judges' decision. A second and third pole may also be selected in order of merit.

As will be seen, this challenge offers almost unlimited scope for dramatic storytelling. A story told by one pole may be funny, while another may be tragic. One pole can portray the emotions of a clan, as well as speaking of its greatness. The stories will have to be thought up first, and probably several changes will be made in both the selection of crests and the incidents shown before the "carvers" raise their adzes for the first stroke of actual work. A pole can tell of real, as well as imaginary, adventures which befell the clan and its members while in camp. Such a pole may be made only of strong cardboard and decorated with cardboard or plywood beaks, ears, crests, and figures; but it can be nicely colored, and even varnished, so that it may serve as the totem pole of a clan during its entire stay in camp.

The presentation of this coup can be made far more picturesque and dramatic by having costumed "actors" sing, dance, and pantomime the stories of certain crests and incidents told on the pole. This was one of the most thrilling features of such pole interpretation ceremonies among the Indians of the American and Canadian Northwest Coast.

This challenge is most effective as a challenge pageant in which the different clans carry their totem poles into the council fire area by torchlight. A drum or drums can head each marching clan, and each clan can have two torch bearers marching one on either side of their pole. After the clans have marched twice around the council fire area, the poles are set up opposite the tribal chief's chair or in some other part of the area for the judges' decision.

COPPER CHALLENGE PAGEANT

The tribal chief proclaims a Copper Challenge Pageant, to be held in about a week. During the days which follow, the clans spend some time in making and painting coppers for the pageant. Each clan should only make one copper. It may be made from very strong cardboard or several sheets of thinner cardboard glued together, or the copper may be cut from a sheet of thin plywood or some other wood from ¼ to ½ inch thick. The size of the coppers should range from 30 to 40 inches high, with a width of from 10 to 20 inches more or less.

COPPER

The coppers should be cut in the form of one of the coppers illustrated. Care should be taken to see that each copper has the distinctive T of the actual coppers of the

Northwest Coast, formed by two grooves meeting and touching on the face of the copper. These shieldlike coppers were usually made of soft native copper, beaten to a thickness of about ⅛ to ¼ inch. They were painted or etched with the owner's crest or with animal or other designs. The earlier coppers of the tribes were usually painted in reds, yellows, and blacks, with white markings. In later coppers, blues and greens of varying shades were also used. However, the colors selected by the clans which contest in the pageant may be left to the painters' imagination. While the actual value of these early coppers ranged from five to perhaps twenty-five dollars, the value set on them by their owners, and generally accepted by the Northwest Coast tribes, began at two thousand blankets and went as high as twelve thousand blankets for one copper. They were often sold for these high amounts, when the owner was willing to part with them.

In ceremonial pagents, the coppers were carried in front of their owners by servants, while frequently other servants or slaves beat them like a gong, to call attention to their beauty and design and the importance of their owners. This method of parading the coppers should be considered by the clan chiefs when the clan coppers are paraded around the council area, accompanied by torch bearers, to the area where the judging takes place.

Awards may be made by the judges, as in the Totem Pole Challenge Pageant. The winning coppers may be exhibited after the council fire by being hung on painted posts in front of the tribal chief's house or in some other place. These coppers can also serve to decorate the council fire area on special occasions.

Each clan should give its copper a name, since every copper on the Northwest Coast has one. Such names as Bright One, Envied One, or Treasured One are appropriate, as will be seen by referring to some of the actual coppers which represented fabulous trading values in blankets to their owners. Around 1900, one famous copper which was traded for eight thousand blankets was named, not without reason, *Makstso,* meaning "All-Other-Coppers-Are-Ashamed-to-Look-on-It." Another copper, traded for five thousand blankets, was called *Lopwlila,* or "Making-the-House-Empty-of-Blankets."

INDEX